T0330234

How Green Were the Nazis?

Ohio University Press
Series in Ecology and History
James L. A. Webb, Jr., Series Editor

Conrad Totman
The Green Archipelago: Forestry in Preindustrial Japan

Timo Myllyntaus and Mikko Saiku, eds.
Encountering the Past in Nature: Essays in Environmental History

James L. A. Webb, Jr.
Tropical Pioneers: Human Agency and Ecological
Change in the Highlands of Sri Lanka, 1800–1900

Stephen Dovers, Ruth Edgecombe, and Bill Guest, eds.
South Africa's Environmental History: Cases and Comparisons

David M. Anderson
Eroding the Commons: The Politics of Ecology in
Baringo, Kenya, 1890s–1963

William Beinart and JoAnn McGregor, eds.
Social History and African Environments

Michael L. Lewis
Inventing Global Ecology: Tracking the Biodiversity
Ideal in India, 1947–1997

Christopher A. Conte
Highland Sanctuary: Environmental History in
Tanzania's Usambara Mountains

Kate B. Showers
Imperial Gullies: Soil Erosion and Conservation in Lesotho

Franz-Josef Brüggemeier, Mark Cioc, and Thomas Zeller, eds.
How Green Were the Nazis? Nature, Environment, and Nation
in the Third Reich

How Green Were the Nazis?

*Nature, Environment, and Nation
in the Third Reich*

Edited by Franz-Josef Brüggemeier,
Mark Cioc, and Thomas Zeller

OHIO UNIVERSITY PRESS

ATHENS

Ohio University Press, Athens, Ohio 45701
© 2005 by Ohio University Press
www.ohiou.edu/oupress/

Ohio University Press books are printed on acid-free paper ⊗ ™

13 12 11 10 09 08 07 06 05   5 4 3 2 1

Cover image: The cover photo depicts a swastika-shaped patch of larch trees in a pine forest in Brandenburg. Presumably a zealous forester planted the sylvan swastika, with a diameter of nearly two hundred feet, in the 1930s as a sign of his allegiance to the Nazi regime. The swastika survived not only World War II but also four decades of East German communist rule. Visible only from the air during the fall and winter months, the larch trees were detected in 1992 and felled in 2000. *Courtesy Reuter Pictures Archive*

Library of Congress Cataloging-in-Publication Data

How green were the Nazis? : nature, environment, and nation in the Third Reich / edited by Franz-Josef Brüggemeier, Mark Cioc, and Thomas Zeller.— 1st ed.
    p. cm. — (Ohio University Press series in ecology and history)
Includes bibliographical references and index.
ISBN 0-8214-1646-4 (cloth : alk. paper) — ISBN 0-8214-1647-2 (pbk. : alk. paper)
    1. Environmental policy—Germany—History—20th century. 2. Germany—Politics and government—1933-1945. 3. Green movement—History—20th century. I. Brüggemeier, Franz-Josef. II. Cioc, Mark. III. Zeller, Thomas. IV. Series.
HC290.5.E5H68 2005
333.7'0943'09043—dc22

2005022300

Contents

Acknowledgments   vii

Introduction   FRANZ-JOSEF BRÜGGEMEIER, MARK CIOC,
                THOMAS ZELLER   1

Chapter 1.   Legalizing a *Volksgemeinschaft*
                Nazi Germany's Reich Nature Protection
                Law of 1935
                CHARLES CLOSMANN   18

Chapter 2.   "Eternal Forest—Eternal *Volk*"
                The Rhetoric and Reality of National
                Socialist Forest Policy
                MICHAEL IMORT   43

Chapter 3.   "It Shall Be the Whole Landscape!"
                The Reich Nature Protection Law and
                Regional Planning in the Third Reich
                THOMAS LEKAN   73

Chapter 4.   Polycentrism in Full Swing
                Air Pollution Control in Nazi Germany
                FRANK UEKÖTTER   101

Chapter 5.   Breeding Pigs and People for the Third Reich
                Richard Walther Darré's Agrarian Ideology
                GESINE GERHARD   129

Chapter 6.   Molding the Landscape of Nazi Environmentalism
                Alwin Seifert and the Third Reich
                THOMAS ZELLER   147

Chapter 7. Martin Heidegger, National Socialism,
and Environmentalism
THOMAS ROHKRÄMER   171

Chapter 8. Blood or Soil?
The Völkisch *Movement, the Nazis, and
the Legacy of Geopolitik*
MARK BASSIN   204

Chapter 9. Violence as the Basis of National Socialist Landscape Planning in the "Annexed Eastern Areas"
JOACHIM WOLSCHKE-BULMAHN   243

Glossary   257
Selected Bibliography   261
Contributors   273
Index   275

Acknowledgments

The editors would like to thank the nine authors who contributed articles to this anthology. We also owe a big debt of gratitude to Gillian Berchowitz, senior editor at Ohio University Press, who guided this project through the publication process so quickly and smoothly. We also wish to thank the press's anonymous readers, whose critiques and suggestions strengthened each of the contributions. Finally, special thanks go to Christof Mauch, director of the German Historical Institute in Washington, DC, for encouraging this project and for providing financial assistance for the preparation of the index.

Introduction

Franz-Josef Brüggemeier, Mark Cioc, and Thomas Zeller

THE QUESTION "How green were the Nazis?" is likely to evoke a different response from Germans than from non-Germans. In Germany, the question sounds downright provocative. The Green Party stands solidly on the left end of the German political spectrum, and its members are active in the fight against neo-Nazism. The Greens, moreover, view themselves as a new political force—one that emerged out of the student and environmental movements of the 1960s and 1970s—with no roots in the Nazi past.[1] Outside Germany, by contrast, the question probably arouses more puzzlement than passion: the Nazis are associated with nationalism, militarism, and racism, but not with environmentalism. "Eco-fascism," of course, has become a media buzzword, and occasionally one actually comes across environmentalist factions that espouse an ideology with Nazi undertones.[2] But such groups reside on the outer fringes of modern-day politics, their antics more annoying than dangerous.

National differences aside, the question "How green were the Nazis?" is laden with linguistic ambiguities: neither "green" nor "Nazi" is easily defined. Green generally carries a positive connotation, but its meaning is highly elastic. The media use the word *green* to describe a multitude of diverse political groupings, institutions, and associations. Advertisers market their products as green, no matter how noxious they actually are for the environment. Multinational corporations—even oil companies and paper mills—try to dress themselves in green garb. Nazi is a term of opprobrium with a more straightforward meaning: it is clearly associated with Adolf Hitler, World War II, and the Holocaust. Yet even this term is more elusive than meets the eye. Scholars have shown that Nazi leaders represented a ragbag of opinions, not a unified ideology. Rarely did Hitler forge a comprehensive approach to a problem or push a clear legislative agenda. Most of his policies emerged in piecemeal fashion, usually after a long and bitter clash of personalities, interests, institutions, and ideas. While the foundation stones of Nazi ideology—racism and anti-Semitism—were already laid in 1933, it was by no means clear whether, how, or how soon they would be translated into what the world came to know as war and genocide.

Given the terminological ambiguities, it makes no sense to blithely claim that "the Nazis were proto-Greens," or that "the Greens are latter-day Nazis," even if these assertions occasionally pop up in polemical discourse. Those who make them want to establish a simple linear relationship between today's Greens and yesteryear's environmentalists, either in order to demonize Green politicians or to find laudable elements in an otherwise damnable dictatorship. Scholars too have sometimes succumbed to this temptation, most famously Anna Bramwell, who claimed in 1985 that the Nazi Party had a "Green wing."[3] Most experts, however, feel that this interpretation is not supported by the evidence and does little to enhance our understanding of today's Greens. Equally unsubstantiated, albeit with a different political bent, is Ramachandra Guha's bold assertion that "To be Green—then or now—is not connected with being Nazi."[4]

The most obvious and fundamental feature of almost all pre-1945 environmentalist movements was their parochialism: for the most part, environmental concerns were local, regional, or state-centered. By contrast, most environmentalists today make the connection between the local and the global a major part of their rallying cry. We do not mean to downplay the important connections between colonialism, imperialism, and environmentalism in the pre-1945 period that environmental historians are examining today. Rather, we are simply pointing out that the physical boundaries of the nation-state largely shaped the mental worlds of most conservationists and environmentalists until after World War II came to an end.[5]

The essays in this book steer clear of polemic, just as they shy away from a monolithic interpretation. They simply ask whether there was an overlap between the goals of National Socialists and environmentalists in the first half of the twentieth century, be it at the level of policies, persons, institutions, or methodologies; and, if so, whether that overlap translated into laws and policies that had a lasting impact on the German landscape. Germany offers a particularly fertile field for exploring these intercon- nections. First, the nature-protection movement was more powerful and articulate in Germany than elsewhere in Europe, and many Nazi voters were sympathetic to its agenda. Second, the Nazi seizure of power opened up new and long-desired opportunities for green ideas finally to come to the forefront. These new opportunities and the sheer fact that both green and brown ideas enjoyed widespread support in Germany in the 1930s make the question "How green were the Nazis?" worthy of investigation. The topic becomes all the more fascinating when one keeps in mind that National Socialism—both as a movement and as a governmental force— reflected the hopes and failings of modern society in its most extreme form.[6]

The notion that National Socialism belongs to "modernity" is rela- tively new to Nazi studies. National Socialism was a criminal regime, one of the most brutal and rapacious in human memory. The longstanding tendency, therefore, has been to interpret Nazism as a wholly reactionary system, a throwback to premodern times. The Nazis themselves encour- aged this interpretation, intentionally or not, by repeatedly expressing nostalgia for the world that existed before the era of the Enlightenment, before the triumph of rational thought, before the birth of modern sci- ence. The Holocaust further reinforced the perception that Nazi Germany was nothing more than a horrendous aberration of German (and West- ern) history. Of course, Germans could not deny that the Nazis drew on traditions and practices that clearly predated 1933, but they could also point to many other traditions that put the German past in a more posi- tive light. In fact, the Federal Republic of Germany (1949–present) has often been held up as proof that there were "good" German traditions upon which a peaceful and democratic German state could be built. Out- side Germany, the task of turning the Nazis into a historical aberration required fewer intellectual acrobatics: nearly everyone was predisposed to believe that fascist policies had nothing to do with what was "truly" mod- ern in their own societies.

Today the pendulum has swung in the opposite direction. Over the past two decades, more researchers are inclined to regard National Social- ism largely as an offshoot and the pathology of modern society, not merely as a reaction to it.[7] They point out that, in some arenas, Nazi Germany was more modern than other European governments—for instance, in its use of propaganda techniques and in its promotion of technology.[8] In other arenas, it was at least on par with other societies—for instance, in the realm of scientific research and in nature conservation.[9] It must be kept in mind, after all, that Hitler did not win elections, or solidify his control over Germany, by promising a return to a past clouded by nostalgia and myth; and he did not sustain his domestic popularity for so many years by offering up old-fashioned nostrums and reactionary rhetoric. Quite a few Germans supported the political persecution, aggressive nationalism, anti-Semitism, and unchecked militarism which were part and parcel of his political agenda. But many were just attracted to the promise of full employment, the policies to overcome class differences, and the promotion of scientific advances and technological breakthroughs. Hitler's vision of Germany was largely dynamic, goal-oriented, and forward-looking—but often this pragmatic approach conflicted with Hitler's and the party's ambitions for a well-ordered, "organic" Germany that was to combine an imagined common history with features of modern life.[10] Agricultural policymakers, for instance, spent a good deal of time promoting organic techniques even while they struggled mightily to feed an ever-growing urbanized population through the use of artificial fertilizers and pesticides. A similar mixture of atavistic and avant-garde ideas could be seen in other arenas as well.

It serves little purpose to weigh the positive and negative aspects of National Socialism on a mental scale; the horrors of war and genocide make a mockery of any such attempt. It also serves little purpose to pit the positive and negative achievements against each other. As the following essays will amply demonstrate, they are far too intertwined to separate. The Nazis, for instance, introduced social policies that adumbrated a modern welfare state (albeit a racially defined one) that far surpassed those of its predecessor, the Weimar Republic. Social historians who write about Germany's modern welfare state must therefore avoid demonizing every measure that the Nazis envisaged and implemented simply because that regime was fundamentally evil. To miss the positive features of National Socialism is to miss why it appealed to so many people. The same holds true for environmental historians: they must see the positive as well as the negative aspects of Nazi conservation policies.

National Socialism was a novel and (in many ways) strange force in German politics, but not an alien one. Nazis, as a rule, did not start from scratch when they forged their policies: they took their cues from debates already taking place within the larger frame of German politics, society, and science. Most of those debates began long before the Nazis were on the political scene. More precisely, the Nazis emerged from within Germany, not from without, and Nazi leaders held a variety of viewpoints, not a unified one. There were, of course, some core beliefs, most importantly racism and anti-Semitism.[11] In addition, the belief in the *Volk*, an almost mystical faith in the goodness of the ethnically pure "common German," was very important. The concept of the Volk colored all aspects of German political, social, and intellectual life after World War I—the nature protection movement most of all—and it was largely through this folkish ideology that green and brown began to blend.

This brings us to the heart of the question: what possible meaning can the phrases "green movement" or "green ideas" have within the context of the first half of the twentieth century? No movement or ideology carried that label. The same can be said for "environment" (*Umwelt*) and "environmental protection" (*Umweltschutz*): neither was part of the discourse. Nonetheless, there were numerous personalities and (after 1904) a sprawling organization, the Deutscher Bund Heimatschutz ("Homeland Protection Association of Germany," or DBH), that embodied certain ideas of "homeland protection" (*Heimatschutz*) and "nature protection" (*Naturschutz*) that today would be subsumed under the green label. These protectionists did not speak in an abstract or universal way. They used the language of protecting the German homeland (*Heimat*) and preserving the German landscape (*Landschaft*). In their view, Germany's mountains, meadows, and rivers bore the peculiar imprint of German history, German culture, and German tastes. German traditions, habits, and attitudes shaped the German countryside just as German architectural styles and building preferences shaped the German city. A new appreciation of local and regional history, architectural preservation, and the conservation of landscapes thus went hand in hand, as educated urban middle classes formed lobbies to protect what they deemed worthy from the encroachments of industrialization and urbanization.[12] Protection carried with it an idea of management and human interference, as long as it was the kind of stewardship favored by the conservationists. Also, as a new way of experiencing nature for middle-class urbanites, the youth movement, with its Wandervogel wing of weekend hikers, exposed an entire generation to organized outings that combined education and recreation. While politically multivalent, the youth movement often served as social cement for those who attained positions of power after 1933.[13]

Homeland and nature protectionists saw it as their task not only to protect rare plants, endangered animals, and natural monuments, but also to preserve local customs and national traditions, following the dictum "keep the German people [*Volkstum*] strong and wholesome."[14] What kept Germans powerful and pure, in turn, was the strength Germans drew from preserving their traditions, monuments, and land. Folk, homeland, and nature were intertwined, each defining the other, and it was only by remaining bundled together that they could survive the universalizing onslaught of the industrial world. Such attitudes embodied, from the outset, a strongly developed sense of nationalism. They also carried a whiff of racism: Ernst Rudorff, the founder of the Homeland Protection Association, struggled with the question as to whether Jews should be allowed to join his organization (though ultimately two Jews signed its founding charter, one of whom was his longtime friend and fellow musician Joseph Joachim).

The Homeland Protection Association had two wings, one mostly concerned with preserving the German past, the other more concerned with shaping the German future. Many of the most important founding members longed nostalgically for the old days. Their ideal was the Germany of 1800 or earlier—before the impact of the industrial revolution and the emergence of big cities—when (in their minds at least) German traditions and customs were in full bloom. Other founding members took a more modernist perspective, among them Paul Schultze-Naumburg, who greatly influenced the organization for many years and later joined the Nazi Party. Human-induced transformations in the landscape were, for him, not automatically a fall from grace. Rather they offered opportunities to shape a future where German traditions and characteristics could be taken into account. The gap between those who looked backward and those who looked forward grew in subsequent decades. Both sides, however, were united in their belief in the power of the Volk, and folkish ideology would help keep them united (and indeed radicalize them) as the years passed.[15] Another source of tension was the ideological tenet of Heimat, a term that had connotations that went beyond the local landscape to include anti-centralist regional visions as well as notions of national unity.[16]

Folkish ideology emerged during the Second Reich (1871–1918), but it was World War I, the Versailles Treaty, and the crises of the Weimar Republic that elevated it to a position of supreme importance in the 1920s and 1930s. The crushing defeat of 1918 led not only to a short-lived revolution and the establishment of a democracy, but also to an aggressively conservative and nationalistic countermovement—a countermovement with a strong folkish tinge. Those who believed in the redemptive power of the Volk saw little prospect that Weimar Germany would be capable of throwing off the "humiliation of Versailles." The battle between capitalism and socialism, they felt, only weakened the nation without providing any solution; hence they saw little purpose to Germany's parliamentary debates. Western democracies added to the problem: first they saddled Germany with the entire responsibility for the war, and then they treated Germany as a pariah in world affairs. The Western world did not, in any case, provide a good model. It was too materialistic and too lacking in cultural traditions. Only the German nation itself—as embodied in the German Volk—offered a way out of its humiliation. The Volk stood for something that was above ideology and above class conflict. It embodied all that was great in Germany: pristine strength, genuine traditions, and a sense of community.

This type of political rhetoric reverberated in homeland-protection circles. Landscape and Heimat preservation experienced something of a renaissance after World War I, and the Homeland Protection Association and its sympathizers had reason to believe that their message was finally being heard. To begin with, the Weimar constitution included for the first time an article that made "nature protection" a national task. Meanwhile, a series of economic and political crises (as a retrospective analysis put it) "made people aware of the need to protect their natural areas and landscapes in their locales." These crises created a "strong spiritual readiness" that "helped foster" nature protection: "for every hundred people that once bemoaned the disfigurement and destruction, there are now a thousand."[17] There were other indices as well. For instance, when the well-known homeland poet Hermann Löns died in 1914, he had sold a mere twenty thousand books. Twenty years later, sales had topped five million.

Unfortunately, the high hopes of the homeland protectionists were not fulfilled. Constitutional protection did not translate into a change in economic policy, let alone into passage of new protection laws. On the contrary, the German landscape continued to deteriorate. Worse yet, from the viewpoint of the Homeland Protection Association, the upsurge in interest in Heimat was all too short-lived. The association continued to sponsor event after event designed to promote German traditions, the singing of folk songs, and a sense of conviviality and belongingness, but attendance at such events was never large. Young people in particular were turned off by the backward-looking nostalgia. The bright lights of the big city and new forms of entertainment such as film, dance, and sport had a much greater allure. The decline triggered different reactions among different homeland protectionists. Some withdrew from the movement, disappointed and embittered. Others, such as Schultze-Naumburg, blamed the failure on the racial decline of the German people. These latter responded by radicalizing their position through race-based notions of rejuvenation of Volk and Heimat. Still others pinned their hopes on technological solutions that entailed even greater interventions in the landscape. In their minds, dams, cities, and other human-created structures should be built in a manner more in keeping with German traditions. It is important to point out that the last two groups really reinforced rather than competed with each other: one provided a technological framework for sculpting the German landscape, while the other provided a race-based rationale for doing it. These synergies became all too apparent during the Nazi era.[18]

With the Nazi triumph in 1933, Volk, racism, and conservation became integrally linked, opening up new vistas for those who wanted to transform the German landscape. As in other arenas, however, Nazi leaders held no unified viewpoint on what was meant by "nature" and "landscape," and therefore the implications for homeland and nature protection were not entirely clear. It was one thing to use the notion of Volk to blur the lines between conservationism and National Socialism. It was quite another to mold the ideas and beliefs that stood behind these words into a coherent whole.

It was in this political and ideological wilderness that Germany's Reich Nature Protection Law of 1935 (Reichsnaturschutzgesetz, or RNG) was finalized. The fact that Hitler's government was the first to pass such a comprehensive piece of legislation is often cited as proof of Nazism's pro-environmental face (even though it has long been recognized that much of the law's stipulations were drafted during Weimar and reflected the longstanding concerns of the Romantics). In "Legalizing a *Volksgemeinschaft*: Nazi Germany's Reich Nature Protection Law of 1935," Charles Closmann provides a fresh perspective on this law. He notes that a vast amount of political maneuvering went into its passage and that its terms only served to paper over the differences between the goals of Nazi leaders and those of the conservationists. The high hopes of the conservationists turned to frustration as they realized that Nazi Germany honored the law mostly in the breach, especially once war preparations came to dominate policy in the late 1930s. Nonetheless, as Closmann makes clear, the Nazis deserve some credit for recognizing the importance of the legislation and for securing its passage.

A similar gap between rhetoric and reality characterized Nazi forest practices, as Michael Imort makes clear in "'Eternal Forest—Eternal *Volk*': The Rhetoric and Reality of National Socialist Forest Policy": even as Nazi leaders extolled the virtues of Germany's forest in bombastic terms, they exploited the country's timber resources aggressively. Imort notes that some Nazi leaders expressed a sincere interest in forest conservation (most notably Hermann Göring), but that most others did not. Inasmuch as they thought about Germany's forests at all, they thought in terms of propaganda: it provided an opportunity to meld the Romantic "love of the woods" to Nazi thinking. Imort notes that it was largely because of Göring that the forestry doctrine known as *Dauerwald* ("eternal" or "perpetual" forest)—first enunciated in the early 1920s—increasingly began to insinuate itself into timber management. It was largely because this practice proved profitable that many timber owners were willing to implement it. The Nazis, however, were not interested in turning Germany into a tree farm: Hitler's military-industrial machine required vast quantities of natural resources, forests included, and it consumed Germany's timber reserves just as it consumed those elsewhere in Europe. As a result, the conservationist principles associated with the concept of Dauerwald were not enshrined in law until the 1970s—long after the Nazi era was over.

Closmann and Imort raise the "continuity" question: does it even make sense to label the Reich Nature Protection Law and the Dauerwald doctrine as "National Socialist" when both predated 1933 and both continued to impact policy after 1945? Neither was the brainchild of a Nazi ideologue, and neither was totally in sync with other Nazi goals and ideas. Had Hitler never triumphed, one could well imagine a scenario in which Weimar politicians would eventually have passed a law not all that different from the RNG, just as one could imagine Dauerwald ideas slowly percolating their way into the minds of forestry officials. Perhaps the pace of change would have been slower, but that does not inherently mean that the German landscape would look fundamentally different today if the

Nazis had never triumphed. And yet, as all the contributors make abundantly clear, the Nazis did in fact impact the landscape in ways far out of proportion to the short twelve years they were in power.

Thomas Lekan's "'It Shall Be the Whole Landscape!': The Reich Nature Protection Law and Regional Planning in the Third Reich" examines in detail just how far-reaching the Nazi impact was on the Rhineland Province. The Rhineland was famous both for its awesome beauty (the "romantic Rhine") and its astonishing industrial output (the coal-rich "Ruhr region"). It also had one of the most vibrant Homeland Protection Associations in the country. As Lekan notes, Rhineland conservationists initially embraced the RNG—and with it a Nazification of the conservationist movement—with great enthusiasm, as did their counterparts elsewhere in Germany. Conservationists had long chafed under the decentralized traditions of the past, whereby each city, region, and state was allowed to protect (or, more often, *not* protect) its own territory as it saw fit. They quickly discovered, however, that centralization had its disadvantages as well, especially in the hands of a regime that championed nature protection mostly for its propagandistic value. Under the Nazis, conservation policies emanated from Berlin, with little or no input from regional conservationists, and they came out in cookie-cutter fashion, not always with much appreciation for local conditions and needs. Once among the avant-garde of German protectionists, Rhinelanders suddenly found themselves on the sidelines, powerless to shape (let alone thwart) Reich policies. Lekan's article is a cautionary tale reminiscent of the advice to "be careful what you ask for": Rhineland conservationists wanted a top-down approach to landscape preservation but got a command-and-control approach to natural-resource exploitation instead.

Homeland and nature protection under the Nazis might well have benefited from more of a bottom-up strategy. Yet, as Frank Uekötter points out in "Polycentrism in Full Swing: Air Pollution Control in Nazi Germany," that was not always the case: air pollution policies under the Nazis might well have benefited from a more comprehensive (and more comprehensible) top-down approach. Despite their much-vaunted ability to ride roughshod over enemies and friends alike, the Nazis were never able to hammer out an umbrella law for air pollution similar to the one they passed for nature protection. There were, as Uekötter points out, simply too many conflicting ideas coming out of too many warring agencies and bureaucracies for a unified policy to emerge. In 1933, for instance, the Munich-based Academy for German Law (Akademie für

Deutsches Recht) began the task of bringing air pollution laws and regulations into conformity with the Nazi concept of *Gemeinnutz vor Eigennutz* (the common good above the individual good). The Reich Food Estate (Reichsnährstand, or RNS), by contrast, was mostly interested in ensuring that individual farmers continued to get adequate compensation for any crop damage caused by industrial pollution. Other bureaucrats, meanwhile, spent their time making sure that air pollution laws did not interfere in any way with Hitler's rearmament program. Given the bureaucratic conflicts, enforcement of Germany's air pollution policies (most of which predated 1933) was haphazard at best. What civil servant was going to try to convince Hitler that farmers—the quintessential Volk—were not central to Germany's resurgence as a world power? What judge was going to decree that rearmament did not encode the notion of the common good? As Uekötter points out, no uniformly applied standards for air pollution policy ever emerged. Instead, Nazi policy was characterized by "a bureaucratic routine that was semiconscious at best."

Nazi Germany, of course, was not just a web of warring bureaucracies. It was also a labyrinth of rival personalities. In "Breeding Pigs and People for the Third Reich: Richard Walther Darré's Agrarian Ideology," Gesine Gerhard takes a new look at the Nazi leader most often identified as a proto-Green: Hitler's first minister of agriculture, Richard Walther Darré. Darré popularized the phrase "blood and soil"—a takeoff on Bismarck's "blood and iron"—in order to highlight the continued centrality of agriculture to the strength of Germany. But as Gerhard amply demonstrates, it is a stretch to view Darré as a proto-ecologist or an apostle of organic farming on the basis of his agrarian policies: "soil" was for him merely "a part of agricultural property," in which environmental considerations played a negligible role. By contrast, "blood" was fundamental to his thinking, as it was to other Nazis—and it served as a justification for Hitler's exterminatory "resettlement" policies in eastern Europe.

Alwin Seifert is the other prominent Nazi most often portrayed as a proto-Green. An outspoken Munich landscape architect, Seifert is best remembered today for his role in co-designing the autobahn network. In "Molding the Landscape of Nazi Environmentalism: Alwin Seifert and the Third Reich," Thomas Zeller analyzes the career of this eccentric landscaper, placing him squarely within the confused jumble of Nazi infighting. Seifert's self-portrayal—especially in his grandiloquent autobiography—tends to embellish his influence over Nazi landscaping policies, while minimizing his role as a Nazi ideologue. As Zeller points out, however, Seifert's influence on the autobahn and similar projects was actually quite limited. In fact, Seifert spent much of his time embroiled in personal and institutional battles with his rivals, not landscaping the autobahn. While Seifert's provocative publications did give rise to intense debates on agriculture, water policy, and highway design, his impact was much more circumscribed than he ever admitted. In the end, as Zeller notes, Seifert played the role of Nazi "environmental court jester and Cassandra rolled into one."

Darré and Seifert were active participants in the Nazi political structure, men who were preoccupied with the day-to-day details of bureaucratic life. In "Martin Heidegger, National Socialism, and Environmentalism," Thomas Rohkrämer turns his attention to a different type of personality: Germany's most famous philosopher during the Weimar and Nazi periods. It is now well known that Heidegger was a Nazi and that he served briefly as the rector of Freiburg University, during which time Jewish professors lost their jobs. He withdrew from politics after 1936, but never denounced the Nazis and never apologized for lending his prestige to Hitler's murderous regime. As Rohkrämer points out, however, his meditations on the environment came to maturity mostly after his enthusiasm for Nazism had subsided, and his writings reflected a growing distrust of all societies (capitalist, socialist, and, to a lesser extent, fascist) that deified science and technology. While he absorbed much of the conservationist rhetoric of his era, his writings have influenced the post-1945 generation far more than Darré and Seifert because his ideas far transcended the blood-and-soil mentality of the Nazi era.

In "Blood or Soil? The *Völkisch* Movement, the Nazis, and the Legacy of Geopolitik," Mark Bassin reexamines the influence of geopolitical ideas on Nazi expansionist policies and racial goals. Geopolitical concepts had been prominent in Nazi circles ever since Hitler came across the works of Karl Haushofer while writing *Mein Kampf,* and because of that connection many scholars have assumed that Haushofer was the "master magician" behind Nazi military strategy. Bassin, however, goes beyond the clichés of Social Darwinism, "blood and soil," and Lebensraum ("living space," a term the geographer Friedrich Ratzel borrowed from ecological theory) to show that Haushofer's theories (like those of Heidegger) were far too sophisticated and complex to fit easily into the Nazi ideological framework. Haushofer, for instance, sought a genuine alliance with the Soviet Union, not the sham Nazi-Soviet Pact of 1939, and he embraced a foreign policy based on notions of space (*Raum*), not race

(*Rasse*). As Bassin points out, Nazi ideologues selected only those aspects of geopolitical thinking that flattered their predispositions, and they ended up employing an eclectic mix of theories that lacked any sense of coherence.

Coherent or not, the hodgepodge of conservationist and geopolitical ideas that Nazi leaders carried in their heads had far-reaching consequences during World War II, as Joachim Wolschke-Bulmahn notes in "Violence as the Basis of National Socialist Landscape Planning in the 'Annexed Eastern Areas.'" Within Germany, conservationists, Nazi landscapers, and architects had to take into account already existing land-use patterns, city plans, dam structures, and the like. In the vast territories conquered in the east, by contrast, they saw the opportunity to create a better, greener future, combining racist and environmental thinking. On 7 October 1939, shortly after the outbreak of World War II, Hitler placed Heinrich Himmler in charge of these territories so that they could be settled by Germans. Himmler's immediate order was couched in euphemisms that gave it an innocent ring, but it set in motion a succession of increasingly radical plans that culminated in the Generalplan Ost. At first, the plan only applied to Poland, but then it was extended to eastern and southeastern Europe, then to the Black Sea, and finally to Siberia. These new territories, according to Himmler, were to be remodeled on the basis of the "latest scientific research"; the campaigns would have "revolutionary results" because the aim was not simply to colonize these territories with Germans but to "radically change the landscape."

World War II was the opportunity that many modernist landscape architects had been waiting for. The Germans, as one of them put it, would be the "first western Volk to implant its very soul in the landscape and thereby achieve for the first time in human history a way of life in which the Volk itself determines its physical and moral well-being in full awareness of local conditions."[19] In other words, Generalplan Ost was about bringing humans, nature, and race into harmony in order to establish a new agrarian way of life for Aryan colonists. Here green and Nazi thinking came together to a degree not seen elsewhere. In order to achieve this vision, the landscape had to be made anew, first by forcibly removing the Slavic population, then by bulldozing away the past, and finally by moving Germans into the newly emptied space. Annexation exposed a side of Nazi-era "conservationism" that was as ugly as it was logical. It was ugly because it was exterminatory. It was logical because only the clearance of the new territories created the opportunity to build a new, green Germany. Polish forests were therefore turned into Nazi hunting grounds, eastern agrarian lands were transformed into German settlement areas, and "inferior" Jews and Slavs were weeded out to make room for "superior" Aryans.

Taken together, these papers offer a more nuanced and historically richer answer to the question "How green were the Nazis?" than previous efforts. While certain ideological elements and practical policies of the National Socialist regime overlapped with conservationists' and ecologists' agendas, other Nazi goals and practices, especially the rapid rearmament, flew in the face of green ideas. For some green-leaning Nazis, however, that was acceptable. For them the war and destruction were necessary evils since they would bring about a new order that would finally allow the establishment of a better and greener Germany. Put in the context of Germany's tumultuous twentieth century, it can neither simply be said that all greens were Nazis nor that all the Nazis were greens. But there were many similarities between both ways of thinking and there were some people—especially among those planning for the postwar world—who felt that Nazi and green thinking went hand in hand.

When Thomas Zeller first broached the question "How green were the Nazis?" at a panel during the American Society for Environmental History conference in 1997, he initiated a debate between German and non-German scholars that eventually culminated in this anthology. We hope these contributions will help move the debate beyond the stereotype that Germans were both "nature lovers" and "violent," and help dispel the notion that there is a clear-cut, black-and-white approach to Nazi-era conservationism. We also hope that our focus on Germany will shed new light on the larger question of twentieth-century environmentalism. The green policies of the Nazis were more than a mere episode or aberration in environmental history at large. They point to larger meanings and demonstrate with brutal clarity that conservationism and environmentalism are not and have never been value-free or inherently benign enterprises.

Notes

1. One of the founding members and erstwhile leader of Germany's Green Party confessed to feeling embarrassed about Nazi Germany's green policies. While acknowledging topical continuities, she also stressed the degree to which the Greens mark a rupture from this past. Manon Andreas-

Griesebach, "Kontinuität und Bruch," *Politische Ökologie* 11 (November 1993): 13–16.

2. Janet Biehl and Peter Staudenmaier, *Ecofascism: Lessons from the German Experience* (Edinburgh: AK Press, 1995), try to lump together environmentalism and Nazi Germany in an ultimately ahistoric fashion. For an analysis of German right-wing parties claiming "green" ground, see Thomas Jahn and Peter Wehling, *Ökologie von rechts: Nationalismus und Umweltschutz bei der Neuen Rechten und den "Republikanern"* (Frankfurt: Campus, 1991); and Jonathan Olsen, *Nature and Nationalism: Right-Wing Ecology and the Politics of Identity in Contemporary Germany* (New York: St. Martin's Press, 1999).

3. Anna Bramwell, *Blood and Soil: Richard Walther Darré and Hitler's Green Party* (Bourne End, Buckinghamshire: Kensal Press, 1985). See also her follow-up book, *Ecology in the 20th Century: A History* (New Haven: Yale University Press, 1989). For a recent critique, see Piers H. G. Stephens, "Blood, Not Soil: Anna Bramwell and the Myth of Hitler's Green Party," *Organization and Environment* 14 (June 2001): 173–87.

4. Ramachandra Guha, *Environmentalism: A Global History* (New York: Longman, 2000), 19.

5. Dick Richardson and Chris Rootes, *The Green Challenge: The Development of Green Parties in Europe* (London: Routledge, 1995); Eeva Berglund, *Knowing Nature, Knowing Science: An Ethnography of Environmental Activism* (Cambridge: White Horse Press, 1998).

6. For a recent assessment in German focusing on conservation, see Joachim Radkau and Frank Uekötter, eds., *Naturschutz und Nationalsozialismus* (Frankfurt: Campus, 2003). See also Douglas Weiner, "Demythologizing Environmentalism," *Journal of the History of Biology* 25 (Fall 1992): 385–411; Colin Riordan, ed., *Green Thought in German Culture: Historical and Contemporary Perspectives* (Cardiff: University of Wales Press, 1997); and Thomas Rohkrämer, "Contemporary Environmentalism and Its Links with the German Past," in *The Culture of German Environmentalism: Anxieties, Visions, Realities,* ed. Axel Goodbody (New York: Berghahn Books, 2002), 47–62.

7. For the historiographical debates, see Ian Kershaw, *The Nazi Dictatorship: Problems and Perspectives of Interpretation,* 4th ed. (London: Arnold, 2000); and Riccardo Bavaj, *Die Ambivalenz der Moderne im Nationalsozialismus: Eine Bilanz der Forschung* (Munich: Oldenbourg, 2003).

8. Karl-Heinz Ludwig, *Technik und Ingenieure im Dritten Reich* (Düsseldorf: Athenäum/Droste, 1979); and Monika Renneberg and Mark Walker, eds., *Science, Technology and National Socialism* (Cambridge: Cambridge University Press, 1994).

9. See the papers in Doris Kaufmann, ed., *Geschichte der Kaiser-Wilhelm-Gesellschaft im Nationalsozialismus: Bestandsaufnahme und Perspektiven der Forschung*, 2 vols. (Göttingen: Wallstein, 2000); and Margit Szöllösi-Janze, ed., *Science in the Third Reich* (Oxford: Berg, 2001); and see Robert Proctor, *The Nazi War on Cancer* (Princeton: Princeton University Press, 1999), 120–72.

10. For two competing interpretations regarding National Socialism's modernity, see Jeffrey Herf, "Der nationalsozialistische Technikdiskurs: Die deutschen Eigenheiten des reaktionären Modernismus," in *Der Technikdiskurs in der Hitler-Stalin-Ära*, ed. Wolfgang Emmerich and Carl Wege (Stuttgart: Metzler, 1995), 72–93; and Anson Rabinbach, "Nationalsozialismus und Moderne: Zur Technik-Interpretation im Dritten Reich," ibid., 94–113.

11. For an overview, see Michael Burleigh and Wolfgang Wippermann, *The Racial State: Germany, 1933–1945* (Cambridge: Cambridge University Press, 1991).

12. Thomas Adam, "Parallele Wege: Geschichtsvereinigungen und Naturschutzbewegung in Deutschland," *Geschichte in Wissenschaft und Unterricht* 48 (1997): 413–28. This trend, of course, was by no means unique to Germany. For Great Britain, see James Winter, *Secure from Rash Assault: Sustaining the Victorian Environment* (Berkeley: University of California Press, 1999).

13. Diethart Kerbs, ed., *Handbuch der deutschen Reformbewegungen, 1880–1933* (Wuppertal: Peter Hammer, 1998); Judith Baumgartner, "Licht, Luft, Sonne, Bergwelt, Wandern und Baden als Sehnsuchtsziele der Lebensreformbewegung," in *Die Lebensreform: Entwürfe zur Neugestaltung von Leben und Kunst um 1900*, ed. Kai Buchholz (Darmstadt: Häusser, 2001), 403–6.

14. See Andreas Knaut, *Zurück zur Natur! Die Wurzeln der Ökologiebewegung* (Greven: Kilda, 1993), 69.

15. Edeltraud Klueting, ed., *Antimodernismus und Reform: Beiträge zur Geschichte der deutschen Heimatbewegung* (Darmstadt: Wissenschaftliche Buchgesellschaft, 1991); William H. Rollins, *A Greener Vision of Home: Cultural Politics and Environmental Reform in the German Heimatschutz Movement, 1904–1918* (Ann Arbor: University of Michigan Press, 1997).

16. For some examples of the considerable Heimat historiography, see Celia Applegate, *A Nation of Provincials: The German Idea of Heimat* (Berkeley: University of California Press, 1990); and Alon Confino, *The Nation as a Local Metaphor: Württemberg, Imperial Germany, and National Memory, 1871–1918* (Chapel Hill: University of North Carolina Press, 1997).

17. Hans Klose, *Fünfzig Jahre staatlicher Naturschutz: Ein Rückblick auf den Weg der deutschen Naturschutzbewegung* (Giessen: Brühlscher Verlag, 1957), 25.

18. Franz-Josef Brüggemeier, *Tschernobyl, 26. April 1986: Die ökologische Herausforderung* (Munich: Deutscher Taschenbuch Verlag, 1998), 155–78; Karl Ditt, "Nature Conservation in England and Germany, 1900–1970: Forerunners of Environmental Protection?" *Contemporary European History* 5 (1996): 1–28; Joachim Radkau, *Natur und Macht: Eine Weltgeschichte der Umwelt*, 2nd ed. (Munich: Beck, 2002), 294–98; Paul Josephson and Thomas Zeller, "The Transformation of Nature under Hitler and Stalin," in *Science and Ideology: A Comparative History*, ed. Mark Walker (London: Routledge, 2003), 124–55.

19. Quoted by Gert Gröning and Joachim Wolschke-Bulmahn, *Die Liebe zur Landschaft. Teil III: Der Drang nach Osten* (Munich: Minerva-Publikation, 1987), 30; Mechtild Rössler and Sabine Schleiermacher, eds., *Der "Generalplan Ost": Hauptlinien der nationalsozialistischen Planungs- und Vernichtungspolitik* (Berlin: Akademie-Verlag, 1993), 132. See also Isabel Heinemann, *"Rasse, Siedlung, deutsches Blut": Das Rasse- und Siedlungshauptamt der SS und die rassenpolitische Neuordnung Europas* (Göttingen: Wallstein, 2003).

CHAPTER 1

Legalizing a *Volksgemeinschaft*

Nazi Germany's Reich Nature Protection Law of 1935

Charles E. Closmann

IN JULY 1935, Germany's National Socialist dictatorship decreed one of the industrialized world's most wide-ranging conservation laws. Known as the Reich Nature Protection Law (Reichsnaturschutzgesetz, or RNG), it impressed observers at the time for several reasons. It created the possibility for protecting entire landscapes and curbing the destructive effects of economic development on the countryside. It provided a unified definition of areas worthy of protection for the entire nation, a long time goal of German advocates for *Naturschutz* (nature protection). It also required any party wishing to alter the terrain through major construction projects to consult with responsible government officials. Spokespersons for leading Naturschutz journals praised the Nazi regime for passing legislation with such far-reaching potential to preserve Germany's natural surroundings; in fact, many of them considered the RNG long overdue.[1]

Not surprisingly, Nazi Germany's nature protection law has proven to be a contentious subject for historians: did this brutal dictatorship really support progressive measures to protect the environment, or did nature protection merely serve as a camouflage for the promotion of other goals, such as Nazi racial policies?[2] Anna Bramwell, in *Blood and Soil* (1985), has suggested that there was an inherent connection between National Socialist ideology and today's Green ideas. She argued that the Nazi minister of agriculture, Richard Walther Darré, should be considered a "Father of the Greens" because he was among the first to support organic farming and the use of low-tech, small-scale agricultural machinery.[3] Similarly, Simon Schama argued in *Landscape and Memory* (1995) that the Nazis' belief in a relationship between their alleged superior racial qualities and the German landscape—the ideology of *Blut und Boden* (blood and soil)—created a sinister bond between barbarism and reverence for nature within the Third Reich.[4]

Others, however, are not convinced that the ties between Nazism and nature were so tightly bound. Raymond Dominick, for instance, feels that the attempt to find a link between Nazi ideas and modern-day environmentalism reflects a "superficial understanding of the history and worldview of today's Greens." The officials who drafted the RNG, he noted, "had no prior organizational and only weak ideological connections to the Nazi cause."[5] High-ranking Nazis who promoted Naturschutz were merely "playacting," using popular conservation laws for propaganda.[6] Similarly, at a conference held in Berlin in 2002 to assess the impact of National Socialism on the environment, Karl Ditt noted that the RNG was an important and progressive measure; but unlike Bramwell he also labeled it "remarkably unideological."[7] Meanwhile, Edeltraud Klueting acknowledged the centralizing tendencies within the Nazi state that encouraged the adoption of major environmental laws, but denied that the Third Reich was fundamentally committed to the protection of natural areas. The needs of the army, the demands of Germany's wartime economy, and major road building projects undermined any potential benefits from Nazi Germany's Naturschutz legislation.[8]

Taken together, Dominick, Ditt, and Klueting challenge the notion of systematic reverence for nature within the Nazi state, first by questioning the ideological connections between the RNG and National Socialism, and then by asserting that the Nazis never implemented the law on a systematic scale. Unlike Bramwell and Schama, they see no reason to view Nazi Germany as an environmentally sensitive state, at least based on the example of RNG and other Naturschutz laws passed during Hitler's regime.

In many ways, however, all of these viewpoints oversimplify the history and significance of the RNG. As this chapter will demonstrate, the RNG was indeed a green law in the sense that it echoed progressive ideas about nature preservation and landscape protection from the standpoint of the 1930s. The RNG also reflected key elements of the National

Socialist worldview when one takes into account the broader ideological context in which German officials drafted this law. The propagandistic statements of Nazi conservationists were not mere symbolism; they effectively infused ideological content into a law that otherwise looked "remarkably unideological."[9] Moreover, government officials attempted to extend nature protection policies, including the RNG, into the occupied portions of Europe during World War II. This attempt to spread the Nazi vision of conservation underscores the dangers present for a society which links reverence for nature—as represented in laws like the RNG—with racism and the brutal suppression of other nations. It also highlights how problematic it is to glibly equate Nazi environmental goals with those of the Greens today.[10]

Provisions of the RNG

For German conservationists of the Weimar era, the RNG represented a decisive legal step forward. First, it established a unified administration to handle nature protection for the entire Reich, a long-standing goal of Germany's Naturschutz community. Since at least the 1920s, leading spokespersons for the Naturschutz movement complained that Germany's federalist traditions allowed each *Land* (state) to pass its own nature protection regulations and designate its own *Naturdenkmäler* (natural monuments) and *Naturschutzgebiete* (nature protection areas).[11] Some states, such as Prussia, were active in this arena, while others were not. In the minds of German conservationists, this state-by-state approach undermined their efforts to breathe life into Article 150 of the Weimar constitution, which read: "The monuments of history and nature as well as the countryside enjoy the protection and care of the state."[12] Sections 7, 8, and 9 of the RNG rectified this problem by elevating the Prussian Office for the Care of Natural Monuments to the national level. In addition, the RNG placed the new Reichstelle für Naturschutz, or Reich Nature Protection Office, directly under the authority of the newly created Reich Forest Office (Reichsforstamt), beneath the command of Hermann Göring. The RNG also unified the definition of natural areas worthy of protection for all of Germany, a clear departure from the 1920s when a patchwork of regulations characterized German conservation law.[13]

Other features of the RNG also made it progressive for its time. Most importantly, section 5 sought to preserve "remaining portions of the landscape in free nature" that "decorate or enliven the appearance of the land-scape" or "lie in the interest of the animal world," especially if they pro-tect "songbirds and small game animals (e.g., trees, groves of trees or bushes, ridges, avenues, old fortifications, hedges, parks, and cemeteries)." Section 19 then authorized nature protection officials to issue specific decrees to implement section 5. Together, sections 5 and 19 created the potential for comprehensive land use planning, beyond the narrow definition of areas worthy of protection that had existed for many years. Finally, section 20 also furthered that goal, requiring all "national, state, and local officials" to consult with responsible nature protection authorities "prior to conducting any project which might lead to essential alterations in the free landscape."[14]

Sections 5, 19, and 20 corresponded not only to the goals of contemporary nature protectionists, but also to those of Germany's *Heimat-schutz* (homeland protection) movement. In addition to individual objects of nature like forests and meadows, the homeland group wanted to preserve and embellish built features of the landscape like culturally significant bridges, footpaths, streets, and buildings. In this respect, sections 5, 19, and 20 reflected evolving notions of *Landschaftspflege* (the care for the landscape), a concept that emphasized curtailing unattractive, unplanned economic development in favor of an aesthetically pleasing ensemble of streams, roadways, buildings, and countryside. Advocates of Landschafts-pflege especially liked those portions of the RNG that emphasized curbs on development or restrictions on advertising signs. As Ditt has pointed out, this aspect of the law also corresponded to changing ecological theories of planning and development. Increasingly, German landscape architects saw the countryside as an organic entity in which one intrusive alteration, such as the regulation of a stream, might have unintended consequences such as erosion. Finally, other features of the law gave authorities impressive, wide-ranging powers to protect the countryside. Section 18, for example, authorized the Reich master of forestry to designate special "Reich Nature Protection Areas," and to expropriate land when necessary. Along the same lines, section 24 denied indemnification claims by aggrieved parties who lost land to the state under the law.[15]

By the standards of 1935, these features of the RNG made Germany more progressive in matters of conservation and landscape planning than other industrialized nations.[16] Although comparisons between nations are inherently difficult, some illustrations make this point. Various British government leaders from 1900 onward attempted to preserve portions of the landscape, curb real estate development, and create a series of green-belts, but Parliament delayed major action on a national law to create nature preserves and national parks until after World War II. Economic problems, two world wars, and opposition from landowners all posed insuperable hurdles to such legislation. Similar problems beset France: the Council of State did not establish its first national parks and nature reserves until 1960, a full quarter of a century after Nazi Germany had adopted the RNG. Other European nations also passed nature protection laws of one form or another beginning in the early 1900s, with the Netherlands leading the way. Yet none of these laws provided the same degree of protection for natural monuments, nature preserves, and settled landscapes as that provided by Nazi Germany. In the Soviet Union, a major state policy to set aside *zapovedniki* (nature preserves) as examples of ecologically valuable communities showed great promise in the 1920s. By 1933, the state had established several million acres of land for such preserves. Yet by the mid-1930s, the Stalinist regime began to deride the biologists who supported the creation of zapovedniki as bourgeois elitists. The state now shifted the focus of its conservation policies, emphasizing the domination of nature, a goal consistent with the huge industrialization schemes of Stalinist Russia. By the beginning of World War II, Soviet officials had converted many such preserves into laboratories for the introduction of exotic species, and by 1947 some 85 percent of all zapovedniki territory no longer existed. Seen in the light of comparisons to the Soviet Union and other European countries, Germany's RNG demonstrated commendable sensitivity to issues of nature and landscape protection.[17]

Yet this does not mean that Nazi officials were the first in Germany to promote nature preservation and landscape protection. Indeed, key passages in the RNG drew upon ideas and legislation dating to the turn of the twentieth century and even earlier. Those portions of the RNG that dealt with the establishment of natural monuments and nature protection areas demonstrate this point. Section 1 stated that natural monuments and nature protection areas should be protected because of their "rarity, beauty, uniqueness," or because their value from the standpoint of "scientific, regional culture, forestry, or hunting reasons" lay in the public interest. Section 3 defined natural monuments as "single creations of nature" such as "rock formations . . . waterfalls, or rare trees." Likewise, section 4 defined nature protection areas as "certain limited regions" whose preservation also served the public interest, mainly for the same reasons stated in section 1.[18]

None of these provisions were new: they reflected the influence of Romanticism, a worldview common among advocates for nature protection in the nineteenth century. As early as the 1870s, the belief that nature could be beautiful and awe-inspiring encouraged middle-class teachers, civil servants, and others to demand the preservation of picturesque river cascades and mountain valleys. One such crusader, the musicologist Ernst Rudorff, called nature a "purifying and uplifting agent" that must "above all remain undesecrated and unadulterated."[19] These conservationists saw nature as a soothing antidote to the unsettling appearance of bustling cities, factories, and tenement apartments. As in other industrializing nations, Germany's nature protection movement grew partly as a reaction against these developments, and spokespersons for the movement frequently articulated their complaints in Romantic terms.[20]

Such Romantic motives inspired the creation of a number of state agencies and laws that clearly presaged the RNG. The Prussian state approved the best known of these agencies: the Prussian Office for the Care of Natural Monuments (which the Nazis would later elevate to the national level). Its first director, the botanist Hugo Conwentz, defined natural monuments as those parts of the landscape that stood out because of their "general, local scientific, or aesthetic interest."[21] Working on a shoestring budget, Conwentz's agency put together teams of volunteers who identified thousands of Naturdenkmäler across the state.[22] Other states took similar (if less well known) measures. The state of Hesse, for instance, adopted a Law for the Protection of Monuments that encouraged the preservation of "water courses, rock formations, trees, and similar items, whose preservation lies in the public interest because of natural scientific reasons, or because of the beauty or unique qualities that such objects add to the landscape." It also permitted protection of wider areas beyond the narrow definition of "natural monuments."[23]

Many of the newly designated natural monuments reflected not only an emphasis on physical beauty, but also the scientific curiosity of Conwentz and other founders of the Naturschutz movement. By virtue of his education and experience in the German city of Danzig (now Gdańsk, Poland), Conwentz was especially concerned about the disappearance of individual plant species through deforestation and agriculture. Hence he spent a good deal of his time on the preservation of scientifically valuable groves of trees, colonies of plants, and other discrete features of the landscape. Conservationists in other parts of Germany—especially Bavaria—followed his lead, concentrating on the preservation of scientifically and aesthetically valuable objects. Those portions of the RNG that dealt with natural monuments and nature protection areas owed much both to the Romantics and to the scientifically based model of nature protection that Conwentz championed.[24]

Other portions of the RNG also drew on earlier models of conservation. Sections 5, 19, and 20—all of which dealt with landscape preservation—were inspired by the Romantic appreciation for "pristine" nature as well as a cultural-pessimistic form of German nationalism. As in Britain and the United States, Germany's nature protectionists increasingly saw the intrusion of modern civilization into the countryside as a form of degradation, and a threat to the nation.[25] Rudorff articulated this belief more eloquently than most in the late nineteenth century, arguing that preserving the "monuments and beautiful objects of nature" would preserve the "*deutsches Volkstum*" (German national character). Writing in 1880, he warned against destruction of the landscape, asserting that the "roots of the German essence" lay within the German people's "deep feeling for nature."[26] In this sense, Rudorff and his followers in the homeland protection movement shared the view of middle-class observers who equated the destruction of their countryside with the destruction of Germany itself. By 1900, hundreds of prominent individuals and many associations across Germany also shared this perspective on their changing society, to one degree or another.[27] Prolific writers like Otto Ammon and Max Nordau reinforced this sense of national decline, diagnosing a kind of "nervousness" among the inhabitants of big cities—a sickness that threatened the reproductive capacity and vigor of the nation.[28]

This brand of antimodernism often shaded into a critique of unchecked capitalism as well. Rudorff lambasted the effects of modern agriculture, which uprooted hedgerows, trees, and bushes. He demanded, on aesthetic grounds, the preservation of waterways in their original, irregular streambeds, and the protection of small meadows for deer. As always, he laced his critique with a social-cultural message, arguing that all humans had the right to set foot on land that inspired their soul, and that only a more complete appreciation for nature—in all of its diversity—would help to reconcile those who possessed property with those who did not. Like other middle-class reformers in Germany and England, he saw the preservation of green space as a solution to the alienation experienced by industrial workers, who often lived in sprawling tenements. The same materialistic forces that transformed and degraded the countryside also degraded the working class, according to this perspective.[29]

Sections 5, 19, and 20 of the RNG alluded to these ideas, to one degree or another. As stated earlier, section 5 allowed the protection of "remaining portions of the landscape in free nature" that "decorate or enliven the appearance of the landscape."[30] Features of section 5 that referenced "hedges," "alleys," and "parks" echoed Rudorff's statements calling for the "consideration of regional characteristics" in order to protect the countryside from the "one-sided priority of material . . . and economic interests." In particular he wanted to limit "excessive construction of paths, stream regulation, and the ruination of streams by surrounding agricultural fields."[31] He also recommended that land-enclosure decisions be submitted for review to panels of responsible experts, knowledgeable in the aesthetic or historical value of the countryside.[32] In this sense, his ideas foreshadowed section 20 of the RNG, requiring all government officials to consult with nature protection experts before taking measures that might defile the landscape.[33]

As in other areas, some states turned these ideas of landscape protection into legal statutes long before the Nazi seizure of power in 1933. Prussia enacted a "Law Against the Disfigurement of Exceptionally Scenic Areas" in 1902 and again in 1907. Although the first legislation applied only to advertising billboards that threatened to disrupt unusually picturesque vistas, the second measure was more ambitious: it allowed public officials to reject *any* construction projects that might potentially disturb areas of "exceptionally scenic countryside." A wide variety of Heimatschutz, gardening, and monument-protection groups lobbied on behalf of this measure. Although the law had its shortcomings from the perspective of Germany's Heimatschutz movement, the campaign for the measure further instilled in the Prussian bureaucracy an awareness of the principles of this movement. One Prussian guideline even recommended that road builders consult with local Heimatschutz groups prior to the final design of major construction projects.[34] Although limited in number, other regulations in Prussia during the 1920s also created the possibility of comprehensive landscape protection. The Prussian Field and Forest Police Law of 1926 is one notable example.[35] In addition, several German states enacted their own versions of Naturschutz and Heimatschutz laws by the 1920s, a reflection of the wide acceptance of these ideas in Germany.[36]

Clearly, some of the principal ideas motivating Nazi Germany's RNG were not unique to the Third Reich. Indeed, conservation policies based upon Romantic and cultural-nationalistic rationales had existed for years, inside and outside Germany. In the United States, for instance, preservationists like John Muir lobbied for the designation of federally protected national parks at Yellowstone, Yosemite, and other locations during the late 1800s. Set aside for "public use, resort, and recreation," these parks expressed that society's unease over the loss of its western frontier, the alleged cradle of American individualism and democracy. In Britain, urban intellectuals idealized the rural countryside, arguing that its destruction could lead to national decline. Although such arguments failed to inspire major legislation until after World War II, their motives differed little from those of the German nature protectionists who fought for passage of the RNG.[37]

The RNG in the Context of Nazi Ideology

Nevertheless, when one more closely examines actual provisions of the RNG and the context in which this law was enacted, it is clear that the legislation reflected some ideas characteristic of the Nazi movement. Among other things, provisions of the RNG regarding landscape protection—sections 5, 19, and 20—echoed the highly nationalistic and racialized views of German conservationists who supported such a measure in the 1920s and 1930s. Increasingly, leaders of the Naturschutz movement argued that Germany's landscape was the foundation for an allegedly superior race of people.[38] Like Alfred Rosenberg, Richard Walther Darré, and other National Socialist ideologues, some leading conservationists were coming to the conclusion that a mystical connection of "blood and soil" existed between the people and the land.[39]

Many conservationists who shared such race-based beliefs also increasingly began to challenge what they considered to be an excessively narrow conception of Naturschutz as practiced by Conwentz and others. The poet and naturalist Hermann Löns was among the first to articulate this critique, arguing as early as 1906 that "the nature protection movement was a struggle for the preservation of the health of the entire people, a struggle for the power of the nation, for the prosperity of the race." The protection of single objects of nature—an unusual rock or a cultural artifact—had little meaning for society in general. Löns called for comprehensive landscape protection in order to prevent the countryside from becoming a "boring grain steppe, without trees or bushes." In the troubling economic and political climate of the 1920s, members of the nature protection movement increasingly began to pick up on Löns's comprehensive approach and to wrap themselves in *völkisch* ideas. Since they portrayed nature protection in cultural terms, they also emphasized a more expansive definition of those portions of the landscape worthy of protection.[40]

The most prominent conservationist who expressed his commitment to landscape protection in terms of a supposed relationship of "blood and soil" was Walther Schoenichen. As director of the Prussian Office for the Care of Natural Monuments during the 1920s, Schoenichen warned in 1926 that "a racial-hygienic collapse threatens our people [*Volk*]."[41] In 1933, he joined the Nazi Party, making him one of the most prominent fascists within the nature-protection movement. In 1934 he stated that "the nature of our homeland, with its woodlands and meadows, . . . has formed the essence of the German people," and that "in order for a new peoples' community to exist . . . the nature-loving soul of our race must break through."[42] Schoenichen's ideas were similar to those of Rudorff, but he expressed them in a new political context. Lamenting the impact of mining, railroads, and canals on Germany's countryside, he stated that "homeland protection in the sense of Rudorff, and a shaping of the landscape in the spirit of the new times, is the goal."[43] He decried the effects of tourism, jazz music, and the unrestricted picking of flowers, activities characterized by the word *Kulturlosigkeit* (a lack of culture).[44] He found advertising billboards, a problem that liberal governments during the Weimar era had been unwilling to address, especially offensive.[45] Those who shared the "National Socialistic worldview" would be responsible for purifying the landscape of such unfortunate consequences of modern society.[46]

Not surprisingly, Schoenichen also believed that a comprehensive Naturschutz law was necessary to achieve such ambitious goals. Among other things, the RNG would create a Nature Protection Office at the national level, empowered to implement unified Naturschutz regulations for the entire Reich. In addition, a team of government commissioners would oversee construction projects that threatened to disrupt the countryside in a manner deemed unsuitable by the regime. Schoenichen's proposals were not completely antimodern. Indeed, he called not for a return to old-fashioned, pastoral values, but for a reconciliation of development with efforts to shape the landscape in a way that preserved nature for the German people. Only then could the German nation succeed in its competition with other peoples.[47] According to Schoenichen, a vigorous nature protection law was necessary since German governments during the time of "parliamentarianism" showed little concern for Naturschutz.[48]

Schoenichen's reference to parliamentary inaction underscores another ideological connection between provisions of the RNG and the National Socialist movement: the idea of a *Volksgemeinschaft* (people's community). Among other things, spokespersons for the Nazi Party appealed to the idea of an ethnically pure society, free from the political bickering and class conflict that many Germans associated with the Weimar Republic. Repeating the slogan, "the common good takes precedence over the individual good," Nazi ideologues also suggested that exaggerated concerns with individual gain and private property would come to an end, buried in the interest of public welfare.[49]

Leading supporters of landscape and nature protection shared such beliefs. In 1927, noted conservationist Professor Hans Schwenkel decried "the predominance of money" and the "over-valuation of productivity," abhorrence of which, he argued, had inspired the nature protection movement.[50] Three years later, Schoenichen lamented the "unscrupulous thirst for profit that holds nothing as holy or worthy of reverence except the welfare of the cash register."[51] In an October 1933 article in the periodical Naturschutz, Schoenichen demanded that the countryside be purified of the "un-German spirit of commerce." This could only happen through a national law forbidding the construction of advertising signs in the countryside.[52] One year later, Schoenichen expressed confidence that Nazi Germany would promote regional planning by adopting a comprehensive Naturschutz law. He was certain that the National Socialists would act differently from previous governments because of their commitment to a Volksgemeinschaft rooted in the soil of the homeland.[53]

Schoenichen's hope that a Volksgemeinschaft would sweep away the spirit of "parliamentarianism" and "commerce" was undoubtedly based on the experience of the prior years. Motivated by public demands for laws to unify Germany's patchwork of Naturschutz ordinances, Weimar-era governments took up and rejected plans for such comprehensive legislation on several occasions.[54] Among other things, the Weimar constitution continued Germany's federal system, guaranteeing that responsibility for issues of natural resource management remained with the states. Consequently, Prussia, Bavaria, Saxony, and other states each adopted their own Naturschutz or Heimatschutz ordinances, contributing to a patchwork quilt of laws across Germany.[55]

More importantly, questions of private property rights undermined attempts during the late 1920s to pass more effective laws for the states or the nation. Specifically, government bureaucrats feared a rash of indemnification claims if another government agency restricted the use of a parcel of land.[56] Meetings between the Prussian ministries of justice, culture, and the interior underscored this point. At a joint conference in 1927, the ministers engaged in a lively discussion on the issue of indemnification claims during which the minister of the interior asserted that this issue was critical to the acceptance of a proposed nature protection law. In fact, all three ministries in Prussia's left-center coalition government agreed that any provision of a law that expropriated land from a property owner would violate the Weimar constitution, and they considered this issue the main impediment to passing a comprehensive Naturschutz law.[57]

By contrast, the Nazi regime was prepared to limit property rights in order to pass such a law. In 1935, Prussian minister of education Bernhard Rust warned that property rights had always impeded past attempts to adopt an RNG, and he noted that Adolf Hitler agreed with this assertion.[58] Other Reich ministers also remained determined to override concerns about the sanctity of private property. Citing the slogan "The common good takes precedence over the individual good," a March 1935 memorandum from the Ministry of Justice stated that future drafts of an RNG would prohibit any claim for indemnification by aggrieved landowners.[59] Consequently, actual provisions of the law specifically limited property rights in the interest of creating a Volksgemeinschaft. While section 18 allowed the Nature Protection Authorities to expropriate land in order to create special Reich Nature Protection Areas, section 24 stated that measures enacted through the RNG "give no reason for a claim of indemnification."[60]

In addition to those sections of the law mentioned above, it is clear that the broader context in which the Nazis adopted this measure created additional ideological connections between the RNG and the Nazi movement. As stated earlier, portions of this legislation mirrored the Romantic, scientific, and cultural motives expressed in legislation predating the Nazi era. Indeed, drafts of the RNG from 1935 closely resembled documents discussed within the Prussian bureaucracy in 1927, several years before the Nazi seizure of power. Also, the draft RNG left Germany's network of voluntary conservationists intact, providing little increase in their funding. In this respect, the Nazis' new law created an apparatus that differed little from that established in Prussia by Conwentz, three decades earlier.[61]

Yet the new political context of the 1930s places this measure in a different historical light and underscores its relationship to Nazi ideology. In addition to the personal connections between völkisch conservationists and the law, a new willingness to override democratic conventions made passage of the RNG possible. Otherwise, concerns about property rights or parliamentary procedure might have forestalled its adoption, just as they had during the 1920s.

The bureaucratic infighting over drafts of the RNG underscores this point. Attempting to retain administrative authority over this field in the spring of 1935, the ministers of justice, the interior, and education grappled for several weeks over control of Naturschutz policies in the Reich, with each ministry asserting its responsibility on the basis of past traditions or perceived competence. In April, Hermann Göring grabbed this field for himself with little debate, subordinating the Prussian Office for the Care of Natural Monuments to his Reich Forest Office and expanding its authority over the entire nation. Moreover, Göring insisted that the law itself be adopted quickly thereafter, before the summer vacation period began, in part so that he could decree a large nature protection area in Prussia. Several weeks later, on July 1, 1935, Nazi Germany formally announced passage of the RNG. Yet even formal passage of the law did not end questions about the expropriation of private property. In the fall of 1936, during discussions concerning amendments to the law, officials in the Ministry for Regional Planning again raised the question of property indemnification claims. Yet once adopted, the amended version of the law continued to deny such property rights claims, the major impediment to this law under the Weimar Republic.[62]

In short, even though the RNG looked like laws drafted under the Weimar Republic, only the Nazis could have adopted this measure. The comments of those Nazi officials who justified the RNG based upon the emergency legislation of 1933, or who appealed to notions of the "common good" taking precedence over the "individual good," underscore this point. Critics might argue that Nazi leaders who espoused such beliefs were hardly sincere. As stated above, Nazi ministers fought desperately to retain authority over the field of Naturschutz, suggesting that bureaucratic power was as much a rationale for supporting the RNG as was a sincere belief in the ideals of "blood and soil" or a mystical Volksgemeinschaft. In this respect the bureaucratic infighting over nature protection differed little from the internal power struggles—the polycentric infighting—that characterized the Nazi regime throughout its existence.[63]

Yet those government officials who drafted this law in 1935 honestly wanted to improve Germany's nature protection and landscape preservation policies. Göring commissioned the well-known conservationist Dr. Hans Klose to draft the RNG, a task that Klose undertook with diligence and sincerity. In the meantime, Göring appointed forestry expert Walter von Keudell as Germany's deputy minister of forest affairs. Among other things, von Keudell was a noted supporter of a more ecologically progressive approach to forestry that encouraged the planting of mixed stands of conifers and hardwood, rather than monoculture plantings of spruce. Writing years later, Klose contended that von Keudell's appointment created a bureaucratic climate favorable to nature protection. Klose and other legal advisors spent seven weeks reviewing drafts of this law, hardly the efforts of those who were not sincere about this particular measure.[64]

Other aspects of the political environment surrounding the RNG reinforce the notion that this legislation reflected Nazi ideology. Attempting to create a unified and authoritarian legal system in the early 1930s, the regime formally abolished Germany's federal structure, making individual states like Prussia or Bavaria subordinate to Wilhelm Frick's Ministry of the Interior, and appointed loyal Nazis to positions in each state.[65] The RNG fully reflected this unitary approach.[66] More importantly, Göring did not proclaim the RNG until 1935, by which time the Nazi regime had already passed a number of other popular conservation measures. In the spring of 1933, Rust's Ministry of Education swept aside bureaucratic wrangling and decreed a new law protecting animals and plants. Other important legislation followed in the next year.[67] Hoping to protect a valuable source of timber and a symbol of national identity, Göring's Reich Forest Office issued tough regulations to reverse the policy of planting only conifers in the woodlands, a practice that destroyed valuable animal habitat and undermined the economic viability of German forests.[68] Familiar motives also inspired Germany's new wildlife management laws. For years, German hunters faced a confusing jumble of hunting decrees. Rules varied widely from state to state, and regulations on licensing, game quotas, and trapping lacked clarity.[69] In addition, populations of game animals like elk, grouse, and partridges were dwindling. Germany needed clear, detailed regulations to restore these game animals and eliminate confusion among hunters. Under Prussia's chief forester, Germany passed a Reich Hunting Law that provided a single body of hunting guidelines for all of the Reich, tight gun licensing rules, and limits on the use of snares, traps, decoys, and other techniques.[70]

German officials extolled these measures in ideological language and portrayed these policies as part of a unified plan to restore national vigor.

In his 1934 book on the subject, Schoenichen proclaimed the importance of defending Germany against the influence of "liberalism" and of preserving woodlands, moors, and heaths in the interest of creating a new Volksgemeinschaft.[71] Germany's new laws all contributed to this goal, according to Schoenichen. Legislation protecting rare plants would guarantee that "the common good takes precedence over the individual good," while the National Socialist state would use its new hunting regulations to restore rare animal species. Schoenichen portrayed the RNG as part of this larger agenda.[72]

Calling the RNG the "Magna Carta" of German nature protection, Klose declared that previous regimes had been unable to pass such a measure because "those essential political and worldview assumptions were lacking."[73] Other conservationists also placed this law in the proper ideological context. The editors of the periodical *Natur und Heimat* announced that "the foundation of the Reich Nature Protection Law states clearly and without a doubt that nature protection is an essential part of the worldview of National Socialism."[74] Such declarations were commonplace during the mid-to-late 1930s. In a 1938 article in the publication *Blätter für Naturschutz,* Schwenkel extolled three great laws that would preserve the "soulfulness and creative powers of the Nordic people."[75] These were the Reich Animal Protection Law, the Reich Hunting Law, and the Reich Nature Protection Law, all of which guaranteed that all Germans—even those living in poverty—would have a chance to enjoy nature. In the same article, Schwenkel gratuitously declared that "since the first book of Moses, the Jews do not know nature protection, since God has given to the children of Israel all the plants and animals for their enjoyment."[76]

Given that the text of the RNG drew heavily from ideas predating the 1930s, the question arises: why should such comments be construed as evidence of ideological connections between the RNG and the National Socialist movement? Could one not argue that Schoenichen's statements were mere propaganda? After all, only the preamble to the law specifically and intentionally referenced the National Socialist worldview, reflecting Klose's comments about the "essential political and worldview assumptions" necessary to pass such an impressive measure. Klose even repudiated this statement years later, pleading (unconvincingly) that no one would be able to find evidence of specific National Socialist thoughts in the text of the law, except for the preamble. A non-Party member, Klose maintained that the Nazi Party objected to the law in principle, and he insisted that another Nazi minister had "smuggled" questionable, ideological language into the preamble, just prior to the law's adoption by the government in July 1935.[77]

Yet the mere fact that well-known conservationists like Schoenichen and Schwenkel praised the RNG in ideological terms is significant. Quite apart from the argument already made in this essay—that sections of the law dealing with landscape protection or property rights *did* reflect elements of National Socialist ideology—it is important to understand that propagandistic statements like those of Schoenichen or Schwenkel can have serious consequences. In a well-known study of architectural design in Germany, Barbara Miller Lane argued that architecture under the Nazis did not actually demonstrate totalitarian control over style. Throughout the 1930s, she pointed out, German architects designed buildings that suggested a diversity of concepts, some radical, some neoclassical, and others traditional. In many cases, Nazi architecture reflected developments common to modern styles of the 1920s and to other countries. Yet the Nazis publicized their new buildings with a great deal of propaganda, associating ideological significance to a variety of buildings and styles. This massive propaganda campaign served several functions. First, it publicly reproduced for observers the many conflicting tendencies within architectural design in Germany during the 1920s and 1930s. Second, it created a public impression of a far greater level of building activity than actually existed, an effect that reinforced notions of National Socialist dynamism, creativity, and vigor.[78]

As with architecture, Nazi propaganda associated with the RNG publicly emphasized the dynamic, authoritarian character of the Nazi regime, and its willingness to undertake bold and dramatic measures in the interest of creating a racially pure society. By the mid-1930s, several prominent conservationists had enlisted in this publicity campaign, including Schoenichen, Klose, and others. These men honestly supported the regime and its nature protection policies, and their commitment to the Nazi state underscores the way that the regime successfully co-opted middle class scientists, teachers, and other professionals.[79] Following Lane's line of reasoning, the propaganda associated with conservation policies served to create and reinforce connections between the idea of "nature" and National Socialist ideas of racial superiority. As Gert Gröning and Joachim Wolschke-Bulmahn have demonstrated in their work on regional planning under the Nazis, there is a danger for society when a regime links concepts of "nature" to political agendas like those of the Nazis. Since many people consider nature, and the protection of nature, to be inherently good, there may be a tendency to assume that the other motives surrounding the protection of nature are good as well.[80]

This sort of ideological confusion was clearly a possibility during the Third Reich. Once World War II began, Nazi experts followed the German army into occupied Poland and immediately began to implement National Socialist planning concepts on a massive scale. They justified the forced removal of thousands of Poles from their homes on the grounds that such an allegedly degenerate race of people could never have a proper relationship to nature and to those portions of the countryside occupied by the German army.[81]

The bureaucrats who were associated with the RNG also participated in this form of environmental imperialism, once the war began. From 1939 to 1943, Klose, now director of the Reich Nature Protection Office, argued for the extension of existing Naturschutz laws into occupied portions of Poland.[82] Indeed, the Nazis installed their own nature protection officials in occupied eastern Europe, and these officials immediately attempted to extend German conservation law into captured lands.[83] In the annexed portion of Poland known as the Warthegau, officials in the Reich Nature Protection Office catalogued numerous plots of land for designation as future nature preserves. Rationalizing this action, Naturschutz official Dr. Kurt Hueck characterized some of this land as uniquely "German" and in need of protection because of the presence of German inhabitants in the region.[84] Some officials—such as Schoenichen—indulged even wilder fantasies, and attempted to create a huge national park in the Bialowieża Forest, an area occupied by Polish and Jewish villagers. Schoenichen was seemingly oblivious to the moral problems and intellectual contradictions associated with the desire to protect a "primeval" woodland by removing or murdering the local inhabitants.[85]

Several things may explain the ability of men like Schoenichen and Klose to resolve such contradictions. Klose was a consummate opportunist, willing to bend his convictions depending upon the regime in power, and always determined to expand the influence of the Reich Nature Protection Office and the RNG. Schoenichen was a more committed Nazi, a firm believer in the racist ideology of "blood and soil" and the belief that landscape shapes national character.[86] These factors may explain why both men, for different reasons, made their peace with a murderous regime.

Regardless of their motives, neither openly questioned the contradictions between the goals of the RNG and the more sinister policies of the

National Socialist movement.[87] In addition, their activities in occupied eastern Europe and their attempts to implement the RNG in regions acquired by conquest demonstrate that there are dangers for a society when such impressive laws are linked with the political goals of a conquering regime. Any obvious contradictions between the protection of nature and a lack of regard for conquered peoples would have been obscured by the ideological rhetoric surrounding this law, regardless of the text of the law itself.

My examination of the RNG and its supporters underscores several points about the current debate on whether or not the National Socialist state was green. Among other things, it demonstrates that National Socialism was hardly monolithic: it was a movement capable of accommodating men like Schoenichen and Klose, in addition to many Nazi officials with little regard for the concerns of nature and landscape protection. The overwhelming indication that ministries within the Nazi regime worked to undermine Naturschutz policies in the late 1930s is ample evidence of the polycentric character of the Nazi movement.[88] More importantly, the example of the RNG demonstrates that current debates about whether this legislation reflected National Socialist ideology may be missing the point. If Nazi officials attached ideological meaning to the RNG, and if only the Nazi regime was capable of passing such a measure, then we can justifiably conclude that it was a law that reflected Nazi ideology. Only by understanding this can we fully appreciate the appeal of National Socialism to members of the Naturschutz movement, and to those Germans who shared a reverence for nature during the 1920s. Finally, the example of the Reich Nature Protection Law demonstrates that historical debates about environmental sensitivity within the Nazi regime are valuable exercises, especially since they underscore the way that political agendas unrelated to the preservation of nature may affect environmental policy.[89]

Notes

1. Some of the following articles and books provide useful discussions of the RNG: Karl Ditt, "Nature Conservation in England and Germany, 1900–1970: Forerunner of Environmental Protection?" *Contemporary European History* 5, no. 1 (1996): 17–18; Ditt, "Naturschutz zwischen Zivilizationskritik, Tourismusförderung und Umweltschutz: USA, England und

Deutschland, 1860–1970," in *Politische Zäsuren und gesellschaftlicher Wandel im 20. Jahrhundert: Regionale und vergleichende Perspektiven,* ed. Matthias Frese and Michael Prinz, special issue, Westfälisches Institut für Regionalgeschichte Landschaftsverband Westfalen-Lippe Münster, 18 (Paderborn: F. Schöningh, 1996): 504–29; and Raymond H. Dominick III, *The Environmental Movement in Germany: Prophets & Pioneers, 1871–1971* (Bloomington, IN: Indiana University Press, 1992), 107–8.

2. For a discussion of how the history of the Reich Nature Protection Law has distressed some scholars, see Thomas Lekan, "Regionalism and the Politics of Landscape Preservation in the Third Reich," *Environmental History* 4, no. 3 (1999): 384. For evidence of contrasting opinions on this subject, see Dominick, *Environmental Movement,* 111–15, 222.

3. Anna Bramwell, *Blood and Soil: Richard Walther Darré and Hitler's "Green Party"* (London: Kensal Press, 1985), 171–200; and Anna Bramwell, "Was This Man 'Father of the Greens'?" *History Today* 34 (September 1984): 7–13. See also the chapter by Gesine Gehard in this volume.

4. Simon Schama, *Landscape and Memory* (New York: Alfred A. Knopf, 1995), 82, 119–20. Also, see Thomas Lekan's discussion of this controversy in "Regionalism and the Politics of Landscape Preservation," 384.

5. See quotes in Dominick, *Environmental Movement,* 111 and 222, respectively.

6. See discussion and quote ibid., 222.

7. Karl Ditt, "Die Anfänge der Naturschutzbewegung in Deutschland und England, 1935/49," in *Naturschutz und Nationalsozialismus,* ed. Joachim Radkau and Frank Uekötter (Frankfurt: Campus, 2003), quote at 119, full discussion at 107–44.

8. Edeltraud Klueting, "Die gesetzlichen Regelungen der nationalsozialistischen Reichsregierung für den Tierschutz, den Naturschutz und den Umweltschutz," in Radkau and Uekötter, *Naturschutz und Nationalsozialismus,* 92–101.

9. Ditt, "Die Anfänge der Naturschutzbewegung," 119.

10. For a discussion of Nazi ideology, see Dominick, *Environmental Movement,* 87–102. For scholarship which discusses the dangers present for a society which fails to see linkages between a political worldview and reverence for nature, see Douglas Weiner, "Demythologizing Environmentalism," *Journal of the History of Biology* 25, no. 3 (Fall 1992): 387–93.

11. Michael Wettengel, "Staat und Naturschutz, 1906–1945: Zur Geschichte der staatlichen Stelle für Naturdenkmalpflege in Preußen und der Reichsstelle für Naturschutz," *Historische Zeitschrift* 257 (1993): 362–64, 367, 378; Hans Klose, *Fünfzig Jahre staatlicher Naturschutz: Ein Rückblick auf den*

Weg der deutschen Naturschutzbewegung (Giessen: Brühlscher Verlag, 1957), 30–32.

12. See quote in Dominick, *Environmental Movement,* 82, and remaining discussion in Klose, *Fünfzig Jahre Staatlicher Naturschutz,* 19–33.

13. See text of the RNG in *Reichsgesetzblatt,* part 1, no. 68, 1 July 1935. See also Ditt, "Nature Conservation in England and Germany," 17; Dominick, *Environmental Movement,* 82, 107–8. Klose, *Fünfzig Jahre Staatlicher Naturschutz,* 19–33.

14. See Sections 5, 19, and 20 of the RNG in *Reichsgesetzblatt,* part 1, no. 68, 1 July 1935. See also portions of text quoted in Ditt, "Nature Conservation in England and Germany," 17–19.

15. Ditt, "Nature Conservation in England and Germany," 12–13, 17–19; Dominick, *Environmental Movement,* 108; Wettengel, "Staat und Naturschutz," 380–81. See Section 24, RNG, in *Reichsgesetzblatt,* part 1, no. 68, 1 July 1935.

16. Raymond Dominick argues that Nazi Germany "adopted the most comprehensive and progressive nature conservation legislation then in effect anywhere in the world." As evidence, Dominick cites the Reich Nature Protection Law, Nazi Germany's Reich Hunting Law, and laws protecting animals and plants. See Raymond H. Dominick III, "The Nazis and the Nature Conservationists," *Historian* 49, no. 4 (August 1987): 508 (quote) and 534–35 (other references to German laws).

17. For evidence on conservation in Great Britain, see Anna Bramwell, *Ecology in the 20th Century: A History* (London: Yale University Press, 1989), 48–49; Ditt, "Nature Conservation in England and Germany," 4–9; John Sheail, "Wildlife Conservation: An Historical Perspective," *Geography* 69, no. 1 (January 1984): 119; Peter Gould, *Early Green Politics: Back to Nature, Back to the Land, and Socialism in Britain, 1880–1900* (Sussex: The Harvester Press, 1988), 147–63. For additional discussions of France's efforts, see Peter L. Nowicki, "National and Nature Park Protection in France," *Parks* 8, no. 2 (July 1983): 4. Regarding other nations besides Germany, Great Britain, and France, see Paul Hochstrasser, "Naturschutz-, Natur-, und Nationalparke," *Naturschutz und Nationalparke* 45, no. 2 (1967): 8–11; and Douglas R. Weiner, "The Changing Face of Soviet Conservation," in *The Ends of the Earth: Perspectives on Modern Environmental History,* ed. Donald Worster (New York: Cambridge University Press, 1988), 253–57.

18. RNG in *Reichsgesetzblatt,* part 1, no. 68, 1 July 1935.

19. See the discussion of Romanticism as an inspiration for *Naturschutz* in Dominick, *Environmental Movement,* 25–30, quote from Rudorff at 26. For a discussion of who supported Naturschutz in the late 1800s, see 58–60 ibid.

20. Ibid., 26–29; Klaus Georg Wey, *Umweltpolitik in Deutschland: Kurze Geschichte des Umweltschutzes in Deutschland seit 1900* (Opladen: Westdeutscher Verlag, 1982), 128–31.

21. See quote on Conwentz's definition of natural monuments in Ditt, "Nature Conservation in England and Germany," 14, and rest of discussion of Conwentz's work in Prussia at 14–15.

22. Dominick, *Environmental Movement*, 53. Wolfgang Erz, "Geschichte des Naturschutzes: Rückblicke und Einblicke in die Naturschutz-Geschichte," *Natur und Landschaft* 65, no. 3 (1990): 104. For a useful summary of Germany's major Naturschutz laws, see Wolfgang Erz, "Zur zeitgeschichtlichen Entwicklung von Naturschutz und Landschaftspflege," in *Erhalten und Gestalten: 75 Jahre Rheinischer Verein für Denkmalpflege und Landschaftsschutz,* ed. Josef Ruland (Neuss: Verlag Gesellschaft für Buchdruckerei AG, 1981), 386–87. See also the overall account of Conwentz and his work at Wettengel, "Staat und Naturschutz," 365–73.

23. See quotes at Wettengel, "Staat und Naturschutz," 364.

24. Walther Schoenichen, *Naturschutz, Heimatschutz: Ihre Begründung durch Ernst Rudorff, Hugo Conwentz, und ihre Vorläufer* (Stuttgart: Wissenschaftliche Verlagsgesellschaft M.B.H., 1954), 39, 54, 69, 178–95, 214, 226, 236–39, 281–83, 289; Klose, *Fünfzig Jahre staatlicher Naturschutz*, 22; Wettengel, "Staat und Naturschutz," 363–79; Wey, *Umweltpolitik in Deutschland*, 137.

25. See quote and discussion in Ditt, "Naturschutz zwischen Zivilizationskritik, Tourismusförderung und Umweltschutz," 518.

26. See quotes from Rudorff at Wettengel, "Staat und Naturschutz," 360.

27. For a general discussion of this movement, see ibid., 359–60. For a discussion of middle-class support for the Heimatschutz movement, see William H. Rollins, "Aesthetic Environmentalism: The *Heimatschutz* Movement in Germany, 1904–1918" (PhD diss., University of Wisconsin, 1994), 172–73. See also Dominick, *Environmental Movement*, 29, 46–47, 51, 53, 57.

28. Both Ammon and Nordau are quoted in Rollins, "Aesthetic Environmentalism," 120.

29. Ibid., 97–117, 126–36.

30. Quoted from Section 5, RNG, in *Reichsgesetzblatt,* part 1, no. 68, 1 July 1935.

31. See quote from RNG, ibid., and quotes from Rudorff in Erz, "Geschichte des Naturschutzes," 104.

32. See the summary of Ernst Rudorff's ideas in Erz, "Geschichte des Naturschutzes," 104.

33. See Section 20, RNG, in *Reichsgesetzblatt,* part 1, no. 68, 1 July 1935.

34. Rollins, "Aesthetic Environmentalism," 147–54, and see specific quotes regarding these laws at 152.

35. Erz, "Zur zeitgeschichtlichen Entwicklung von Naturschutz und Landschaftspflege," 386. See also Wey, *Umweltpolitik in Deutschland,* 141–45.

36. Klose, *Fünfzig Jahre Staatlicher Naturschutz,* 30–32; Wey, *Umweltpolitik in Deutschland,* 132–39.

37. More than anyone else, Alfred Runte has emphasized the cultural, aesthetic roots of the American national park system. Runte states that the original impetus behind America's first national parks was "the search for a distinct national identity" and not any particularly ecological or environmental concerns. See Alfred Runte, *National Parks: The American Experience* (Lincoln: University of Nebraska Press, 1997), xxii. See also Karl Ditt, "Naturschutz zwischen Zivilizationskritik, Tourismusförderung und Umweltschutz," 500–504, 508–12; and Ditt, "Nature Conservation in England and Germany," 4–9, 15–19.

38. Wettengel, "Staat und Naturschutz," 372–81.

39. Dominick, *Environmental Movement,* 87–90, 93–101, 114.

40. See quotes in Wettengel, "Staat und Naturschutz," 373, and remaining discussion at 372–77.

41. Quote from Dominick, *Environmental Movement,* 88–89. See also evidence that Schoenichen joined the Nazi Party in 1933, ibid., 98–102. For evidence of his support for a comprehensive Naturschutz law, see Walther Schoenichen, *Naturschutz im Dritten Reich: Einführung in Wesen und Grundlagen zeitgemäßer Naturschutz-Arbeit* (Berlin-Lichterfelde: Hugo Behrmühler Verlag, 1934), 85.

42. Quoted in Wettengel, "Staat und Naturschutz," 379.

43. Quoted ibid., 380.

44. Schoenichen, *Naturschutz im Dritten Reich,* 82.

45. Ibid., 84.

46. Ibid., 82.

47. Ibid., 75–85.

48. Ibid., 84.

49. Dominick, *Environmental Movement,* 85–90, 92–96.

50. Quoted in Dominick, "The Nazis and the Nature Conservationists," 514. For evidence that Schwenkel supported a Reichsnaturschutzgesetz during the 1930s, see Hans Klose, "Der Schutz der Landschaft nach § 5 des Reichsnaturgesetzes," in Hans Klose, Hans Schwenkel, and Werner Weber, *Der Schutz der Landschaft nach dem Reichsnaturschutzgesetz* (Neudamm: Verlag von J. Neumann, 1936), 7.

51. Quoted in Dominick, "Nazis and the Nature Conservationists," 514.

52. Walther Schoenichen, "'Das deutsche Volk muß gereinigt werden.'—Und die deutsche Landschaft?" *Naturschutz* 14, no. 11 (1933): 207.

53. Walther Schoenichen, "Vom Naturschutz im neuen Staat," *Naturschutz* 16, no. 1 (1935): 4.

54. Klose, *Jahre Fünfzig staatlicher Naturschutz,* 30–33. Various groups protested the lack of action of the part of German governments during the 1920s. See the letters of protest to the Prussian government in the archives of the Prussian State at Geheimes Staatsarchiv Preußischer Kulturbesitz (hereafter designated as GStA), HA Rep. 90a, Nr. 1798; Rep. 151, Nr. 155.

55. Wey, *Umweltpolitik in Deutschland,* 134–38.

56. Ibid., 137.

57. Meeting of the Prussian ministries of justice, the interior, and culture, GStA HA Rep. 90a, Nr. 1798, 260–69. Throughout the 1920s and until 1932, Prussia was a bastion of support for Weimar's republican government. In 1927, it was governed by a coalition of the Social Democratic Party of Germany and the Center Party. See V. R. Berghahn, *Modern Germany: Society, Economy, and Politics in the Twentieth Century* (Cambridge: Cambridge University Press, 1987), 80, 92, 109.

58. Reich Ministry of Science, Education, and Culture, "Betrifft: Entwurf eines Naturschutzgesetzes," 6 March 1935, Bundesarchiv Potsdam (BAP), R II 43/227.

59. Quoted in the meeting, "Vorläufige Begründung zum Entwurf eines Naturschutzgesetzes," March 1935, BAP, R II 43/227.

60. See RNG in *Reichsgesetzblatt,* part 1, no. 68, 1 July 1935.

61. See ibid. For evidence that this law echoed earlier versions, see Wettengel, "Staat und Naturschutz," 382–99. See also portions of a draft of the 1927 Prussian Nature Protection Law, 17 January 1927, GStA HA Rep. 90a, Nr. 1798, 260–77. For a discussion of Hugo Conwentz's Prussian Office for the Care of Natural Monuments, see Dominick, *Environmental Movement,* 51–53, 108.

62. The debate over this measure within the Nazi regime is well documented by several scholars. For references to the competition for control of nature protection, see Dominick, *Environmental Movement,* 107; Wettengel, "Staat und Naturschutz," 382–85; Klueting, "Die gesetzlichen Regelungen." For evidence that some Nazi ministers continued to be concerned about property rights in 1936 and for the ability of the regime to override those concerns, see various memoranda in files of the Reich Ministry of Finance, BAP, R 2/4730. For a discussion of infighting in Nazi Germany, see Berghahn, *Modern Germany,* 152.

63. See Dominick, *Environmental Movement,* 107; Wettengel, "Staat und Naturschutz," 383; Berghahn, *Modern Germany,* 152.

64. Klose, *Fünfzig Jahre staatlicher Naturschutz,* 33, 36; Wettengel, "Staat und Naturschutz," 382–87. For more details on mixed woodland forestry, see

Aldo Leopold, "Deer and Dauerwald in Germany: I. History," *Journal of Forestry* 34, no. 4 (April 1936): 374.

65. Klaus Fischer, *Nazi Germany: A New History* (New York: Continuum, 1995), 278–79, 319–21.

66. Ditt, "Nature Conservation in England and Germany," 17–18.

67. Dominick, "The Nazis and the Nature Conservationists," 534–36.

68. Anna Bramwell, *Ecology in the 20th Century*, 199; Aldo Leopold, "Deer and Dauerwald in Germany: I. History," 366–75. See also the chapter by Michael Imort in this volume.

69. Erich Gritzbach, *Hermann Goering: The Man and His Work* (London: Hurst & Blackett Ltd., 1939), 49.

70. Ibid., 58–65; *Prussian Hunting Law of 18 January 1934*, 2d ed. (trans. n.d.; Berlin: Paul Parey, 1934), 1; Aldo Leopold, "Naturschutz in Germany," *Bird Lore* 38, no. 2 (March–April 1936): 103–5, 110.

71. Schoenichen, *Naturschutz im Dritten Reich*, 3.

72. Ibid., 46, and rest of discussion at 85.

73. Klose, "Der Schutz der Landschaft nach § 5 des Reichsnaturgesetzes," 5, 7.

74. "Im Zeichen des Reichsnaturschutzgesetzes," *Natur und Heimat* 3, no.1 (January–March 1936): 1.

75. Hans Schwenkel, "Vom Wesen des deutschen Naturschutzes," *Blätter für Naturschutz* 21, no. 3/4 (October 1938): 74.

76. See quote, ibid., 74, and full discussion at 74–75.

77. See discussion and quote in Klose, *Fünfzig Jahre Staatlicher Naturschutz*, 34. See discussion of Klose's status in Dominick, *Environmental Movement*, 119, 222.

78. Barbara Miller Lane, *Architecture and Politics in Germany, 1918–1945* (Cambridge: Harvard University Press, 1968), 212–16.

79. This argument is put forward by Raymond Dominick in *Environmental Movement*, 96–115.

80. Gert Gröning and Joachim Wolschke-Bulmahn, "Politics, Planning and the Protection of Nature: Political Abuse of Early Ecological Ideas in Germany, 1933–1945," *Planning Perspectives* 2 (1987), 127–48; Gert Gröning and Joachim Wolschke, "Naturschutz und Ökologie," *Die Alte Stadt* 10 (1983): 1–16. See also Weiner, "Demythologizing Environmentalism," 385–93.

81. Gröning and Wolschke-Bulmahn, "Politics, Planning and the Protection of Nature," 135–39.

82. See memoranda on Klose's actions in his letter to the Reich Forest Office, 11 December 1939, Reichsstelle für Naturschutz, Bundesarchiv Koblenz (BAK), B 245/88, 254–60; "Betrifft: Einführung des Reichsnaturschutzgesetzes im Regierungsbezirk Kattowitz," 2 February 1940, BAK, B 245/197, 510–19.

Regarding the Sudetenland, a magazine article indicated that Nazi officials implemented the Reichsnaturschutzgesetz in that part of Czechoslovakia. See "Verordnung zur Einführung des Reichsnaturschutzgesetzes im Reichsgau Sudetenland. Vom 25. Oktober 1939," *Nachrichtenblatt für Naturschutz* 16, no. 12 (1939): 121.

83. See notes 79–81, and see also Hans Klose to Otto Tumm, 4 February 1943, BAK, B 245/137, 14–17.

84. Kurt Hueck, "Bericht über die Bereisung des Reichsgaues Wartheland im Oktober und November 1940," n.d.; BAK, B 245/137, 20–82.

85. See Gröning and Wolschke-Bulmahn, "Politics, Planning and the Protection of Nature," 133–35; Schama, *Landscape and Memory,* 70–71.

86. For evidence of their ideological convictions, see Dominick, *Environmental Movement,* 111–23; Wettengel, "Staat und Naturschutz," 380–87.

87. See Klose's comments about the RNG in Klose, *Fünfzig Jahre staatlicher Naturschutz,* 34. Regarding Schoenichen, none of the works cited here demonstrate that he publicly questioned his own role in spreading German Naturschutz policies into occupied lands. See especially Dominick, *Environmental Movement,* 111.

88. Dominick, *Environmental Movement,* 106–15; Wettengel, "Staat und Naturschutz," 387–97.

89. See Douglas Weiner's cautionary note about environmentalism, "Demythologizing Environmentalism," 385–93.

CHAPTER 2

"Eternal Forest—Eternal *Volk*"

The Rhetoric and Reality of National Socialist Forest Policy

Michael Imort

THE TERM MOST frequently associated with German forest policy during the Nazi era is *Dauerwald,* best translated as "perpetual forest" or "eternal forest." Dauerwald is a form of *naturgemäße Waldwirtschaft,* or "natural forest management," and as such it corresponds closely to what is today called "close-to-nature" forestry or ecoforestry. As a holistic form of silviculture, the Dauerwald doctrine rejects many of the mechanistic tenets of "scientific forestry," a form of forestry that was conceived in Germany in the eighteenth century in response to the perceived threat of a wood shortage caused by a rapidly expanding economy. The principal difference is that scientific foresters concern themselves with maximizing wood production, while Dauerwald advocates also seek to improve the health of the forest ecosystem, arguing that in the long run their practices produce both healthier forests and more sustainable yields.

In 1934, the Nazis mandated the Dauerwald as the official silvicultural doctrine for the German Reich. Puzzling contradictions, however, mark its implementation. For instance, some policies enacted by the self-anointed *Reichsforstmeister* or "Reich master of forestry" Hermann Göring and his lieutenants were ecologically aware to a degree not seen again until the 1980s, when the swelling Green movement forced mainstream politics to embrace environmental perspectives. At the same time, many other measures clearly undermined the principle of ecological sustainability inherent in the Dauerwald. Finally, still other regulations obfuscated the underlying forestry concerns by employing the racist jargon of the Nazis, trumpeting measures to ensure "racial purity" and the "eradication of stands of poor race" so as to "cast out the unwanted foreigners and bastards that have as little right to be in the German forest as they have to be in the German *Volk*."[1]

Reconciling these contradictions is no easy task. Do they simply reflect a lack of conceptual coherence on the part of forest policy makers? Rare is the country that has a wholly consistent forestry practice, especially in times of political and economic upheaval. Or are the inconsistencies symbolic of the polycentric character of the Nazi state? It is well known, after all, that Nazi industrialists, agriculturalists, and other groups fought fiercely with each other over land, water, and other natural resources. Or do the contradictions simply reflect the Nazis' underhanded way of co-opting environmentalism for their ideological purposes? Most German foresters today seem to favor the ideological explanation. "Forestry during the Nazi period," states a well-known bon mot, "was like the forest itself: green on the surface, brown underneath."

This chapter analyses the contradictions that accompanied the adoption and adaptation of the Dauerwald doctrine between 1933 and 1945. First, I examine whether the Nazis simply marshaled Dauerwald terminology for their own goals, both within and outside the forestry sector, or whether there was indeed some green substance behind the brown rhetoric. Second, I examine whether the forest policies enacted by Nazis left at least some kind of positive environmental legacy, regardless of their ideological foundations. I argue that the Dauerwald doctrine was proclaimed mainly because it offered the Nazis an abundance of propagandistic analogies between German forest and German Volk. At the same time, several of the laws enacted during the Dauerwald period were technically sound and ecologically progressive enough to either remain in force for decades after the end of the Third Reich or serve as models for postwar forest policies in West Germany. This means that these Nazi policies produced a positive environmental legacy. How are we to understand this tension between brown intentions and green outcomes—or, as the case may be, between green intentions and brown outcomes? Or, put differently: "How green were the Nazis?"

The question as such suggests that the Nazis employed concepts (whether out of conviction or as a smoke screen) that we would label green or environmental today. Obviously, the notion of green as we know it today did not exist in the 1930s. It follows that the Nazis must have been referring to a different (though comparable) concept when they stressed the importance of what we now call green forestry or ecoforestry. Similarly, if we assume that a green veneer is suitable for providing cachet for another, less respectable idea, we tacitly accept that the term *green* has a mainly positive connotation. If green has a positive connotation today, it is only because environmental thinking moved from the radical fringe into the mainstream of public awareness in the 1980s. Within forestry, the Dauerwald concept had "ecological" and positive connotations that are comparable to those we ascribe to the term green today. In other words, the organic view of nature that underlay the Dauerwald model in the 1930s corresponds to a large degree with what we would label holism, environmentalism, sustainability, biodiversity, habitat protection, and ecological management today. Where foresters in the 1930s spoke of the forest as an organism, we would now use the term ecosystem; where they used the term organic, we would think green.

The notion that the Nazis promoted green or environmentally aware forest policies is based almost entirely on the fact that they made the Dauerwald model mandatory for all German forests. To appreciate how much of a break with tradition the imposition of the Dauerwald approach represented at the time, we must first understand the main differences between the "scientific forestry" that had been practiced during the previous centuries and the "eternal forest" of the Nazi "reformers."

From Scientific Forestry to Dauerwald:
A Primer in German Silviculture

Beginning in the late eighteenth century, German foresters developed the theories and methods necessary for restocking over-exploited forests and reforesting marginal soils that had been cleared for agriculture. In its most basic form, scientific forestry was based on the idea that a properly managed forest should be planted, thinned, and cut in even-aged management blocks of equal area. The blocks were planted as monocultures with frugal yet fast-growing species such as Norway spruce (*Picea abies*) and Scots pine (*Pinus sylvestris*). As the stands matured, they were gradually thinned and then clear-cut and replanted, producing graduated age classes that were arranged in a systematic "felling series" across space and time: the perfect *Normalwald,* or "normal forest." Ideally, the strict implementation of this system over several rotation periods leads to a forest structure that provides a sustained yield: an equal quantity of wood of equal dimensions is grown and cut each year in perpetuity. In fact, it was in the context of the normal forest that the theory of *Nachhaltigkeit* or "sustained yield" was first developed.

At first, scientific forestry appeared to be a panacea: within a few decades, the quickly maturing conifer plantations had doubled the productivity of the forest, providing the booming German economy with mine props, railway ties, and construction wood of all dimensions. Scientific forestry developed into one of Germany's premier intellectual exports as more and more countries hired German foresters or sent their foresters to study in Germany at the newly founded forestry academies. But even as German forestry practices were celebrated around the globe, the forestry sector at home deteriorated in unexpected ways. The recession of 1873–79 strangled the wood market and led to a collapse of revenues for producers. At the same time, the fixed costs incurred by thinning and other silvicultural measures prescribed by scientific forestry began to mount. To make matters worse, cheap wood imports flooded into Germany from Russia and other countries that still practiced exploitation forestry.[2]

Meanwhile, a serious ecological crisis began to compound the economic troubles of forest owners. Scientific forestry was founded on plantation methods and it shared the same problems as other monocultures. First, it exhausted the forest soil. Second, it made the stands vulnerable to pests and disease, or felling by wind, hoarfrost, and snow. The collapse of entire stands led to a growing disenchantment with scientific forestry, and beginning around 1850, foresters began to publish on the virtues of silviculture based on uneven-aged, mixed stands of site-adapted species. In essence, these foresters argued that a profitable and sustainable forestry could not ignore ecological constraints but had to adapt to them. Foresters such as Gottlob König, Emil Adolf Roßmäßler, and Karl Gayer sounded the clarion call of "Back to Nature," recognizing that each species in the forest played an important role in the well-being of the forest as a whole. Consequently, they demanded mixed forests instead of pure stands; continuous uneven-aged stands instead of even-aged blocks; retention or reintroduction of broadleaf species such as beech and maple; and a return to natural regeneration methods instead of clear-cutting followed by planting.[3]

Around 1920, Professor Alfred Möller of the Prussian Forestry Academy at Eberswalde refined these critiques of scientific forestry into a complex new approach to forestry, which he was the first to call Dauer-wald.[4] The general idea was to manage the "forest organism" (what we would call "forest ecosystem" today) rather than just the trees.[5] To ensure the continual presence and health of all components of the forest organism from the dominant trees all the way down to the soil fungi, Möller demanded that the forest canopy never be removed: no ecological shock such as clear-cutting was to disrupt the permanence and harmony of the forest. The main tenets of the Dauerwald concept were:

1. continual selective cutting rather than periodic clear-cutting;

2. natural regeneration rather than planting;

3. multilayered structure rather than uniformly tall, even-aged stands;

4. the use of a variety of site-adapted species rather than monoculture; and

5. maximization of sustainable yield in terms of value rather than volume.

The overall intention was to create a diverse forest structure that was more stable in ecological and economic terms. Immediately after its publication, Möller's Dauerwald idea sparked a lively debate, with reformers and traditionalists squaring off at forestry conventions and expending much ink on the topic. Möller died in 1922 before his approach was field-tested, but his ideas continued to fuel debate to the point where the "Dauerwald question" became the main point of dissension among German academic foresters in the 1920s. Nonetheless, only a handful of forest owners actually switched to a management plan based on Dauerwald tenets, and no state forest administration declared it official policy. That makes it all the more surprising that the Nazis so quickly embraced this largely untested approach to forestry and imposed it on the entire German forest. The sense of surprise felt by contemporaneous observers is palpable in a comment by Aldo Leopold: "The Germans, who taught the world to plant trees like cabbages, have scrapped their own teachings and gone back to mixed woods of native species, selectively cut and naturally reproduced. . . . In their new Dauerwald the hard-headed Germans are now propagating owls, woodpeckers, titmice, goshawks, and other useless wildlife."[6] Leopold left no doubt about what he thought of the new policy: "The Germans realized that increment bought at the expense of soil health, landscape beauty, and wildlife is poor economics as well as poor public policy."[7]

Were Leopold and others blinded by the green veneer of National Socialist forest policy? Did the Nazi government indeed mandate the Dauerwald policy because it wanted to put an end to the negative ecological consequences of traditional scientific forestry? Or were there other reasons, economic or political, that informed this decision? In the following three sections I will argue that the Nazis appropriated the Dauerwald concept not primarily for ecological reasons, but because of Göring's personal preference for the idea, the economic circumstances of the early 1930s, and particularly the suggestive potential of the Dauerwald for *völkisch* propaganda. This last point will return us back full circle to Göring's paramount role, for, as we will see in the subsequent sections, no other Nazi figure was more active in putting that potential to work for the aims of the Nazi regime.

Göring and Dauerwald

Probably the single most important reason for the Nazis' adoption of the Dauerwald idea was the personal *Waldgesinnung* or "forest-mindedness" of Göring, the second most important leader in the Nazi state. An avid huntsman and self-proclaimed forest lover, Göring went to great lengths to bring German forestry under his personal control—and to change the entire German forest into a Dauerwald. The forest historian Rubner suggests that Göring's love affair with the Dauerwald idea began in the spring of 1932, when he was invited to the forest estate of Walter von Keudell, a retired Reich minister of the interior and one of the few prominent practitioners of Dauerwald forestry. Von Keudell introduced his guest to the ecological and economic advantages that he saw realized through the application of Dauerwald forestry to his estate—and Göring was greatly impressed.[8] While it is impossible to reconstruct the exact reasons from the surviving records, one may speculate that, as a private individual, Göring was probably taken with the good hunting opportunities. As an astute *homo politicus,* however, Göring likely realized the enormous propagandistic potential of the "primeval" appeal of an "organic" Dauerwald compared to the "mechanistic" monotony of a Normalwald. To the Nazis, the Dauerwald offered a commonsense metaphor for an "organic" Germanic heritage to which they could hark back in their propaganda.

Whatever the exact reasons, Göring soon used his power to implement the Dauerwald in all forests under his rapidly expanding jurisdiction. When Göring became prime minister of Prussia, he made von

Keudell chief of the Prussian State Forest Office. Promptly, in a series of decrees beginning as early as September 1933, von Keudell mandated Dauerwald principles for the tending of all Prussian forests.[9] At the same time, Göring began grooming von Keudell's staff in the Prussian State Forest Office into the cadre of a future Reich forest ministry. On 3 July 1934, the cabinet indeed transferred jurisdiction over forestry and hunting to a new Reichsforstamt (Reich Forest Office), which was headed by Göring as the Reichsforstmeister (Reich master of forestry). Göring picked von Keudell as his deputy (*Generalforstmeister*) and gave him the task of "synchronizing" German foresters and their professional associations with the Nazi state and bringing the Dauerwald concept to bear on all German forests. While not called a Reich ministry, the new Reichsforstamt nonetheless functioned as such and its de facto minister Göring embarked on setting forestry guidelines for the entire Reich. There was some initial insistence upon the vestiges of *Länder* (state) jurisdiction with regard to forest policy, but soon most state forest services saw themselves forced to follow the instructions Göring handed down through his increasingly powerful Berlin office.[10] One of the first actions of the Reichsforstamt was to expand the Dauerwald doctrine from Prussia to the entire Reich. Now, all German forest owners had to adhere to the following regulations:

1. refrain from cutting conifer stands under fifty years of age (offenses were punishable by up to one year in jail);

2. refrain from clear-cutting more than 2.5 percent of their forest;

3. use single-tree-selection cutting principles rather than clear-cuts;

4. cut the worst rather than the best trees so as to improve the overall quality of the stand and allow only the best specimens to reproduce;

5. refrain from cutting the oldest and biggest trees, and instead cut in the lower age and volume ranges to meet the harvest quota;

6. take measures to promote a mixed species composition and uneven-aged structure; and

7. revisit stands and perform improvement cuts at least every third year.

These rules reflect an approach to forestry that we would today call ecoforestry, for they placed an emphasis on small-scale management, selective cutting in short intervals, avoidance of clear-cuts, and promotion of a mixed, uneven-aged structure across the entire stand. Then as now, such an approach stands in marked contrast to the established normal forest model of scientific forestry that governs most sustainable forestry operations.

Radical as it was, the policy change paralleled the mandate of the new Reichsforstamt to promote "the maintenance of the protective functions of the forest" (*Wohlfahrtswirkungen*), which included habitat protection, watershed management, and recreation.[11] The preamble to the Law of 3 July 1934 Concerning the Transfer of Forestry and Hunting Affairs to the Reich stated clearly that the new Reichsforstamt, and the centralized legislation it was expected to generate, should promote these ecological functions on par with those functions of the forest relating to wood production and labor markets. This represented a dramatic departure from the emphasis on the economic importance of the forest that had traditionally been at the center of political debates about forestry. Obviously, the Dauerwald concept with its emphasis on the perpetual maintenance of natural processes fit well with this new mandate. Still, the question arises: was the adoption of the Dauerwald policy a consequence of the new mandate? More likely the reverse was the case: it stands to be argued that it was Göring's preference for the Dauerwald idea that led him to dictate the new mandate.

The new rules as listed above also illustrate that the policy change went well beyond the ecological dimension: most of the new rules actually told forest owners when and how they could harvest and market their forests and thus represented far-reaching impositions on their freedom to utilize their property. This leads us to the second circumstance that facilitated, if not favored the imposition of the Dauerwald concept as forest policy: the depressed economic conditions of the early 1930s.

Dauerwald in the Economic Context of the 1930s

There can be no doubt that the imposition of the Dauerwald policy represented an abrupt break with German silvicultural dogma. The effect of the new policy on forest owners' economic freedom, however, was less dramatic than one might think because German forest owners were already accustomed to restrictive forest laws. Many nineteenth-century state forest laws obligated German forest owners to manage their estates in ways that preserved both the forest area and the growing stock. Furthermore, forest owners were obligated to prevent any forest devastation and to maintain the cultural landscape. With forest owners already accustomed to state interference, the Nazis found it relatively easy to impose policies that further circumscribed individual forest owners' freedom to pursue economic goals and instead obligated them to manage their forest in a way that was primarily beneficial to the Volk or nation as a whole. This de facto socialization of the forest was frequently couched in slogans such as "The German forest is a national property" (*Volksgut*). Accordingly, Reichsforstmeister Göring insisted that "those who have it on fief from the people" had to shoulder "the duty of furthering the economic welfare of the entire nation," a goal that was "more important than financial success." In other words, the forest was to be managed for maximum collective productivity, rather than individual profit.[12]

Yet there was another important factor contributing to forest owners' acquiescence in accepting the economic restrictions of the Dauerwald policy: the depressed wood market of the early 1930s. Revenues from the forest are tied to the demand for wood. A slow economy depresses wood prices, prompting all but the most cash-strapped forest owners to postpone cuts and let their growing stock compound in the hope of better days to come. With this mechanism in mind, a parallel can be drawn between the depressed economic situation in Germany in the early 1920s and the early 1930s, and the popularity of the Dauerwald concept during those respective years. This parallel builds on the fact that Dauerwald forestry eliminates certain expenses (by not requiring clearing, planting, and weed control), allows the postponement of other expenses (by not prescribing a rigid management plan), and maximizes future product value (by concentrating growth on the largest, most valuable trees). For these reasons, the Dauerwald model can be very appealing under the conditions of a depressed wood market. In Germany, this was the case during the inflationary crisis of the early 1920s, when the Dauerwald theory was first introduced. Similarly, the effects of the Great Depression and intense import competition from low-cost producers such as Poland and the Soviet Union had halved producer prices for wood between 1928 and 1932. Thus, when the Nazis imposed the Dauerwald doctrine in 1933, some forest owners might well have acquiesced to a policy that reduced their fixed short-term costs, even if they did not necessarily welcome the limitations the new policy imposed on their cherished silvicultural freedom, or *Waldbaufreiheit.* In the long run, the Dauerwald method also had the additional advantage of concentrating growth on the biggest and most valuable trees, which meant that the latter were becoming disproportionately more valuable with every additional year. In economic terms, the Dauerwald method thus combined immediate savings with the promise of increased future revenues.

From the preceding arguments we might conclude that the Nazis mandated the Dauerwald policy because it represented a rational management approach for the German forest under the conditions of the early 1930s—and because Hermann Göring wanted the Dauerwald. Why do we seem less surprised by the latter than by the former? The answer has as much to do with the apparent ad hoc character of decision-making within the Nazi regime as with the "evidence" the Nazis themselves left behind in the form of their prolific propaganda, much of which was concerned with expounding Göring's view that the Dauerwald supposedly exemplified Germandom and National Socialism in its purest form. Quite possibly, this consistent conflation of "green" organicism and Germandom in the propaganda is one of the reasons we ask the question "How green were the Nazis?" today. Our next task will thus be to take a critical look at how exactly the Nazis employed the Dauerwald concept in their propaganda, both within and outside of the forestry sector.

The Dauerwald Rhetoric in Nazi Propaganda

Why would the Nazis be interested in using the Dauerwald concept for their propaganda? The answer is that it allowed "commonsense" analogies to be drawn between individual trees and the forest on one hand, and individual citizens and the nation on the other. Specifically, by emphasizing that the Dauerwald had an "organic" structure, that it comprised only *bodenständige* (native) species, and that it was a collective and perpetual entity that had no fixed morphology or lifespan, the Nazis were able to naturalize their ideal of a classless, racially pure, and "eternal" *Volksgemeinschaft* or national community.

1. Only native, site-adapted tree species were allowed to be a part of the Dauerwald forest; similarly, only those Germans that were of the "proper" racial heritage could be *Volksgenossen* or members of the national community.

2. Individual trees played an important role as components of the Dauerwald forest, but they did so at their "proper station," with some

dominating and others serving within the greater organic whole; similarly, every Volksgenosse was assigned to a task and a position that most benefited the corporatist Volksgemeinschaft, rather than himself or herself.

3. The best trees in the Dauerwald forest were to be privileged in terms of light and space so a greater share of the growth might accrue to them; similarly, those Volksgenossen of the "best race" were to receive incentives and rewards for child rearing and other ways of "serving the nation."

4. Selective cutting, thinning, and pruning ensured that the stand was continually improved in terms of phenotype and "race"; similarly, those individuals who did not fit the National Socialist vision of "race" were to be "removed" from the collective of the Volk.

5. Selective cutting meant that while individual trees were removed constantly, the stand was never cleared entirely and the forest as a whole was perpetual; similarly, while the individual Volksgenossen were dispensable and lived only for a relatively short time, the Volksgemeinschaft as a whole was perpetual, or, in Nazi parlance, "eternal."

Evidently, most of these analogies are not contingent on the Dauerwald model but are just as easily constructed on the basis of the normal forest model of scientific forestry. As we will see shortly, Nazi propaganda in fact did not limit itself to the exploitation of Dauerwald-specific analogies but frequently used the forest in general to extol the National Socialist ideal of community and malign the democratic emphasis on the individual. Yet it was those analogies that were unique to the Dauerwald idea that were particularly useful to the Nazis. For example, the first analogy, based on the Dauerwald's exclusion of introduced, "foreign" species, conveniently naturalized the Nazis' own racial precepts.[13] It was the last analogy, about the timeless and permanent "organism," however, that made the Dauerwald idea most appealing to the National Socialists. Its emphasis on the permanence of the collective over the ephemerality of the individual fit perfectly with the vision of a Thousand Year Reich. As a professor of silviculture at the prestigious Forestry Academy at Tharandt trumpeted, "The new tendency in silviculture has its foundation in National Socialist philosophy and includes the principle . . . of biological sustained yield corresponding to the idea of the eternity of the German people within its living-space."[14]

Not surprisingly, the Nazified forestry journals of the mid-1930s were full of articles celebrating this supposedly natural and eternal bond between forest and Volk with never-ending comparisons of silviculture and politics in general, and Dauerwald forestry and National Socialism in particular.[15] Reichsforstmeister Göring himself made the analogy between Dauerwald and National Socialism more than explicit: "Forest and people are much akin in the doctrines of National Socialism. The people is [*sic*] also a living community, a great, organic, eternal body whose members are the individual citizens. Only by the complete subjection of the individual to the service of the whole can the perpetuity of the community be assured. *Eternal forest and eternal nation are ideas that are indissolubly linked.*"[16] In the same vein, one of the most vocal proponents of the Dauerwald idea explained the affinity thus: "The *Dauerwald* idea has much in common with our National Socialist idea of life, of the state, of race, blood, and soil. . . . Hence it is not surprising that the new leadership adopted this novel idea of the forest immediately after coming to power."[17] Finally, still other foresters were even more succinct: "Ask the trees, they will teach you how to become National Socialists!"[18]

Why would the editors of forestry periodicals spend so much effort on trying to indoctrinate their readers with the analogy between Dauerwald and National Socialism? The answer is that foresters, with their exceptionally high reputation among the German populace, were frequently called upon as local dignitaries. The journals assisted foresters by expounding the obligatory party line, with some even providing exemplars of speeches laced with opportune analogies foresters could use in their public speaking engagements. To further "reeducate" them for their public duty, foresters were drafted into *Weltanschauliche Schulungslager* (ideology camps) to receive "ideological and physical training."[19] The fact that foresters shared this "honor" with relatively few other professions such as teachers and university lecturers indicates how important the National Socialists thought foresters were as public role models in the rural districts.[20]

For example, in 1935, all Saxon state foresters under the age of 55 had to spend one week in the NS-Gauführerschule (National Socialist District Leader Training School) at Augustusburg castle. At this boot camp, foresters of all ranks (even full professors!) had to eat, sleep, and wash in common quarters with bunk beds. They exercised in "forest runs" and "battle games," formed "potato-peeling kitchen detachments," and had to pass spot inspections of their quarters while standing at attention in their pajamas. Yet the "strict regime of military and athletic duties" was only meant to provide the "framework" for "ideological presentations as the core of the entire training."[21] The *Reichsstatthalter* (Reich governor) of Saxony himself spelled out the purpose of this training camp: "Apply and carry through in the outside world everything you hear and experience here. Do so as the loyal soldiers of the Führer—soldiers who can march and shoot if need be."[22] The whole idea behind reeducating foresters in this way was to enable and exhort them to "comprehend the nature of the forest that surrounds you daily, and apply the spirit of its community of life to the German Volk."[23] In essence, foresters were asked to help reform the Volk according to the laws of nature as the Nazis saw them realized in the Dauerwald.

Evidently, the Nazis saw foresters as multiplicators of public opinion who were important to win over. But the notion of the eternal forest and its supposed lessons for the German Volksgemeinschaft were also grafted onto art exhibitions, trade shows, coffee table books, and other cultural products in entertainment and education that were designed for the general population.[24] For example, in the preface to a 1936 biology textbook for middle school, the respected natural historian Konrad Guenther explained that the book "shows us that the balance among the components of the forest is maintained through the consumption of those who are superfluous, and that the survivors are those who are stronger and healthier, so that both the struggle and its victims serve the community. Thus the forest teaches us the foundational laws of a völkisch and racially aware state such as the National Socialist one. And that is no coincidence."[25] From an early age, the lessons of the forest thus were to educate German pupils about both the nature of the state and their role in society.

With such völkisch "education" being ubiquitous in the Nazi state, it is not surprising that the message of "The Eternal German Forest" was also pitched in the movie theaters. In 1936, a propaganda film with the title *Ewiger Wald* (Eternal Forest) premiered in German cinemas. It presented a sequence of vignettes on the two-thousand-year history of the German Volk with images of historical figures and events emerging from the forest. Using the new technique of fading, the film suggested the interchangeability of Germans and trees by dissolving one into the other. The film was not coy about telling the audience how it should further connect the specifics of forestry, and particularly the practice of improvement cutting as employed in Dauerwald forestry and as shown in the film, to the life-or-death question of race, blood, and soil. Thus one scene shows an axe in close-up while a chorus exhorts the audience from the off: "Excise what is of foreign race and sick." In the next shot, the axe cleaves the dead wood of a dry tree. Before the tree crashes to the ground, the axe appears once more in a close-up and the chorus spells out the mission of the New Germany:

> From the multitude of species,
> Create the new community of the eternal forest,
> Create the eternal forest of the new community.[26]

This carefully selected "new community" was the racially pure Volksgemeinschaft, its "eternal forest" the Dauerwald. Both were to protect and help reproduce one another: the Volksgemeinschaft maintained the "eternal forest," which in turn provided the physically challenging and spiritually nourishing environment that was necessary for the continual honing of the "German race." The film left no doubt that Germans were to glean from the "natural" example of the Dauerwald forest how to prune and racially purify the human forest: just as the eternal Dauerwald tolerated only healthy specimens of native, site-adapted species, the Volksgenossen were encouraged to take up the axes of euthanasia and other forms of systematic murder and "excise what is of foreign race and sick" from society.

Despite this blatant and ubiquitous injection of ideology into books, films, and other cultural products dealing with the forest, we should not assume that this represented an entirely new phenomenon. Since the turn of the century there had been a swelling current of völkisch propaganda that used the forest in a similar way as an analogy of the German state and nation.[27] In fact, the Nazis likely adopted the völkisch analogy between forest and nation precisely because it was an idea with which the public was quite familiar already. What was new about the way the Nazis used the forest and especially the Dauerwald idea in their propaganda was how they distorted the organic (what we would now call green) perspective into a Social Darwinist one: much of the Nazi propaganda argued from the ecological necessity of a healthy, resilient, and diverse German forest (represented by the Dauerwald) to the perceived social necessity of an equally healthy, resilient, and stratified German Volksgemeinschaft. It is because of this unsavory association of the "green" Dauerwald idea with rabid National Socialist propaganda that we feel uneasy today about even considering the possibility that the Nazis could have promoted forest policies that had positive environmental consequences. And yet it appears that they did just that: the Nazis decreed several regulations that claimed to protect the environment in general and the forest in particular. Will this claim stand up to scrutiny once we cut through the smoke screen of propaganda and examine the concrete laws and regulations? In other words, were there Nazi forest policies that turned out to be ecologically beneficial in practice?

The "Green" Record of National Socialist Forest Policy

As we saw in the preceding sections, Göring and his Reichsforstamt were quick to issue laws, decrees, and directives for the German forestry sector. While many of those regulations were designed to bring forestry and foresters politically in line with the emerging one-party state, there were also many of exclusively or primarily technical content. Overall, we can distinguish three intentions behind the legislative activities of the Reichsforstamt: Göring's desire to reform German silviculture through the application of Dauerwald forestry; the determination of high-ranking forestry officials to centralize jurisdiction over all public and private forests in a Reich Forest Office that had the power to issue Reich-wide regulations; and the Nazis' goal of achieving autarky in wood and wood products. When looking merely at the number of regulations issued between 1933 and 1945, it is easy to lose sight of the first two intentions because, as soon as the German economy was revived through massive state expenditures and wood demand went up sharply, regulations were overwhelmingly and explicitly concerned with increasing both the cutting quota and the utility value of the forest.

For instance, as early as 1935, Göring had to raise the cutting quota in all publicly owned forests to 150 percent of the sustained yield in order to meet the wood demand of the booming German economy; in December 1936, the same quota was imposed on all private forest owners as well.[28] In February 1937, the Reichsforstamt was ordered to report on its contingency plan in case of a war and how it planned to improve its preparedness.[29] As the newly appointed plenipotentiary for the Four-Year Plan, Göring now had to sacrifice his love of Dauerwald principles and take measures to ramp up the wood output of the German forest at all cost. To avoid violating its own regulations, the Reichsforstamt was forced to issue new regulations that allowed cuts to exceed the limits set by the 1934 Dauerwald regulations. When it became obvious that the Dauerwald figurehead von Keudell was not willing to adjust to the new realities, Göring replaced him with the jurist Friedrich Alpers, a party functionary and SS officer. Within weeks, a new set of silvicultural regulations was issued that relaxed the Dauerwald policies.[30]

Ironically, it was Alpers's comparative ignorance in forestry matters that allowed the experts in the Reichsforstamt to draw up a compromise that retained the best principles of the Dauerwald policy—those calling for the (re)establishment of a mixed, uneven-aged forest structure—while granting individual foresters more freedom regarding when and how to cut in order to fulfill the new quotas. In general, forest owners were free to devise their own management plans as long as they remained true to the general idea of "close-to-nature" (naturgemäß) forestry and as long as they produced the required quota of wood. While effectively marking the end of the Dauerwald era sensu stricto, the new regulations thus also enshrined some of the Dauerwald principles as fundamental management rules for German forestry. For example, the new regulations repeated the stipulation that forestry had to be "close-to-nature," which in essence meant that the composition, structure, and management of the German forest had to be appropriate for the ecological site conditions—even though the primary function of the forest was to supply wood. This emphasis on ecologically aware productivity was expressed in the compound name for the new policy—*naturgemäßer Wirtschaftswald*—in which the noun *Wirtschaftswald* (commercial forest) was qualified by the adjective *naturgemäß* (close-to-nature). Until the regulations of 1 December 1937, these two terms would have been understood as mutually exclusive.

With the new regulations in force, however, foresters now had to reconcile the two approaches and find common ground in order to execute the orders of the regime: to produce as much wood as possible with the most ecologically benign methods available. The shift from Dauerwald to naturgemäßer Wirtschaftswald in the years 1936–37 thus marks a watershed in the legislative activities of the Nazis concerning the forest: until that point, the emphasis was on restructuring the German forestry sector and on improving the ecological and economic stability of the forest. After that time, the autarky goal can be seen as the dominating influence on German forest policy right up to the end of the Third Reich. With that distinction in mind, we will inspect some of the milestones of National Socialist forest policy with a view to their ecological impact and legislative legacy, both of which extended well beyond 1945.

The Dauerwald Decrees

Through von Keudell, Göring began to prescribe Dauerwald forestry as the silvicultural doctrine as early as September 1933. The Silviculture Decree of 17 January 1934 Concerning Tending of Individual Trees and the Silviculture Decree of 30 May 1934 Concerning Tending Blocks mandated new treatment guidelines for the Prussian forests that were subsequently extended to all of Germany. The goal was to rebuild the German forest into a mixed, uneven-aged perpetual forest with a high percentage of deciduous species. This forest was to be managed as an "organism" or ecosystem with the intent of maintaining its "health" or ecological integrity in perpetuity—essentially the same ecological goals that underlie the management principles of contemporary ecoforestry. When the Dauerwald decrees were revised into the new policy of the naturgemäßer Wirtschaftswald in 1937, those ecological goals were retained as the general principles for forestry operations—even beyond 1945. In fact, following the devastation caused by acid rain in the 1980s and wind storms in the early 1990s, most German state forest administrations declared naturgemäße Waldwirtschaft or "close-to-nature forest management" the guiding principle of their operations in the hopes of improving the ecological stability of their forests.

The Dauerwald decrees thus had a positive ecological legacy in that they introduced foresters at all levels to a holistic view of the forest that emphasized the forest rather than the stand or individual trees as the basic management unit. Seen from this perspective, the imposition of Dauerwald principles was a first step toward loosening the grip of the normal forest model on German forest policy and introducing holistic ideas of forest management. Partly for this reason, renowned West German foresters have described the Dauerwald era under von Keudell as "halcyon years of German forestry."[31]

The National Afforestation Program

In 1934, the Nazis initiated a National Afforestation Program whose initial purpose was as a workfare scheme that put unemployed men to work in the forest. While not specifically the result of a forestry sector initiative, the program nonetheless can be seen as part of the overall forest policy, as Göring's new Reichsforstamt quickly stamped its imprint on it. Under the provisions of the Law for the Reduction of Unemployment of

1 June 1933, landowners could apply for loans to pay for subsidized labor detachments of the Freiwilliger Arbeitsdienst (Voluntary Labor Service, made compulsory and renamed Reichsarbeitsdienst in 1935) to plant forests on their land. The concluding passage of the application instructions issued by the Reichsforstamt suggests distinctly ecological intentions behind the program: "The great social economic value of this national afforestation program is assured not alone by its scope, but more significantly by the manner of its execution. To be avoided, under all circumstances, is the creation of forests which owing to inappropriate composition will be seriously threatened by calamities of various sorts, such as storms, insects, and fungi; especially pure conifer forests. In all cases the aim must be to use those methods of establishing the stand which will result in a mixed forest. . . . Certain broadleaf trees, the 'stepchildren of forestry,' also deserve special consideration."[32] Besides stressing the creation of ecologically stable and aesthetically pleasing mixed forests, the program also had a positive impact on the development of the total forest area in Germany, with 40,000 hectares (98,800 acres) afforested in the first year of the program alone.[33] Between 1933 and 1945, the total net balance of forest area remained positive with an average of 1,500 hectares of new forest created every year.[34] Obviously, this did not amount to a substantial increase in the total German forest area of more than 10 million hectares (which the program hoped to increase by a full 2.5 million hectares). Yet the positive net balance must nonetheless be seen as an ecological achievement, particularly in view of the intense pressure on forest lands caused by the intensification of agriculture, the expansion of military areas, and the construction of the autobahn network.[35]

The Reich Laws of 1934 and 1935

During the years 1934 and 1935, the Nazis promulgated several Reich laws concerning forestry matters that had the effect of holding forest owners to stricter standards of ecological diversity and sustainability. Several of these laws were considered beneficial enough to remain in effect for decades after 1945 and thus imparted long-lasting legacies on the German forestry sector. The first Reich-wide forestry law was the Law Against Forest Devastation of 18 January 1934, which prevented forest owners from clear-cutting more than 2.5 percent of their estate. In addition, the cutting of any conifers under fifty years of age was banned, as was reducing the standing volume of a forest to less than 50 percent of the age-standardized target volume. Finally, all cut-over areas had to be reforested according to "proper forestry principles." The law has been called "progressive for its time" by forest historians because it prevented private forest owners from meeting current account deficits by liquidating the standing forest capital.[36] This is all the more surprising as the law to some degree impeded the mobilization of all forest resources for the war preparations that were to begin only two years later. In fact, even during the war years, with the demand for wood being higher than ever before, any cut that exceeded the sustainable annual cut by more than 60 percent had to be authorized by the Reichsforstamt.[37] The laudable intention of ensuring both ecological and economic sustainability of the forest was recognized by the policy makers of the Federal Republic of Germany and the law remained in effect in West Germany until a comprehensive Federal Forest Law superseded it in 1975.

The second Reich law of ecological consequence was the Law of 13 December 1934 Concerning the Protection of the Racial Purity of Forest Plants. Assessing the ecological value of this law is tantamount to a tightrope walk, as it is difficult to separate bona fide ecological intentions behind the law from the openly racist attitude its wording betrays (see n. 1). Without doubt, the law fit with the Nazi goal of enforcing the "racial principle" in all aspects of German society, in this case the seemingly mundane question of whether a certain provenance of seed produced straight or crooked trees. At the same time, however, foresters could point to sound silvicultural reasons why seeds should be certified: too many stands were collapsing because they had grown from seeds that were inappropriate for the ecological site conditions. To prevent such costly mismatches, the new law allowed only the best phenotypes for certified seed production. Obviously, humans have always employed selective breeding principles to improve the productivity or resilience of domesticated animals and plants, including forest trees. In the context of the Nazi regime, however, the law's emphasis on "racial" selection takes on an ominous dimension, as it foreshadowed the Nuremberg racial laws that applied those same principles to humans within a year's time. In light of this, can we legitimately assess the ecological dimension of this law separately from its ideological dimension? If we decide that the answer is yes, we must acknowledge that the law indeed filled an ecological need in that it ensured a better match between site conditions and phenotype and thus increased the ecological appropriateness of the forest stand. Apparently, the lawmakers of the Federal Republic shared this view, as they waited until 1957 to revise the law. At that time the wording, but not the intent, of the law was changed.

The third Reich law of ecological consequence was the Reichsnatur-schutzgesetz (Reich Nature Protection Law, or RNG) of 26 June 1935. It is connected to the forestry sector in that it placed all aspects of nature con-servancy under the jurisdiction of the Reichsforstamt.[38] Consequently, as of 1935, Göring was not only Reichsforstmeister and Reich master of the hunt but also the supreme commissioner for nature conservancy. From this trinity of positions, Göring was effectively able to legislate in all as-pects concerning the natural and cultural landscapes, with the exception of agricultural landscapes, which fell under the jurisdiction of Richard Walther Darré and his Reichsnährstand (Reich Food Estate).[39] With only four full-time academic personnel, the nature conservancy branch of the Reichsforstamt was only sparsely staffed compared to the forestry and hunting branches with their combined staff of 71 academics. This was ex-plained with the argument that "proper" forestry, and particularly Dauer-wald forestry, already practiced "exemplary" nature conservancy as a matter of course, and that the entire forest administration supported na-ture conservancy efforts ex officio.[40]

Despite its meager personnel complement, the nature conservancy branch in the Reichsforstamt pursued three national park projects, until all had to be shelved as nonessential to the war effort. By the beginning of the war, nonetheless, almost eight hundred smaller-scale nature pro-tection areas (*Naturschutzgebiete*) had been created, many of them in forested areas.[41] In the context of a densely populated country such as Germany, where total protection across extensive areas is an elusive goal, such local and regional preserves provide important exclusion zones where activities and practices that could be detrimental to flora and fauna are either prohibited or subject to prior authorization. Similarly, the Reich law compiled the existing state and regional lists of protected species into a Reich-wide list that made protection efforts more consis-tent and effective. Thus, while German nature conservancy may have been at the mercy of the Nazi state, it should not be overlooked that the Reich Nature Protection Law helped slow the deterioration of overall ecological conditions in Germany. In terms of its ecological legacy, the law provided for measures toward the in situ protection of plant and animal species, in effect amounting to an early form of habitat protec-tion. The law remained in force until 1976, at which time it was enlarged into the Federal Nature Conservancy Law.

With the exception of the Reich Nature Protection Law, the regulations decreed by the Nazis for the forestry sector were never intended to be more than temporary "Band-Aids," as the goal was to replace them with a comprehensive Reich Forest Law that was to put German forestry on a new ecological, social, economic, and political footing. That law never progressed past the draft stage, however, and the "temporary" laws remained on the books. The fact that many did so for decades after the end of the Third Reich can be seen as a testimony to their technical quality, notwithstanding their ideological birthmarks. Yet, as we will see in the final section, the draft of the elusive Reich Forest Law probably exerted a more lasting and ecologically beneficial influence on German forestry than any of the actual legislation passed by the Nazis. This is largely the result of a fundamental reconceptualization of the German forest from a private commodity to a public ecological resource, a process that, cynically enough, was facilitated by the dictatorship's ability to disregard the objections of private forest owners.

The Reich Forest Bill

For the better part of its eleven years of existence, the Reichsforstamt was busy preparing a Reich Forest Bill that was to reflect the state of the art in German silviculture, forest policy, and civil administration. Admittedly, the bill was a product of its authoritarian time in that it called, for example, for the abolition of traditional rights in favor of a centralized and uniform Reich-wide forest administration, and the autarkist maximization of wood production. On the other hand, it contained many laudable principles that obligated forest owners to manage their forest so as to improve the ecological, social, and economic well-being of society as a whole. Although the bill never became law, many of these principles resurfaced after 1945 in a number of West German state forest laws and eventually in the Federal Forest Law of 1975.[42] In these reincarnations, the ecological and social principles of the Reich Forest Bill have informed West German forest policy to the present day. This was possible because, as contemporary German forest historians have asserted, the draft was "largely free of National Socialist ideas."[43] Instead of yielding to overblown political demands from forces outside forestry, the draft concentrated on laying the foundation for a forestry sector that was ecologically healthy, economically sustainable, and socially stable in the long term. An English version of the draft published in 1936 identified the following paramount tasks for German forestry:

1) cultural interests of people: formation of more intimate relations between forest and people, care for the beauty of the forest;

2) cultural interests of the land: improvement of conservation effects of forest (climate, protection from wind, water protection, prevention of erosion, etc.);

3) defensive economics: production of raw material in emergencies;

4) national economics: supply of all demands for the products of the forest; and

5) social interests: co-operation in unemployment schemes.

The fulfilment of all these tasks is guided by the principles of sustained yield and maximum economic efficiency.[44]

Thus, while all five tasks ultimately were to be accomplished within the limits set by an all-encompassing wood supply management plan, they were also to be governed by ecological, social, and economic sustainability. Moreover, the ranking of the tasks and the elaborate explanations in the preamble indicated that the main task of the forest was now understood as providing services to society, rather than the individual forest owner. This newly defined public character of the forest required that *all* forest owners—states, municipalities, corporations of public law, private individuals—were subject to the same laws. Consequently, the Reich Forest Bill for the first time delineated universal standards that held for *all* forests in Germany, regardless of who owned them and whether they were situated in Hesse, Bavaria, or Prussia. This meant that private forest owners could no longer evade the strict silvicultural standards (such as longer rotation periods and higher standing volume per hectare) that earlier state laws had already imposed only on publicly owned forests; at the same time, they now also had a right to technical and financial assistance from the centralized forest administration, which enabled them to pursue said standards.

With its new wording, its new ranking of the functions of the forest, and its claim to universality, the Reich Forest Bill stressed for the first time the overarching ecological and social importance of the forest for society as a whole. In today's terminology, the "cultural interests of people" are equivalent to the recreational and socio-hygienic functions of the forest, while the "cultural interests of the land" are what we today call ecological benefits, such as watershed management, erosion control, avalanche prevention, soil amelioration, and flood control. By declaring "cultural interests" the first and second priorities of German forestry, the Reich Forest Bill underscored the ecological importance of the forest for nature and society. After 1945, this recognition resurfaced in the forest laws of the Federal Republic, all of which stress the equal importance of the productive, protective, and recreational functions of the forest.[45] The Reich Forest Bill represented the first time that the protective ecological function of the forest was codified, and so imparted an important and lasting environmental legacy to German forestry. This leaves us with a final, intriguing question: if the Reich Forest Bill was indeed the pièce de résistance of forest policy in the New Germany, and if its scientific foundations were obviously sound enough to be built upon after 1945, why did it stall?

The first reason for the failure of the bill is that it became a casualty of turf wars in the polycentric Nazi state. To begin with, internal rivalries in the Reichsforstamt thwarted progress, as party functionaries and politically uninterested experts fought over how much of a political imprint the bill should carry. More important, though, Göring's declared goal of bringing all German forests under his sole and absolute jurisdiction alarmed his colleagues in cabinet, who saw the integrity of their own portfolios threatened. Walter Darré, for one, insisted that his Reichsnährstand retain jurisdiction over privately owned forests (mostly by farmers). This blocked Göring's plans for a universal Reich Forest Law until the beginning of the war, when the dovish Darré was sidelined in a cabinet shuffle. Thus it was only in January of 1940 that a first full draft of the bill could be printed and circulated to obtain the necessary placet from the ministries of agriculture, finance, justice, labor, and the interior.

Alas, the subsequent discussions about the massive document, with 199 sections and more than a hundred pages of commentary, proved just as difficult as before Darré's ouster. Now the strongest opposition came from the Interior Ministry, which resisted Göring's attempt to detach his forest administration from the hierarchy of general administration and invest it with independent planning, policing, and other powers over forested land. Other unforeseen difficulties arose when the Nazi leaders of recently annexed Austria refused to agree to a Reich Forest Bill that would have required them to more or less hand over jurisdiction over much of their forest to a centralized Reichsforstamt in Berlin. The final roadblock to the realization of the Reich Forest Law in 1940, however, was the fact that the war had brought substantial foreign forest resources under German control. In 1934, the German Reich had produced 44 million cubic meters of wood. By 1938, the autarky measures had forced this figure to 60 million, an increase largely effected by raising the annual cut to 150 percent of the sustainable yield. By 1940, the rapid advance of the Wehrmacht had brought the forests of Czechoslovakia, Poland, France, and Norway under German control, while Romania, Sweden, and Finland were bullied into "cooperation" with the monopolistic German wood marketing board. From these sources, the German market now had access to an additional eight million cubic meters per year from annexed Austria alone, another three from the Sudetenland, and more than six from France. Meanwhile, the army simply cut whatever it needed locally, amounting to approximately two million cubic meters per year in France, but more than ten times that number on the eastern front.

During the mid-1930s, Göring had repeatedly argued that a Reich Forest Law was urgently needed to make Germany self-sufficient in wood. Now that the forests of other countries could be plundered instead, this argument backfired: to the same degree that the pressure on the domestic forest eased, the perceived urgency to pass a comprehensive Reich Forest Law declined too. In turn, this enabled the Interior Ministry in particular to insist on changes that made a second draft necessary. Alas, just when the revised second draft was finally ready in 1942, the changing fortunes of war dealt the final blow to the Reich Forest Bill: Hitler shelved it and all other laws that were "nonessential to the war effort" until after the war.

In the end, the Reich Forest Law was delayed and eventually scuttled by factors and interests external to the forestry sector: ideological disagreements over the role of the state, jealous protection of turfs and competencies, regional animosities, and, finally, the fortunes of war proved more powerful obstacles to reforming German forestry than any professional debates over the silvicultural merits of the Dauerwald doctrine ever could. In fact, it could be argued that the progressive Dauerwald idea and the ecologically aware components of the Reich Forest Bill could only survive the demise of the Third Reich and be resurrected in the forest policies of West Germany because they were not implemented in earnest during the Nazi regime. Had they been implemented, the green aspirations of German foresters between 1933 and 1945 (such as they were) would doubtless have been sullied even more by the brown outcomes of their policies—which in turn would have made the question "How green were the Nazis?" an even more delicate one.

This chapter has attempted to assess the rhetoric and reality of National Socialist forest policy. The analysis has shown that any examination of the ecological intentions and legacy of forest policy during the Nazi period is complicated by the often contradictory statements and actions of the regime itself, as well as by the very effective utilization of the forest in propaganda, which continues to blur the subject matter to this day. Despite these difficulties, several conclusions can be drawn, with the caveat that they not be seen as definitive results, but rather as starting points for further investigation.

First, if analyzed in isolation from the political circumstances of the Nazi regime (an admittedly problematic suggestion), several of the forest laws and decrees of the years 1933–45 can be characterized as mostly beneficial in purely ecological terms. They severely limited clear-cuts, proscribed plantation-style silvicultural techniques, and improved the species composition and age structure of forest stands. The progressive character of these laws is reflected in the fact that they remained in force for decades after the end of the undemocratic regime that issued them.

Second, the war saved the Nazi regime from having to prove in the long term how serious it was about implementing either the Dauerwald idea or the abortive Reich Forest Law. Prior to the war, the Nazis quietly undermined their own Dauerwald doctrine by ramping up Germany's wood production in the name of rearmament and autarky. Once the war started, the pressure on the domestic forest eased as German foresters followed behind the front lines to exploit the forest resources of occupied countries. Ironically, the increased supply reduced the urgency of passing the Reich Forest Law and so delayed a fuller implementation of ecologically aware forestry until after 1945.

Third, the most far-reaching and long-lasting ecological legacy of National Socialist forest policy was the fundamental revaluation of the forest developed in the Reich Forest Bill. The bill represented a conceptual advance over previous forest policy in that it gave *equal* standing to the ecological, recreational, and economic functions of the forest. Where economic considerations used to dominate the debates about the utility of the forest, the Reich Forest Bill stressed its ecological importance for the well-being of both nature and society. It also obligated *all* forest owners to manage their forest with due care, in a sustainable fashion, on the basis of a plan, with the proper techniques, and for the benefit of the cultural landscape and the human population. In effect, forest owners were told that owning forest property brought with it just as many public obligations as it did private entitlements. After 1945, the West German forest laws at the state and federal levels reprised and refined the ideas laid out in the Reich Forest Bill and so made the ecological intentions of the bill become reality.

Fourth, as the discussed examples of National Socialist propaganda have shown, the regime did not tire of representing the forest, and particularly the Dauerwald, as an analogy of the German Volk and state and as the cornerstone of National Socialist ideas of race, community, and eternity. The effect of this intensive use of the forest in propaganda inside and outside the forestry sector was a lingering "brown" taint of forestry and foresters—one that continues to complicate any appreciation of their "green" achievements, such as those discussed in this chapter.

Notes

1. Wilhelm Parchmann's explanation of the Law of 13 December 1934 Concerning the Protection of Racial Purity of Forest Plants, as quoted in H. Knuchel, "Was geht forstlich in Deutschland vor?" *Schweizerische Zeitschrift für Forstwesen* 86, no. 3 (1935): 92. Parchmann was the head of the Forestry Policy Unit (Forstpolitischer Apparat) of the Nazi Party.

2. Heinrich Rubner, *Forstgeschichte im Zeitalter der Industriellen Revolution* (Berlin: Duncker & Humblot, 1967), 130–50.

3. Gottlob König, *Die Waldpflege aus der Natur und Erfahrung neu aufgefasst* (Gotha: Becker'sche Verlags-Buchhandlung, 1849); Emil Adolf Roßmäßler, *Der Wald: Den Freunden und Pflegern des Waldes geschildert* (Leipzig: Winter, 1860); Karl Gayer, *Der Waldbau* (Berlin: Paul Parey, 1880); Karl Gayer, *Der Gemischte Wald* (Berlin: Paul Parey, 1886).

4. Alfred Möller, *Dauerwaldwirtschaft* (Berlin: Julius Springer, 1921); Alfred Möller, *Der Dauerwaldgedanke: Sein Sinn und seine Bedeutung* (Berlin: Julius Springer, 1922).

5. Möller's use of the term *organism* was criticized even then, a decade before Tansley introduced the term *ecosystem* in 1935. Most critics suggested Möller use the term *Lebensgemeinschaft* or "community of life" instead.

6. Aldo Leopold, *A Biotic View of Life* (paper given at the Meeting of the Ecological Society of America on June 21, 1939).

7. Aldo Leopold, "Deer and Dauerwald in Germany," *Journal of Forestry* 34, nos. 4 and 5 (1936): 366–75, 460–66.

8. Heinrich Rubner, *Deutsche Forstgeschichte, 1933–1945: Forstwirtschaft, Jagd und Umwelt im NS-Staat,* 2nd ed. (St. Katharinen: Scripta Mercaturae Verlag, 1997), 65–68.

9. Decree of 27 September 1933 Concerning Growing Stock, in *Ministerialblatt des Preußischen Landwirtschaftsministeriums und der Landesforstverwaltung* (Prussian Law Gazette of the Agriculture Ministry and State Forest Administration, hereafter *LwMBl*) (1933), column 535–36; Decree of 17 January 1934 Concerning Tending of Individual Trees, in *LwMBl* (1934), column 42–46; and Decree of 30 May 1934 Concerning Tending Blocks, in *LwMBl* (1934), column 375–79.

10. For an account of the events leading to the establishment of the Reichsforstamt, see Rubner, *Deutsche Forstgeschichte,* 95–103.

11. Preamble to the Law of 3 July 1934 Concerning the Transfer of Forestry and Hunting Affairs to the Reich, in *Reichsgesetzblatt* (Reich Law Gazette), part 1, 1934, 534–35.

12. Quoted from the official English summary of a Göring speech on the role of forest and forestry in German national affairs, in Hermann Göring, "Deutsches Volk—Deutscher Wald," *Zeitschrift für Weltforstwirtschaft* 3 (1935–1936): 651–61 (English summary at 655–58). This was a special issue on Germany called "Sonderheft Deutschland."

13. While the Dauerwald idea indeed called for utilizing as many species as possible, this does not necessarily contradict the Nazis' quest for "racial purity" of the German Volk: all tree species deemed desirable in the Dauerwald were native to the area in the first place, just as all acceptable members of the Volksgemeinschaft by definition were of German "racial heritage." Thus, it might be helpful to see the equivalent of tree species not in human "races," but in the variety of occupational estates, or *Berufsstände,* in the corporatist Nazi society.

14. Quoted from the English summary of Konrad Rubner, "Neue Wege und Ziele des Waldbaus in Deutschland," *Zeitschrift für Weltforstwirtschaft* 3 (1935–1936): 796–803 (English summary at 804).

15. For example: Fritz Loetsch, "Wald und Volk," *Allgemeine Forst- und Jagdzeitschrift* 109, May (1933): 170–71; Fuchs, "Wald und Volk," *Der Deutsche Forstbeamte* 2, no. 19 (1934): 345–48; Eduard Krca, "Wald und Volk," *Sudetendeutsche Forst- und Jagdzeitung* 37, no. 19/20 (1937): 185–86; Holle, "Deutscher Wald, Deutsches Volk," *Der Deutsche Forstwirt* 17, no. 65 (1935):

785–87; Schmidt, "Deutscher Wald—Deutsches Volk," *Deutsche Forst-Zeitung* 7, no. 18 (1938): 659–60; A. Weißker, "Wald, Volk und Forstwirtschaft im Nationalsozialistischen Staate," *Der Deutsche Forstbeamte* 2, no. 30 (1934): 610–14; and Eberhard Groß, "Gedanken zum Dauerwald," *Der Deutsche Forstwirt* 17, no. 4 (1935): 31–33.

16. Göring, "Deutsches Volk—Deutscher Wald," 656. Grammar and emphasis in the original.

17. Früchtenicht, *Deutsche Waldwirtschaft,* Vorabdruck aus Heft 17 der "Mitteilungen" (Hannover: Selbstverlag der Hannoverschen Hochschulgemeinschaft, 1937), 12.

18. A. W. Modersohn, "Weltanschauung und beruflicher Einsatz," *Deutsche Forst-Zeitung* 8, no. 15 (1939): 602–3.

19. Loetsch, "Sachsens Forstbeamte auf der NS-Gauführerschule," *Deutsche Forstbeamtenzeitung* 1, no. 13 (1935): 311–12.

20. Norbert Frei, *National Socialist Rule in Germany: The Führer State, 1933–1945* (Oxford: Blackwell, 1993), 88. Foresters' organizations also praised "young, field-tested foresters" as "doubtless the best leaders" for the Reichsarbeitsdienst (Reich Labor Service) and offered to liaise between projects in search of leaders and interested foresters; see the public notice in *Der Deutsche Forstwirt* 16, no. 50 (1934): 503. Foresters were apparently keen to embrace the opportunity: more than four hundred foresters applied to be trained as "camp leaders" for the Labor Service—more than eight times the number of available positions. "Forstliches Führerschulungslager Hann.-Münden," *Deutsche Forst-Zeitung* 48, no. 21a (1933): 437. It is likely that the reason for the strong interest was the high unemployment rate among young foresters.

21. Loetsch, "Sachsens Forstbeamte," 311.

22. "Erster Lehrgang für Sächs. Staatsforstbeamte in der Gauführerschule der NSDAP auf der Augustusburg," *Der Deutsche Forstwirt* 17, no. 68 (1935): 830–31.

23. Holle, *Deutscher Wald—Deutsches Volk!* 455. Also in *Der Deutsche Forstwirt* 17, no. 65 (1935): 785–87.

24. For example, the 1936 art exhibition "Der Wald" in Berlin. See the review by Richard Bertold Hilf, "Der Wald des Künstlers: Zur Kunstausstellung 'Der Wald,' Berlin, 6. Juni bis 12. Juli 1936," *Forstarchiv* 12, no. 13 (1936): 250–52; and "Ausstellung 'Der Wald,'" *Deutsche Forstbeamtenzeitung* 2, no. 13 (1936): 405–6. Among the many coffee table books were Josef Nikolaus Köstler, *Offenbarung des Waldes: Ein Beitrag zur künstlerischen Gestaltung deutschen Naturerlebens* (Munich: Bruckmann, 1941); and Hubert Schrade, *Baum und Wald in Bildern deutscher Maler: 50 Bilder ausgewählt und beschrieben von Hubert Schrade* (Munich: Albert Langen-Georg Müller, 1937)

25. Preface by Konrad Guenther in Hugo Keller, *So lebt die Waldgemeinschaft: Eine Bildreihe in 3 Heften. 1. Heft: Biologische Gemeinschaftskunde* (Leipzig: Ernst Wunderlich, 1936), v–vi.

26. Albert von Pestalozza, *Ewiger Wald: Allegorie über die Geschichte und das Leben* (author's transcript), 1936.

27. See Rudolf Düesberg, *Der Wald als Erzieher* (Berlin: Paul Parey, 1910); Raoul Heinrich Francé, *Ewiger Wald* (Leipzig: Richard Eckstein, 1922); Raoul Heinrich Francé, *Vom deutschen Walde* (Berlin: Deutsche Buch-Gemeinschaft, 1927); Eduard Zentgraf, *Wald und Volk* (Langensalza: Hermann Beyer & Söhne, 1923).

28. Decree of 30 October 1934 Concerning Cutting Quotas and Wood Utilization for 1935, in *LwMBl* (1934), columns 749–752 (this decree was followed by similar decrees for subsequent years); and Directive of 7 December 1936 Concerning the Increased Supply of Raw Materials, in *Reichsgesetzblatt*, part 1, 1936, 1011.

29. Rubner, *Deutsche Forstgeschichte*, 119–20.

30. Decree of 1 December 1937 Concerning Principles, Purpose, and Importance of Silvicultural Planning, in *Reichsministerialblatt der Forstverwaltung* (Law Gazette of the Reich Forest Administration) (1937), 343–45.

31. Rubner, *Deutsche Forstgeschichte*, 68.

32. Quoted in English in Franz Heske, *German Forestry* (New Haven: Yale University Press, 1938), 332.

33. "Das nationale Aufforstungswerk des Reichsministers Darré: Oedland wird Wald!" *Der Deutsche Forstwirt* 15, no. 78 (1933): 489–91; and "160,000 Morgen neuer Wald!" *Der Deutsche Forstwirt* 16, no. 50 (1934): 501.

34. Rolf Zundel and Ekkehard Schwartz, *50 Jahre Forstpolitik in Deutschland* (Münster-Hiltrup: Landwirtschaftsverlag, 1996), 13.

35. Not surprisingly, the regime repeatedly cited the increase as proof of its commitment to preserving the "truly" German landscape of the forest. For a collection of newspaper reports on the Afforestation Program, see Bundesarchiv Berlin, R 113/45–50.

36. Peter-Michael Steinsiek and Zoltán Rozsnyay, "Grundzüge der deutschen Forstgeschichte 1933–1950 unter besonderer Berücksichtigung Niedersachsens," *Aus dem Walde (Mitteilungen aus der Niedersächsischen Landesforstverwaltung)*, no. 46 (1994): 18.

37. Rubner, *Deutsche Forstgeschichte*, 123.

38. Rubner (in *Deutsche Forstgeschichte*, 110–11) relates the high-handed methods Göring employed against his ministerial colleagues to ensure that the nascent public nature conservancy would come under the umbrella of his new "superministry" of forestry, hunting, fishing, and nature conservancy.

39. The Reich Food Estate was distinct from the Ministry of Agriculture (also headed by Darré) and had been created in September 1933 to submit all persons and organizations involved in food production to strict central control. The fact that Darré was able to retain jurisdiction over those forests that were part of farm property (approximately 25 percent of the total German forest area) was a constant source of friction within the Nazi cabinet and, as we will see shortly, prevented Göring from gaining universal and exclusive control over all German forests through a Reich Forest Law.

40. The leading author of the law and the divisional head for nature protection in the Reichsforstamt, Hans Klose, repeatedly publicized this view in the forestry journals. See, for example, Hans Klose, "Das Reichsnaturschutzgesetz und die Forstwirtschaft," *Jahresbericht des Deutschen Forstvereins* (1935): 314–42.

41. Rubner, *Deutsche Forstgeschichte*, 111.

42. For example, in the state laws of North Rhine-Westphalia (1950), Rhineland-Palatinate (1950), and Hesse (1954), as well as the second generation of laws in Rhineland-Palatinate (1977) and Hesse (1978). See Zundel and Schwartz, *50 Jahre Forstpolitik in Deutschland*, 13, as well as Zoltán Rozsnyay and Uta Schulte, *Der Reichsforstgesetzentwurf von 1942 und seine Auswirkungen auf die neuere Forstgesetzgebung* (Frankfurt a. M.: Sauerländer, 1978), 200.

43. Rozsnyay and Schulte, *Der Reichsforstgesetzentwurf*, 201.

44. Heinrich Eberts, "Die Neuordnung des Forstwesens in Deutschland," *Zeitschrift für Weltforstwirtschaft* 3 (1935–1936): 667–77 (English summary at 677).

45. While this chapter deals only with the legacy of the National Socialist forest policies and laws in West Germany, the developments in East Germany can be sketched briefly as follows. During the 1950s, the government prescribed a policy akin to the Dauerwald doctrine that was called *Vorratspflegliche Waldwirtschaft* or "stock-preserving forestry." This was followed during the 1960s by a modified policy called *Standortgerechte Forstwirtschaft* or "site-adapted forestry." Increasing economic difficulties during the 1970s and 1980s caused the East German government to officially turn away from ecologically aware forestry and to foreground the production of raw wood volume. After reunification, the East German state forest administrations declared *naturgemäße Waldwirtschaft* or "close-to-nature forest management" their official policy.

CHAPTER 3

"It Shall Be the Whole Landscape!"

The Reich Nature Protection Law and Regional Planning in the Third Reich

Thomas Lekan

IN 1934, A YEAR after the Nazi seizure of power, the Rhenish regional planner and Heimatschutz member Wernher Witthaus declared that the Third Reich had ushered in a new era of environmental stewardship.[1] "Die ganze Landschaft soll es sein!" (It shall be the whole landscape!), he exclaimed, noting that the "total state" being developed in Germany was "fundamentally related to the way we perceive and want to see space and landscape. The relationships to the landscape have developed beyond specialized knowledge; they want to create the whole."[2] Witthaus's faith that the National Socialist state would advance a holistic approach to the design of Germany's living space, or Lebensraum, was echoed among planners, nature conservationists, and landscape architects throughout the country. They foresaw a new era of "organic" land use planning that stressed long-term sustainability over short-term profitability. These environmental professionals believed that the liberal era's environmental degradation and aesthetic disarray, which had reached their nadir in the Weimar Republic, had come to an end. In their place, the Third Reich would elevate the ideal values of homeland (*Heimat*) and landscape to new heights as part of its commitment to restoring Germany on the basis of "blood and soil."

Organic planning promised a new status for nature conservation (*Naturschutz*) and homeland protection (*Heimatschutz*) within German society and politics. Whereas Naturschutz traditionally had sought to set aside scenic or scientifically valuable natural monuments or nature conservation regions on a case-by-case basis, the new trend toward *Landschaftspflege* (literally "the care of the landscape," or landscape preservation) and organic planning called for a functional integration of natural landscapes into a comprehensive regional land use plan. The framers of the Reich Nature Protection Law (Reichsnaturschutzgesetz, or RNG), Germany's first nationwide nature conservation law, had given regional planning new legal status by including provisions specifying that local environmental protection officers be contacted before a permit could be issued for buildings or other land uses in the countryside. For regional planners, Heimatschutz advocates, and nature protection officials, Germany seemed to be entering a golden age of environmental concern, characterized by a total approach to planning that recognized the interdependent relationship between land use, ecology, social stability, and national identity.

Many observers have regarded the RNG as one of the Third Reich's most successful environmental protection efforts, for it provided the legislative foundation for German Naturschutz up to 1958. The law's passage has also confirmed the Third Reich's reputation as a "green" regime for several scholars, as Charles Closmann notes in the first chapter of this volume.[3] Yet few historians who have touted the Nazi regime's environmental record have examined the RNG's impact at the regional level, even though Germany's landscape protection institutions remained highly decentralized even after the so-called *Gleichschaltung* (synchronization) of nature conservation in 1933. To evaluate the Nazis' environmental agenda, therefore, scholars need to focus on the provinces: did the RNG provide Rhenish officials and Heimat advocates with new regulatory means for protecting the natural landscape, and what were the effects of such measures? Of equal importance, we need to examine the ideological implications of the RNG: did the Nazi regime manage to co-opt Naturschutz into its racist "blood and soil" ideology, or did the cultural meaning of Heimat and landscape remain wedded to older traditions of regional identification and romantic-aesthetic appreciation?

In this essay, I examine the RNG's impact on organic land use planning using examples from the former Prussian provinces of the Rhineland and Westphalia to investigate the reception, implementation, and contradictions of Nazi environmental policy at the local and regional levels. These provinces contained some of Germany's oldest and most effective

Naturschutz and Heimatschutz organizations, which had dedicated themselves to protecting and preserving the natural landscape decades before
the Nazi seizure of power and the passage of the RNG. Numerous organizations—including the Westphalian Homeland Association and Provincial Museum for Natural History in Westphalia, and the Beautification
Society for the Siebengebirge and the Rhenish Society for Monument
Preservation and Homeland Protection (Rheinischer Verein für Denkmalpflege und Heimatschutz, or RVDH) in the Rhineland—worked
alongside provincial officials in protecting scientifically, aesthetically, or
recreationally valuable natural monuments and nature conservation regions. The leaders of Westphalia's Provincial Museum for Natural History led the way in transforming Westphalia's Provincial Committee for
Natural Monument Preservation (a regional affiliate of Hugo Conwentz's
Prussian Office for the Care of Natural Monuments) into the most effective regional nature conservation organ in Prussia, protecting over fifty-six
nature conservation regions by 1932.[4] Rhenish conservationists registered
more modest success, although the Beautification Society for the Siebengebirge, working closely with provincial and municipal officials from the
surrounding region, helped to create the Siebengebirge nature park as a
gateway to the romantic Rhine Gorge in 1898–99.[5]

Heimatschutz members, landscape architects, and provincial officials
from both provinces also helped the Ruhr Settlement Association (Ruhrsiedlungsverband), founded in 1920, to provision green spaces in the
Ruhr coal-mining and industrial manufacturing districts.[6] This region,
once a sleepy agricultural area, was transformed within the space of five
decades into the heartland of Germany's coal-mining, iron, steel, paper,
and chemical industries.[7] Settlement Association planners sought to
overcome the patchwork of municipal land use ordinances, creating a holistic planning mechanism that improved workers' health and recreational opportunities through urban forestry, protected meadow, and
better transportation to parks and recreational facilities.[8] In this way,
noted one planner, "the contrast between city and countryside, industry
and agriculture, urban economy and agricultural economy is subordinated to a structure of organically determined functions that all stand in
a particular relationship to the overall plan."[9] Through such efforts, the
Settlement Association was able to protect approximately 141,000 hectares,
or 37 percent of the Ruhr coal-mining region, as green space despite an
influx of well over five hundred thousand new workers into the area during the course of the 1920s.[10] The existence of large-scale and expanding

manufacturing districts alongside rich natural heritage thus made these provincial landscapes ideal candidates for the organic planning envisioned by the 1935 law.

Despite its promise to centralize and regulate regional government programs, the totalitarian Third Reich was unable to fully "synchronize" Rhenish and Westphalian provincial landscape preservation organs, either institutionally or ideologically, due to the competition among government and party agencies within the Reich's polycentric power structure. The lack of institutional streamlining at the national level enabled regional organs, such as the Rhineland's Provincial Association (Provinzialverband) under provincial governor Heinrich Haake, to assume the dominant role in designating nature protection regions and developing land use plans. The ideological Nazification of Naturschutz and Landschaftspflege therefore remained uneven and incomplete, with traditional references to protecting the bucolic Heimat landscape coexisting uneasily alongside racist demands for purifying Germany's Lebensraum of the traces of "Jewish" capitalist exploitation. The environmental benefits of the law were also uneven and disappointing. Regional planning certainly broadened the aims of Naturschutz to include ameliorating the environmental and social effects of urban sprawl, tourism, roadway construction, and even pollution. Yet regional preservationists found themselves unable to keep pace with the National Socialists' massive public works projects, such as the land reclamation activities carried out during the Battle for Production as part of the Four-Year Plan of 1936. The discourse of organic planning meshed well with Nazism's corporatist approach to economic intervention and its promise to create a *Volksgemeinschaft* (people's community) based on natural laws, but the instrumentalist approach to the environment characteristic of modern capitalist and militarized states remained intact.

Regional Perspectives on the Reich Nature Protection Law

Germany's regional nature protection, homeland protection, and landscape protection clubs and organizations greeted the Nazi seizure of power with enthusiasm. In 1933, Hans Klose, the provincial director of nature protection in the Prussian province of Brandenburg, announced that "several favorable comments and signs demonstrate that national and socialist Germany is ready to take Heimatschutz and Naturschutz concerns much more seriously than ever before." Klose proclaimed confidently that "[we preservationists] can trust that the government led by Reich Chancellor Hitler has heard the call of Heimat and will know how to co-operate with Heimat- and Naturschutz systematically in rebuilding the German nation."[11] Klose had good reason to be optimistic about the new regime, as several National Socialist leaders, including Richard Walther Darré, Walter von Keudell, and Fritz Todt, held environmentally friendly views on agriculture, forestry, and road-building, respectively.[12] Regional preservationists believed that such high-level support for environmental issues would also result in a favorable climate for the expansion of nature and landscape protection in the Third Reich.

Nature preservationists' support for National Socialism reflected a broader middle-class frustration with Weimar's parliamentary system in the early 1930s, a period that witnessed an erosion of support for liberalism across German society. Preservationists readily assimilated key aspects of Nazi ideology into their own conservative, bourgeois, anti-materialist framework. Nazi leaders' references to Heimat as the emotional foundation for the new Volksgemeinschaft, for example, suggested that the Nazis supported regionalism and tapped into local nature conservationists' provincial distaste for Berlin.[13] Nazism's anti-Marxism also resonated among bourgeois preservationist leaders in the Rhineland and Westphalia, who feared the "red menace" in the industrial districts of Cologne, Duisburg, and the Ruhr coal-mining region. For these back-to-nature advocates, Nazism's reinvigoration of German nationalism would supplant class warfare with a newfound appreciation for the eternal values of homeland.

The failure of the Weimar Republic to pass a nationwide nature protection law was, however, local preservationists' major grievance against the parliamentary system.[14] The Düsseldorf Naturschutz officer Robert Rein noted that "we Rhinelanders have very often bitterly experienced the lack of a comprehensive nature protection law." Rein explained that a paucity of effective legislation had doomed preservationists' efforts to protect areas surrounding Lake Laacher near Andernach and to prevent the building of a hotel on one of the Eifel region's lakes. According to Rein, drafts of a nationwide nature protection law surfaced annually at the national nature protection conference in Berlin during the Weimar era, but "just as quickly disappeared into the drawer, because a single draft could not be passed due to the conflict between different interest groups and parties."[15] Nature conservationists had also felt threatened by Weimar urban modernity, whose proponents had ridiculed Naturschutz and Heimatschutz proponents as dreamy idealists unable to cope with the hard realities of industrial society.[16]

In 1935, the National Socialist regime answered nature preservationists' call for state support in protecting the natural environment by passing the Reich Nature Protection Law, which replaced the country's patchwork of conflicting and often ineffectual state, provincial, district, and municipal ordinances with a national framework for Naturschutz. Rhenish and Westphalian nature preservationists quickly applauded the new legislation, which they viewed as the fulfillment of long-cherished hopes crushed by Weimar economic limitations and bureaucratic inertia. The Rhineland Province's cultural affairs officer Hans Kornfeld wrote that the law's passage "was a load off the minds of nature's friends. Their decades-long efforts had finally found the resonance that raised the care of nature from a hobby to a duty for the entire people."[17] Kornfeld viewed the RNG as a symbol of the close alliance between Nazism and Naturschutz. He remarked: "It was left up to the National Socialist state, which is founded on 'blood and soil,' to pass the Reich Nature Protection Law. The 'parliamentary system' had repeatedly endeavored to do this, but the spiritual conditions were missing to make it a reality."[18] The RNG's rapid passage thus confirmed for preservationists the advantages of Nazi authoritarianism over Weimar democracy.

Preservationists were pleased by the RNG's stricter and more uniform standards for designating natural monuments and protecting the rural countryside. The law's provisions expanded the range of criteria used for designating a site worthy of protection beyond the vague and increasingly outdated aesthetic concept of "exceptional scenic beauty," a cornerstone of the 1902 and 1907 Prussian Laws Against the Disfigurement of Exceptionally Scenic Areas. Under the RNG, a variety of sites could receive protection under the law, including not only ecologically unique plants and animals but also "remaining portions of the landscape in free nature" whose preservation "lies in the general interest" because of rarity, beauty, scientific study, or even Heimat feeling (sections 5 and 19).[19] Private and state conservationists in the heavily urbanized portions of the Rhineland and Westphalia welcomed these latter clauses as a way to protect the cultural landscape in areas that lacked the "undisturbed" forests and moors cherished by Conwentz's natural monument tradition. As one Rhenish preservationist remarked, the Rhineland, especially the industrialized Ruhr region, contained "the bloodiest wounds of the German landscape," and every area having even the "hint of primordial character" was an "unassailable shrine."[20] The Third Reich also established the Reich Office for Nature Protection to coordinate these tasks at the national level and to compile a list of Germany's natural monuments (*Naturdenkmäler*) and nature conservation regions (*Naturschutzgebiete*) in the so-called Reich Nature Protection Book.

Advocates of holistic planning believed that the RNG's greatest promise lay in its landscape protection clauses. Section 20 of the RNG required state and local officials to contact nature protection officers before granting permits for development projects that might lead to "significant modifications of the open landscape."[21] This commitment to total planning was buttressed by other legislation and government agencies created in the same year as the RNG. In March 1935, for example, the regime passed the Law Concerning the Regulation of Land Requirements for the Public Service, which called on the state to regulate government land use so as to achieve a balance between the conflicting demands of the military, transportation ministries, forestry service, agricultural service, and nature protection offices. The regime established the Reich Office for Spatial Planning (Reichstelle für Raumordnung) to coordinate these tasks, while states and provinces created affiliate agencies to develop plans suited to unique regional conditions. Regional planners within the Rhineland's Heimatschutz organization praised the new approach to Raumordnung. They commended the Third Reich as "the first [government] that gave planning, whose end goal must be the reestablishment of an organic relationship between people and space, the political significance that it deserves and raised Reich and regional planning to a priority task for the state."[22] This attention to spatial planning for the entire Lebensraum, argued the Württemberg nature protection officer Hans Schwenkel, was fully in line with Adolf Hitler's long-term goal for Germany. "We don't want merely to create a Germany of power," wrote Schwenkel, citing the Führer's own words, "but also a Germany of beauty."[23]

The RNG's landscape protection clauses echoed the tendency within late-Weimar nature conservation circles to shed their reputation as antimodern Romantics by linking Naturschutz closely to Landschaftspflege and future-oriented regional planning. Already before World War I, the president of the Homeland Protection Association of Germany (Deutscher Bund Heimatschutz, or DBH), Paul Schultze-Naumburg, had argued that it was possible to reconcile nature and technology in the countryside through careful planning and more rational land use. It was only in the late 1920s, however, that nature conservationists and homeland protectionists seriously promoted Landschaftspflege as an alternative to traditional natural monument protection as they sought new ways to reconcile Naturschutz with Weimar modernization processes. In 1926, for example, new DBH president Werner Lindner argued that Heimatschutz proponents needed to rethink the movement's earlier anti-industrialism in light of modern building technologies that enabled architects to embed factories, bridges, and dams into the landscape "without damage to landscape beauty or for the native countryfolk."[24]

Following Lindner's lead, organic planners in the Third Reich sought to "naturalize" technological features by embedding them into the contours of the existing cultural landscape, but they also went beyond these aesthetic goals by emphasizing the ecological benefits of such planning. In his 1941 essay, "The Tasks of Landscape Design and the Care of the Landscape," Schwenkel argued that Landschaftspflege utilized aesthetic and "biological" insights in its search for a harmonious balance between human priorities and the natural environment. In Schwenkel's view, the RNG would enable Heimatschutz members to serve as consultants on questions concerning historic preservation and new construction to ensure that the owners used colors, roof lines, wall heights, and exterior decoration that fit the historic character of the town or city center. They could also identify scenic portions of the landscape on a regional map and enter these areas into the Reich Nature Protection Book. In these areas, environmental users would avoid "disfiguring" environmental impacts by locating mines, factories, garbage dumps, high-tension wires, rail lines, and billboards away from heavily traveled roads and hiking paths.

Such aesthetic improvement also brought ecological benefits. Schwenkel noted that by protecting historic hedgerows in the countryside, for example, farmers enhanced microclimatic and "biozonal" (*biozönotisch*) conditions. Schwenkel claimed that hedgerows moderated disturbances in the "biological balance" caused by agricultural exploitation, secured the soil against desiccating winds and drops in the groundwater level, maintained air humidity, and served as habitat for birds. Unlike the liberal era, which had allowed untrained individuals to make haphazard and uninformed decisions about the natural and built environment, Schwenkel foresaw a time when properly educated building inspectors (*Baupolizei*) and nature protection officials would "rap the knuckles" of the "masses" (*die Vielzuvielen*), admonishing them to pay heed to the aesthetic demands of the whole community.[25]

Scholars who have argued that *völkisch* antimodernism motivated such authoritarian aspirations have largely overlooked nature conservationists' enthusiasm for future-oriented Landschaftspflege.[26] Hans Kornfeld remarked that the new friend of Heimat "not only wants to preserve, but also to create." He argued that conservationists would assume a new and indispensable role in the Battle for Production in the countryside, a key part of the Four-Year Plan. This plan, whose ultimate goal was to achieve greater agricultural and industrial self-sufficiency in preparation for war, would entail massive new efforts at land reclamation, waterway regulation, and dam construction. Kornfeld applauded this effort to secure the German people "on its own soil" and assured fellow conservations that the RNG would enable Naturschutz authorities to make sure the environmental impact of these activities did not inflict damage on "the healthy and natural."[27]

In the realm of town planning, the goal was similarly forward-looking, using historic town centers and agrarian landscapes as models, not templates, for fashioning aesthetically balanced, nature-centered, and economically viable communities throughout Germany. The Munich landscape architect Alwin Seifert underscored this modern approach by noting that homeland protectionists' goal was not "to transform Germany into an open-air Heimat museum or to stick people of urban origins and urban careers into *Lederhosen.*" Rather, the goal of Heimatschutz was a blending of tradition and modernity that enabled the individual to feel himself a part of the larger community. "We demand that each new housing development," he remarked, "incorporate elements of the togetherness of the old Germanic village.[28] Regional planning under the auspices of the RNG would thus transform the public perception of nature conservation from an outmoded, elitist critique of mass society to an instrument of modern spatial planning.

Several nature conservation leaders also hoped to modernize their movement by fusing its aims with the goals of Nazi racial hygiene. Though the RNG's preamble was surprisingly free of racist or anti-Semitic references, these nature preservationists readily adapted Landschaftspflege goals to the new ideological climate. Schultze-Naumburg, who joined the Nazi Party in 1930, laid the conceptual framework for a thoroughly Nazified view of landscape in his essay "The Creation of the Landscape" of the same year.[29] Schultze-Naumburg cast aside the cultural landscape tradition of Wilhelm Heinrich Riehl and Heimatschutz founder Ernst Rudorff, who had viewed the landscape as the product of centuries-long historical interaction between a "people," defined as a spiritual and cultural community, and its natural surroundings. Riehl and Rudorff had blamed Germany's environmental degradation on the materialistic forces of *Zivilisation,* a modern worldview that robbed nature of its divine and patriotic essence.[30] After his conversion to Nazism, by contrast, Schultze-Naumburg spoke of the *racial* causes for landscape "disfigurement," arguing that the visual appearance of the landscape reflected the inherited racial character of the human beings living in a particular geographic space. Unlike their pure-blooded ancestors, Schultze-Naumburg asserted that "Nordic Germans" had ignored the laws of natural selection since the mid-nineteenth century, allowing miscegenation and the birth of the "hereditarily ill" to go unchecked. These "sick" individuals had subsequently stamped their surroundings with diseased characteristics. The result was an unhealthy, "degenerate" landscape marked by smoking factories, overcrowded cities, and insatiable natural resource exploitation. In this racialized vision of landscape, neither capitalism nor industrialization per se were thus at fault for Germany's environmental woes; rather, "Jewish capital" and "diseased" individuals had diverted economy and society from their organic foundations in the soil of Heimat.

Other Heimatschutz leaders followed Schultze-Naumburg's lead in touting the racial foundations of the Heimatschutz aesthetic. Werner Lindner noted in his 1934 work *Homeland Protection in the New Reich* that the affinity that Germans felt for their historic town centers and rural countryside was an expression of racial energies. The clarity and harmony of the "old," he asserted, was "nothing more than our own blood in an older form. Proportion, rhythm, color, materials, the continuity of contours were thus elements of the total unity."[31] Heimatschutz advocates who assisted the regime in expunging traces of liberal decay thus envisioned their own form of environmental and cultural eugenics; in fact, Schwenkel asserted that such individuals would aid the regime in its battle against "incompetence, capitalist thinking, and all Jewish-American relicts of a bygone era."[32]

Synchronizing the Provinces: Regional Planning in the Rhineland

Despite the much-vaunted claim that the Third Reich would overcome liberal arbitrariness through streamlined central planning, the institutional *Gleichschaltung* of nature conservation and the implementation of the RNG remained uneven and disappointing. The call to centralize and nationalize Naturschutz according to Nazi principles faltered due to in-fighting and competition among a maze of state and party institutions. In the early years of the Nazi regime, both Alfred Rosenberg's Fighting League for German Culture and Werner Haverbeck's Reich League for Volkstum and Heimat (RVH) vied for control of the Naturschutz movement.[33] This lack of direction and confusion continued throughout 1933 and 1934, as Rosenberg's Fighting League reconstituted itself as the National Socialist Cultural Community and then was itself absorbed by the Deutsche Arbeitsfront (German Labor Front, or DAF) in 1934. Regional preservationists were dismayed by such confusion in a regime that had promised to synchronize Naturschutz according to Nazism's hierarchical principles. Rhenish Heimatschutz leader Oskar Karpa left the RVH's 1933 Kassel conference with the impression that the organization suffered from a "complete lack of direction and confusion" over competencies.[34] Regional preservationists remained unsure which agency controlled nature conservation until Haverbeck gained leadership over the Cultural Community and disbanded the RVH in 1934. The confusion ended only after Hermann Göring, the chief of forestry in the Third Reich, pushed through the RNG and established the Reich Nature Protection Office in 1935.[35]

The institutional Gleichschaltung of the Heimatschutz movement was similarly uneven due to infighting among Nazi leaders. Despite Schultze-Naumburg's prominence in Rosenberg's Fighting League for German Culture, the DBH and the RVDH affiliated initially with Haverbeck's RVH, but soon left the group in 1934 because of the organization's chaotic structure and the perceived threat to regional autonomy.[36] The Rhenish provincial governor Heinrich Haake, who had become president of the DBH in 1933, announced that the DBH would become a self-standing organization, with a loose affiliation to the German Gemeindetag. The Rhenish governor declared "the current state must end, where there are always a huge number of offices active in the same area."[37] Haake also rationalized the DBH's structure by designating one regional organization in each state, free city, or Prussian province as that area's representative Heimatschutz organization.[38] While the RNG had envisioned a centralization of Naturschutz authority in the Reich Office, these conflicts over jurisdiction at the national level ultimately allowed Haake, as well as other provincial and state officials, to chart their own approaches to landscape preservation.

With Haake at the helm, Rhenish nature conservation and landscape planning entered a new phase in which traditional aesthetic and regionalist discourses of provincial landscape preservation, modern demands for functional spatial planning, and National Socialism's racializing tendencies all found expression. Haake, who held power from April 1933 until the regime's collapse in 1945, was one of the Third Reich's most important defenders of regional self-administration and regional identity. The lack of cultural-political direction from Berlin led Haake to reemphasize traditional discourses of regional autonomy as the best solution to executing administrative tasks and building national character. Haake proclaimed that "every German has a duty to his more familiar Heimat, where he first truly experienced things and where he grew up, on par with his membership in the greater German Volksgemeinschaft. The German landscape and the German person are not uniform in their appearance, but rather German life is embodied in a diversity of forms that in their totality represent Germandom."[39] According to Haake, provincial self-administration helped to rationalize the state's activities, taking care of tasks that "do not belong in the hand of Reich, party, professional or local self-administration" so that the Reich as a whole would be rendered "bureaucratically streamlined."[40] Haake's veneration of Germany's landscape diversity thus resurrected the regionalist thrust of the cultural landscape tradition in order to reassert the advantages of provincial autonomy within the Nazi regime's constantly shifting power alliances.

Haake's defense of regional autonomy and provincial government proved far more effective than top-down standardization in bringing Heimatschutz and Naturschutz organizations into line with the regime's broader ideological purposes. Haake's patronage brought concrete advantages to the work of nature protection in the province, leading to greater financial stability and enhanced professional status for Rhenish nature protection. Whereas Reich funding for Naturschutz remained minuscule, provincial monies for Naturschutz increased substantially between 1934 and 1937, although they leveled off during the remaining years of the regime. In 1934, for example, Naturschutz offices reported receiving approximately 6,800 Reichsmark (RM), with RM 4,000 coming from the provincial administration and RM 1,800 from the Prussian *Oberpräsident* for the Rhineland Province.[41] In 1937, on the other hand, the provincial administration reported granting approximately RM 26,500 for Naturschutz.[42] The sum of RM 26,500 was paltry in comparison to the province's overall cultural affairs budget of RM 1,250,000 and paled in comparison to the province's outlays for road-building, land reclamation, and social welfare programs. Yet local preservationists viewed Haake's support as a significant improvement over the Weimar era, since it helped them to maintain and to ensure the protected status of several nature protection regions, including the Siebengebirge, Rodderberg, the Wahner Heath, and the Urfelder Heath.[43]

To help achieve these goals of comprehensive regional planning, Haake established the Rhenish Society for Spatial Planning, the regional affiliate of the national Reich Office for Spatial Planning, in 1936.[44] Haake called on the RVDH to work closely with this agency to create comprehensive land use plans for the Rhineland Province. The society brought together provincial nature protection offices, agricultural, road-building, and military authorities, landscape architects, and other authorities to make critical decisions about provincial land use. It also promoted measures to foster economic growth and improve the province's infrastructure, including agricultural land reclamation, highway expansion, dam construction, and new public housing projects on the urban fringe.[45] Despite the potential environmental impact of such activities, Haake assured Rhinelanders that such planning could be accomplished in an organic fashion that "is creatively based and therefore precisely [reflects] harmony with Nature."[46] Whereas initial planning efforts centered on "defending against damages left behind by the liberal period," noted a 1936 issue of Haake's official newsletter, *The Rhine Province*, the Nazi regime demanded a "creative new ordering of the entire space."[47] This creative ordering would produce an organic landscape both functional and beautiful, attuned to aesthetic needs and the health of the population.

Planning would also ensure that the regime's de-urbanization schemes would not result in careless rural development. In his 1939 treatise *The New City*, the Nazi urban theorist Gottfried Feder argued that the regime could heal the "cancer of modernity" by dispersing urban populations into the hinterland, distributing them into small- and medium-sized Garden Cities that maintained their communal character. Feder believed that small-town living would ameliorate the population's alienation from the land, thus binding them more closely to the Fatherland, though he conceded that urban renewal in big cities according to organic principles could serve similar purposes.[48] Cologne Heimatschutz member Wilhelm Schürmann warned that maintaining a balance between urban and open space required that new housing settlements should not "reach long arms out into the landscape," but rather should grow organically from existing town centers and be partitioned into separate zones for residential, transportation, commercial, and industrial uses.[49] This would also facilitate efficient electricity and gas provision, shorter streets, and easier police protection and administration.[50] Density, rather than dispersion, became a hallmark of organic regional planning, as Heimatschutz advocates touted preindustrial villages as models of a more efficient and environmentally sustainable future.

Rhenish preservationists were most concerned about overdevelopment in the Rhine Valley, the province's cultural heartland. Though they recognized that the Rhineland was a man-made cultural landscape, rather than a wilderness in the American sense, Naturschutz advocates believed that the relationship between humans and their environment had remained harmonious in the region until the last quarter of the nineteenth century. Since that time the river valley had been undergoing continuous degradation. As Kornfeld argued in his 1936 essay, "Hopes for the Protection of the Rhine Landscape," the liberal period had allowed individuals to "stamp . . . their untrammeled personality" on the environment and wound the "epidermis" of the majestic landscape.[51] In Kornfeld's view, wounds from this time remained visible in the landscape's physiognomy, including factories that destroyed pleasant views of the river islands from steamships, gaudy hotels that upset the "holistic view" of the surrounding foliage, and oil slicks from ships that polluted fish habitat and caused unsightly marks on the river's surface. Kornfeld claimed that the flat, barren agricultural fields crisscrossed by high-tension wires that were increasingly commonplace in the Rhine Valley reminded him of an "American petroleum field," rather than an authentic German Heimat.[52] He also feared that creeping sprawl, shoddy hotels, and tacky souvenir shops threatened to transform the Rhine, "the proud river, the symbol of German freedom,"[53] into a commercialized wasteland. Kornfeld called on the government, municipalities, and private owners to design a regional plan for the entire area bordering the river and to enter the region into the Reich Nature Protection Book.

Other observers focused on the environmental threats resulting from economic prosperity in the mid-1930s. Schürmann noted that the spread of automobiles had enabled many Rhinelanders to reside a considerable distance outside urban centers such as Cologne and Düsseldorf. They tended to live in isolation from their neighbors, rather than in closed settlements; the result was "chains" of single homes in rows along the river's banks or creeping up hillsides. Schürmann maintained that such scattered development was destroying the pleasing transition between villages and open landscape that made river travel so enjoyable.[54] Schürmann also noted that Rhinelanders' desire to "get back to nature" had multiplied the number of weekend houses in the Rhine Valley. Hikers who experienced scenic vistas far from the city wanted to retain their piece of "untouched" nature by building a small cottage on the site. Schürmann was not willing to condemn such developments outright. He believed they stemmed from a desire to lead a "healthy" life that was "close to nature," but called on Rhinelanders to build their weekend houses hidden from view, behind hilltops and trees rather than facing the valley. Other Rhineland preservationists were more forceful in their criticisms. They complained about the mushrooming numbers of hotels, souvenir shops, and coffee shops in the Rhine Valley that "robbed . . . almost every mountain and every castle of their peacefulness [and] degenerated almost every visited town into a real fairground."[55] These preservationists hoped that the RNG and other laws would enable provincial officials to regulate land use more carefully.

Sentiments such as those voiced by Kornfeld and Schürmann soon spurred plans for designating the entire Middle Rhine Gorge from Mainz to Cologne as a landscape protection zone under section 20 of the RNG. In 1937, Haake's call for a "Rhine protection action" resulted in a series of excursions along the river in 1937 and 1938. The boat trips assembled over three hundred participants to discuss the need for better planning in the Rhine Valley, including national conservation leaders such as Klose and Walther Schoenichen, the head of the Prussian Government Office for Natural Monument Preservation, Rhenish preservationists such as Oskar Karpa and Herbert Iven, landscape advocates from the autobahn project such as Reinhold Hoemann, industrial spokesmen, and representatives from agricultural, river transportation, and railway ministries.[56]

The discussions that occurred during these trips focused primarily on the aesthetic damage to the Rhine Valley. Participants spoke about the impact of road and railway construction, agricultural reclamation, factory construction, and excessive tourism along the river's banks. On several trips, however, they also bemoaned the polluting effects of industrial effluent such as phenol and untreated municipal wastewater on the river, anticipating postwar concerns about the ecological and public health effects of toxins in the environment.[57] The result of these trips was a comprehensive landscape protection ordinance for the Middle Rhine Gorge that recognized the Rhine as a "natural monument of the first order, the glorious site of the greatest of German history and völkisch experience, the life vessel of German culture, art, and economy." Stressing the need for both organic planning and environmental restoration, the ordinance called for the "energetic rebuilding of the Rhine landscape according to its own law."[58] While the plan allowed most existing economic practices to continue in the area undisturbed, it forbade any modifications of the landscape within the protection zone that would "disfigure" the landscape's appearance or detract from the enjoyment of nature. The plan restricted commercial or industrial development to a select number of areas, called for the removal of unsightly billboards and garish building colors, directed local officials to consult nature protection authorities before allowing transportation or other major developments, and specified that only "native," or *bodenständig,* sources be used for building materials and plantings. Though Schoenichen touted the plan as a model for the rest of Germany and Rhenish nature protectionists celebrated its provisions as a triumph of Heimatschutz principles, the plan was never realized due to the onset of war in 1939.[59]

Residential planning was another area of environmental reform that incorporated Heimatschutz aesthetic ideals. Echoing the so-called flat-roof controversy of the late 1920s, Haake embraced Heimatschutz members' critique of Modernist architecture, proclaiming its "steel and iron" boxes as unfit for German people's comrades. He inveighed against the architectural "arbitrariness" that had disturbed the "healthy organism" of German towns during the liberal epoch.[60] The Third Reich, he asserted, would put an end to "limitless individualism," in which each owner built whatever he liked, in favor of "native" styles that fit into the existing natural environment and cited surrounding historical styles with "nuance and honesty."[61] To avoid these "sins" from the past required not only "purification" through urban renewal, but also a revolution in the German population's perception of built environments. Haake argued that state and municipal involvement in planning and architecture was not enough; "truthful and deep-seated renewal can only occur when it follows from a new spirit that breathes life into everyone," he wrote.[62] For Haake, every Rhinelander needed to feel responsible for his or her surroundings, to be a "carrier of living thoughts of Volkstum and Heimat."[63]

To combat such individualist tendencies and to place architectural and urban design on a more organic footing, Haake assisted DBH president Lindner in organizing a traveling exhibit, "The Beautiful City: Its Regeneration and Design," which was devised to popularize Heimatschutz design principles, now recast as examples of "healthy" National Socialist architecture and city planning. With the exhibition traveling to more than a hundred German cities, its organizers adopted the method developed in the 1937 "Degenerate Art" exhibit, showing examples of "good" and "bad" architecture side by side. Bad architecture included both the austere, functionalist structures of international modernism and those that had succumbed to "false Romanticism" in the form of "inauthentic renovations," kitschy historicism, or garish colors. Good architecture, on the other hand, was both functional and organic, embracing modern building technologies while embodying virtues such as order, cleanliness, clarity, functionality, simplicity, and attention to context. This context included the natural landscape and existing urban ensembles; designers and builders should incorporate native plants and materials wherever possible.[64] Haake emphasized that the new city would not only be visually pleasing, but also a site of emotional and physical health. "The beautiful city . . . is not only a city of formal, aesthetic beauty, it is also a city of health and a powerful feeling of life. Every house within it must feel like home for a German person."[65] A combination of urban renewal and proper Heimat design of new structures would inevitably "exterminate the traces of decay, the manifestations of an evil past," thus regenerating the city as a healthy and organic Lebensraum.[66]

Other exhibits from the Nazi era envisioned residential and landscape design as a way to secure attachment to Heimat and nation. Whereas Modernist apartment complexes alienated workers from nature, exhibitors asserted, single-family cottages in a vernacular style would bind the proletariat to the Fatherland. The 1937 "Productive People" (*Schaffendes Volk*) exhibition in Düsseldorf, for example, showcased detached, historicist cottages with small gardens, curvilinear streets, extensive groves of trees, and free-flowing streams. As one Rhenish architect remarked, manual laborers who traditionally had not enjoyed the benefits of home ownership would feel comfortable and healthy in such surroundings, thus binding them to the family and strengthening their love of Heimat and Fatherland. "There is scarcely anything more necessary than strengthening the love of Heimat through settlement, through rooting with the soil, through activities on the land, through connection of ownership."[67] Such feelings of attachment were politically imperative in the Rhenish borderlands, where another architect described the working-class families in the settlements as a "firmly fit-together human wall" and a "powerful bulwark against international ideas."[68]

Binding workers to the national soil was only one goal of Nazi residential planning. Another aim was to provide a healthy home environment in which to boost the birthrate among "racially fit" comrades.

According to Alwin Seifert, such a racial home would integrate "German Volk trees," such as indigenous lindens and oaks, instead of "foreign" species such as the blue spruce and the acacia.[69] Charged with helping the "healthy tribe of industrial workers" to find "healthy dwellings," the Rhenish Homestead Association, with the assistance of the Rhenish Regional Planning Society and the German Labor Front, completed 6,850 small houses and settlements in garden suburbs between 1933 and 1936, targeting workers who were of "limited means" but sound racial health. The association argued that the complexes' attention to "healthy" open space and garden plots would encourage workers to produce large families of "hereditarily healthy" (*erbgesund*) children.[70] Like Landschaftspflege, therefore, back-to-nature residential design drew selectively upon modernist impulses, departing from the geometric forms of high modernism while infusing the 1920s rhetoric of "light, air, and sun" with new racist meanings.

The Ideological and Environmental Limits of the RNG

Both the Naturschutz and Heimatschutz movements thus made significant strides during the first half of the Third Reich in protecting portions of the natural environment and developing more sustainable urban growth patterns. Yet the overall record of both ideological indoctrination and environmental protection in the Third Reich remained mixed. While Heimatschutz and nature conservation leaders such as Schultze-Naumburg sought to bring landscape preservation's goals into line with Nazi racism, regional conservationists' vision of landscape planning remained overwhelmingly aesthetic and provincial rather than racist and nationalist. Despite the Gleichschaltung of landscape preservation, many local nature conservationists still tended to emphasize the environment, or "soil," of Heimat, rather than race, or "blood," when discussing the aims of Nazi "blood and soil" rhetoric. In his 1934 "The German and his Landscape," the Westphalian nature conservationist Wilhelm Lienenkämper noted that "just as race and family researchers see 'blood' as their area of activity, so too would we [Naturschutz advocates] not want to neglect reconnecting the old relationship to the 'soil.'"[71] Racial strength and landscape vitality went hand in hand; only through nature protection could the regime achieve its goal of völkisch rebuilding.

The environmental benefits of the RNG were also disappointing. Regional preservationists continued to see regional planning as a vehicle for protecting the aesthetic values of areas like the Romantic Rhine without considering the more dire ecological impacts of road building and water pollution. Moreover, despite preservationists' faith that the law would establish a Golden Age of environmental awareness, there were few institutional differences between the former Prussian Government Office for the Care of Natural Monuments and the Nazi state's Reich Office for Nature Protection. Rather than being in the effective control of true civil servants (*Beamte*), German nature protection affairs remained in the hands of unpaid regional volunteers (*Beauftragte*) who lacked the political or financial clout to implement the RNG effectively. As Lienenkämper noted in a surprisingly pointed critique of the RNG and its provisions, local conservationists lacked money, manpower, and regime support: "[the law] sees the work of [nature protection] as a side occupation, as an honorary post. Whoever perceives his role seriously and takes it as an affair of the heart is not in a position, despite his best efforts, to carry out the spirit and letter of the law alongside his main career (*Brotberuf*)."[72] Comparing it to "Adolf Hitler's highways and the construction of monumental buildings," for which ample funds were available, Lienenkämper noted that "the preservation of the actual remaining traces of primordial Germany (*Urdeutschland*) through the Reich Nature Protection Law is an equally important task which cannot be carried out without enough money." Lienenkämper also complained bitterly that the regime's propaganda apparatus had failed to disseminate Naturschutz ideals while building entire ministries for "often the most profane things on this earth."[73] With such a lack of resources and power, local Naturschutz activities remained limited to traditional tasks with little widespread impact: creating inventories of ecologically valuable sites, researching local natural monuments, or holding lectures about environmental protection. Clearly, the RNG had not established the regulatory controls or monetary means that nature preservationists needed to achieve their goals.

With so little financial or bureaucratic power, preservationists were unable to keep pace with the Nazi regime's numerous public works programs. Among the most environmentally detrimental were the land reclamation efforts of Robert Ley's Reich Labor Service, which employed thousands of workers to create new farmsteads in an effort to boost Germany's domestic food production. These programs included a number of traditional beautification measures, such as cleaning up fields or replanting trees in denuded areas. Yet they also adopted many environmentally questionable methods, such as draining marshy areas, securing embankments, straightening streams, or building dams and dikes.[74] Nature preservationists such as Rudolf Hoffmann bemoaned the destruction of swamps and marshes, which the Labor Service deemed "wastelands," because these parcels of land provided vital habitat for birds and small mammals.[75] Regional nature protectionists also argued that the new dams created stagnant waters that were intolerable for local fish species, which were accustomed to migrating through swiftly moving stream and river currents.[76] Karl Oberkirch, the nature protection officer for the Ruhr Settlement Association, warned that land reclamation projects were upsetting the entire "household of nature" by changing local climate conditions, lowering the groundwater table, and desiccating the soil.[77]

Despite these preservationist concerns, the National Socialists accelerated their land reclamation efforts in 1936 as part of the Battle for Production, with little input from nature conservationists. Göring called on Darré's Agricultural Ministry to limit the country's dependence on foreign raw materials and foodstuffs, which led to an expansion of cultivated land often referred to as "inner colonization." Inner colonization's drive toward autarky included swamp drainage and dam construction; planners forecast the conversion of over two million hectares of "wasteland" into arable farms by 1940.[78] Westphalian nature protection officer Wilhelm Münker noted that inner colonization—under the motto, "Change wasteland into arable land!"—led farmers to clear away "trees, bushes, hedgerows" in a "careless drive for output" that was transforming "field basins into monotonous steppeland."[79] In the context of inner colonization, in other words, environmental sympathies appeared incompatible with war preparation.

With the onset of war in 1939, the regime's need for military installations and its thirst for raw materials endangered Germany's remaining natural monuments and conservation regions. Military planners viewed open landscapes through a militarist lens: the Wahner Heath near Cologne, for example, was used as a shooting and drill range, while the Haardt Forest in the Ruhr region hid antiaircraft artillery.[80] In November 1939, the district nature protection officer and mayor of Bonn pleaded in vain with the local antiaircraft division not to fell a nearby acacia grove, which had been designated a natural monument. Citing the RNG, local friends of nature claimed that the trees were first-order natural monuments serving as both unique ecological specimens and as sites of memory in numerous "Heimat stories about the city of Bonn."[81] Yet homeland narratives that linked trees to municipal identity were of far less importance to the

Third Reich than military expansion. Even Germany's one official national park, the Lunebürger Heath near Hamburg, was not safe from military planners. From 1936 to 1941, the regime considered developing aircraft landing strips, experimental petroleum drilling fields, and hospitals for victims of air strikes in the region. While landscape architects claimed that they could restore the landscape to its former appearance, nature preservationists recognized that the ecological and cultural significance of the area would be lost forever.[82]

The Nazi regime's passage of the RNG in 1935 promised a new era of environmental reform for Germany after over a decade of failed attempts to pass a nationwide nature protection law. Preservationists celebrated the law's comprehensive protection of the country's remaining natural monuments and its pledge to involve them in future-oriented, organic planning that would reconcile industrial development and environmental protection. Like middle-class groups across Germany, preservationists embraced Nazism's rejection of liberal individualism and Marxist materialism, but they had an added incentive to support the new regime: its promise to found the new Volksgemeinschaft on "blood and soil," timeless, organic virtues dictated by the natural order rather than shifting political alliances. Preservationists interpreted this promise as an affirmation of Naturschutz and Heimatschutz ideals, an opportunity to overcome the spiritual barrenness and political gridlock of Weimar liberalism in favor of the ideal goals of Heimat. They also saw the RNG as a means to modernize traditional preservation concerns by linking Landschaftspflege to the regime's call for a new, centrally planned, functionally efficient, and environmental sound Lebensraum for Germany. By participating in organic regional planning, they sought to reclaim their role as stewards of the Heimat landscape, a duty they believed had been denigrated and devalued under the liberal Weimar Republic. Not surprisingly, the passage of the RNG solidified preservationists' enthusiasm for the Nazi regime in its early years.

Given the apparent ideological affinity between Nazism and Naturschutz, the regime expected a rapid Gleichschaltung of nature protection organizations, but this process faltered due to infighting among Nazi leaders and bureaucratic confusion. The failure to create a streamlined Naturschutz apparatus at the national level left the day-to-day tasks of environmental protection in the hands of regional authorities, much as they had been in the Wilhelmine and Weimar eras. Though nature protection organizations received increased financial support from regional authorities, nature protection officers remained honorary commissioners with insufficient funds to achieve adequate regulatory oversight over local development projects. The incomplete institutional Gleichschaltung also produced an uneven ideological coordination of nature protection groups. As the initial euphoria about Nazism faded, Schultze-Naumburg's and Schoenichen's bold attempts to racialize the meaning and practice of landscape preservation found decreasing resonance among local environmentalists. The result was an uneasy amalgam of competing visions of nature and environmental reform, including a bourgeois aesthetic tradition emphasizing nature as a pathway to moral strength, a modernist variant touting the public health advantages and functional efficiency of organic planning, and a Nazified worldview glorifying the biological connection between a healthy environment and racial fitness. In the end, however, Nazism failed to fully displace the older bourgeois aesthetic, environmentalist, and regionalist vision of Heimat that had formed the basis of grassroots Naturschutz since 1900.

Regional nature conservationists' disillusionment with the Nazi regime also reflected their profound disappointment with the Third Reich's record on nature conservation and landscape preservation. Rather than proving itself a stable and reliable advocate of such environmentalist causes, the fascist state posed a far greater menace to local Naturschutz than the supposedly "materialist" and "arbitrary" Weimar system. Despite small accomplishments such as a new Naturschutz registry, the Middle Rhine Gorge Plan, and model garden city developments, all of which borrowed from stalled Weimar reform efforts, the Third Reich subordinated nature protection to economic development, war preparation, and racist expansionism. Nazi public works projects and industrial mobilization created new environmental threats such as the autobahn system and the inner colonization program that mechanized the countryside, destroyed valuable animal habitat, and endangered local natural monuments. In this context, preservationists' oft-repeated call for government agencies and military planners to heed the RNG and Hitler's dictum that "the natural beauties of the German Fatherland . . . are the sources of power and strength for the National Socialist movement" displayed their profound naïveté about Nazism's inner dynamic and their insignificance to a regime bent on launching a catastrophic war of racial expansion.

Notes

1. An earlier version of this chapter appeared in Joachim Radkau, ed., *Naturschutz und Nationalsozialismus* (Frankfurt: Campus Verlag, 2003). The revised and translated version is printed here with permission.

2. Wernher Witthaus, "Die ganze Landschaft soll es sein!" *Nachrichtenblatt für Rheinische Heimatpflege* 5, no. 5/7 (1933–1934): 172.

3. See the chapter by Charles Closmann in this volume.

4. See Karl Ditt, *Raum und Volkstum: Die Kulturpolitik des Provinzialverbandes Westfalen, 1923–1945* (Münster: Aschendorff, 1988), 134–44. On the RVDH, see Karl Peter Wiemer, *Ein Verein im Wandel der Zeit: Der Rheinische Verein für Denkmalpflege und Heimatschutz von 1906 bis 1970* (Cologne: Rheinischer Verein für Denkmalpflege und Landschaftsschutz, 2000).

5. On the Siebengebirge, see Elmar Heinen, "Naturschutzgebiet Siebengebirge gestern—heute—morgen," *Rheinische Heimatpflege* 27 (1990): 112–21; Frieder Berres and Christian Kiess, *Siebengebirge: Naturpark—Orte—Sehenswertes,* 2nd ed., ed. Heimatverein Siebengebirge (Siegburg: Rheinlandia Verlag, 1994); and Thomas Lekan, *Imagining the Nation in Nature: Landscape Preservation and German Identity, 1885–1945* (Cambridge: Harvard University Press, 2004), 36–49.

6. On the Ruhr Settlement Association, see "Die Tätigkeit des Siedlungverbandes Ruhrkohlenbezirks: Nach einem Vortrag der Verbandsleitung am 20 July 1926 vor dem Wohungsausschuss des preussischen Landtages," in Archiv des Landschaftsverbandes Rheinland (hereafter ALVR) 12466; Heinrich Hoebink, *Mehr Raum—Mehr Macht: Preussische Kommunalpolitik im rheinisch-westfälischen Industriegebiet* (Essen: Klartext, 1990); and Heinz Günter Steinberg, "Die Entwicklung des Ruhrsiedlungverbandes," in *Ruhrgebiet und Neues Land,* Band 2, *Beiträge zur neueren Landesgeschichte des Rheinlandes und Westfalens,* ed. Walter Först (Cologne: Grote, 1968), 115–52.

7. Recent works that contain useful information on Ruhr environmental problems include Franz-Josef Brüggemeier and Thomas Rommelspacher, eds., *Blauer Himmel über der Ruhr: Geschichte der Umwelt im Ruhrgebiet, 1840–1990* (Essen: Klartext, 1992); Ulrike Gilhaus, *"Schmerzenskinder der Industrie": Umweltverschmutzung, Umweltpolitik und sozialer Protest im Industriezeitalter in Westfalen, 1845–1914* (Paderborn: F. Schöningh, 1995); Jürgen Büschenfeld, *Flüsse und Kloaken: Umweltfragen im Zeitalter der Industrialisierung, 1870–1918* (Stuttgart: Klett-Cotta, 1997); and Mark Cioc, "The Impact of the Coal Age on the German Environment: A Review of the Historical Literature," *Environment and History* 4, no. 1 (1998): 105–24.

8. Steinberg, "Die Entwicklung des Ruhrsiedlungverbandes," 115–18.

9. Albert Kloeckner, "Landesplanung und Landschaftsgestaltung," *Kölnische Volkszeitung*, 13 November 1930.

10. Steinberg, "Die Entwicklung des Ruhrsiedlungverbandes," 121; Klaus-Georg Wey, *Umweltpolitik in Deutschland: Kurze Geschichte des Umweltschutzes in Deutschland seit 1900* (Opladen: Westdeutscher Verlag, 1982), 141–46.

11. Hans Klose, "Heimatschutz im nationalen Deutschland," *Naturdenkmalpflege und Naturschutz in Berlin und Brandenburg*, no. 17: 205, 207; quoted in Burckhardt Riechers, "Nature Protection during National Socialism," *Historical Social Research* 21, no. 3 (1996): 47.

12. These individuals are discussed in the contributions by Gesine Gerhard, Michael Imort, and Thomas Zeller, respectively, in this volume.

13. On the ideological overlap between Nazism and Heimat organizations, see Karl Ditt, *Raum und Volkstum*, 21, and Raymond Dominick, *The Environmental Movement in Germany: Prophets and Pioneers, 1871–1971* (Bloomington: Indiana University Press, 1992), 85–90.

14. Dominick, *Environmental Movement in Germany*, 85.

15. Richard Rein, "Die heimische Landschaft wird geschützt: Das neue Reichsnaturschutzgesetz und das Rheinland," *Düsseldorfer Nachrichten*, 28 July 1935.

16. Hans Schwenkel, "Gegner des Heimatschutzes," *Mitteilungen des Landesvereins Sächsicher Heimatschutz* 20, no. 9/12 (1931): 116–18.

17. Hans Kornfeld, "Erste Sitzung der Rheinischen Provinzialstelle für Naturschutz," 12 December 1936, 1, in ALVR 11138.

18. Kornfeld, "Erste Sitzung," 1.

19. Rein, "Die heimische Landschaft wird geschützt: Das neue Reichsnaturschutzgesetz und das Rheinland"; "Reichsnaturschutzgesetz vom 26 June 1935," *Reichsgesetzblatt*, part 1, 1935, 821–25; Wettengel, "Staat und Naturschutz," 382–83.

20. Kornfeld, "Erste Sitzung," 6.

21. See Werner Weber, *Das Recht des Landschaftsschutzes* (Berlin: J. Neumann-Neudamm), 81–82; Hans Klose, Hans Schwenkel, and Werner Weber, *Der Schutz der Landschaft nach dem Reichsnaturschutzgesetz* (Berlin: J. Neumann-Neudamm, 1937), 5; and chapter 1 in this volume.

22. "Landesplanungsgemeinschaft Rheinland," *Die Rheinprovinz* 12 (September 1936): 596.

23. Hans Schwenkel, "Aufgaben der Landschaftsgestaltung und der Landschaftspflege," *Der Biologe* 10, no. 4 (1941): 11.

24. Werner Lindner, *Ingenieurwerk und Naturschutz* (Berlin: Hugo Bermühler, 1926), vii.

25. Schwenkel, "Aufgaben der Landschaftsgestaltung und der Landschaftspflege," 11–13.

26. See, for example, Wettengel, "Staat und Naturschutz," 379–82. Historians have begun to emphasize the modern roots of Nazi environmental concern. See, for example, John Williams, "'The Chords of the German Soul are Tuned to Nature': The Movement to Preserve the Natural *Heimat* from the Kaiserreich to the Third Reich," *Central European History* 29, no. 3 (1996): 339–84.

27. Kornfeld, "Erste Sitzung," 1.

28. Alwin Seifert, "Heimat und Siedlung," *Zeitschrift des Rheinischen Vereins für Denkmalpflege und Heimatschutz* 30, no. 2 (1937): 8.

29. Paul Schultze-Naumburg, "Die Gestaltung der Landschaft," in *Der deutsche Heimatschutz: Ein Rückblick und Ausblick,* ed. Gesellschaft der Freunde des deutschen Heimatschutzes (Munich: Kastner and Callwey, 1930): 11–17.

30. On Heimatschutz landscape ideals, see William Rollins, *A Greener Vision of Home: Cultural Politics and Environmental Reform in the German* Heimatschutz *Movement* (Ann Arbor: University of Michigan Press, 1997).

31. Werner Lindner, *Der Heimatschutz im neuen Reich* (Leipzig: E.U. Seemann, 1934), 19.

32. Schwenkel, "Aufgaben der Landschaftsgestaltung und der Landschaftspflege," 11–13.

33. See Dominick, *Environmental Movement in Germany,* 102–4, for a detailed depiction of this institutional rivalry.

34. Oskar Karpa, "Bericht über meine Teilnahme an der 20. Tagung für Naturdenkmalpflege in der Staatlichen Stelle für Naturdenkmalpflege zu Berlin am 9. December 1933," 12 December 1933, ALVR 11122.

35. Wettengel, "Staat und Naturschutz," 381.

36. "Niederschrift über die Arbeitstagung des Deutschen Bundes Heimatschutz im Provinzialständehaus zu Hannover am 10 April 1937," ALVR 11125.

37. Prussian Gemeindetag Speech, 5 April 1940, 8–10, ALVR Nachlass Haake 86.

38. On the reorganization of the DBH, see letter from Haake to Rhenish Heimat Organizations, ALVR 11145 (1938?).

39. "Entwurf für die Rundfunk Reportage über die Forschungsstelle 'Rheinländer in aller Welt,'" (n.d.), 1, ALVR Nachlass Haake 63.

40. Prussian Gemeindetag Speech, 5 April 1940, 8–10, ALVR Nachlass Haake 86.

41. Karpa, "Übersicht über den Aufbau des Naturschutzes in Preussen," 3 October 1934, ALVR 11122. On provincial outlays for cultural affairs, see also "Die Kulturaufgaben der Rheinprovinz: Ein umfassendes Programm ist durchgeführt," *Düsseldorfer Nachrichten,* 13 June 1937.

42. "Bericht über Ausgaben für Rechnungsjahr 1937," 21 April 1938, and "Beihilfe für den Naturschutz," 22 April 1937, ALVR 11123.

43. Elmar Heinen, "Naturschutzgebiet Siebengebirge," *Rheinische Heimatpflege* 27 (1990): 119.

44. On the founding of the Rhineland Landesplanungsgemeinschaft, see "Pressenotiz: Landeshauptmann Heinrich Haake," April 1943, 2, ALVR Nachlass Haake 43; "Landesplanungsgemeinschaft Rheinland," *Die Rheinprovinz* 12 (September 1936): 593–96; *Der Planungsraum Rheinland: Seine Struktur und Entwicklungsrichtung. Referate der Regierungspräsidenten in Düsseldorf, Köln, Aachen, Koblenz und Trier erstattet auf der 1. Sitzung des Beirats der Landesplanungsgemeinschaft Rheinland am 23. Februar 1938 in Düsseldorf* (Düsseldorf: Droste, 1938).

45. "Die Rheinische Provinzialverwaltung: Ein Bericht aus dem umfangreichen Arbeitsbereich in den Jahren 1933–1936," *Westdeutsche Landzeitung Geldern,* 10 June 1937.

46. Haake, Prussian Gemeindetag Speech, 5 April 1940, 5, AVLR Nachlass Haake 86.

47. "Landesplanung, Wohnungs- und Siedlungswesen," *Die Rheinprovinz* 13 (May 1937): 332–40. The Rhenish Society for Spatial Planning also assisted in four-year planning for the province, as well as the provision of military installations and strategic locations for sensitive industries.

48. Gottfried Feder, *Die Neue Stadt: Versuch der Begründung einer neuen Stadtplanungskunst aus der sozialen Struktur der Bevölkerung,* 2nd ed. (Berlin: Julius Springer, 1939). For a brief discussion of Feder's influence on urban planning, see Rudy Koshar, *Germany's Transient Pasts: Preservation and National Memory in the Twentieth Century* (Chapel Hill: University of North Carolina Press, 1998), 156–57.

49. Wilhelm Schürmann, "Siedlung und Landesplanung," *Zeitschrift des Rheinischen Vereins für Denkmalpflege und Heimatschutz* 30, no. 2 (1937): 33–38.

50. Schürmann, "Siedlung und Landesplanung," 31–33.

51. Hans Kornfeld, "Wünsche zur Erhaltung der Rheinlandschaft," *Die Rheinprovinz* 12 (July 1936): 462–69.

52. Kornfeld, "Wünsche zur Erhaltung der Rheinlandschaft," 467.

53. Kornfeld, "Erste Sitzung," 5.

54. Schürmann, "Siedlung und Landesplanung," 34–38.

55. Kornfeld, "Erste Sitzung," 5.

56. Josef Ruland, ed., *Festschrift für Franz Graf Wolff Metternich* (Neuss: Gesellschaft für Buchdruckerei, 1974), 55–57.

57. Ibid., 55–58.

58. "Endgültiger Entwurf, Verordnung zum Schutz der Landschaft des Mittelrheins," (1941?), ALVR 11241.

59. Ruland, ed., *Festschrift für Franz Graf Wolff Metternich*, 58; "Endgültiger Entwurf, Verordnung zum Schutz der Landschaft des Mittelrheins" and "Begründung einer für das Rheintal zu erlassenden Schutzverordnung nebst kritischer Würdigung des Entwurfes Becker und der Abänderungsanträge der beteiligten Behörden," ALVR 11241. See also Walther Schoenichen, *Naturschutz als völkische und internationale Kulturaufgabe* (Jena: Gustav Fischer, 1942), 33, 55.

60. "Die Ausstellung: 'Die schöne Stadt,' Zur Schau in der Kunsthalle: Ihre Entschandelung und Baugestaltung," *Düsseldorfer Nachrichten*, 11 September 1941.

61. Haake, Speech before Dutch Architects, 1, ALVR Nachlass Haake 86.

62. "Die Schöne Stadt: Ihre Entschandelung und Gestaltung," Exhibition Catalog, 7, AVLR Nachlass Haake 86. See also "Wann ist eine Stadt 'schön'? Wege aus dem Alten ins Neue—An das öffentliche Gewissen," *Rheinische Westfälische Zeitung*, 14 September 1941.

63. "Die Ausstellung: 'Die schöne Stadt,' Zur Schau in der Kunsthalle: Ihre Entschandelung und Baugestaltung," *Düsseldorfer Nachrichten*, 11 September 1941.

64. Haake, "Begleitschrift der Lehrschau, 'Die Schöne Stadt.'"

65. Haake, Speech before Dutch architects, 2, AVLR Nachlass Haake 86. See also *Zeitschrift des Rheinischen Vereins für Denkmalpflege und Heimatschutz* 30, no. 2 (1937).

66. Haake, "Begleitschrift der Lehrschau, 'Die Schöne Stadt,'" 5.

67. F. Schmidt, "Heimatschutz und Siedlung," *Zeitschrift des Rheinischen Vereins für Denkmalpflege und Heimatschutz* 30, no. 2 (1937): 15.

68. Günther Wohlers, "Der rheinische Siedler und sein Haus," *Zeitschrift des Rheinischen Vereins für Denkmalpflege und Heimatschutz* 30, no. 2 (1937): 45–46.

69. Seifert, "Heimat und Siedlung," 6–9.

70. "Landesplanung, Wohnungs- und Siedlungswesen," *Die Rheinprovinz*, 337–40. Reform architects and garden city planners from the 1920s had already argued for the use of planning to support eugenic goals; see Wolfgang Voigt, "The Garden City as Eugenic Utopia," *Planning Perspectives* 4, no. 3 (1989): 295–312.

71. Wilhelm Lienenkämper, "Der Deutsche und seine Landschaft: Vom gegenwärtigen Stand der Naturschutzbewegung," *Heimatliebe—Heimatschutz* 80, no. 31 (March 1934).

72. Wilhelm Lienenkämper, "Die Arbeit der Naturschutzbeauftragten: Planvolles Schaffen oder Armeleutebetrieb," n.d., in ALVW, C 70, nr. 184, bd. 1, fol. 227.

73. Lienenkämper, "Die Arbeit der Naturschutzbeauftragten," fol. 228.

74. See Rudolf Hoffmann, "Landschaftsschutz und Bauaufgaben im nationalsozialistischen Staat," *Die Rheinprovinz* 12 (April 1936): 249.

75. Hoffmann, "Landschaftsschutz und Bauaufgaben im nationalsozialistischen Staat," 249.

76. Memorandum from Karl Oberkirch, Bezirksbeauftragter für Naturschutz in the Ruhrsiedlungsverband, 11 November 1935, fol. 237–38, and letter from Vogelschutzverein Haltern und Umgebung to Oberkirch, 15 November 1935, fol. 239–40, Bundesarchiv Koblenz (hereafter BAK), B 245/24; Memorandum from Dr. Menke to Iven, Provinzialbeauftragter für Naturschutz, 9 December 1942, ALVR 11136.

77. "Naturschutztagung im Oberpräsidium Koblenz am 16. Mai 1938," ALVR 11123.

78. Hoffmann, "Landschaftsschutz und Bauaufgaben im nationalsozialistischen Staat," 249; Riechers, "Nature Protection during National Socialism," 47–49. Michael Wettengel has referred to 1936 as a *"generelle Zäsur"* in Nazi support for environmental protection measures. See "Staat und Naturschutz," 386.

79. Wilhelm Münker, "Erhaltet—Schützt—Pflanzt! Ein Notruf in letzter Stunde für die bedrohte Natur," Heimat und Naturschutz-Ausschuss des Sauerländischen Gebirgsvereins (1935?), ALVW, C 70, Nr. 192a, fol. 31.

80. Letter from Iven to Dr. Gobbin concerning closure of hiking and recreation areas in the Rhineland Province, 20 July 1939, BAK, B 245/18; on the Haardt Forest, see BAK, B 245/24, fol. 63–69.

81. Correspondence between Dr. Schmeisser, Cologne District nature protection officer, and Reich Forest Ministry, 28 November 1939, BAK, 245/18, fol. 76–77.

82. On the Lunebürger Heath in the Nazi era, see BAK, 245/82, fol. 343, fol. 395, fol. 414, fol. 462. The Nazis scrapped plans for the aircraft landing strip on the heathlands; unfortunately, I have not been able to determine from available documentation whether the other projects were completed.

CHAPTER 4

Polycentrism in Full Swing

Air Pollution Control in Nazi Germany

Frank Uekötter

SCHOLARS HAVE LONG known that Nazi policymaking was character-ized by an enormous amount of administrative confusion and bureau-cratic infighting. "The ruling class of National Socialist Germany is far from homogeneous," Franz Neumann wrote in *Behemoth: The Structure and Practice of National Socialism* (1942). "There are as many interests as there are groups."[1] Similarly, in *The Origins of Totalitarianism* (1951), Han-nah Arendt pointed out "the peculiar 'shapelessness' of the totalitarian government," refuting the idea that a totalitarian state would necessarily have a monolithic structure.[2]

Since then, many others have commented on the "polycracy of de-partments" and the "administrative anarchy" of the Third Reich.[3] "The polycratic regime consisted of a number of oligarchies that differed in ide-ology, interests, personnel, internal structure, and style of working," Peter Hüttenberger wrote in 1976.[4] "Never before in German history has there been a government that had extreme powers like Hitler's *Führerstaat* while simultaneously being characterized to a large extent by contradictory ele-ments and by bitter disputes over respective areas of responsibility in the uncharted terrain of a confused administrative organization," Dieter Rebentisch added in 1998.[5] Hans Mommsen has carried this argument one step further, noting that the Nazi regime displayed "an unparalleled institutional anarchy" and that Hitler therefore appeared to be "in some respects a weak dictator."[6]

Critics have pointed out that the polycentric model of the Third Reich tends to overly marginalize Adolf Hitler: Nazi leaders were able to accomplish many things in Nazi Germany without Hitler's explicit endorsement, but nothing could happen against the Führer's declared will.[7] This was certainly true as regards the central issues of the regime, from rearmament to genocide. However, on issues that the Führer considered less important, or at least less in need of his direct attention, bureaucrats found plenty of room to maneuver and fight among themselves. Air pollution was one such issue. Hitler never took an official public stance on air pollution control. Nor was there anything in his writings and memoranda that could be construed as a support for a certain position. Consequently, the administrative chaos of Nazi Germany came into full swing, making the history of air pollution control during that time period a showpiece of the polycentric character of Nazi policy.

At no point did a single official Nazi position emerge on air pollution issues between 1933 and 1945. Instead, three different approaches emerged, based on conflicting rationales. The first was largely ideological, the second largely tactical, the third largely practical. The Munich-based Academy for German Law (Akademie für Deutsches Recht) took an ideological approach: it sought a fundamental reorganization of German law, including pollution control laws, to bring them into conformity with the Nazi notion of *Gemeinnutz vor Eigennutz* (the common good above the individual good). The Reichsnährstand (Reich Food Estate) took a more tactical approach: it encouraged farmers to be more aggressive in seeking compensation for crop damage caused by industrial pollution as a way of improving the financial situation of farmers. Those involved with rearmament took a more practical approach: they recognized that some pollution-control laws (most notably those that required a special license to construct hazardous plants) had the potential to compromise military secrets. They therefore supported changes to these regulations, often without taking a stance on air pollution itself.

This chapter will investigate these three positions in detail and examine the degree to which they implied a departure from, or a reaction to, previous practices. I will show that, despite these challenges, the dominant characteristic of air pollution control after 1933 was a continuation of previous procedures. This held true until around 1942–43, when the pace of wartime production began to undermine all bureaucratic efforts to control pollution. Finally, I will discuss the impact that the Nazi era had on air pollution control after 1945.

Gemeinnutz vor Eigennutz:
The Ideological Challenge to Air Pollution Law

Soon after 1933, a discussion arose among juridical experts as to whether the existing legal provisions for air pollution problems were compatible with the ideological principles of National Socialism. The focal point of the debate was Paragraph 906 of the Civil Code (*Bürgerliches Gesetzbuch,* or *BGB*). This paragraph contained some of the key provisions for conflicts over air pollution. In a nutshell, it provided citizens with protection from industrial emissions unless these emissions were either "insignificant" (*unwesentlich*) or consistent with "the local norm" (*ortsüblich*). Although Paragraph 906 looks modest at first glance, it drew a fair amount of criticism from jurists embracing the ideology of National Socialism because it seemed to conform to the principles of liberalism and individualism. "In discussing the juridical questions in conflicts over emissions, the guiding principle is that all economic activity is a tribute to the nation at large (*Dienst am Volksganzen*)," Ernst Eiser, a Berlin lawyer, wrote in 1938. "The formulation of Paragraph 906 of the Civil Code does not leave enough room (at least in its current interpretation) to take this point of view into account. . . . Only the National Socialist conception of property rights might provide some wiggle room to the provisions of Paragraph 906."[8] Similarly, Heinz Schiffer asked in 1936 whether Paragraph 906 allowed a resolution of pollution conflicts "pursuant to principles that are in accordance with the legal philosophy of National Socialism." His answer: "a resounding 'no.'"[9]

The discussion of Paragraph 906 was part of a broader debate that took place in Nazi Germany, most prominently in the Academy for German Law. As historian Dennis LeRoy Anderson has argued, it was "the declared Nazi intention [to replace] the priority of the individual and his rights to property with the principle of 'Gemeinnutz vor Eigennutz'"[10] The profit for the nation at large, rather than for the individual, was to be the central yardstick; from this perspective, the dispute over air pollution legislation was part of a fundamental challenge to the German legal system. Also, it was by all means typical that the dispute over air pollution centered around a provision of the Civil Code. "In many ways, the BGB was the symbol of liberalism, individualism, materialism, and legal positivism, all anathema to the National Socialist concepts of the *Führer-staat* and the *Volksgemeinschaft*," Anderson noted.[11]

The most important result of this ideological challenge was a law of 13 December 1933 that limited the rights of those citizens who lived or worked in the vicinity of facilities that were considered important for the physical training of the people. Neighbors of such facilities could not demand that these facilities be closed, nor could they force the installations to reduce their deleterious impact. In other words, neighbors were powerless to eliminate the nuisance itself; the only option they had was to apply for monetary compensation. However, the law of 13 December 1933 did not offer blanket protection to all sports facilities. Rather, it gave special status to specific, highly important installations, and this special status could only come from the Ministry of the Interior (Reichsinnenministerium). In granting this status, the ministry placed the facility under certain conditions and regulations; it could repeal its decision at any time, in which case the facility would again fall under the terms of the Civil Code. Finally, the ministry also settled issues of monetary compensation to neighbors by incontestable decree.[12] This law was followed by a similar law of 18 October 1935 that extended this type of special status to hospitals, nursing homes, and similar installations.[13]

In explaining the intentions of the 1933 law, the *National Socialist Handbook for Law and Legislation* (*Nationalsozialistisches Handbuch für Recht und Gesetzgebung*) referred to Point 21 of the Nazi Party program, which called for "the greatest support for all associations that seek the physical training of young people."[14] At the same time, however, the *Handbook* was quick to point out that the protection of the burgeoning sports movement was by no means the only intention of the law: "Its provisions also imply the first decisive step towards a renunciation of the individualistic and liberalistic concept of property which stresses the rights of the property owners while ignoring the owners' obligations," the *Handbook* stated. The phrases "the common good above the individual good" and "the supreme interests of the *Volksgemeinschaft*" occurred in subsequent sentences, further highlighting this point.[15] In a similar vein, a comment in the *Juristische Wochenschrift* (a renowned legal journal) declared that, although this law had gone largely unnoticed, it was in fact "of the highest significance with regard to the future development of the Civil Code in the Third Reich." The author spoke enthusiastically of a "sensitive breach" in a heretofore dominant concept of property, predicting that this was only "the beginning of a corresponding development."[16]

However, the general transformation that these jurists envisioned never materialized: the two laws of 1933 and 1935 remained singular acts. In fact, it may be safely assumed that the impact of these laws was very limited. Even a governmental decree pursuant to the law of 1935 stated that complaints about nuisances from hospitals and similar installations were "generally rare." More commonly a hospital *suffered* from industrial or nonindustrial emissions; but for cases of that kind, the new laws left everything unchanged.[17] There is other evidence that the new laws were largely inconsequential as well. An overview article of 1936 only referred to the two laws "in passing."[18] And in 1937, Friedrich Klausing, a prominent member of the Academy for German Law, concluded that there had been "no fundamental changes" of traditional legal provisions as a consequence of these laws.[19]

The failure of the ideological challenge to existing air pollution law was somewhat typical for initiatives of the Academy for German Law. Even the most ambitious project of the Academy, the *Nation's Code* (*Volksgesetzbuch*), would have had little chance of implementation even if it had ever been completed.[20] "In spite of many publications and numerous conferences, the Academy for German Law had little influence on legislation, due to the resistance of the ministerial bureaucracy," an article on the academy notes.[21] Nazi jurists, however, were not just struggling with the reluctance of the bureaucratic establishment but also with the inconclusiveness of their own directives. It was easy to invoke the principle of "the common good above the individual good" in order to demand the primacy of the national interest. But it was difficult—if not altogether impossible—to transform this slogan into law.

The trouble began as soon as jurists attempted to define the national interest. While it was relatively easy (and uncontroversial) to declare that hospitals and sports facilities were in the national interest, such pronouncements gave little guidance when it came to everyday conflicts over air pollution. For instance, who was representing the national interest when an industrial facility's emissions did damage to cropland—the industrialist or the farmer? Friedrich Klausing tried to answer that question by stating that it was important to find "a sensible balance of interests in accordance with the demands of the national economy." But formulations of that nature just raised more questions than they solved.[22] Similarly, Heinz Schiffer urged all parties "to tackle the problem from the point of view of the community." The victim of pollution and the polluter itself should "show consideration for each other" and "make sacrifices."

And if the individual conditions of the case in question did not allow for such a solution, the case had to be judged "exclusively with regard to the well-being and the flourishing of the entire German nation."[23] The vagueness of Schiffer's formulations is plainly apparent.

With the general direction of reform blurred, the concrete proposals soon became documents of disorientation. It was not even clear whether there was actually an urgent need for a new law. Klausing, for example, argued that the key was "a more appropriate interpretation and use of the existing legal provisions on the basis of the new juridical philosophy." To be sure, he did not exclude new legislation on principle; rather, he warned against "partial reforms" since the ultimate goal would have to be "a comprehensive reordering of our entire property law."[24] By contrast, Schiffer argued in favor of special commissions of experts that could deal with complaints in a flexible way, making them an alternative to formal court proceedings.[25] In a similar vein, Eiser stressed that there was a need for an "elastic jurisdiction." Countering contemporary attempts to define certain measurable standards, he called for a consideration of "all the peculiar conditions" of each individual case. But he also stated: "It is the task of the law to create an order that provides for the best possible result for the nation as a whole."[26] Apparently, it never occurred to him that his calls for a new overarching juridical order, and for greater flexibility in dealing with individual cases, were somewhat inconsistent.

The confusion over ways and means reached its peak in a session of the Committee on Land Law (*Ausschuß für Bodenrecht*) of the Academy for German Law in February 1938. In his introduction, the chairman of the session argued that the topic of pollution control was to be used as an exemplary case of the much-desired general juridical transformation because the basic direction that the ideological transformation would need to take had already become reasonably clear.[27] However, the discussion itself proved otherwise. Proposals were plentiful, but most of them were contradictory, incoherent, and vague; the only thing they shared was that someone was willing to defend them on the grounds they conformed to Nazi ideology. In the end, the committee did not even come close to agreeing on any concrete legislative proposals. For example, one speaker stressed the "communal relationship" (*Gemeinschaftsverhältnis*) of neighbors, arguing that on the basis of this communal relationship, "we can trust the judge if he takes all aspects into account."[28] A few moments later, the same person proposed to name members of both parties as jurors in order to assist the judge in making his decision.[29] Another speaker argued that neighbors should only have to tolerate "small imponderables" (*kleine Imponderabilien*) and that "large imponderables" should be forbidden. However, Paragraph 906 of the Civil Code already required the toleration of "insignificant" emissions, making it unclear what the speaker's suggestion would have done to improve the legal status quo.[30] Yet another speaker stressed the duty of landowners "to maintain their property in such a way as to keep the well-being of the nation (*Wohl der Volksgemeinschaft*) in accordance with the law and popular sentiment (*gesundes Volksempfinden*)."[31] He then flip-flopped as he strove to be more concrete. One should not be able to prohibit emissions "if one could expect someone to tolerate it, taking into account all the details of the case, especially the local situation of the property in question."[32] Moments later, he acknowledged "that these provisions, taken by themselves, are not very meaningful," and so he proposed "to enlarge the present law and to make it more flexible."[33] Another speaker stressed "the idea of the folk character (*Volkstümlichkeit*) of the law" since one was dealing with smallholders and ordinary people in this field.[34] What exactly "folk character" meant was left unclear. Meanwhile, others added confusion to the notion of *Ortsüblichkeit* (the local norm). While several Nazi jurists were known to believe that this principle was incompatible with National Socialistic ideology, someone in this session declared that this formulation would have to stay. It was only the interpretation of this provision that would have to change: one had to take into account "the local norms as a whole" (*Ortsüblichkeit im Ganzen*)—whatever that meant.[35]

Clearly, the ideological premises of the Academy for German Law did not provide a sufficient compass for a reformulation of air pollution law. The key problem was that the Academy never dared to tackle the concept of individual property head-on. As long as there were landowners, there would be conflicts over the use of property; with emissions being common in an industrial society, a fair amount of these conflicts would center upon air pollution problems. In other words, the Nazi jurists tended to argue as if conflicts over pollution grew out of contempt for the demands of the *Volksgemeinschaft,* while it was actually the sheer existence of divergent interests that lay at the root of the problem. If one accepted the legitimacy of these interests, there was basically no way to keep the parties from fighting for these interests in court. This was the fundamental irony of the efforts of the Academy for German Law in the field of air pollution control: in emphasizing the *Dienst am Volksganzen,* the jurists tried to urge the different parties to work together. Ultimately, the reality

of divergent interests was stronger than the ideology of National Socialism: one could demand cooperation in the name of a unified Reich, but
one could not thereby guarantee unanimity among competing groups, all
of which could claim to be representing the national interest.

Supporting the Case of the Farmers:
The Policy of the Reich Food Estate

While the first challenge to existing air pollution measures was essentially
ideological, the second challenge was more tactical in nature. Numerous
documents indicate that the Reich Food Estate, the farmers' organization
in Nazi Germany, encouraged farmers to be more aggressive with damage
claims. For example, when the German organization of heavy industry
(Wirtschaftsgruppe Metallindustrie) conducted a poll among its members about their experiences in dealing with air pollution problems, several companies mentioned activities of the Reich Food Estate during the
1930s. The Kupferwerk Ilsenburg reported that in settling damage claims
of three farmers, it had consulted two experts "at the instigation of the
Reich Food Estate."[36] In Saxony, the Reich Food Estate supported a law-
suit of a number of beekeepers against the state-owned metalworks.[37] In
a conflict over a branch factory of the Vereinigte Deutsche Metallwerke
near Frankfurt, the Reich Food Estate approached the company on behalf
of several farmers; in this instance, the factory succeeded in fending off
the complaints.[38] The Reich Food Estate assumed a similar role in a conflict over a plant of the Gewerkschaft Zinnwalder Bergbau in Freiberg;
the case was still pending when the company wrote its report.[39] In some
cases, even Reich Peasant Leader (*Reichsbauernführer*) Richard Walther
Darré, the head of the Reich Food Estate, became active. In 1937, the Reich
peasant leader sent a letter to the Gutehoffnungshütte in Oberhausen in
which he urged an "amicable settlement" of pending damage claims.[40] And
as late as December 1943, the Reich peasant leader tried to negotiate a deal
in a conflict over the emissions of the Rütgerswerke near Dresden.[41]

For industrialists to haggle with farmers or forest owners over monetary compensation for damage to plants and trees was, of course, nothing
new. In fact, money had been one of the most common ways for polluters
and their neighbors to settle their disputes since the late nineteenth century.[42] But until 1933, it had been relatively rare that a farmers' association
became involved in conflicts of this kind. Moreover, it was a testimony to
the strength of the Reich Food Estate's activity that it provoked a reaction

from industry. In 1941, a number of industrial associations agreed to set up a Research Institute for Air Pollution Damage (Forschungsstelle für Rauchschäden).[43] In explaining its motives in supporting this initiative, the organization of the German chemical industry (Wirtschaftsgruppe Chemische Industrie) referred to the "strong and well-organized organization" of the Reich Food Estate, which commanded a comprehensive network of experts that put industry "severely at a disadvantage."[44] If a farmers' association was able to provoke such a decisive reaction, it seems reasonable to assume that the aforementioned activities were part of a general strategy, rather than isolated events.

Unfortunately, the surviving files of the Reich Food Estate do not include documents on the subject, making it difficult to evaluate the precise extent of the association's activities.[45] However, it is clear from documents in other archives that the Reich Food Estate at least tried to develop a full-scale policy initiative on the subject. In 1935, the Reich peasant leader asked its local branches to report pollution conflicts in their area. Mentioning a number of unfavorable court decisions during the previous years, the Reich peasant leader took the initiative "to raise the question of compensation for damage effected by the emissions of industrial enterprises, with the goal of reaching a fundamental and permanent arrangement." The Reich Peasant Leader also hinted at the direction in which he was thinking. According to his decree, it was imperative "to check whether a change of the existing legal provisions is necessary, specifically with a view to enlarging the obligation of liability for compensation pursuant to Paragraph 26 of the Trading Regulations (Gewerbeordnung)."[46] However, the Trading Regulations were within the jurisdiction of the Ministry of Trade and Commerce (Reichswirtschaftsministerium), and in order to make a convincing case, the Reich peasant leader sought to collect information about individual conflicts. It is indeed not difficult to find a motive for this initiative: after all, the Reich Food Estate had by no means an easy standing among the farmers. The *Erbhof* Law of 1933 had led to "a groundswell of protest," contributing to the "general failure" of the Nazi's *Erbhof* policy.[47] In the implementation of this law, the Reich Food Estate had shown itself to be driven primarily by ideological motives, rather than a concern for the individual farmer.[48] Also, it is important to realize that there was constant "bickering between the [Reich Food Estate] and the normal administrative machinery." And with the Four-Year Plan of 1936, "the *Reich Food Estate* lost any sort of independence which it may ever have enjoyed and simply became an outright instrument for the mobilization of the agrarian sector and its adaptation to a wartime economy."[49] In supporting the case of the farmers in conflicts over pollution damage, the Reich Food Estate was probably using one of its last remaining options to operate independently.

It is important to notice that the Reich Food Estate's standpoint was somewhat ambivalent. It was, of course, in favor of broader and higher compensation for crop damage, but not as an end in itself. If farmers received too much compensation in this way, they might neglect their agricultural work, which in turn would conflict with the goal of higher agricultural production in preparation for the war.[50] Interestingly, the Reich peasant leader occasionally found himself arguing in favor of *limited* compensation: "from the point of view of the Reich Food Estate, it is not a desirable goal to breed so-called 'pensioners' on a large scale," he declared in his letter to the Gutehoffnungshütte.[51] In this regard, the position of the Reich Food Estate merged with that of members of the Academy for German Law who pointed to the negative side effects of monetary compensation. "In the light of the interests of all parties involved, the 'pension farmer' in the environs of industrial plants is not a pleasant phenomenon," Eiser noted in an article of 1938.[52] According to his description, one could occasionally notice that, upon construction of a new plant, neighboring farmers would neglect their ordinary work, apparently keen to profit from the new enterprise as much as they could. In a similar vein, Klausing declared that it was "unacceptable if landowners receive single or regular payments for emission damage while leaving everything else unchanged," arguing in favor of a transformation of agricultural production that took into account the peculiar conditions of the location. Klausing maintained that farmers should assume more than "the passive role of the recipient of compensation."[53]

The Reich peasant leader's decree of 1935 was obviously written with a view to formulating a legislative proposal. However, such a proposal never surfaced, and, lacking documentation of discussions within the Reich Food Estate, it is a matter of speculation why that was the case. But it seems probable that the initiative of the Reich Food Estate suffered from a problem similar to that of the Academy for German Law: both were seeking a goal that was difficult, or even impossible, to decree by law. After all, how could one be assured that a farmer would use his compensation in a productive way? Eiser proposed to give out compensation in non-monetary terms as far as possible, but a productive transfer of goods was almost as difficult to define as a productive investment.[54] One basically had to control the entire business of each single farm in order to assure an appropriate use of goods and money. Even disregarding the amount of bureaucratic work that this would have required, it is certain that such an intrusion would have been anything but welcome to farmers. And given that the most probable motivation of the Reich Food Estate in dealing with the issue was to improve its standing among farmers, it seems clear that the Reich Food Estate was essentially dealing with contradictory rationales. When the Reich Peasant Leader decided not to come up with a legislative proposal, it was probably serving its own interests best.

How to Control a Secret Plant:
The Impact of Rearmament on Air Pollution Control

When the Nazis took power, it was a firmly established bureaucratic practice that dangerous industrial installations had to obtain a special license. This practice ultimately went back to the Prussian Trading Regulations (Gewerbeordnung) of 1845. These regulations required all entrepreneurs to file their construction plans with the local authorities, which then checked them for fire, health, and other potential hazards. As part of the licensing procedure, the project had to be made public, giving everyone four weeks (later reduced to two weeks) to file objections against it.[55] Of course, this requirement was somewhat at odds with the Nazi goal of rearmament; after all, it effectively meant that everybody could check the plans of a war production plant. Consequently, a new paragraph (Paragraph 22a) was added to the Trading Regulations in the summer of 1934 that provided for a secret licensing procedure. The necessary requirement was that construction of the installation in question had to be "in the public interest."[56] As the German Ministry of Trade and Commerce declared in a decree of 30 October 1934, this would regularly be the case "if we are dealing with plants producing military supplies."[57]

The decree did not elaborate on the process that led to the creation of this new procedure. But presumably the experience of World War I had played an important role: war production between 1914 and 1918 had led to a juridical quagmire that must have remained fresh in the memories of bureaucrats. Jurists had to stretch their imagination quite a bit to allow war production to progress without formal licensing procedures. For example, in dealing with a munitions factory in 1915, the Prussian Ministry of War urged local authorities "to postpone the licensing procedure until the war is over."[58] The Bavarian Ministry of War, meanwhile, declared that the provisions of the Trading Regulations only pertained to permanent installations, arguing that all war production in Bavaria was "temporary."[59] The state of Württemberg used an even more daring juridical concept: it argued that the Trading Regulations did not explicitly require the states to prosecute those installations that lacked a license; in other words, war production might technically violate the law, but the government was under no obligation to enforce it.[60] Given this backdrop, it is understandable that the Nazi government would have wanted to create procedures for the licensing of war production plants that avoided the need for this sort of legal legerdemain.

Interestingly, it was apparently not the intention of the Nazi government to free war production plants from all regulations. The decree of 30 October 1934 specifically ruled that the procedure pursuant to Paragraph 22a did not imply a limitation of the usual examination of the plans, since that would mean "a disadvantage to the workers, the neighbors, and the public at large."[61] Also, experience had shown that the reaction of the public was generally unimportant for the decision of the bureaucracy.[62] Finally, it is important to realize that this decree clearly envisioned licensing procedures of this kind to be the exception: the license had to be granted by the state government, with local authorities assuming a preparatory role only. However, all this only referred to the legal side of the matter, which surely did not determine the administrative reality in all its details. There was obviously no intentional negligence regarding air pollution from war production plants. For example, the Ministry of Trade and Commerce issued a decree in 1936 to inquire about problems with the awful smell of viscose factories, a type of production that was of high importance in the context of the Four-Year Plan.[63] When the ministry discovered that 9 of the 28 factories were faced with complaints from neighbors, the ministry issued a second decree that gave guidelines for mitigating this problem.[64] Still, it is important to remember that, in spite of such initiatives, the Nazis' rearmament program and the subsequent rise of war production necessarily meant more pollution. Also, it seems reasonable to assume that, in licensing a war production plant, the bureaucracy was faced with somewhat limited possibilities as compared to a normal licensing procedure. But before discussing the actual impact of the licensing procedure pursuant to Paragraph 22a in more detail, it is necessary to briefly describe air pollution control as commonly practiced in interwar Germany.

Continuity Reigning Supreme:
The Everyday Practice of Air Pollution Control

Since the nineteenth century, Germany had developed a complex system of legal provisions on air pollution problems. The most important regulations were spread over three different bodies of legislation, two of which have already been mentioned: Paragraph 906 of the Civil Code; the licensing procedure pursuant to the Trading Regulations; and the general police law. In fact, even the Prussian Ministry of Public Welfare conceded in a decree of 1931 that the legislative status quo was "not simple" to determine since there were "no coherent legal provisions."[65] In general, however, it can be said that these provisions provided decent, though certainly not perfect, working conditions for air pollution control. As a ministry official wrote in 1930: "If there is a singular case of air pollution of excessive proportions, the person affected can be assured of the necessary juridical protection."[66] The main weakness in the legal structure was that it made it difficult to handle the cumulative impact of pollution damage from many sources. As soon as an air pollution problem resulted from a multitude of sources or traveled beyond a plant's immediate surroundings, the ministry official saw "little chances for success."[67] However, while this was by no means a marginal restriction of the powers of the bureaucracy, it would be wrong to overemphasize this deficit. The key problem was not a lack of legal provisions, it was the negligent enforcement of these provisions.[68]

In bureaucratic terms, the control of air pollution was essentially no-man's-land. Health authorities, factory inspectors, building inspectors, and the general police force occasionally dealt with the issue, but none of them felt that air pollution was a central issue, at least for their own agencies. No one knew who was responsible for air pollution control, but all agreed that it was certainly not themselves. Consequently, enforcement of the existing legal provisions was highly unsystematic, if not chaotic; as a general rule, the administration did not become active unless someone applied for a license or filed a complaint. And with air pollution being seen as an issue of marginal importance, the administration usually tried to get rid of the issue as quickly as possible. Therefore, German bureaucrats displayed a high degree of flexibility in dealing with complaints. Even the Prussian Ministry of Public Welfare urged officials to refrain from a legalistic approach: "It has been our experience so far that faster and better solutions can be obtained through amicable advice (*gütliche*

Einwirkungen und Belehrungen) by factory inspectors and other expert officials than through prosecution and coercion by the police," the ministry noted in its decree of 1931.[69]

Therefore, in a strict sense, Germany did not have a policy on air pollution: it had bureaucratic routine. Air pollution control as it stood in 1933 was neither anti-Nazi nor pro-Nazi—it was administrative normality. To be sure, people sometimes referred to the Nazi regime in order to hammer home their point. For example, a local Nazi representative (*Ortsgruppenleiter*) in the city of Bielefeld wrote in a letter to the authorities responsible for a smoking municipal plant, "I hereby demand instant abatement, especially since there is a widespread opinion that under the past political system, there has never been air pollution of this magnitude."[70] However, the tactical nature of this statement is only too apparent. After all, arguing that air pollution would decline under the Nazis was all too easily belied by reality: a booming economy, an obvious goal of the Nazi regime, would almost certainly result in more, rather than less pollution. As a medical official in the city of Leipzig wrote in a 1940 report: "I do not think that I am estimating too high when I say that the intensity of production has doubled or tripled on the average [as compared with 1933–34], even excluding the war economy. Should we be surprised if during the same time period, the airborne smoke and dust have increased twofold, threefold, and more?"[71]

Interestingly, the presumable increase of air pollution did not stimulate a reform discussion. During the Nazi era, people could run into the topic for ideological, tactical, or juridical reasons—but few people took the actual state of the atmosphere as their point of departure, and those who did failed to get off the ground. The proposal of a Breslau official named Hoffmann provides a case in point. During the 1930s, Hoffmann had organized a campaign against the smoke nuisance in the city of Breslau. However, since the campaign was mainly based on free advice, it failed to gain momentum; even Hoffmann himself wrote that the practical result of his work was "poor."[72] Consequently, Hoffmann came up with a call for an "air hygiene law" to overcome current provisions that were allegedly written "under the decisive influence of a pervasive capitalist egocentricity."[73] Hoffmann's paper was sent to the Prussian Institute for Water, Soil, and Air Hygiene (Preußische Landesanstalt für Wasser-, Boden- und Lufthygiene), which was the highest authority on questions of environmental pollution in Germany at the time. But the institute's response spelled the sudden and unheroic death of his initiative: referring to several "factual errors" in passing, the institute claimed to see "nothing basically new" in Hoffmann's proposal.[74] To be sure, this distaste for reform was by no means a peculiarity of the Nazi era: those attempting to bring about discussions of this kind had always had a hard time in the history of German air pollution control, and, during the Weimar Republic, similar reform initiatives had been especially rare. Hoffmann's proposal basically stood in a tradition of sporadic initiatives during the interwar years that had two things in common. First, they rarely if ever had a chance of success, and second, they were rarely well conceived.[75] However, one should add in the interest of fairness that it was indeed hard to come up with a good reform proposal. It would have been relatively easy to argue for a better approach if there had been a specific law or decree that lay at the root of the problem, but criticizing a bureaucratic routine that even long-time observers could barely identify was quite a different matter.

Given this bureaucratic practice, neither the activities of the Reich Food Estate nor the introduction of a secret licensing procedure implied a fundamental challenge to established practices. The German system of air pollution control was already flexible to such an extent that it could easily accommodate these initiatives. If a war plant was to be licensed pursuant to Paragraph 22a, the factory inspectorate could certainly not check the plans as critically as it could have done with a normal installation. But it had long been an unwritten rule that the specific conditions that went along with the license could vary tremendously from case to case, and the secret licensing procedure was ultimately nothing more than one more cause for these variations. Similarly, if the Reich Food Estate allowed farmers to be more aggressive in their complaints about pollution damage, this was basically nothing more than a variation in a long-standing conflict—for disputes over the amount of compensation were only too familiar to farmers, polluting companies, and bureaucrats alike.

In fact, the Academy for German Law was missing the point when it centered its discussion around legal provisions: the key impediment to an effective air pollution control policy was the mentality of the German bureaucracy, which tended to think "from case to case" without a general system—in fact, without ever even thinking that there *should* be a system.[76] "The control authorities will decide from case to case what kind of dust filters will have to be built—or whether they have to be built at all—to prevent a nuisance to neighbors," the Prussian Institute for Water,

Soil, and Air Hygiene replied to an inquiry about specific standards in 1934.[77] With this general orientation, the stage was set for the persistence of air pollution control routines far into World War II.

Normalcy during Abnormal Times: Air Pollution Control during World War II

In the spring of 1940, the Leipzig district organization (*Kreisleitung*) of the Nazi Party filed a complaint against the licensing of an iron and steel foundry. Arguing that residents had been suffering from soot and stink for years, the agency demanded that the foundry be built in another area.[78] However, the foundry in question was not an ordinary plant: the company was producing mainly for the war economy. Moreover, the plant was one of only three of its kind in Germany, two of which were located in the western part of Germany and thus closer to the enemy, and the new foundry was part of an urgent rearmament program (Sofort-Programm des Generalinspekteurs für das deutsche Straßenwesen, Abteilung Rüstungsbau).[79] With France and Great Britain at war with Germany, the Nazi Party's petition (which the mayor of Leipzig chose to ignore) appears somewhat untimely, to say the least. But when compared with other activities in the field of air pollution control during that time period, the petition barely stands out, because complaints were not infrequent. For example, a resident of Essen complained in 1941 that smoke from a nearby mine was soiling her laundry.[80] Two years later, a conflict arose in the same city over a coffee roasting plant that produced surrogate coffee for the military; the conflict ended after the company installed a special filter and agreed not to process certain raw materials during morning hours.[81] In 1942, a producer of artificial silk in the city of Krefeld built special cleansing towers in reaction to numerous complaints, although the company had some trouble in getting the necessary workers, especially bricklayers. "The demands of the war are stronger than the good will of the company," an official commented on the factory's efforts.[82] In 1942, a long-standing conflict between a furniture factory and the factory inspectorate of the state of Baden ended with the installation of a new boiler.[83]

Even when the demands of air pollution control were in direct conflict with war conditions, the bureaucracy's reaction was by no means automatic, as yet another case, this time in Bielefeld, showed. In July 1941, a printer asked the local authorities to grant him permission to dismantle a smokestack on his premises. "I have noticed that during the last two air-raids on Bielefeld, the enemy pilots regularly used my chimney as a target when they threw bombs in the environs of my factory," the printer wrote.[84] However, the local administration declined, and the factory inspectorate, to which the printer sent a similar request, sustained this decision; the decisive argument was that a lower chimney would almost certainly create a smoke nuisance.[85] Even the intensification of war production pursuant to the appointment of Albert Speer as minister for armament and ammunition (*Reichsminister für Bewaffnung und Munition*) in February 1942 did not spell the end to all efforts.[86] A mining company in the Harz region agreed to pay compensation for forest damage of RM 15,578 in November 1943.[87] And on 19 May 1944, half a dozen officials met in the city of Lüdenscheid in southern Westphalia to discuss the damage that the emissions of a local aluminum smelter were doing to the trees near the local stadium.[88]

The ministerial decrees of this period displayed a similar normality. To be sure, the government did make significant concessions to the war conditions: in 1941, the Ministry of Trade and Commerce introduced a temporary license for war production plants that was designed for those cases "where an unrestricted license would have been unacceptable with regard to the protection of the neighbors." But once again, the government tried to keep the damage within limits: the decree clearly argued for a "limited" use of this option.[89] About three months later, the same ministry ruled that companies did not have to pay fees for the licensing of installations which replaced those destroyed by enemy force.[90] On 20 August 1943, the Ministry of the Interior clarified how to proceed when a smoke screen for camouflage purposes damaged useful plants.[91] And on 18 February 1942, the Ministry of Trade and Commerce even issued a decree that effectively strengthened air pollution control: in licensing a number of plants, the ministry urged the local authorities to consult with the experts at the Prussian Institute for Water, Soil, and Air Hygiene.[92] In doing so, the ministry followed a suggestion of the institute itself; the list of installations in the decree was almost identical with a list that the institute had sent to the ministry about a month earlier.[93]

It is not difficult to envision the motive behind the institute's initiative: the decree promised more work for the institute, underscoring the importance of its mission and demonstrating that none of its staff members was dispensable for military duty. Of course, this idea was never written down, but it can be inferred from the surprising fact that as the war progressed, a discussion arose within the administration on how to reform air pollution regulation—a discussion that was completely dormant when the war started. For example, on 25 June 1941, the Ministry of Trade and Commerce took the initiative to revise the list of plants that required a special license—three days after the German attack on the Soviet Union.[94] In 1944, work started on a new version of the *Technische Anleitung,* a handbook for licensing plants that offered technical information and standards.[95] A memorandum of the Institute for Water, Soil, and Air Hygiene of 1942 spoke of "a reform of Paragraph 16 of the Trading Regulations [which dealt with the licensing procedure] after the end of the war."[96] In a letter of January 1944, a member of the institute acknowledged that "the air in industrial areas is barely better now than a generation ago"—in earlier years, the institute had given a much more positive description of the status quo.[97] "After the war, there will be an urgent need to control air pollution in industrial areas in a better way than heretofore," an official of the Ministry of the Interior wrote in an internal document in 1943.[98] Of course, these initiatives were a far cry from the discussions that would actually take place in the 1950s and 1960s. But nevertheless, it is noteworthy that World War II was in an indirect way a stimulation for reform initiatives. In spite of the lack of interest that bureaucrats had displayed in the problems of atmospheric pollution in earlier years, the issue was useful to demonstrate that they were indispensable and should not be conscripted and sent to the front, for there was still so much paperwork to do.

The Impact of the Nazi Era on Air Pollution Control after 1945

In 1943, the building department of the Auschwitz concentration camp (Zentral-Bauleitung der Waffen-SS und Polizei Auschwitz) wrote a letter to the Prussian Institute for Water, Soil, and Air Hygiene. Referring to a correlating request of the local authorities, it asked whether the institute would be ready to write an expert report; the project in question was "the construction of a heating plant at the Auschwitz camp."[99] The institute, eager to get as much work as possible in order to demonstrate the indispensability of its staff, was generally willing to write such a report. Consequently, it asked for a map that showed the environs of the projected plant within a radius of five kilometers. That may explain why the report was never written.[100] This exchange of letters was perhaps the most obscene type of communication that one could imagine in the field of air pollution control. It is not clear whether the "heating plant" was in fact a crematorium (though it is worth pointing out that the letters were written at a time when the SS started to use the large crematoriums of the Birkenau extermination camp). But to even think of air pollution control in the context of these camps is grotesque. This communication is stark evidence of one of the great ambivalences of the Nazi era: the unsettling coexistence of monstrous crimes and bureaucratic routine.[101] It shows, once again, that air pollution control was not something exceptional or sensational in Nazi Germany, but part of administrative normality.

With the continuation of pre-1933 traditions being the dominant feature of air pollution control during the twelve years of Nazi rule, denazification was not a prominent issue in this field. In legislative perspective, the only leftover of the Nazi era was Paragraph 22a of the Trading Regulations, and even this paragraph did not stimulate discussion until well into the 1950s. In a memorandum of 1948, a ministry official noted that Paragraph 22a was "still in force," but "its premises do not generally exist any more"; after all, the paragraph provided for the licensing of secret production facilities, which a demilitarized Germany simply did not have.[102] Consequently, the validity and the role of the provision were somewhat unclear. In 1955, the Ministry of Labor of the state of Schleswig-Holstein asked for "a clarification of the applicability of Paragraph 22a."[103] Not surprisingly, the Ministry of Defense was in favor of the provision: in a letter of 24 September 1958, it declared "that the deletion of this regulation would amplify the problems of the German government in building up a military force in an orderly and timely fashion."[104] However, contrary to what this assertion might lead one to expect, Paragraph 22a did not achieve major significance in the Federal Republic of Germany. The Ministry of Defense argued that the motives behind the creation of the provision in 1934 did not matter, but that viewpoint was anything but uncontroversial; for example, an official of the federal Ministry of Labor said that there would necessarily be "certain doubts" about the use of the paragraph, "for reasons of the rule of law (*Rechtsstaatlichkeit*)."[105] In 1958, the conference of the trading law experts of the states agreed that the paragraph was still valid, but simultaneously urged that the secret licensing procedure be limited to "special cases." The general line of argument was that the "public interest" that Paragraph 22a presupposed had to be defined in a narrow way.[106] In the highly industrialized state of Baden-Württemberg, only two companies had applied for a license pursuant to Paragraph 22a by the early 1970s. One of the applications was refused by the state authorities, the other was withdrawn after a modification of production plans.[107]

Not surprisingly, Paragraph 22a never became a prominent issue in policy discussions of the 1950s and 1960s. The reform of air pollution regulations during that period took place without any explicit reference to the Nazi era. If there was an influence, it was an indirect one: soon after the war, engineers found themselves confronted with the slogan "the curse of technology" (*Fluch der Technik*). Now largely forgotten, this catchphrase was widely heard among the German populace in the immediate postwar period. It concerned the Verein Deutscher Ingenieure (Association of German Engineers, or VDI) enough that it held two conferences devoted to the theme of designing technology that benefited people.[108] Years later, in fact, the VDI would even set up a special clean air committee (VDI-Kommission "Reinhaltung der Luft"). When asked to explain why this organization was taking the lead on such an issue, a VDI spokesperson explained: "During recent years, the VDI has been attacked violently as a result of the negative impact of technology, putting the association on the defensive. Consequently, there is a need for a demonstration that the VDI is doing something for the general public."[109] To be sure, this was not the only reason the VDI became active; the clean air committee was also established to prevent an unwelcome politicization of air pollution control.[110] Nevertheless, talk of the *Fluch der Technik,* clearly a reflection of Nazi and wartime experiences, played an important role in the creation of the clean air committee of the VDI, which assumes a key role in the German system of air pollution control up to the present day.

In the 1970s, controversy raged between those who viewed the Nazi government as a monolithic dictatorship and those who emphasized its polycentric character. The debate has now lost much of its steam, and much of its bitterness, as scholars have begun to appreciate the merits of both interpretations. As Dieter Rebentisch has noted: "In a certain way, the polycentric organization of the German administrative system was a precondition for the autocracy of Hitler; after all, a powerful administrative body with institutionalized expert knowledge would have prejudged and rationalized the Führer's decisions to a larger extent than would have been compatible with Hitler's ideological maxims."[111] Kershaw's recent biography of Hitler can be read as an attempt to reconcile the two perspectives.[112] A recent historiographic survey even asserted that the controversy's use for empirical research had been "rather limited," but such a perspective certainly overstates its point.[113]

As the history of air pollution control in Nazi Germany shows, the issue of polycentrism is still a current, and indeed important, one. Only by stressing the polycentric character of the Nazi state does it become possible to explain why there were three distinct and conflicting reform initiatives during the Nazi era: the attempts of juridical experts to formulate a distinctly "German" nuisance law; the activities of the Reich Food Estate to protect farmers; and the legislative reforms to mitigate conflicts between war production and pollution laws. All three initiatives claimed, in one way or another, to contribute to a key goal of the Nazi regime, and it is impossible to identify the "true" Nazi line of reasoning in retrospect.

In spite of the differences, the three reform initiatives had one thing in common: air pollution was not their most immediate concern. Rather, those involved in the debates and controversies all saw air pollution within a wider context: the restitution of a "German Law," the strengthening of the Nazi regime's legitimacy among farmers, or the development of a war economy. Thus, all three initiatives missed the key point that any successful reform initiative would have had to tackle: implementation and enforcement. Traditionally, there had been a marked difference between grandiose statements from top officials, on the one hand, and bureaucratic normalcy, on the other—and this difference remained basically unchanged during the Nazi era. Enforcement was haphazard, based on an official's ad hoc decision on whether pollution was "excessive" or not, and it always treated air pollution as a local problem, ignoring that the impact of emissions stretched far beyond the immediate vicinity of a plant. Tellingly, none of the three groups ever came close to discussing this issue in depth.

At first glance, this may sound like a classic phenomenon: the failure of Nazi efforts due to resistance from the bureaucracy. However, in this context, it seems that such an interpretation would bestow too much honor upon the bureaucracy. After all, such an interpretation would presuppose a determined, or at least conscious, effort to defend the existing policy. However, the everyday practice of air pollution control during the 1930s reveals that there was no policy in the strict sense of the word, but rather a bureaucratic routine that was semiconscious at best. The bureaucratic approach to air pollution control was first and foremost the result of the administration's desire to process complaints as quickly and smoothly as possible. This desire was anything but new in the 1930s. Reform initiatives during the 1950s and early 1960s certainly did a lot to strengthen air pollution measures—but these efforts were once again oblivious of the issue of implementation.[114] In fact, it has only been within the past three decades that environmentalists have managed to bring the issue of implementation to the forefront of environmental debates—long after the Nazis were gone.[115]

Notes

1. Franz Neumann, *Behemoth: The Structure and Practice of National Socialism, 1933–1944* (New York: Octagon Books, 1963 [1942]), 396.

2. Hannah Arendt, *The Origins of Totalitarianism* (San Diego: Harcourt Brace Jovanovich, 1979 [1951]), 395.

3. Hans Mommsen, "Hitlers Stellung im nationalsozialistischen Herrschaftssystem," in *The "Führer State": Myth and Reality,* ed. Gerhard Hirschfeld and Lothar Kettenacker (Stuttgart: Klett-Cotta, 1981), 51; Martin Broszat, *Der Staat Hitlers: Grundlegung und Entwicklung seiner inneren Verfassung* (Munich: Deutscher Taschenbuch Verlag, 1976), 363.

4. Peter Hüttenberger, "Nationalsozialistische Polykratie," *Geschichte und Gesellschaft* 2, no. 4 (1976): 442.

5. Dieter Rebentisch, *Führerstaat und Verwaltung im Zweiten Weltkrieg: Verfassungsentwicklung und Verwaltungspolitik, 1939–1945* (Stuttgart: Steiner, 1989), 533.

6. Hans Mommsen, "Nationalsozialismus," *Sowjetsystem und demokratische Gesellschaft: Eine vergleichende Enzyklopädie,* vol. 4 (Freiburg: Herder, 1971), c. 702.

7. For a strong version of this argument, see Klaus Hildebrand, "Monokratie oder Polykratie? Hitlers Herrschaft und das Dritte Reich," in *The "Führer State": Myth and Reality,* ed. Gerhard Hirschfeld and Lothar Kettenacker (Stuttgart: Klett-Cotta, 1981), 73–97.

8. Ernst Eiser, "Die Behandlung industrieller Einwirkungen in der neuen Rechtsprechung des Reichsgerichts," *Zeitschrift der Akademie für Deutsches Recht* 5 (1938): 112.

9. Heinz Schiffer, "Immissionen: Ein Beitrag zur Neugestaltung des Nachbarrechts," *Zeitschrift der Akademie für Deutsches Recht* 3 (1936): 1079.

10. Dennis LeRoy Anderson, *The Academy for German Law, 1933–1944* (New York: Garland, 1987), 251.

11. Ibid., 250.

12. "Das Gesetz über die Beschränkung der Nachbarrechte vom 13. Dez. 1933," *Juristische Wochenschrift* 63, no. 4 (1934): 204; Hans Frank, ed., *Nationalsozialistisches Handbuch für Recht und Gesetzgebung* (Munich: Zentralverlag der NSDAP, 1935), 1003; Wilhelm Liesegang, "Die Bedeutung der chemischen Luftuntersuchung für die gewerbepolizeiliche Genehmigung von Industrieanlagen," *Kleine Mitteilungen für die Mitglieder des Vereins für Wasser-, Boden- und Lufthygiene* 12 (1936): 404; *Deutsche Justiz* 95 (1933): 862n; *Reichsgesetzblatt*, part 1, 1933, 1058n.

13. *Reichsgesetzblatt*, part 1, 1935, 1247n. See also Hauptstaatsarchiv Düsseldorf: Regierung Aachen No. 13633, Der Reichs- und Preußische Wirtschaftsminister to the Preußische Regierungspräsidenten, 14 November 1935.

14. Frank, *Nationalsozialistisches Handbuch*, 1002; Walther Hofer, ed., *Der Nationalsozialismus: Dokumente, 1933–1945* (Frankfurt: Fischer, 1957), 30. On the sports movement in Nazi Germany, see Wolf-Dieter Mattausch, "Sport," in *Enzyklopädie des Nationalsozialismus*, ed. Wolfgang Benz, Hermann Graml, and Hermann Weiß (Munich: Deutscher Taschenbuch Verlag, 1997), 251–56; and Hajo Bernett, *Der Weg des Sports in die nationalsozialistische Diktatur* (Schorndorf: Hofmann, 1983).

15. Frank, *Nationalsozialistisches Handbuch*, 1003.

16. "Gesetz," 203.

17. Hauptstaatsarchiv Düsseldorf: Regierung Aachen No. 13633, Der Reichs- und Preußische Wirtschaftsminister to the Preußische Regierungspräsidenten, 14 November 1935.

18. Liesegang, "Bedeutung," 404.

19. Friedrich Klausing, "Immissionsrecht und Industrialisierung," *Juristische Wochenschrift* 66, no. 3 (1937): 68.

20. Anderson, *Academy*, 294.

21. Angelika Königseder, "Akademie für Deutsches Recht," in *Enzyklopädie des Nationalsozialismus*, ed. Wolfgang Benz, Hermann Graml, and Hermann Weiß (Munich: Deutscher Taschenbuch Verlag, 1997), 353–54.

22. Klausing, "Immissionsrecht," 72.

23. Schiffer, "Immissionen," 1083.

24. Klausing, "Immissionsrecht," 68.

25. Heinz Schiffer, "Zum Verfahren in Immissionssachen," *Zeitschrift der Akademie für Deutsches Recht* 4 (1937): 276–77.

26. Eiser, "Behandlung," 116, 112.

27. Bundesarchiv Koblenz (hereafter BAK), R 61/144, 2.

28. Ibid., 34.

29. Ibid., 40.

30. Ibid., 41.

31. Ibid., 43.

32. Ibid., 46.

33. Ibid., 46n.

34. Ibid., 59.

35. Ibid., 37.

36. BAK, R 154/31, attachment to a letter from the Wirtschaftsgruppe Metallindustrie, 11 March 1940, 8.

37. Ibid., 12.

38. Ibid., 17.

39. Ibid., 19n.

40. Hauptstaatsarchiv Düsseldorf, NW 354, No. 42, Der Reichsbauern-führer, Verwaltungsamt, to the Gutehoffnungshütte Oberhausen, 11 May 1937, 1.

41. BAK, R 154/11969, Der Reichswirtschaftsminister to the Reichsanstalt für Wasser- und Luftgüte, 25 May 1944.

42. See Frank Uekötter, *Von der Rauchplage zur ökologischen Revolution: Eine Geschichte der Luftverschmutzung in Deutschland und den USA, 1880–1970* (Essen: Klartext, 2003), chap. 10.

43. BAK, R 154/12026, Memorandum by Liesegang of 9 December 1941.

44. BAK, R 154/12026, Wirtschaftsgruppe Chemische Industrie to the Reichswirtschaftsministerium, 12 November 1941.

45. For the files of the Reich Food Estate, see BAK, R 16.

46. Stadtarchiv Ludwigshafen am Rhein: Bestand Oppau No. 1084, Reichs-nährstand, Kreisbauernschaft Kirchheimbolanden, Rundschreiben No. 11/35, 21 May 1935.

47. John E. Farquharson, *The Plough and the Swastika: The NSDAP and Agriculture in Germany, 1928–1945* (London: Sage, 1976), 120; Friedrich Grundmann, *Agrarpolitik im "Dritten Reich": Anspruch und Wirklichkeit des Reichserbhofgesetzes* (Hamburg: Hoffmann und Campe, 1979), 151.

48. Grundmann, *Agrarpolitik*, 153n; Gustavo Corni, *Hitler and the Peasants: Agrarian Policy of the Third Reich, 1930–1939* (Oxford: Berg, 1990), 152.

49. Farquharson, *Plough*, 87, 106. Emphasis in the original.

50. Joachim Lehmann, "Agrarpolitik und Landwirtschaft in Deutschland 1939 bis 1945," in *Agriculture and Food Supply in the Second World War*, ed. Bernd Martin and Alan S. Milward (Ostfildern: Scripta Mercaturae Verlag, 1985), 29–49; Günter Fahle, *Nazis und Bauern: Zur Agrarpolitik des deutschen Faschismus 1933 bis 1945* (Cologne: Pahl-Rugenstein, 1986).

51. Hauptstaatsarchiv Düsseldorf, NW 354, No. 42, Der Reichsbauernführer, Verwaltungsamt, to the Gutehoffnungshütte Oberhausen, May 11, 1937, 2.

52. Ernst Eiser, "Die industriellen Einwirkungen auf die Umgebung und ihre Behandlung in der bisherigen Rechtsprechung zu § 906 BGB," *Zeitschrift der Akademie für deutsches Recht* 5 (1938): 86.

53. Klausing, "Immissionsrecht," 69, 71.

54. Eiser, "Die industriellen Einwirkungen," 86.

55. Michael Kloepfer, *Zur Geschichte des deutschen Umweltrechts* (Berlin: Duncker & Humblot, 1994), 42n. For the juridical status quo around 1900, see Kurt von Rohrscheidt, *Die Gewerbeordnung für das Deutsche Reich mit sämmtlichen Ausführungsbestimmungen für das Reich und für Preußen* (Leipzig: Hirschfeld, 1901), 53–90, 776–808.

56. *Reichsgesetzblatt*, part 1, 1934, 566.

57. Hauptstaatsarchiv Düsseldorf, Regierung Aachen No. 12974, Der Reichswirtschaftsminister und Preussische Minister für Wirtschaft und Arbeit to the Regierungspräsidenten, 30 October 1934.

58. Bayerisches Hauptstaatsarchiv München, MH 14541, Kriegsministerium to the Königliches stellvertretendes Generalkommando, IV. Armeekorps, 8 July 1915.

59. Bayerisches Hauptstaatsarchiv München, MWi 654, Kriegsministerium to the Staatsministerium des Kgl. Hauses und des Äußern, 30 May 1918.

60. Bayerisches Hauptstaatsarchiv München, MWi 654, Remarks of the State of Württemberg, 10 June 1918.

61. Hauptstaatsarchiv Düsseldorf, Regierung Aachen No. 12974, Der Reichswirtschaftsminister und Preussische Minister für Wirtschaft und Arbeit to the Regierungspräsidenten, 30 October 1934. Also see Bayerisches Hauptstaatsarchiv München, MWi 658, letter to the Regierungspräsident München, 27 September 1940.

62. Badisches Generallandesarchiv Karlsruhe, Abt. 233/26102, Vorschläge für die Änderung des Genehmigungsverfahrens, attachment to Reichsarbeitsminister to the Sozialministerien der Länder, 1 February 1928, 5.

63. Hauptstaatsarchiv Düsseldorf, BR 1050 No. 8, 93–94. On the Four-Year Plan, see Dieter Petzina, *Autarkiepolitik im Dritten Reich: Der nationalsozialistische Vierjahresplan* (Stuttgart: Deutsche Verlags-Anstalt, 1968).

64. Staatsarchiv Münster, Regierung Arnsberg No. 1569, 5–8.

65. Stadtarchiv Bielefeld, MBV 037, Der Preussische Minister für Volkswohlfahrt, Berlin, 27 July 1931.

66. G. von Meyeren, "Die Rechtslage bei der Bekämpfung von Luftverunreinigungen," *Kleine Mitteilungen für die Mitglieder des Vereins für Wasser-, Boden- und Lufthygiene* 6 (1930): 318. On the origin of this article, see BAK, R 154/88.

67. Meyeren, "Rechtslage," 318.

68. For a more extensive discussion of this topic, see Frank Uekötter, "A Look Into the Black Box: Why Air Pollution Control Was Undisputed in Interwar Germany," in *The Modern Demon: Pollution in Urban and Industrial European Societies*, ed. Christoph Bernhardt and Geneviève Massard-Guilbaud (Clermont-Ferrand: Presses Universitaires Blaise-Pascal, 2002), 239–55.

69. Stadtarchiv Bielefeld, MBV 037, Der Preussische Minister für Volkswohlfahrt, Berlin, 27 July 1931. For further information, see Uekötter, *Rauchplage*, 212n.

70. Stadtarchiv Bielefeld, Hauptamt, Betriebsamt, 165, vol. 2, Nationalsozialistische Deutsche Arbeiterpartei, Ortsgruppe Kesselbrink to the Magistrat der Stadt Bielefeld, 3 August 1934. I would like to thank Jürgen Büschenfeld for pointing me to this document.

71. Stadtarchiv Leipzig, Stadtgesundheitsamt No. 234, 70.

72. F. Hoffmann, "Die Rauch- und Rußbekämpfung: Erfahrungsbericht über Abwehrmaßnahmen in Breslau," *Heizung und Lüftung* 16 (1942): 41–45.

73. BAK, R 154/17, attachment to Reichsarbeitsgemeinschaft für Schadenverhütung to the Reichsgesundheitsamt, 31 July 1936.

74. BAK, R 154/17, Landesanstalt für Wasser-, Boden- und Lufthygiene to Arbeitsgemeinschaft für Schadenverhütung, 20 August 1936.

75. Uekötter, *Rauchplage*, 217n.

76. Against this background, it also becomes clear that the Nazi jurists' call for compromise and cooperation was far less innovative than they proclaimed. At one point, even Friedrich Klausing acknowledged that the factory inspectorate and other authorities "have already hitherto been trying, in many cases with considerable success, to work towards a peaceful communication between the parties involved." Klausing, "Immissionsrecht," 73.

77. BAK, R 154/66, Landesanstalt für Wasser-, Boden- und Lufthygiene to Vereinigte Oberschlesische Hüttenwerke AG, 3 March 1934.

78. Stadtarchiv Leipzig, Stadtgesundheitsamt No. 234, 57.

79. Ibid., 57R.

80. Stadtarchiv Essen, Rep. 102 Abt. XIV No. 93, Frau Albert Vogt to the Oberbürgermeister der Stadt Essen, 10 February 1941.

81. Stadtarchiv Essen, Rep. 102 Abt. XIV No. 94, Nobel-Kaffee KG to Oberbürgermeister der Stadt Essen, 11 June 1943.

82. Hauptstaatsarchiv Düsseldorf, BR 1015/101, 233–34, 253, quotation 253R.

83. Badisches Generallandesarchiv Karlsruhe, 455/Zug. 1991–49 No. 1336, Erläuterungsbericht zum Baugesuch der Firma A. Stoll, Stuhlfabrik, 6 March 1942.

84. Stadtarchiv Bielefeld, MBV 038, J. D. Küster Nachf. to the Oberbürgermeister, Abt. Baupolizei, Bielefeld, 9 July 1941.

85. Stadtarchiv Bielefeld, MBV 038, Oberbürgermeister als Ortspolizeibehörde to J. D. Küster Nachf., 2 August 1941; ibid., Gewerbeaufsichtsamt Bielefeld to J. D. Küster Nachf., 21 August 1941.

86. On the impact of Speer's appointment, see Alan S. Milward, *The German Economy at War* (London: Athlone Press, 1965), 72n; Ludolf Herbst, *Der Totale Krieg und die Ordnung der Wirtschaft: Die Kriegswirtschaft im Spannungsfeld von Politik, Ideologie und Propaganda, 1939–1945* (Stuttgart: Deutsche Verlags-Anstalt, 1982), 176n; R. J. Overy, *War and Economy in the Third Reich* (Oxford: Clarendon Press, 1994), 356n.

87. Niedersächsisches Staatsarchiv Wolfenbüttel, 12 Neu 15 No. 3868, Vergleich zwischen der Forstgenossenschaft Lüttgenberg und den Unterharzer Berg- und Hüttenwerken GmbH, 22 November 1943.

88. Staatsarchiv Münster, Regierung Arnsberg 6 No. 217, Reisebericht zum Termin am 19. Mai 1944.

89. Badisches Generallandesarchiv Karlsruhe, Abt. 233/26103, Reichswirtschaftsminister to the Landesregierungen, 20 February 1941.

90. Bayerisches Hauptstaatsarchiv München, MWi 655, Reichswirtschaftsminister to the Reichsstatthalter in den Reichsgauen and the Landesregierungen, 29 May 1941.

91. BAK, R 18/3754, Runderlaß des Reichsministers des Innern, 20 August 1943.

92. BAK, R 154/12026, Runderlaß des Reichswirtschaftsministers, 18 February 1942.

93. BAK, R 154/12026, Landesanstalt für Wasser-, Boden- und Lufthygiene to the Reichswirtschaftsminister durch die Hand des Reichsministers des Innern, 11 January 1942.

94. Bayerisches Hauptstaatsarchiv München, MWi 655, Der Reichswirtschaftsminister to the Reichsstatthalter in den Reichsgauen Danzig-Westpreussen und Wartheland, the Landesregierungen, the Preußische Regierungspräsidenten and the Polizeipräsident in Berlin, 25 June 1941.

95. Arnold Heller, "Soll man in Deutschland das Abgasproblem, insbesondere bei Feuerstätten, gesetzlich regeln?" *Gesundheits-Ingenieur* 75 (1954): 390; Helmut Köhler, "Die durch die Technische Anleitung zur Reinhaltung der Luft zu erwartende rechtliche Situation," *IWL-Forum* 2 (1964): 308.

96. BAK, R 154/12026, Memorandum of Liesegang, 20 June 1942.

97. BAK, R 154/39, Reichsanstalt für Wasser- und Luftgüte to Rüder, 14 January 1944.

98. BAK, R 18/3754, memorandum on "Arbeitsgebiet Trinkwasserhygiene, Abwasserbeseitigung, Luftreinhaltung," ca. August 1943, 2.

99. BAK, R 154/48, Zentral-Bauleitung der Waffen-SS und Polizei Auschwitz to the Reichsanstalt für Wasser- und Luftgüte, 1 March 1943.

100. BAK, R 154/48, response of 23 September 1943.

101. See the classic by Hannah Arendt, *Eichmann in Jerusalem: A Report on the Banality of Evil* (New York: Penguin, 1994 [1963]).

102. Hauptstaatsarchiv Düsseldorf, NW 50 No. 1249, 14.

103. BAK, B 149/10407, Der Minister für Arbeit, Soziales und Vertriebene des Landes Schleswig-Holstein to the Bundesminister für Arbeit, 30 November 1955, 1.

104. BAK, B 106/38374, Der Bundesminister für Verteidigung to the Bundesminister für Arbeit und Sozialordnung, 24 September 1958, 2.

105. Bayerisches Hauptstaatsarchiv München, MWi 26077, Niederschrift über die 17. Tagung der Gewerberechtsreferenten der Länder am 24. und 25. April 1958 in Bonn, 15.

106. Ibid., 16.

107. Hauptstaatsarchiv Stuttgart, EA 8/301 Büschel 464.

108. Landesarchiv Schleswig-Holstein, Abt. 761 No. 14, Niederschrift über die Konferenz für Arbeitsschutz (Gewerbeaufsicht) am 5. und 6. Dezember 1951 in Königswinter, Anlage 2.

109. Hauptstaatsarchiv Düsseldorf, NW 50 No. 1215, 32R.

110. Uekötter, *Rauchplage,* 460n.

111. Rebentisch, *Führerstaat,* 552. Similarly, see Hans-Ulrich Thamer, *Verführung und Gewalt: Deutschland, 1933–1945* (Berlin: Siedler, 1986), 340. For summaries of this debate during the 1980s, see Ian Kershaw, *The Nazi Dictatorship: Problems and Perspectives of Interpretation* (London: Arnold, 1985), chap. 4; and Manfred Funke, *Starker oder schwacher Diktator? Hitlers Herrschaft und die Deutschen: Ein Essay* (Düsseldorf: Droste, 1989).

112. Ian Kershaw, *Hitler, 1889–1936: Hubris* (New York: Norton, 1999), and *Hitler, 1936–45: Nemesis* (New York: Norton, 2000).

113. Ulrich von Hehl, *Nationalsozialistische Herrschaft* (Munich: Oldenbourg, 1996), 62.

114. Uekötter, *Rauchplage,* 489.

115. Renate Mayntz, *Vollzugsprobleme der Umweltpolitik: Empirische Untersuchung der Implementation von Gesetzen im Bereich der Luftreinhaltung und des Gewässerschutzes* (Stuttgart: Kohlhammer, 1978).

CHAPTER 5

Breeding Pigs and People for the Third Reich

Richard Walther Darré's Agrarian Ideology

Gesine Gerhard

BLUT UND BODEN—"blood and soil"—was a metaphor frequently used in Nazi propaganda: it implied that there was an intimate connection between the "racial health" of the German people and "the land."[1] This ideology was used to flatter peasants and recruit them as supporters of the Nazis. It also justified the killing of "less valuable" members of the community in the euthanasia program. And it laid the theoretical groundwork for the conquest and settlement of eastern Europe. Over the course of the Third Reich, the ideology of "blood and soil" lost some of its aura, because of the economic demands of a society at war. The gradual fall of Richard Walther Darré, the minister of food and agriculture, Reich peasant leader (*Reichsbauernführer*), and head of the SS Race and Settlement Office, symbolizes this shift in priorities.[2] His final dismissal in 1942 highlights the tension that existed between the agrarian ideal and the requirements of a modern industrial state engaged in war. The existence of competing and shifting priorities over the twelve years of the Third Reich did not, however, weaken the centrality of "blood and soil" ideology or its persistence as a justification for territorial expansion and racial extermination. From the early days of Darré's rural campaign in 1930 to his service as the head of the SS Race and Settlement Office and even beyond Darré's dismissal in 1942, "blood and soil" was one of the ideologies that fueled Nazi action.

This is a controversial thesis. Contemporaries as well as historians have judged the impact of the ideology of "blood and soil" and Darré's role differently.[3] Some have gone so far as to claim that Darré's desire to preserve a pristine rural world constituted a precocious "green" program, and thus that the Nazis anticipated some of the ideas that modern environmental parties are founded upon.[4] Anna Bramwell's book *Blood and Soil: Richard Walther Darré and Hitler's "Green Party"* is a sympathetic biography of Darré that tries to distinguish his ideas from Heinrich Himmler's imperialistic visions and today's Green Party platforms.[5] For Bramwell, Darré remains a misunderstood proponent of a true peasant nation and organic farming whose ideas found a space in the Nazi platform for a short period during the early 1930s. She argues that in the mid-1930s his ideas were betrayed by the Nazis, and Darré was demoted and ultimately replaced by Herbert Backe, the more practical food policy expert who toed the party line alongside the powerful Nazi leaders Martin Bormann, Hermann Göring, and Himmler. Historians Gustavo Corni and Horst Gies disagree strongly with this representation of Darré as a harmless peasant romantic who did not share Hitler's expansionist racist ideology. In their view, it is impossible to separate Darré's racial ideology of "blood and soil" from the claim for world dominion; Darré lost his power not because his views clashed with the official party line but because of political rivalries and problems in food policy under his leadership.[6]

I will argue that, while Nazi agrarian ideology ultimately became "bloody red" with the occupation and "resettlement" of peasants on land in the east, Darré's peasant vision cannot be considered a "green" start.[7] Nazi agricultural ideology—its anti-Semitic reification of small peasant farming and its claim to "save" the peasant world from the threat posed by industrialization and urbanization—was based on a pseudoscientific racism that regarded the "Nordic race" as superior.[8] From the outset, it provided the theoretical rationale for a program that aimed at the racial "renewal" of the German people, the elimination of Jews, and the conquest of Lebensraum (living space) in eastern Europe for Germans. In addition to its ideological importance, the Nazis also used the rural ideology for political purposes. "Blood and soil" worked well to win rural electoral support. It fostered peasant allegiance (even as national government policies increasingly worked against rural interests) and therefore contributed to the stability of the Nazi regime until the very end.

The Ideology of Blood and Soil

What lies behind the mystique of "blood and soil"? How did the Nazis implement their agrarian ideology and what role did peasants play in it? Peasants were considered the source of German economic and cultural vitality. According to this rural ideology, a long tradition of settlement and inheritance patterns had shaped the German people. Germans had entered history as peasants and had always despised urban areas. For the Nazis, this stood in stark contrast to nomadic peoples, especially the "desert-dwelling" Jews, who lacked this presumed geo-cultural linkage of race and place.[9] The special connection between the German people (blood) and the land (soil) was regarded as the historical basis for Germany's survival and the reason for its cultural dominance. Industrialization and urbanization threatened peasant farming, and with it the very foundation of the German people. The defense of small peasant farms was understood as a prerequisite for the restoration of Germany's "racial integrity."[10]

Long before the Nazis, however, others had explicitly made the connection between the words "blood" and "soil." Agrarian romanticists in the nineteenth century had stressed the "organic unity" of people and the soil and had depicted peasants as the healthy "backbone" of society.[11] Ernst Moritz Arndt had linked peasant romanticism with nationalism when he called for the state to protect peasants as the foundation of the German people, and sociologist Wilhelm Heinrich Riehl had stressed the political value of peasants as a conservative bloc in society.[12] The fast pace of industrialization and urbanization toward the end of the nineteenth century caused unease and inflamed the debate. These ideas cannot simply be regarded as "antimodern" or as a direct forerunner of Nazi ideology. As recent research has shown, movements such as the *Heimatschutz* were not necessarily backward-looking but promoted ways to lessen the destructive impact of urbanization and industrialization on rural communities and the environment.[13]

Darré gave the idea of "blood and soil" a new connotation. He wanted "blood" to be understood as "race."[14] While until then peasants had been regarded as the "fresh blood" that provided cities with people, Darré called the peasantry the "life source of the Nordic race."[15] In several books and articles Darré elaborated on the idea of creating a new ruling class that was rooted in the agrarian community.[16] Darré was a specialist in genetic livestock selection, and he applied his findings from animal breeding to human beings.[17] Just as in the animal world, this committed Social Darwinist proposed a system of racial selection in order to "breed" a new rural nobility and to achieve the "breeding goal of the German people."[18] Darré suggested marriage restrictions for Jews and "less valuable" non-Jews, strict state control of all marriages and fertility, and sterilization of those members of the community who were considered to be a threat to the "racial purity" of the German people. The Nazis used all of these measures in the subsequent years, even though the idea of a new rural political elite was never fully adopted.

In addition to the racial component, Darré added another connotation to the idea of "blood and soil." While the nineteenth-century romanticists had thought of the soil as character-giving to the German people, Darré used the idea to justify Germany's right to acquire land in the east and to settle ethnic Germans there. Germany was considered to be too small to produce enough food for strategic self-sufficiency. More territory was regarded to be the prerequisite for Germany's future.[19] This expansion implied that people who were considered to be less capable of tilling the soil and settling down could be dispersed. In other words, the Nazis' murderous policy in the occupied eastern lands after the outbreak of the war found its justification also in this agrarian ideology.[20]

Darré as Minister of Agriculture during the Third Reich

Darré's expertise in the field of animal breeding and its application to human beings opened the door for him to be introduced to Adolf Hitler. Darré was born to German emigrants in Argentina and had studied agronomy and zoology at the University of Halle. His service in World War I interrupted his studies, and he had difficulties finding his academic and professional niche after the war. In the late 1920s he worked in agricultural administration and left a record of publications on livestock selection and agriculture heavily indebted to racial theories. His two books, *Das Bauerntum als Lebensquell der nordischen Rasse* (1929) and *Neuadel aus Blut und Boden* (1930), made his name well known in right-wing intellectual circles. Through his membership in the Artamanen youth group and the Stahlhelm organization, he met future Nazi leaders, including Himmler. Darré's first meeting with Hitler took place in 1930 and was organized by Darré's publisher, Julius Friedrich Lehmann, at the architect Paul Schultze-Naumburg's residence in Saaleck. According to Darré,

Hitler knew his name and was intrigued by his research, but Hitler felt that Darré had not emphasized the "Jewish problem" enough in his writings.[21] Darré apparently succeeded in explaining to Hitler his true political and racial beliefs, since the meeting turned out to be the beginning of Darré's meteoric career as one of the chief ideologues of the Nazis. Impressed by his active publication record on racial topics and his experience in agricultural administration, Hitler appointed Darré to organize the peasants and win them over for the Nazi Party. In 1932, he became the head of the newly founded SS Race and Settlement Office. Darré was able to make agrarian questions an integral part of the party program. Hitler realized that desperate peasants, dogged by seasonal economic distress, systemic agrarian crises, and the fear of foreclosure, were a constituency that could be used to his own political advantage.

Hitler's choice was well made. Within two years, Darré had brought all the agricultural interest groups into "synchronization" (*Gleichschaltung*), uniting the bitterly divided groups and fulfilling the dream of a united "green front" that could give agriculture one voice in its struggle against urban and industrial interests. He did this with the familiar Nazi tactics of discrediting other political parties, the infiltration of existing interest groups, and intimidation and terror directed at leading representatives of agriculture.[22]

The powerful propaganda campaign included the organization of countless meetings of peasants and the publication of a Nazi agrarian news magazine that addressed specifically peasant issues.[23] An important tool for the Nazification of the countryside was a new rural organization, the Agrarian Apparatus, created by Darré. It extended over the whole Reich and gained control over the farmers' associations. A network of Apparatus advisors and officials reached even the smallest village and facilitated communication and coordination throughout the country.[24] One official proudly announced that there was "no farm, no estate, no village, no cooperative, no agricultural industry, no local organization of the RLB [Reichs-Landbund, the main agrarian interest organization in the 1920s], no rural equestrian association, etc. etc., where we have not—at the least—placed our LVL [*Landwirtschaftliche Vertrauensleute*, or "agrarian agents"] in such numbers that we could paralyze at one blow the total political life of these structures."[25] By 1932, the task was completed successfully. Darré could report to Hitler that the countryside had been won for the Nazi Party.

Darré's role in making "blood and soil" one of the pillars of Nazi ideology expanded when he became minister of food and agriculture and

Reich peasant leader in 1933. Several agricultural policies reflect the centrality of this idea. Soon after he had become minister, Darré created the Reich Food Estate (Reichsnährstand, or RNS), a mass organization embracing 17 million members. Compulsory membership included not only peasants but also anyone engaged in the processing and selling of agricultural products and food items. All areas of the food and agriculture industry were represented. Darré tried to fulfill the old demand for one single and powerful interest organization that would overcome the regional and other rivalries that had splintered agricultural interest groups in the 1920s.[26] The RNS was conceived as a self-governing body linked to the state only through Darré's dual position as head of the organization and minister of agriculture.[27] The RNS's autonomy, however, was mostly an ideal of its leader; in reality it was limited and hindered by rivalries with other ministries and mass organizations such as the German Labor Front (Deutsche Arbeitsfront, or DAF). Tensions arose especially with Robert Ley, the head of the German Labor Front, over the representation of rural laborers and food prices for workers.[28]

Although Darré later claimed that the Reich Food Estate was autonomous from the Nazi Party and was in conflict with other Nazi organizations, the Reich Food Estate played an undeniably important role in the Third Reich's economy.[29] The massive bureaucratic body consisted of more than 50,000 honorary posts, about 16,000 paid officials and more than 17,000 employees.[30] It oversaw and managed every aspect of food production and reached every village in the Reich. As such, it managed food production that was crucial for war preparations. Without the Reich Food Estate, food supply could not have been maintained and the support of the Nazi regime might have faltered. The lesson of World War I had not been lost on anybody, least of all on Darré, in his endless struggle for recognition of his work.[31]

Another piece of agricultural legislation inaugurated by Darré soon after he came to power also shows the imprint of the ideology of "blood and soil": the *Erbhof* Law (Law of Hereditary Entailment), which guaranteed farm holdings would pass undivided to a single and racially selected heir.[32] This inheritance law was pushed through despite opposition from academics, the business community, and rural leaders. Economists feared that the law would hamper economic incentives for peasants. Businessmen were worried about the loss of landed property for the market. And large landowners felt that it treated them unfairly. Even the agronomist Max Sering, who shared Darré's interest in protecting peasant holdings, opposed the law, since it allowed no flexibility for peasant families and would ultimately hurt the peasant economy. But Darré—with the support of Hitler—defended the law emphatically. Critics of the law were publicly discredited, money was spent on education campaigns, and public debate was outlawed.[33] For Darré, the Erbhof Law was an important part of his racial goal of creating a rural elite that would become the new ruling class in a corporate society.

As in many other cases, the original idea—to legally protect forms of undivided inheritance and shelter the family farm from the capitalist market—was not new. But the Nazis twisted its original purpose and subordinated it to their racial program. In its content, the inheritance law secured the right to will a farm to an *Erbhofbauer* (peasant male heir)—typically the oldest or "most deserving" son—and then made his inheritance subject to economic restrictions and legal protections. The farm could not be bought, sold, or mortgaged. The size of the inheritance was regulated: it could not be smaller than 7.5 hectares and generally not larger than 125 hectares (although no maximum limit was strictly enforced). The privileged position of an Erbhofbauer was reserved for Germans with "flawless moral conduct."[34]

In practice, the Erbhof Law met with resistance from the very people it was supposed to benefit—the peasants—many of whom resented the unfair treatment of noninheriting children. It hampered the social mobility of younger and female siblings, and hindered economic investment in farm modernization by taking farmland off the market and limiting mortgaging of land. Peasant resentment crystallized in numerous appeals to the newly created special courts. The actual number of *Erbhöfe* (inheritance estates) turned out to be much smaller than was originally envisaged, partly because the special courts allowed so many exceptions to the regulations and circumvented the law in favor of local customs or requests for female inheritance.[35] Nonetheless, the law remained intact until September 1943, at which time acting Agricultural Minister Herbert Backe loosened some of the restrictions.[36]

The Erbhof Law was not the only agricultural policy that was unpopular with peasants. Peasants resented the enforced production quotas and the increased state interference in rural affairs. By the late 1930s economic demands overruled the ideological goals of food policies.[37] Early on, Darré had envisioned a German food self-sufficiency that would ensure consumption and allow high domestic prices and an aggressive foreign policy. Germany, however, had become a food-importing country by the end of the nineteenth century. The Four-Year Plan that was adopted in 1936 called for a dramatic increase in home production that could only be achieved by embarking on large-scale mechanization. This clearly stood in opposition to the picture of a static peasant economy praised so highly in the ideology of "blood and soil." Conflicts between Darré and Hjalmar Schacht, minister of economics, could hardly be avoided. In 1936 Göring became head of the Four-Year Plan. At first, Darré seemed happy about this change, since Göring shared Darré's goal of food self-sufficiency.[38] Soon, however, it became clear that the preparation for war forestalled any hopes for major increases in agricultural production at home. Resources, land, and finances were used to support the war machine, and the Battle for Production—as the demand for increased food production was labeled—was a major failure.[39] This weakened Darré's position and empowered the food expert Backe, who was then put in charge of food policies. With the launching of the war and the occupation of other countries, especially in the East, the problem of food sufficiency was tackled in Nazi terms. Regions such as the Ukraine were regarded as "food baskets" for German needs and were ruthlessly exploited.[40] With these land grabs, raising food production and transforming rural life in Germany took on lower priority.

Why Darré Was Not Green

Does the sacrifice of pro-rural policies because of economic necessities eliminate the centrality of the agrarian ideology for the Third Reich? Was Darré therefore really just a harmless dreamer whose ideas were never implemented by the Nazis? He appears as an ambiguous figure in post-1945 descriptions. The picture varies from the unremorseful proponent of eugenics to the peasant romanticist, from the close friend of Himmler to the demoted Nazi, from the calculating food minister to a foolish and weak man, from the first Green to a smart propagandist. Who, in short, was Darré? The study of archival sources gives us a picture that more fully explains this man's historical role.[41]

The apologetic picture of Darré as the benign peasant romanticist and outsider of the Nazi elite was first painted by Darré himself at the so-called Wilhelmstraße proceedings, held in Nuremberg in 1949.[42] Like other ministry-level leaders, Darré was on trial for his role in the Third Reich. He based his defense on the fact that his influence on Nazi politics ceased after 1938 and that he was replaced by Backe in 1942. This uncritical depiction has been generally adopted by Bramwell, who supports her argument with quotes from Darré's diaries.[43] She sees a clear division of labor (and moral character) between Darré and Backe. Backe had been the second man in the Ministry of Agriculture and was made food commissioner for the Four-Year Plan in 1936. Bramwell describes him as an "archetypical National Socialist,"[44] a strong-willed, rational, and cynical colleague of Darré, who, according to Darré's own account, had planned early on to replace a "weak and soft Darré" who would never be able to stand up to his rivals Göring, Himmler, and Ley. To achieve his ultimate goal, Backe was thought to be willing to "walk over dead people."[45] Darré's replacement by Backe in 1942 completes this picture of Backe as a rival, even though Backe was not given the title of minister until 1944.[46]

Seen in this rosy light, Darré appears to be not guilty of the worst Nazi crimes. He was used as long as the party could benefit from his work, but then he was humiliated and demoted. According to Darré's lawyer in the war-crime trial, Darré's "fall" occurred in three steps. In 1936, his power was diluted when Backe was put in charge of food policy in the context of the Four-Year Plan. With the outbreak of the war in 1939, Darré was barred from any real power. Then, in 1942, he was fired.[47] To justify his dismissal, he was declared to be sick or even insane.[48] The last three years of the war he spent in bitterness and isolation. In prison for five years after the war, he polished this strategy of exculpation and promoted the picture of a relentless protector of peasants. Until his death in 1953, Darré maintained that he had nothing to do with the murderous policies of the Nazi regime.

Darré described himself and his organization, the Reich Food Estate, as in opposition to the party and to other mass organizations of the Third Reich.[49] Among his enemies were Göring, architect of the Four-Year Plan; Ley, head of the German Labor Front; and Martin Bormann, the head of the Party chancellery.[50] His most powerful enemy (at least according to Darré's recollections in 1945) was Himmler, head of the SS. Initially, Darré had made a strong impression on Himmler and the two had shared ideas on settlement and other racial questions. Both men considered the SS to be the appropriate "breeding ground" for their racial goals and had founded the SS Race and Settlement Office in December 1931. Darré and Himmler maintained a close relationship during the early 1930s.[51] Darré claims that he distanced himself from Himmler after 1936. In 1938 Darré resigned from his position as director of the SS Race and Settlement Office and requested to leave the SS, but this wish was not granted.

According to Darré, the relationship came to a complete halt in 1939, when Himmler became Reich commissioner for the strengthening of Germandom (Reichskommissar für die Festigung des deutschen Volkstums).[52]

According to Bramwell, Darré's loss of power was the result of his unique plans for the rural future of Germany, a vision that eventually clashed with Nazi policies. She supports her argument with Darré's position on anthroposophical or biodynamic farming. She claims that Darré was a supporter of this alternative farming method and in fact protected other proponents of it from Gestapo persecution.[53] In the realm of agriculture, the new school of anthroposophy led by Rudolf Steiner suggested that plants and the soil had to be handled in accordance with magnetic laws of the cosmos. Artificial fertilizers were condemned because they threatened the organic unit of man and nature.[54] Darré launched a campaign that researched peasants' attitudes toward biodynamic farming in 1940 and 1941 and tried to protect organic farmers.[55] Since the official Nazi line condemned anthroposophical farming,[56] Bramwell considers Darré to be a martyr who in fact had very different ideas from the Nazi Party. According to Bramwell, the Nazis only used Darré to win over the peasantry; they never seriously planned to implement Darré's ideas.

This argument, however, is not supported by the historical record.[57] The Nazis' stand on anthroposophical farming was not uniform—as Bramwell herself points out. Other leading Nazis supported organic farming and saw a link between environmental purity and racial purity.[58] Hitler and Himmler themselves were vegetarians, and during the Third Reich experimental organic farms were set up and used to supply the SS.[59] Jost Hermand even talks about a "green wing" of the Nazi Party that included, besides Darré, also Rudolf Hess, Fritz Todt, and Alwin Seifert.[60] Darré's limited interest in organic farming practices did resonate with individual members of the Nazi Party. But in the end, everyone, including Darré himself, agreed that it was the wrong moment to embark on any projects with organic farming. Germany's food situation was too fragile and depended on efficient farming that included using chemical fertilizers. Any projects were to be put on hold at least until after the war.[61] Nazi agricultural and environmental policies cannot be simply called green.[62]

The fact that Darré interfered with the harassment of organic farmers and their proponents does not make him an "early Green," nor does it diminish his share of responsibility for Nazi crimes. As an agricultural scientist and proponent of peasant farming, it is not surprising that he would show an interest in alternative farming models. Yet Darré remained skeptical of supporters of Steiner and treated biodynamic farming more as an intriguing theoretical possibility than anything else.[63] Moreover, his support was always hindered by practical priorities during his time as minister of agriculture. Only after the war and his release from prison in 1950 did he show commitment to anthroposophical ideas and new anthroposophical circles.

The dominant factor in Darré's writings and work during his career was his emphasis on "blood," race, and genetics. As described above, one of the main pieces of Darré's agricultural policies, the Erbhof Law, stated that only Germans—in fact, only "Aryans"—were able to settle on land or inherit farms. This was the framework for his vision of Germany, rather than any ecological or "green" vision. Here lies the main reason why I consider Bramwell's thesis flawed and the title of her book not only misleading but wrong.

In any case, Darré's anthroposophical escapades were only a very small part of his agrarian thinking and certainly do not characterize him in any meaningful way. At the heart of his rural vision—Germany's "re-agrarianization" and settlement—was the racial conviction that the German people needed to find their way back to the "purity" of the Nordic race living off the land. This was the program he wanted to implement during the Third Reich through policies like the inheritance law, the Reich Food Estate, and market regulations. Agrarian policy was racial policy for Darré. His articles and books published before the Nazis came to power are filled with racist and *völkisch* ideas. Since Darré's agrarian program was also closely linked with aggressive foreign territorial expansion after 1939, it is impossible to whitewash Darré as a peasant romantic or even "early Green."

In fact, ecological problems or nature itself—as implied in the word "soil"—were not of great concern to Darré.[64] For him, "soil" was just part of agricultural property. It had no biodynamic value; it was simply part of the equation of the rural economy. He was an animal geneticist for whom the improvement of breeds and people was a precise scientific activity with economic and political goals. For Darré, "soil" was a functional and familiar metaphor that fit his racial ideology. At least during the 1930s, Darré did not want to be seen as an agrarian romanticist, but rather as a pragmatic modernizer.[65]

Darré's strategy of exculpation was partially successful. He was found not guilty of crimes against peace and charges of anti-Semitism leading to Jewish extermination. He was, however, held responsible for the "compulsory purchase of Jewish-owned farmland," for overseeing discriminatory food rations for Jews, for "expropriating and reducing to serfdom hundreds of thousands of Polish and Jewish farmers in the course of the ethnic German resettlement," and for plunder and destruction in Poland.[66] Given the seriousness of his crimes, his prison term was light; he was condemned to seven years including those he had already served in Nuremberg. Because of "good conduct" he was released early in 1950 and died in 1953.[67] Darré has largely escaped the postwar memory and has often been regarded as a marginal figure among Nazi leaders. Only in the context of new agricultural and environmental history has Darré's role been analyzed more critically.

The historical record shows that any attempt to minimize Darré's share of responsibility cannot be upheld. National Socialist ideology was a mix of conflicting ideas, and priorities shifted during the twelve years of the Third Reich. It is therefore not surprising that some Nazi leaders did not share Darré's rural vision for Germany. The ideology of "blood and soil," however, was never dismissed. It remained a crucial part of Nazi ideology long after Darré had supposedly fallen into disgrace. Darré's rural ideology continued to be the theoretical foundation for a new Germany, a vision that was temporarily put on the backburner to make room for the economic necessities of a country fighting its way to world dominance. Food and agricultural policies under Darré and his successor Backe contributed to the stability of the regime and were pillars of the Nazi state. Without Darré's groundwork, the system might have collapsed much earlier. Darré lost power after 1938 and he lost it permanently in 1942, but his ideas continued to determine Nazi action until Germany's surrender in 1945.

Notes

1. An earlier version of this chapter appeared in Joachim Radkau, ed., *Naturschutz und Nationalsozialismus* (Frankfurt: Campus Verlag, 2003). The revised and translated version is printed here with permission. I would like to thank the University of the Pacific for funding an extensive research trip to the German archives with the Eberhardt Research Fellowship. My special thanks to archivist Gregor Pickro in the Federal Archives in Koblenz, to Daniela Siepe for helpful advice, and to Inge Gerhard for her hospitality during my work in the archives. I would also like to thank Cynthia Dobbs, Amy Smith, Edie Sparks, Ulrike Gerhard, Ute Gerhard, and Greg Rohlf for their valuable critique of different drafts of the article.

2. Darré headed the SS Race and Settlement Office from its beginning in December 1931 until 1938. He served as minister of food and agriculture from 1933 until 1942 when he was replaced by Herbert Backe. The SS Race and Settlement Office was responsible for the "racial purity" of the SS and oversaw settlement of Germans in the occupied eastern territories. The office also monitored marriage licenses for SS men according to racial criteria. See SS-order no. 65, 31 December 1931. Partially reprinted in Gustavo Corni and Horst Gies, *"Blut und Boden": Rassenideologie und Agrarpolitik im Staat Hitlers* (Idstein: Schulz-Kirchner Verlag, 1994), 81.

3. For two opposing points of view, see Anna Bramwell, *Blood and Soil: Richard Walther Darré and Hitler's "Green Party"* (Abbotsbrook, Buckinghamshire, UK: Kensal Press, 1985), and Corni and Gies, *Blut und Boden*.

4. See Anna Bramwell, *Ecology in the 20th Century: A History* (New Haven: Yale University Press, 1989), and Bramwell, *Blood and Soil*.

5. Bramwell claims that today's Green parties actually "bear more resemblance with those pre- and proto-Nazi groups that sprang up during the 1920s in an outbreak of quasi-religious prophecy and radicalism." Bramwell, *Blood and Soil*, 200.

6. Corni and Gies, *Blut und Boden*, and Gustavo Corni and Horst Gies, *Brot, Butter, Kanonen: Die Ernährungswirtschaft in Deutschland unter der Diktatur Hitlers* (Berlin: Akademie Verlag, 1997).

7. Here I am paraphrasing Tucholsky as quoted in Bramwell, *Blood and Soil*, 129.

8. On fascist ecology, see Peter Staudenmaier, "Fascist Ideology: The 'Green Wing' of the Nazi Party and its Historical Antecedents," in *Ecofascism: Lessons from the German Experience*, ed. Janet Biehl and Peter Staudenmaier (Edinburgh: AK Press, 1995), 5–30.

9. Richard Walther Darré, *Das Bauerntum als Lebensquell der nordischen Rasse*, 4th ed. (Munich: Lehmann, 1934), 26.

10. See Darré, *Das Bauerntum als Lebensquell*, and the collection of his articles and speeches in Richard Walther Darré, *Um Blut und Boden: Reden und Aufsätze*, 4th ed. (Munich: F. Eher, 1942).

11. For an overview of agrarian romanticism, see Klaus Bergmann, *Agrarromantik und Grosstadtfeindschaft* (Meisenheim a. Glan: Hain, 1970). See also Gesine Gerhard, "Bauernbewegung und Agrarromantik in der Weimarer Republik: Die Bauernhochschulbewegung und die Blut-und-Boden-Ideologie des Nationalsozialismus" (master's thesis, Technische Universität Berlin, 1994).

12. Ernst Moritz Arndt, "Über künftige ständische Verfassungen in Deutschland (1814)," in *Agrarpolitische Schriften*, ed. W. O. W. Terstegen (Goslar: Blut und Boden Verlag, 1938), 278, and Wilhelm Heinrich Riehl, *Die*

Naturgeschichte des deutschen Volkes als Grundlage einer deutschen Socialpolitik, 4 vols. (Stuttgart: Cotta, 1851–69), 2:41.

13. William H. Rollins, *A Greener Vision of Home: Cultural Politics and Environmental Reform in the German* Heimatschutz *Movement, 1904–1918* (Ann Arbor: University of Michigan Press, 1997).

14. See Darré's presentation on 18 January 1937, Stadtarchiv Goslar (hereafter SA Goslar), NL Darré, vol. 431 a, 2. See also Mathias Eidenbenz, *"Blut und Boden": Zur Funktion und Genese der Metaphern des Agrarismus und Biologismus in der nationalsozialistischen Bauernpropaganda R. W. Darrés* (Bern: Peter Lang, 1993), on usage of the word pair, 3–4.

15. This is the title of Darré's book *Das Bauerntum als Lebensquell der nordischen Rasse.*

16. See Richard Walther Darré, "Blut und Boden als Lebensgrundlagen der nordischen Rasse, 29.9.1933," in Darré, *Um Blut und Boden: Reden und Aufsätze,* 17–29; and other articles and speeches in Darré, *Um Blut und Boden.*

17. The title of one of his articles, written in 1927, was "The Pig as a Criterion for Nordic People and Semites" (*Das Schwein als Kriterium für Nordische Völker und Semiten*).

18. Richard Walther Darré, "Das Zuchtziel des deutschen Volkes, 1931," in *Um Blut und Boden,* 30–40.

19. See Darré's written notes from a talk he gave on 18 January 1931, in SA Goslar, NL Darré, vol. 431 a, 6.

20. See also Corni and Gies, *Brot, Butter, Kanonen,* 29. Anna Bramwell disputes this claim and states that the resettlement program was an "improvised response to a sudden emergency" and represented a "fusion of Darréan Blut und Boden ideology, demographic-national aims, and agrarian reform." Bramwell, *Blood and Soil,* 169.

21. See Darré's letter to Kenstler of 25 April 1930, in SA Goslar, NL Darré, vol. 94. Bramwell uses this alleged lack of anti-Semitism in Darré's work as an argument to support her claim that Darré did not go along with the Nazis' racial extermination policies. See Bramwell, *Blood and Soil,* 191. However, Darré himself said that Hitler was not well informed about his writings. In fact, Darré's early writings are clearly anti-Semitic. Without mentioning Jews directly, he leaves no doubt whom he considers to be a good example of nomads: Jews.

22. By 1932, the agricultural interest organizations had been infiltrated and the most important agrarian party, the Christian National Peasants' and Rural People's Party, had lost all its seats in the parliament. See Larry Eugene Jones, "Crisis and Realignment: Agrarian Splinter Parties in the Late Weimar

Republic, 1928–1933," in *Peasants and Lords in Modern Germany: Recent Studies in Agricultural History,* ed. Robert G. Moeller (Boston: Allen & Unwin, 1986), 198–232; Horst Gies, "The NSDAP and Agrarian Organizations in the Final Phase of the Weimar Republic," in *Nazism and the Third Reich,* ed. Henry A. Turner (New York: Quadrangle Books, 1972), 45–88; and Horst Gies, "Die nationalsozialistische Machtergreifung auf dem agrarpolitischen Sektor," *Zeitschrift für Agrargeschichte und Agrarsoziologie* 16 (1967): 210–32.

23. The *Nationalsozialistische Landpost* was first published in September 1931.

24. John E. Farquharson, "The Agrarian Policy of National Socialist Germany," in *Peasants and Lords in Modern Germany: Recent Studies in Agricultural History,* ed. Robert G. Moeller (Boston: Allen & Unwin, 1986), 233–59.

25. "Der nationalsozialistische landwirtschaftliche Fachbearbeiter," in Gies, *The NSDAP and Agrarian Organizations,* 51.

26. On agricultural interest organizations in the 1920s, see Stephanie Merkenich, *Grüne Front gegen Weimar: Reichs-Landbund und agrarischer Lobbyismus, 1918–1933* (Düsseldorf: Droste Verlag, 1998). On interest groups during the Empire, see Hans-Jürgen Puhle, *Agrarische Interessenpolitik und preussischer Konservatismus im wilhelminischen Reich, 1893–1914: Ein Beitrag zur Analyse des Nationalismus in Deutschland am Beispiel des Bundes der Landwirte und der Deutsch-Konservativen Partei* (Hannover: Verlag für Literatur und Zeitgeschehen, 1967). See also Gesine Gerhard, "Peasants into Farmers: Agriculture and Democracy in West Germany" (PhD diss., University of Iowa, 2000), chapter 1.

27. See Gustavo Corni, *Hitler and the Peasants: Agrarian Policy of the Third Reich, 1930–1939* (New York: Berg, 1990), 66–86.

28. Tensions continued even after a leadership agreement between Darré and Ley in 1935, the "Bückeberger Agreement," that incorporated those parts of the RNS concerned with wage earners into the German Labor Front. Bramwell, *Blood and Soil,* 109. See also Corni, *Hitler and the Peasants,* 80–81.

29. In his own defense during the "Wilhemstraße proceedings" in 1949, Darré argued before the military tribunal that the autonomy of the RNS and the hostility of other organizations toward the RNS was yet more proof of his deviation from the official Nazi line. See Darré, Bundesarchiv Koblenz (hereafter BAK), N 1094 I, Nr. 1, fols. 9–17.

30. Corni, *Hitler and the Peasants,* 74.

31. See, for example, Darré's letter to Göring of 1 November 1936. Darré wrote this letter while recuperating from a long illness. It is a stubborn defense of the RNS against badmouthing from other sides. SA Goslar, NL Darré, vol. 146.

32. The law of hereditary entailment was issued on 29 September 1933. On the law, see especially Friedrich Grundmann, *Agrarpolitik im 3. Reich: Anspruch und Wirklichkeit des Reichserbhofgesetzes* (Hamburg: Hoffmann und Campe, 1979).

33. Corni, *Hitler and the Peasants*, 145–48.

34. Ibid., 144

35. Ibid., 151.

36. Corni and Gies, *Brot, Butter, Kanonen*, 420–21.

37. On the Nazis' food policy, see Corni and Gies, *Brot, Butter, Kanonen*, esp. 251–395 for food policy before the outbreak of the war.

38. See the exchange of letters between Darré and Göring in October–November 1936, SA Goslar, NL Darré, vol. 146. Darré congratulates Göring on his new responsibilities and offers his advice. See esp. the eighteen-page-long letter from Darré of 1 November 1936, in which he confides in detail his own weaknesses and his worries about some of his co-workers.

39. Corni, *Hitler and the Peasants*, 174–75.

40. For an explanation of how food policies influenced the murderous policies in the East, see Christian Gerlach, *Krieg, Ernährung, Völkermord: Deutsche Vernichtungspolitik im Zweiten Weltkrieg*, 2nd ed. (Zürich: Pendo Verlag, 2001). See also Susanne Heim, *Kalorien, Kautschuk, Karrieren: Pflanzenzüchtung und landwirtschaftliche Forschung in Kaiser-Wilhelm-Insituten, 1933–1945* (Göttingen: Wallstein Verlag, 2003), and Corni and Gies, *Brot, Butter, Kanonen*, chap. 5.

41. Darré's personal papers are in Stadtarchiv Goslar (SA Goslar) and Bundesarchiv Koblenz (BAK). An abridged version of Darré's diaries is available in Goslar and in Koblenz.

42. The trial got its name from the street where several of the Nazi ministries had been located. Minutes of the trial are in the archives in BAK, N 1094 I; a copy is also available in the archives of the United States Holocaust Memorial Museum in Washington, DC, RG-06-019.01.

43. Darré's original diaries were edited after the war by his former assistant, Hanns Deetjen. The original diaries were burned at the request of Darré's wife, who felt that they shed bad light on Darré. See Deetjen's explanation from November 1972, BAK, N 1094, fol. 65a, 1. Bramwell insists that the diaries are a reliable source since archivists have testified to their originality. Bramwell, *Ecology in the 20th Century*, 270n19. The diaries, however, should be used with great caution since they are not complete and have been edited purposefully to burnish Darré's image.

44. Bramwell, *Blood and Soil*, 127.

45. Statements entered in court in Darré's defense, BAK, N 1094 I, vol. 1, 10–11.

46. Backe's role needs to be studied further. His personal papers are in BAK, N 1075. Backe hanged himself in the Nuremberg prison on 6 April 1947. On Backe's life, see Bramwell, *Blood and Soil,* 93–100, and Heim, *Kalorien, Kautschuk, Karrieren,* 28–33.

47. BAK, N 1094 I, vol. 1, 11.

48. A newspaper article dated 27 September 1953 described Darré as mentally unstable and depressed. His father committed suicide, perhaps also his brother. The report uses this information to explain Darré's mental situation in 1941–42 and hints at the idea that this was a reason to dismiss him. BAK, N 1094, vol. 1, fol. 11.

49. According to Darré, the party considered the RNS an alien organization (*Fremdkörper*) within the Nazi system, calling it the "Reichsquerstand" (Recalcitrant Office) or "Reichsreaktionärstand" (Reactionary Office). Statements made in defense of Darré, BAK, N 1094 I, vol. 1, 13. In his self-report written in the prison cell in Nuremberg, Backe confirms this picture of the RNS as a "state within the state" that was a thorn in the side of the party. See BAK, N 1075, vol. 3, 37.

50. See the newspaper article dated 27 September 1953 in BAK, N 1094 I, vol. 52. On the conflict with Ley, see note 28 above.

51. There are numerous letters from the 1930s where the two addressed each other affectionately as "Lieber Heini" (Dear Heini). See, for example, BAK, N 1094 I, vol. 10.

52. Statements made in defense Darré, BAK, N 1094 I, vol. 1, 14–15. See also Bramwell, *Blood and Soil,* 129.

53. In 1941, Darré wrote a letter to Hitler informing him about recent harassment of Anthroposophists by the Gestapo. Dr. Eduard Bartsch and Dr. Hans Merkel, the latter of whom would later become Darré's lawyer in the Wilhelmstraße proceedings, were among those arrested. Bartsch was the director of the Union of Anthroposophist Farmers, an organization that was banned by the Gestapo in 1935. Darré assumes that Hitler will be sympathetic to the Anthroposophists since he recalls that Hitler himself was eating only vegetables from biodynamic farms. Letter from Darré of 26 June 1941, BAK, NS 19, 3122, fol. 54. See also Bormann's response in a letter of 18 June 1941, where he denies any support of biodynamic farms. BAK, NS 19, 3122, fol. 56. See also Bramwell, *Ecology in the 20th Century,* 201. See also Uwe Werner's study on anthroposophy in the Third Reich, *Anthroposophen in der Zeit des Nationalsozialismus (1933–1945)* (Munich: Oldenbourg Verlag, 1999).

54. Bramwell, *Ecology in the 20th Century,* 200–201.

55. Darré summarizes the results of this questionnaire in a letter of 19 May 1941. BAK, NS 19, 3122, fols. 46–48.

56. See Heydrich's letter of 18 October 1941, BAK, NS 19, 3122, fol. 59. See also Bormann's letter in BAK, NS 19, 3122, fols. 55–56.

57. For a more thorough analysis of Darré's stand on anthroposophical farming, see Gesine Gerhard, "Richard Walther Darré—Naturschützer oder 'Rassenzüchter'?" in *Naturschutz und Nationalsozialismus,* ed. Joachim Radkau and Frank Uekötter (Frankfurt: Campus Verlag, 2003), 257–71.

58. Staudenmaier, *Fascist Ideology,* 15–17.

59. Bramwell, *Ecology in the 20th Century,* 204. See also Heim, *Kalorien, Kautschuk, Karrieren,* 172–93.

60. Jost Hermand, *Grüne Utopien in Deutschland: Zur Geschichte des ökologischen Bewußtseins* (Frankfurt: Fischer Taschenbuch Verlag, 1991), 112–19.

61. Even Darré was willing to postpone a serious discussion of the question of biodynamic farming until after the war. BAK, NS 19, vol. 3122, fols. 48, 67–72.

62. See other chapters in this volume. See also Radkau and Uekötter, *Nationalsozialismus und Naturschutz.*

63. BAK, NS 19, vol. 3122, fols. 46–48.

64. I disagree with Bramwell, who in her preface says that Darré "headed a group of agrarian radicals who, among other issues, were concerned with what we now call ecological problems." Bramwell, *Blood and Soil,* v.

65. See Eidenbenz, *Blut und Boden,* 11–12.

66. Bramwell, *Blood and Soil,* 188. See also BAK, N 1094 I, vol. 2.

67. BAK, N 1094 I, vol. 2.

CHAPTER 6

Molding the Landscape of Nazi Environmentalism

Alwin Seifert and the Third Reich

Thomas Zeller

IN 1937, the biographical encyclopedia *Who's Who of Munich Cultural Life* described Alwin Seifert as a passionate gardener through whose work "all of Germany has become his garden."[1] With this laconic statement, landscape management was elevated to a national endeavor, and Seifert anointed as the nation's gardener. A seemingly apolitical and private act of gardening thereby received the blessing and support of a powerful nation-state. State sponsorship of landscaping was, of course, a recurrent feature of industrialized countries in the twentieth century. But certain characteristics of gardening—growing, selecting, raising, and weeding—assumed a particular urgency within the ideological world of Nazi Germany.[2] Garden tending was akin to nation building: desirables were to be cultivated, undesirables weeded out.[3]

This poignant parallel between gardening and racial selection is at the core of some of the most uncomfortable questions regarding the "green" Nazis. Indeed, some historians have argued that gardeners and landscape architects like Seifert were a fitting match for the Nazi regime.[4] While it is tempting to draw this conclusion, it is necessary to examine the changing ideologies and complex effects of National Socialist environmental management by looking behind the facade of theatrical self-portrayals which included references to nature. Therefore, this chapter seeks to clarify the question whether ecological consciousness was indeed a feature of Nazi Germany by examining the political biography of Seifert, an avid conservationist, professional landscape architect, and major public figure in the Nazi regime.

Seifert's public life encapsulated the history of the environmental movement in Germany, and his activities reflected the main preoccupations and concerns of early and mid-twentieth-century conservationists. Seifert was the most prominent environmentalist in the Third Reich, as expressed in the illustrious yet legally meaningless title, *Reichslandschaftsanwalt* (Reich landscape advocate), bestowed on him by the regime. Professionally, Seifert found a niche as the leading adviser for the landscaping of the autobahn. By building personal alliances and igniting well-planned scandals, he instigated many debates on conservation, agriculture, urban planning, and modern technology in general, always testing the limits of his role in the Nazi system of power.[5] Yet Seifert's position within the Nazi regime was more tenuous than previously known; while he catapulted himself to a position of relative influence in environmental matters during the Third Reich, the regime kept tight restraints on his activities as well.

By using the lens of a political biography, the relationship between Seifert's individual goals, achievements, successes, and failures, on the one hand, and larger historical and societal trends, on the other, becomes clearer. Furthermore, in examining the major tenets of Seifert's public life, he can be understood as a politically savvy environmentalist—not in the sense of an elected official, but as an individual who understood how to build alliances and continuously forged them, as someone who tried to divert resources for issues that he deemed worthy and who used his own rhetorical resources accordingly. In other words, Seifert displayed a highly developed sensibility regarding power and its mechanics; his acumen flourished even while his moral sensibility failed him. At the same time Seifert professed to be a man of deep convictions who would not easily waver. Indeed, he claimed to have been driven by a love of landscape and ideological predispositions that changed very little over the course of his life from 1890 to 1972, spanning four political systems in Germany: the authoritarian Second Reich, the democratic Weimar Republic, the dictatorial Nazi regime, and finally the democratic Federal Republic.

The Personal and Structural Factors that Affected Seifert's Career

By all accounts, Seifert's personality reflected the firmness of his beliefs. He was described as devoted to the point of being dogged, and sharp to the point of being "arrogant, brusque of manner, pragmatic and eccentric."[6] In his dealings with the civil engineers designing the autobahn, he himself admitted to having been "really insufferable."[7] The death notice published in the local newspaper by his colleagues at the Technical University of Munich gave a kinder rendition of his haughtiness, stressing his "never-failing courage and unnerving tenacity, the secret of his success."[8] For all his stubbornness and perseverance, Seifert nonetheless molded his persona to the National Socialist regime and learned how to adapt to the bureaucratic confusion and ideological controversies that confronted him. Seifert, in short, evinced a lifelong commitment to landscape planning, but not necessarily to democracy.

Seifert's basic ideological tenet was grounded in a particular notion of landscape. It was not "wilderness" or "nature" that motivated and propelled him into action; it was a belief in the normative quality of landscape and the constant desire to redress it in order to "heal" it. The conspicuous absence of the notion of unadulterated nature from these discussions marked a distinctly continental European approach and opened the door to debates on designing and redesigning landscapes.[9] Starting with the establishment of geography as an academic discipline in the late nineteenth century, the basic distinction of rare and elusive "natural landscapes" (*Naturlandschaften*) and omnipresent "cultural landscapes" (*Kulturlandschaften*) was not only the guidepost for geographical research, but also became a common marker of educated discourse. Landscape was a culturally charged space, where humans and nature interacted.[10] If the exchange was appropriate and harmonious, landscape would become attractive and beautiful; if the relationship was disturbed, the consequences were aesthetic distortion and ugliness.[11] What is more, the landscape discourse was increasingly framed in the parameters of the nation-state.[12] The geographer Gerhard Hard states that "landscape" became one of the central categories of German publications, even a signature of the times, between 1890 and 1940, with a clear upsurge of titles on landscape in aesthetics, art history, literary studies, and poetry between 1930 and 1940.[13] Authors such as Rudolf Borchardt, editor of a classical anthology of German landscape writing, claimed in 1925 that the drive to discover, describe, and design landscape was uniquely and genuinely German.[14]

For Seifert and many of his contemporaries, at the heart of these beliefs was the connection between the landscape and the human soul. According to this vein of thought, landscape was the product of a particular type of human soul, be it Nordic or Southern European.[15] Landscape was seen as the outcome of centuries of cultural work on the landscape—and culture here meant primarily agriculture—and thus embodied the values of a specific community whose characteristics were increasingly coming to be seen as based on race. This ethnic-based view of landscape as the interaction site between culture and nature was compatible with a new embrace of industrialization and modernization for some architects, landscape architects, and engineers in the 1920s and 1930s. They asserted that they could capture the "soul" of the landscape by implementing landscape-sensitive designs of buildings and the surrounding landscapes.[16] Rather than seeing himself as a conservationist who tried to set aside tracts of land for preservation, Seifert openly embraced the designing of landscapes in order to preserve the spirit of and the essential link between nature and culture, as expressed in a typical landscape—an attitude which increasingly put him at odds with those conservationists who sought to preserve nature from the encroachments of modernity.

Seifert's professional life before 1933 reflected the budding professionalization of landscape architecture in Germany. Born into a middle-class Munich family that owned a construction company, he studied architecture at the Technical University of Munich. The faculty there favored a regionalist architectural style that was antithetical to the universalism of the Bauhaus. Traditional architectural styles, such as those of Bavarian farmhouses, were seen as a successful blend of humans and nature in a healthy landscape. Regionalist architects of the early twentieth century emphasized the need to carefully embed buildings into their surrounding scenery, while also paying attention to their functional requirements. This attention to harmony was supposedly a distinctively southern German (as opposed to Prussian) style of architecture.[17] This school strongly influenced Seifert, who (after serving in the army during World War I) worked as a lecturer at the University of Munich. He turned to landscape architecture—which at the time was the profession of a few dozen men in Germany who designed gardens for wealthy clients and occasionally parks for cities—as an additional source of income.[18] By the late 1920s, Seifert was also publishing on garden architecture and designs. He adopted organic farming in 1930 and later became one of its most ardent proponents, following the methods of Rudolf Steiner.[19] Like many other architects, he was hit hard by the depression of the early 1930s.

Seifert's passion for conservation matched his interest in landscape. In the 1920s, he joined the Bavarian-based Bund Naturschutz, one of Germany's most important conservation leagues. He worked on its subcommittees for architecture and landscape and contributed to reformulating the conservationist agenda in those years so that it embraced technology and industry.[20] This helps explain why Seifert eagerly sought work on the Nazi autobahn when the opportunity presented itself in 1933. After the project of building a highway network had been announced, conservationists invited Fritz Todt, the engineer in charge, to speak at their convention. Todt declined, yet promised that "legitimate matters regarding landscape protection" would be considered.[21] One of the speakers at the convention was Seifert, who lambasted "outdated romanticism" and "sentimental flower painting" on the part of those conservationists who continued to look backwards. Rather, he recommended the quest for "timeless, great, and simple basic forms" in architecture.[22] After the groundbreaking ceremonies for the autobahn emphasized the alleged effects on employment and not the landscape aspects of the roads, Seifert introduced himself to Todt with a letter outlining the importance of landscaping.[23] He criticized agriculture for leading to the clearing of landscapes of hedges and shrubs, thus creating ecological problems such as desertification, deterioration of the soil, the endangerment of bird life, and a loss of beauty and balance in the landscape. Since farmers had made these mistakes, he argued, the state should now set a good example by planting the embankments along transportation routes. Either native species should be chosen, or, "in a deliberate artistic contrast to the landscape," monumental tree plantings four to eight rows deep could be used.[24] Todt responded affirmatively, yet vaguely, and commissioned Seifert to take a look at the project of the road leading southeast from Munich to the Austrian border.[25] Seifert's idea of avoiding one of the worst aspects of the past—roadside ditches—was shared by Todt, who had spoken of the future autobahn as a *Parkstrasse*, thus alluding to the parkways that were being built in the United States at the time.[26]

This collaboration proved to be the starting point for Seifert's engagement with the Third Reich; it also revealed how the relationship between Seifert and Todt was one of client and patron. Seifert volunteered to offer advice, hoping for professional employment and social status; Todt received the expertise and decided whether to reward it with praise and payment. Generally, Todt defined the parameters of their relationship, while Seifert sought to define its content. In January 1934, Todt named Seifert his adviser for landscape matters. Seifert himself selected fifteen colleagues (all males), who came to be known as *Landschaftsanwälte* (landscape advocates). Seifert acted as a leader of this group. These landscape advocates followed a professional ethic of forming cultural capital through natural improvement and were a socially and ideologically quite homogeneous group. Rather than theorizing about holistic concepts, they preached and practiced organic farming in their own gardens, embraced hiking as a social activity, and sought to know nature through the culturally rewarding work of gardening and landscaping. Interestingly enough, Todt almost never stipulated what specific advice, opinion, or reports he preferred. Rather, he used his power to reward or ignore the expertise provided.

Seifert and the Third Reich's Political Landscape

This entangled relationship conditioned the landscaping of the autobahn, the most prominent task for Seifert and his clique during the Third Reich. Todt's agency agreed to pay landscape architects for advising civil engineers during the planning period. Their task, however, remained ill defined until the end of the autobahn project in 1941, creating a great deal of frustration for the landscape architects. Their correspondence with Seifert, who acted as the liaison with Todt, gives ample evidence of the bureaucratic confusion of the autobahn project, whose speed of construction was one of the key propaganda elements for "Adolf Hitler's roads."[27] In obvious contrast to the carefully orchestrated publicity, the landscape advocates were armed with only their persuasive skills or the possibility of funneling their protest through Seifert if they were to convince civil engineers about their design ideas. As the road building administration provided no institutional basis for them, their status as advisers remained unclear.

The landscape architects fought acrimonious battles with the civil engineers over design features such as whether the roads should follow curvilinear patterns and the contours of the landscape, as the American parkways did, or whether they should be as straight as possible, as railways had been built for decades. Especially during the first years of autobahn building, fast, unadorned thruways rather than the "sweeping" roads celebrated by the autobahn propaganda were the result of the Nazis' most important peacetime infrastructure project. Only by the late 1930s were the landscape architects able to make some headway. The tensions between the engineers and the architects, two distinct professional groups with different agendas, were not resolved during the Nazi years, only covered up by the fast pace of the overall project. Additionally, Todt did not agree with many of the landscape architects' ideas, preferring roads which enabled visual consumption from a speeding car.[28] Even the ebullient Seifert conceded that each stretch of the finished road reflected the peculiarities of both the landscape advocates and the regional road building administration.[29] On the whole, the success of the landscape advocates involved with the autobahn was considerably less pronounced or complete than the regime's propaganda would have it. Caught up in the maze of competing levels of bureaucracy, institutions, and ideologies, the advocates, along with Seifert, pursued a strategy of growing shrillness in order to maintain their position.

It is in this light that the debate over the use of indigenous plants alongside the autobahn should be seen. Seifert did not make the use of native plants mandatory when he first introduced his ideas to Todt. When some landscape advocates began to feel professionally marginalized during the hectic construction phase, they sought refuge in a racialized version of current ecological theories of phytosociology and of the climax community and its disturbance by modern agriculture and silviculture.[30] Reintroducing native plants to the landscapes around the autobahn, they now argued, was a national task which would enable Germans to rejuvenate themselves as a race based on a healthy soil. In particular, Seifert's rhetoric became exclusivist and transcended floristic xenophobia into crass ecological nationalism: "We like sloes and whitethorn, *Pfaffenhütchen* [*Euonymus planipes*] and hazel shrubs, wild pears, linden trees, and wild cherries at the edge of the forest better than all the red oaks and Douglasia of the world. And most of all, they are closer to our heart! With never waning tenacity and unshakeable optimism, we will achieve our goal that the edges of the forests next to the autobahn will be authentic and rich edges; right next to the greatest technical work of all times, the most original landscape will have its home again."[31]

This was overheated rhetoric—even by Nazi standards—and it was designed to impress upon the road builders, who were reluctant to allocate funds for landscaping, that they could not overlook the power of the landscape advocates.[32] The more Todt's bureaucracy appeared resistant to landscape planning, the more passionate and overtly racist the advocates' rhetoric became, as they tried to align their professional agenda with racial definition and exclusion, one of the core tenets of Nazi ideology. Actually, Todt's agency did sponsor phytosociologists' research on native species, especially on those that were hearty enough to survive on their own. But it resisted planting to the extent that the landscape advocates proposed. After much discussion, Todt finally settled the matter to his satisfaction: the chief purpose of roadside plants was to enhance the driving experience, not to act as agents of—in today's terms—ecological restoration.[33]

In general, Seifert realized that his most useful strategy would be one of public appeals and constant alarms, if he wanted to achieve the influence at which he aimed. Seifert's idea of action was to speak up, to make enemies, and to test the strength of his protection in the intellectual and social environment of the Third Reich. While the concept of a "public sphere" is not very useful for understanding the orchestrated publicity in Nazi Germany, it can be understood as the arena for competing beliefs, professional alliances, and ideological battles. Seifert's tenacious personality was well suited for this field, as was his easily accessible, provocative, and constantly polemical writing style. In a telling aside, Todt called Seifert his "conscience."[34]

His first campaign outside the realm of the autobahn was his dire warning of an impending desertification (*Versteppung*) of Germany. While he had warned of desertification as early as 1932, it was the Third Reich that offered Seifert a platform for his views.[35] With the blessing of Todt, they were published in *Deutsche Technik*—Todt's own journal, which sought to bridge the gulf between culture and technology with an increasingly racialized notion of "German" technology.[36] As intended, the article caused quite an uproar among hydraulic engineers, who saw their position being attacked in a journal published by the Third Reich's chief engineer.[37] In line with contemporaneous "holistic" understandings of ecology, Seifert's paper started with a general view of an impending sea change in understanding nature: the mechanistic, rational view of nature was to be supplanted by an intuitive, respectful view of nature as the "alma mater." Seifert's holistic rhetoric gained new urgency by way of his parallel between the new view of nature and a "new Reich"; he popularized the idea of organicism that was prevalent in the ecology of the 1920s and 1930s both in North America and western Europe. Nature was an interconnected whole, in which every part was in tune with everything else, "from the smallest spot of meadow to the entire universe."[38] But his particular line of attack was against the current theory and practice of hydraulic engineering. For decades, Seifert claimed, the goal of water experts had been to lead rainwater out of the countryside as fast as possible—and the result had been a diminishment of local water supplies. River straightening and dam construction led to more and faster high water, leading in turn to destruction downstream. But the devastating effects of hydraulic engineering could also be seen upstream, where coppices growing on the banks had been cut down, upsetting the delicate balance of water circulation in the valleys. The effect of all these measures was the draining of Germany, with destructive ecological and economic results. Seifert's cautionary example was the Dust Bowl in the United States, where fertile landscapes had been simply obliterated.[39] In the same years, the American ecologist Paul Sears issued his dire warnings of desertification under the impression of these catastrophic events. The solution Seifert offered was a technology "close to nature": instead of building large dams (which Seifert felt were more appropriate for Texas and Colorado), Germany needed to build mill and fish ponds that would retain water and renaturalize its streams.[40] His closing argument blended ecological management with racial politics: nature-friendly technology, agriculture, and forestry would lead the new generation of German youth to rejuvenate the nation's racial stock, love the country for its nature, and therefore be all the more willing to defend it.

Seifert's polemic, while introducing his topic in ecological terms, hinged on this nexus of nature and nation. Taking this position, he reduced the debate to an ideological one, especially in the face of his critics. After reviewing the claims that hydraulic engineering had bettered the livelihoods of millions in an industrially advanced Germany, he claimed that, in the end, the debate boiled down to whether Germany's landscape belonged to the hydraulic engineers or to the *Volk;* that is, to a special interest group or to everyone (the "mythical oneness" that the word *Volk* implied).[41] While this argument might have sufficed to make his views unassailable in the Germany of 1937, he went on to add that the United States Soil Conservation Service was implementing measures similar to those he proposed, with shelterbelts and the reintroduction of beavers. Oscillating between merciless ideological arguments and calls for the adaptation of new policies implemented in other countries, Seifert marshaled whatever evidence or opinion would speak in his favor. Not only experts, but government officials were enraged. The minister of agriculture, Richard Walther Darré, asked Todt to silence Seifert and his "wrongheaded, fantasy-ridden scribblings."[42] While Darré at times entertained ideas about ecological farming, he was not persuaded by Seifert's musings with their grounding in the mysticism of Steiner's biologic-dynamic farming.[43] In reply, Todt made it clear that Seifert enjoyed his protection and pointed out that Rudolf Hess, Hitler's deputy, supported Seifert as well.[44] While Todt admonished his protégé in private not to attack engineers per se, he defended him in public against criticism from other government agencies.[45]

Yet Seifert's rhetorical avalanches and his dire warnings of desertification did not result in widespread changes in hydraulic engineering or agriculture. While it was relatively easy for Todt to carve out a polemical niche for the landscape advocates, he was less successful in convincing other state agencies to abandon their practices and embrace Seifert's vision. When thousands of men cultivated land, thinned out forests, corrected rivers, and drained bogs as part of their national service in the Reichsarbeitsdienst (Reich Labor Service), the emphasis was on mobilizing labor and creating employment, not on ecological management. But the landscape advocates sought to extend their dominion, and asked Todt to convince the Labor Service's leaders to use them as advisers.[46] The Labor Service employed five landscape advocates on a trial basis.[47] After one year, the advocates were frustrated by the discrepancy between the leadership's willingness to listen and the unwillingness of the engineers on the ground to utilize their expertise.[48] In 1936, the Labor Service issued a half-hearted decree that all plans should be checked by a "landscape expert" (though not necessarily one of Seifert's group).[49] As with many other environmental policies of the Nazi regime, no records exist of this policy's enforcement. In the end, the landscape advocates as a group remained marginal whenever they tried to expand their reach outside of Todt's zone of relative protection.

Seifert, however, was constantly trying to extend his influence. The chaotic style of governance in Nazi Germany matched his strategy of molding alliances, especially since he enjoyed the tacit protection of his two most powerful patrons, Hess and Todt. With Hess, he shared an interest in Steiner's methods of "biologic-dynamic" agriculture. Seifert designed a garden for Hess's private home and bragged to a colleague that he would do likewise for Hitler "after the war."[50] In 1939, Hitler awarded Seifert the title of professor, and Todt issued a document one year later declaring Seifert as his Reich landscape advocate as a birthday present.[51]

Indeed, Seifert's informal connections were often more powerful than the established channels of bureaucratic procedures. For instance, he acted as a go-between for the Anthroposophical Society and the Nazi state; while anthroposophical societies were banned for some time after 1933, bio-dynamic farming flourished. Only after Hess's flight to England in 1941 were all anthroposophical institutions, including the Steiner schools, outlawed.[52] Seifert spoke on their behalf; he was not a member of the Steiner community himself, but had adapted much of their thinking, especially on farming, as part of his own.

Seifert's Expanding Influence and Ever-Increasing Enemies

In his dealings with the Nazi leaders, his robust style served him well. He managed to extend his sphere of action in accordance with Todt's increasing power.[53] Outside of the realm of the autobahn, Seifert judged that waterways and hydroelectric power projects were in need of his consultancy. Only a few months after starting to work on the roads, Seifert asked Hess to duplicate the structure of Todt's road building administration for the entire sphere of water management in the Reich.[54] After the start of World War II, the transportation secretary agreed to use Seifert's men as consultants when planning new river corrections, but apparently did so only sporadically.[55] Seifert saw an increasingly urgent need to act after the annexation of Austria in 1938 and the Nazis' plans to use hydroelectric power from the Alps on a large scale for the war economy.[56] Work on a huge dam in Kaprun in the Tauern Ridge of the Alps started in May of the same year; Seifert asked Hess to intervene, fearing "irreparable damage" to the mountain landscape.[57] Seifert was able to prevent some of the ecologically most devastating plans for this power plant, which began small-scale operation in 1944, angering the German engineers by his brashness and earning himself the nickname "wild Alwin."[58] Besides Hess's protection, Seifert enjoyed the general backing of Todt, whose sphere after 1941 extended to the management of water and energy. The Reich landscape advocate's plans and reports written for the Danube hydroelectric plant in Ybbs-Persenbeug, another gigantic plan, were used only after the war when the erstwhile Nazi project was executed in the Republic of Austria.[59]

It should be noted that Todt and Hess offered only general and often vague encouragement for Seifert, letting him fend for himself with varying degrees of success. On the ground, his sense of self-importance and the receptiveness among parts of his audiences for environmentally more benign design solutions were paramount. While nature *protection* in Nazi Germany received more legal attention and a new nationwide bureaucracy, landscaping was left to several competing agencies and informal alliances. Seifert and his personally selected group of landscape advocates just managed to accumulate more power than others. Hans Klose, the director of the Reich's nature protection agency, stated flatly in 1942 that Seifert's connections to higher echelons were better than his own.[60] Indeed, even the nation's first nature protection law (1935) excluded the entire sphere of road building since Todt's office was unwilling to relinquish its control.[61] After the beginning of World War II, the landscape advocates engaged in a debate over how to reorganize the fields of conservation and landscape design after the war. Most supported the idea of leaving the preservation of existing landscapes to the established bureaucracies, but creating a nationwide network of landscape advocates, led by Seifert, which would have to be consulted every time major landscape change was imminent. True to the jargon of the time, one of the younger landscape architects labeled Seifert's group a "raiding party" against the established conservationists, thus reflecting a sense of momentum.[62]

The military expansion of Nazi Germany offered the landscape architects an opportunity to partake in the monumental efforts to Germanize the landscape in the occupied territories. After the murder, resettlement, and subjugation of local eastern Europeans, the land was to be redesigned in order to attract settlers from Germany.[63] The landscape advocates offered their rhetorical support and hoped for continuous employment. Seifert's group, however, encountered the entanglements of Nazi politics, where several agencies competed over the occupied territories. Todt's office mostly lost out, and landscaping of the "East" was mainly assigned to SS leaders, who relied on the advice of the Berlin professor, Heinrich Wiepking-Jürgensmann, Seifert's archenemy. Seifert's only influence on the territories was seen in the legal protections under Todt's decrees declaring road planning off limits to the SS.[64] While Wiepking and his students redesigned the occupied East, some of Seifert's men used their landscaping skills in camouflaging the *Westwall*, a fortification wall against French tanks built after 1938. The military also used them to camouflage buildings in preparation for aerial war.[65]

Seifert's closeness to the elites of the Third Reich becomes all the more apparent if we examine his knowledge of sludge experiments conducted at the extermination camp in Auschwitz. Himmler was apparently interested in generating gas from the feces of the camp inmates and kept Seifert abreast of progress on these model plants while Werner Bauch, one of Seifert's landscape advocates, worked in the camp for the SS.[66] Before the beginning of the mass exterminations, Himmler had envisioned Auschwitz as a model town and agricultural station for eastern Europe.[67] In reality, the camp's inmates loathed the work in the fields; a United States report in 1947 claimed that construction of the sludge experimental station had claimed the lives of thousands of camp prisoners.[68] No records exist of an actual visit by Seifert to Auschwitz, but he was well acquainted with the organic herb garden at the Dachau concentration camp close to his home.[69]

There can be little doubt that Seifert was one of the most prominent environmentalists in Nazi Germany. He owed his position to his patronage and his personality as well as to his skills in maneuvering his way through the fragmented body politic. In his quest to restore what he saw as a truly German landscape, he was willing to engage in coalitions that would further his professional, personal, and political goals, even if they involved the most murderous agencies of Nazi Germany. Yet the tenuous position he enjoyed among the Nazis became clearer after Hess's flight to England in 1941 and Todt's death in an airplane crash in 1942. Starting in late 1941, Seifert was under surveillance, though he was never arrested. He was aware that he was being watched and once even mockingly volunteered, in a letter to Oswald Pohl, the main SS business manager, to work in the organic herb farm in Dachau in the event he was arrested.[70] Even though he became a member of the Nazi Party, he was considered too self-willed to be entirely trustworthy.[71] His mentor had planned to give Seifert a country retreat as a reward for his work—a feudal gesture sponsored by the construction industry, Todt's profiteers.[72] But after Todt died, Seifert rallied his academic friends at the Technical University in Munich in order to obtain a chair there in lieu of the Alpine abode. He appears to have been backed by Hitler himself at first.[73] Yet when Seifert appeared to have condoned student dissent in 1943, before ever holding a chair, his academic career was put on "probation." In the spring of 1944, the Reich Chancellery declared him "unfit" for a professorship.[74] After the war, Seifert used this episode to portray himself as a victim of the Nazi regime and was finally briefly hired as a professor before the mandatory retirement age.

When asked to justify his role in Nazi Germany during his "denazification" proceedings in 1947, Seifert proclaimed himself to be—rather grandiosely—the "trustee, the faithful savior of the German landscape."[75] Denying affinity with Nazism, he claimed his core beliefs were apolitical: "In the future, I will use my knowledge, my skills, and my experience for Germany no differently than before and after 1933, notwithstanding who governs it. For governments come and go, but the land stays put, as homeland (*Heimat*) of the Germans, as the home of occidental culture."[76] This rhetorical strategy of depoliticizing what had been immensely political not only served to whitewash Seifert and downplay his prominent position in Hitler's regime, but also portrayed his efforts as worthwhile regardless of their political connotations. Yet it had been precisely the political reality of Nazi Germany that enabled Seifert to launch his crusades.

In sum, Seifert's political biography is remarkable on three levels. First, an underemployed landscape architect from Munich was propelled within a few years into a position of formidable informal power over landscape matters in the Nazi dictatorship. It was through, for, and by means of the state that he sought to implement his ideas. He established personal ties with high-ranking Nazi officials, notably Todt, the chief engineer of the Third Reich, and Hess, the Nazi Party secretary with a predilection for organic farming. Characteristically, his appointment as Todt's official landscape advocate entailed no administrative clout or legal standing, but flattered with an illustrious title his presumption to being the landscape's guardian. His vain ambition was to develop and design German landscapes while satisfying both the demands of modernization and his own sense of aesthetics. The Nazi regime's disregard for established administrative structures, and the competition of individual government agencies, were important preconditions for Seifert's public rise and fall. While relying on the backing of his two most powerful patrons, Todt and Hess, he constantly sought to test the limits of his ambivalent role as the Nazis' environmental court jester and Cassandra rolled into one.

At the same time, Seifert popularized some of the most up-to-date ideas in ecology and land management as well as the less scientifically formal views of Steiner's organic agriculture. He himself was no laboratory researcher. His contribution was limited to polishing and publishing the latest findings and policies in outlets provided to him in the Nazi arena. Provocation and scandalization were his tools; pointed exchanges and occasionally bruised relationships with academics were the results. Seifert did try to convince the Nazi regime to implement organic farming on a large scale in Germany, but ultimately failed when the preparation for war overruled any possibility of experimentation. In his essays, he predicted an imminent drought—a Versteppung—as a consequence of extensive farming and hydraulic engineering, and as a countermeasure proposed replanting the countryside with bushes and trees. The straightening of rivers and creeks also drew his criticism.

Yet while some of these proposals might sound like a European version of Aldo Leopold's ideas, it is important to note that, in these debates, Seifert increasingly sought to undergird his arguments with racial beliefs in line with the ideological tenets of the Nazi regime. The more time he spent fighting his enemies in the chemical industry, in hydroengineering, and in civil engineering, the shriller and more openly racist his rhetoric grew. This suggests that his racism was generally more opportunistic than born of full ideological conviction. Yet his firm belief in the essentialist link between national character and landscape provided him with considerable ease in adjoining and overlapping with Nazi ideology. While he failed many times to realize his visions, he was successful in halting or mitigating plans for large-scale hydroelectric plants in the Alps which would have entailed the flooding of entire valleys. He was able to prevent major damage by pointing out possibilities of minor intrusion, thus introducing compromise when his own rhetoric had been marked by unwavering battle cries to bolster his self-importance.

Finally, after the liberation of Germany in 1945, the Allies held Seifert captive for some months. He was cleared in the denazification process due to letters of recommendation by friends and colleagues and reestablished his business as a landscape architect.[77] He failed in his desire to work for the autobahn administration of the Federal Republic, where road building no longer was the task of a centralized agency, but of the individual states. His major postwar project was the channelization of the Moselle river. It appears that Seifert was more successful in a political realm where personal relationships, alliances, and relative degree of access to powerful individuals shaped policies than with publicly negotiated bureaucratic structures in a democratic context. His legacy, however, is broadly established by two books which he published in his later years: his autobiography, in which he reworked his ambivalent career in Nazi Germany into an apolitical fight for nature, and a how-to book on composting that has sold hundreds of thousands of copies all over Europe since the 1950s and is still in print today.[78] In a sense, Seifert did become "Germany's gardener," by virtue of thousands of compost heaps rotting in backyards.

During the Nazi dictatorship, his single-minded ideological vision for landscape planning occasionally coalesced with the regime's ideas. Above all, he was driven by a wish to replace what he considered to be an old-fashioned type of piecemeal conservationism with a broader and more regional approach in the hands of a professional elite. In personal terms, he quickly rose to a prominent position in Nazi Germany but became increasingly isolated when his mentors Todt and Hess vanished from the political scene. An emblematic conservationist, Seifert symbolizes the transition from a conservation movement based on romantic perceptions of loss to one that more openly embraced industrial change and tried to manage it. He also served an important role as a popularizer of ecological ideas, be it in farming or hydroengineering. Crossing the boundaries between established science and marginal beliefs, he touted his appropriated ideas as revelations, couched in aggressive rhetoric. At the same time, his ideological predisposition and his conservative and reactionary leanings helped him form close alliances with the Nazi regime. Seifert's political allegiance, maneuvering, and personal responsibility show that environmental ideas are not necessarily married to progressive political views and can be used by different regimes. His environmentalism was that of self-assured experts, not of a popular democratic movement. He eagerly awaited the end of the rational, industrial age and the advent of a new, organic economy and technology. The fact that parts of the Nazi elite encouraged his shrill calls did not mean that the regime as a whole was environmentally benign. Yet it shows that the permutations of modernity in the Germany of the 1930s, far from monolithic, included ideas of ecologically motivated restraint, even if protagonists such as Seifert became increasingly marginalized as Nazi governance evolved. This complex intertwining has been overlooked in the broad rhetoric concerning "blood and soil" both during and after the Nazi period, but it is indispensable to disentangle these strands for a better understanding of environmentalism in the twentieth century.

Notes

1. Peter Breuer, *Münchner Künstlerköpfe* (Munich: Callwey, 1937), 327. An earlier version of this chapter appeared in Joachim Radkau, ed., *Naturschutz und Nationalsozialismus* (Frankfurt: Campus Verlag, 2003). The revised and translated version is printed here with permission.

2. James C. Scott, *Seeing Like a State: How Certain Schemes to Improve the Human Condition Have Failed* (New Haven: Yale University Press, 1998).

3. For these reasons, the gardener is one of the central metaphors of totalitarian modernity for Zygmunt Bauman. See *Modernity and the Holocaust* (Oxford: Polity Press, 2000), 70, 229.

4. Gert Gröning and Joachim Wolschke-Bulmahn, *Grüne Biographien: Biographisches Handbuch zur Landschaftsarchitektur des 20. Jahrhunderts in Deutschland* (Berlin: Patzer, 1997), 361–63; Janet Biehl and Peter Staudenmaier, *Ecofascism: Lessons from the German Experience* (Edinburgh: AK Press, 1995); Anna Bramwell, *Ecology in the 20th Century: A History* (New Haven: Yale University Press, 1989); Reinhard Falter, "Ein Leben für die Landschaft: Die Biographie des Naturschutzes im 20. Jahrhundert; In memoriam Alwin Seifert (1890–1972)," *Novalis* 49, no. 3 (1995): 38–42.

5. Alwin Seifert, *Ein Leben für die Landschaft* (Düsseldorf: Diederichs, 1962). This grandiloquent autobiography needs to be countered with the evidence in Seifert's personal papers reflecting the struggles, successes, and failures of his tenure as Reichslandschaftsanwalt. The Alwin Seifert Papers (hereafter ASP) are mainly housed at the Chair for Landscape Architecture and Design, Technical University of Munich-Weihenstephan.

6. John Charles Guse, "The Spirit of the Plassenburg" (PhD diss., University of Nebraska, 1981), 154.

7. Seifert, *Leben*, 50.

8. Obituary, March 1972 (newspaper clipping), Historical Archive, Technical University Munich, Personal Files Alwin Seifert, fol. 322.

9. For recent debates on the wilderness concept in the United States, see William Cronon, "The Trouble with Wilderness; or, Getting Back to the Wrong Nature," in *Uncommon Ground,* ed. William Cronon (New York: Norton, 1995), 69–90; and the debate among William Cronon (7–28, 47–55), Samuel P. Hays (29–32), Michael P. Cohen (33–42), and Thomas R. Dunlap (43–46) in *Environmental History* 1, no. 1 (1996). For the role of the landscape concept in contemporary geography, see Denis E. Cosgrove, *Social Formation and Symbolic Landscape,* 2nd ed. (Madison: University of Wisconsin Press, 1998); and Kenneth R. Olwig, "Recovering the Substantive Nature of Landscape," *Annals of the Association of American Geographers* 86, no. 4 (1996): 630–53.

10. David N. Livingstone, *The Geographical Tradition: Episodes in the History of a Contested Enterprise* (Oxford: Blackwell, 1993); Hans-Dietrich Schultz, *Die deutschsprachige Geographie von 1800 bis 1970: Ein Beitrag zur*

164 | Thomas Zeller

Geschichte ihrer Methodologie (Berlin: Freie Universität, 1980); Jürgen Osterhammel, "Die Wiederkehr des Raumes: Geopolitik, Geohistorie und historische Geographie," *Neue Politische Literatur* 43, no. 3 (1998): 374–97.

11. This notion was particularly valid for landscape planners in Nazi Germany. Stefan Körner, *Der Aufbruch der modernen Umweltplanung in der nationalsozialistischen Landespflege* (Berlin: Technische Universität, 1995), 9.

12. Mark Bassin, "Turner, Solov'ev, and the Frontier Hypothesis: The Nationalist Signification of Open Spaces," *Journal of Modern History* 65 (1993):
473–511; Hans-Dietrich Schultz, "Land-Volk-Staat: Der geographische Anteil
an der 'Erfindung' der Nation," *Geschichte in Wissenschaft und Unterricht* 51
(2000): 4–16.

13. Gerhard Hard, *Die "Landschaft" der Sprache und die "Landschaft" der
Geographen: Semantische und forschungslogische Studien zu einigen zentralen
Denkfiguren in der deutschen geographischen Literatur* (Bonn: Dümmler,
1970), 22f. This finding is based on mention of the word "landscape" in book
titles and academic papers listed in national bibliographies.

14. Rudolf Borchardt, *Der Deutsche in der Landschaft* (1925; repr., Frankfurt: Insel, 1999), 461. See also Friedmar Apel, *Deutscher Geist und deutsche
Landschaft: Eine Topographie* (Berlin: Siedler, 2000), 27. This essentialism is
increasingly challenged today as it becomes apparent that other nations incorporated ideas about landscape into their national discourses with little dis-
cernible difficulty. For England and the USA, see David Matless, *Landscape
and Englishness* (London: Reaktion Books, 1998); Stephen Daniels, *Fields of
Vision: Landscape Imagery and National Identity in England and the United
States* (Cambridge: Polity Press, 1993); and Richard Muir, *Approaches to
Landscape* (Lanham, MD: Barnes and Noble, 1999). For Italy, see Gabriele
Zanetto, Francesco Vallerani, and Stefano Soriani, *Nature, Environment, Land-
scape: European Attitudes and Discourses in the Modern Period; The Italian
Case, 1920–1970,* Quaderni del Dipartimento di Geografia 18 (Padova: Uni-
versità di Padova, 1996).

15. "The manner in which the soul reaches out into its world fashions the
geographical area of this world into a 'landscape.' A landscape is not something that the soul alights upon, as it were, something readymade. Rather, it
is something that it fashions by virtue of its species-determined way of viewing its environment." Ludwig Ferdinand Clauss, *Racial Soul, Landscape, and
World Domination* (originally *Die nordische Seele: Eine Einführung in die
Rassenseelenkunde,* 1932), as quoted in George L. Mosse, *Nazi Culture: Intellectual, Cultural, and Social Life in the Third Reich* (London: W. H. Allen,
1966), 65. While having provided some of the buzzwords for Nazi ideology,

Clauss secretly defied the racial politics of Nazi Germany. Peter Weingart, *Doppel-Leben: Ludwig Ferdinand Clauss zwischen Rassenforschung und Widerstand* (Frankfurt: Campus, 1995).

16. Paul Schultze-Naumburg, *Kulturarbeiten,* vols. 1–9 (Munich: Callwey, 1902–17). Volumes 7–9 deal with "Die Gestaltung der Landschaft durch den Menschen," the designing of landscapes by man. See also Norbert Borrmann, *Paul Schultze-Naumburg, 1869–1949: Maler—Publizist—Architekt* (Essen: Bacht, 1989); and John Alexander Williams, "'The Chords of the German Soul are Tuned to Nature': The Movement to Preserve the Natural *Heimat* from the Kaiserreich to the Third Reich," *Central European History* 29, no. 3 (1996): 339–84.

17. Winfried Nerdinger, ed., *Architekturschule München, 1868–1993: 125 Jahre TU München* (Munich: Klinkhardt und Biermann, 1993).

18. Gröning and Wolschke-Bulmahn, *Grüne Biographien,* 5–8; Ulrich Eisel and Stefanie Schultz, ed., *Geschichte und Struktur der Landschaftsplanung* (Berlin: Technische Universität, 1991).

19. Verband Deutscher Gartenarchitekten, to its members, 14 April 1930, ASP, folder 215. For anthroposophical farming, see the preceding chapter.

20. See William H. Rollins, *A Greener Vision of Home: Cultural Politics and Environmental Reform in the German* Heimatschutz *Movement, 1904–1918* (Ann Arbor: University of Michigan Press, 1997).

21. Tag für Denkmalpflege und Heimatschutz, Geschaftsführender Ausschuß, to Todt, 31 August 1933, Bundesarchiv Potsdam (hereafter BAP), 46.01/1486. Todt to Tag für Denkmalpflege und Heimatschutz, 1 September 1933, BAP, 46.01/1486. On the overall enthusiasm of conservationists after the Nazi seizure of power, see Raymond H. Dominick, *The Environmental Movement in Germany: Prophets and Pioneers, 1871–1980* (Bloomington: Indiana University Press, 1992).

22. *Denkmalpflege und Heimatschutz im Wiederaufbau der Nation: Tag für Denkmalpflege und Heimatschutz im Rahmen des ersten Reichstreffens des Reichsbundes Volkstum und Heimat, Kassel 1933* (Berlin: Deutscher Kunstverlag, 1934), 84–89, quotes 84.

23. Seifert to Todt, 18 November 1933, BAP, 46.01/1487.

24. Seifert, "Aufgaben der öffentlichen Hand zur Landschaftsgestaltung," enclosure to letter, 18 November 1933, BAP, 46.01/1487.

25. Todt to Seifert, 23 November 1933, Deutsches Museum, Munich, Archives (hereafter DMA), NL 133/56.

26. For one of the U.S. parkways of the period, see Timothy Davis, "Mount Vernon Memorial Highway: Changing Conceptions of an American

Commemorative Landscape," in *Places of Commemoration: Search for Identity and Landscape Design*, ed. Joachim Wolschke-Bulmahn (Washington, DC: Dumbarton Oaks, 2001), 123–77.

27. Thomas Zeller, "'The Landscape's Crown': Landscape, Perceptions, and Modernizing Effects of the German *Autobahn* System, 1934–1941," in *Technologies of Landscape: Reaping to Recycling*, ed. David Nye (Amherst: University of Massachusetts Press, 1999), 218–38; Zeller, *Straße, Bahn, Panorama: Verkehrswege und Landschaftsveränderung in Deutschland 1930 bis 1990* (Frankfurt: Campus, 2002), 41–209. For autobahn propaganda, see Erhard Schütz and Eckhard Gruber, *Mythos Reichsautobahn: Bau und Inszenierung der "Straßen des Führers," 1933–1941* (Berlin: Christoph Links, 1996).

28. For theories of visual consumption, see John Urry, *The Tourist Gaze* (London: Sage, 1991); and Urry, *Consuming Places* (London: Routledge, 1995).

29. Seifert, *Leben*, 89.

30. For a discussion of the main ecological theories of that era (most of which were advanced by Anglo-American botanists), see Ronald C. Tobey, *Saving the Prairies: The Life Cycle of the Founding School of American Plant Ecology* (Berkeley: University of California Press, 1981).

31. Alwin Seifert, "Von bodenständiger Gartenkunst," in *Im Zeitalter des Lebendigen: Natur—Heimat—Technik* (Planegg: Langen Müller, 1942), 198.

32. For a different interpretation stressing the ideological similarities between Seifert and the regime at large, see Gert Gröning and Joachim Wolschke-Bulmahn, "Some Notes on the Mania for Native Plants in Germany," *Landscape Journal* 11, no. 2 (1992): 116–26.

33. "Vorläufige Richtlinien über die Bepflanzung der Kraftfahrbahnen auf Grund der Besprechung beim Generalinspektor vom 11.11.1936," ASP, 116.

34. Todt to Mayor Kurz, Pforzheim, 16 October 1935, BAP, 46.01/135.

35. Seifert to Lindner, 23 May 1932, ASP, 5; Lindner to Seifert, 11 June 1932, ASP, 5; Seifert to Lindner, 16 October 1932, ASP, 5.

36. Helmut Maier, "Nationalsozialistische Technikideologie und die Politisierung des 'Technikerstandes': Fritz Todt und die Zeitschrift 'Deutsche Technik,'" in *Technische Intelligenz und "Kulturfaktor Technik": Kulturvorstellungen von Technikern und Ingenieuren zwischen Kaiserreich und früher Bundesrepublik Deutschland*, ed. Burkhard Dietz, Michael Fessner, and Helmut Maier (Münster: Waxmann, 1996), 253–68.

37. Alwin Seifert, "Die Versteppung Deutschlands," *Deutsche Technik* 4 (1936): 423–27, 490–92. Todt authorized the publication of 7,000 offprints documenting Seifert's attack, engineers' reactions, and Todt's "final" statement: *Die Versteppung Deutschlands? (Kulturwasserbau und Heimatschutz): Sonderdruck*

mit Aufsätzen aus der Zeitschrift "Deutsche Technik" (Berlin: Weicher, [1938]). Also, see Alwin Seifert, "Die Versteppung Deutschlands," in *Zeitalter*, 24–51.
    38. Seifert, *Zeitalter*, 24–25.
    39. Paul B. Sears, *Deserts on the March* (Norman: University of Oklahoma Press, 1935). Seifert cited Harlow Stafford Person, *Little Waters: A Study of Headwater Streams and Other Little Waters, Their Use and Relations to the Land* (Washington, DC: United States Government Printing Office, 1936). This booklet published by the U.S. Soil Conservation Service broadly confirms Seifert's assessment with a statement by Aldo Leopold: "I have just returned from Germany, and I am much impressed by the almost nation-wide error which has been made there in straightening small streams" (27). See also Donald Worster, *Dust Bowl: The Southern Plains in the 1930s* (Oxford: Oxford University Press, 1979).
    40. The architect Schultze-Naumburg had reached similar conclusions years before Seifert did—but with aesthetic, not ecological, arguments. Paul Schultze-Naumburg, *Die Gestaltung der Landschaft durch den Menschen*, 3rd ed. (Munich: Callwey, 1928), 109–19.
    41. Seifert, *Zeitalter*, 34.
    42. Darré to Todt, 14 January 1937, BAP, 46.01/864.
    43. See Gesine Gerhard's paper in this volume and Gunter Vogt, *Entstehung und Entwicklung des ökologischen Landbaus im deutschsprachigen Raum* (Bad Dürkheim: Stiftung Ökologie und Landbau, 2000), 136–42.
    44. Todt to Darré, 27 February 1937, BAP, 46.01/864. Seifert had known Hess since 1919, when they met in a "small völkisch club" in Munich. Seifert to Hauptdienstleiter Saur, Reichsministerium Speer, 21 September 1943, 4, Amtsgericht Munich, Denazification Files Alwin Seifert, (hereafter AGM), Amt für Technik.
    45. Todt to Seifert, 1 March 1938, ASP, 33; Fritz Todt, "Abschließende Stellungnahme zu den verschiedensten Erörterungen über die Gefahren einer Versteppung Deutschlands," *Versteppung Deutschlands?* 1–3. In 1940, Seifert launched a campaign against sewage farming: *Über die landwirtschaftliche Verwertung städtischer Abwässer: Ein Meinungsaustausch zahlreicher Fachlente angeregt von Alwin Seifert* (Berlin: Franckh, 1942).
    46. Seifert to the landscape advocates, 27 September 1934, ASP, 116; Todt to Reichsarbeitsführer Hierl, 8 April 1935, BAP, 46.01/1487.
    47. Schwarz to Meyer-Jungclaussen, 12 July 1934, ASP, 150.
    48. Max K. Schwarz, *Bericht über meine einjährige Tätigkeit als Landschaftsanwalt bei den Gauleitungen des Reichsarbeitsdienstes: 17, in Bremen–18, in Hannover–19, in Oldenburg*, 16 June 1936, BAP, 46.01/862.

49. Seifert to Todt, 20 July 1936, BAP, 46.01/862. See also Kiran Klaus Patel, *"Soldaten der Arbeit": Arbeitsdienste in Deutschland und den USA, 1933–1945* (Göttingen: Vandenhoeck & Ruprecht, 2003) 319.

50. Seifert to Generalinspektor Schulze, 7 July 1937, BAP, 46.01/138; Seifert to Hirsch, 16 February 1940, ASP, 131. Seifert also designed a greenhouse for Hitler's mountain retreat on the Obersalzberg near Berchtesgaden, helped to find a gardener for the property, and ensured delivery of organic vegetables: Seifert to Siegloch, 5 April 1935 and 23 April 1937; Siegloch to Seifert, 20 April 1937 and 16 October 1937, all ASP, 153.

51. Circular, 12 August 1940, 2, ASP, 117.

52. Uwe Werner, *Anthroposophen in der Zeit des Nationalsozialismus (1933–1945)* (Munich: Oldenbourg, 1999), 88–9, 268–70; Vogt, *Entstehung*, 145–47; Institut für Zeitgeschichte, Munich (hereafter IfZ), ED 32 (Correspondence Seifert-Hess).

53. Franz W. Seidler, *Fritz Todt: Baumeister des Dritten Reiches* (Frankfurt: Ullstein, 1988).

54. Seifert to Hess, 18 September 1934, IfZ, ED 32, fol. 111; Seifert to Hess, 7 December 1937, IfZ, ED 32, fol. 75.

55. Seifert, "Rundschreiben an die Landschaftsanwälte bei den Reichsautobahnen," 12 April 1940, ASP, 117. During the war economy, their expertise became increasingly peripheral. Seifert, "Wasserkraftbau gestern und morgen," Appendix 1 to circular, 5 February 1944, 1–9, ASP, 117.

56. Karl-Heinz Ludwig, *Technik und Ingenieure im Dritten Reich* (Königstein: Athenäum, 1979), 179–82; Maria Magdalena Koller, *Elektrizitätswirtschaft in Österreich 1938–1947: Von den Alpenelektrowerken zur Verbundgesellschaft* (PhD diss., Karl-Franzens-Universität Graz, 1985); Roman Sandgruber, *Strom der Zeit: Das Jahrhundert der Elektrizität* (Linz: Veritas, 1992), 212–19.

57. Seifert an Hess, 1.6.1936, IfZ, ED 32, fol. 58.

58. Helmut Maier, "'Unter Wasser und unter die Erde': Die Westtiroler Wasserkraftprojekte des Rheinisch-Westfälischen Elektrizitätswerks (RWE) und der Natur- und Landschaftsschutz während des Dritten Reiches," in *Die Veränderung der Kulturlandschaft*, ed. Günter Bayerl and Torsten Meyer (Münster: Waxmann, 2003), 139–75.

59. Koller, *Elektrizitätswirtschaft*, 101, 114–15, 205–6; Sandgruber, *Strom*, 213, 221; Ludwig, *Technik*, 180–81; Seidler, *Todt*, 273.

60. Klose to Emeis, Flensburg, 18 June 1942, Bundesarchiv Koblenz (hereafter BAK), B 245/232, fol. 47. For nature protection, see the papers by Charles Closmann and Thomas Lekan in this volume and Michael Wettengel, "Staat und Naturschutz 1906–1945: Zur Geschichte der Staatlichen Stelle

für Naturdenkmalpflege in Preußen und der Reichsstelle für Naturschutz," *Historische Zeitschrift* 257, no. 2 (1993): 355–99.

61. "Aktenvermerk betr. Landschaftsgestaltung," 23 December 1935 [no author given], BAP, 46.01/861; Schoenichen to Reichsforstmeister, 14 April 1937, BAK, B 245/170, fols. 395–401.

62. Circular, 30 January 1940, 4–5, ASP, 117; Circular, 3 March 1940, 3 ("raiding party"), 10–15, ASP, 117; "Kritische Betrachtungen zu den Rundbriefen, Anhang 9 zum Rundbrief," December 1942, 1–7, ASP, 118; Circular, 8 December 1941, 1, ASP, 119.

63. Mechtild Rössler and Sabine Schleiermacher, eds., *Der Generalplan Ost: Aspekte der nationalsozialistischen Planungs- und Vernichtungspolitik* (Berlin: Akademie-Verlag, 1993); Bruno Wasser, *Himmlers Raumplanung im Osten: Der Generalplan Ost in Polen, 1940–1944* (Basel: Birkhäuser, 1993); Gert Gröning and Joachim Wolschke-Bulmann, *Die Liebe zur Landschaft. Teil III: Der Drang nach Osten: Zur Entwicklung der Landespflege im Nationalsozialismus und während des Zweiten Weltkrieges in den "eingegliederten Ostgebieten"* (Munich: Minerva, 1987); Alwin Seifert, *Die Heckenlandschaft* (Berlin: Stichnote, 1944).

64. See the chapter by Joachim Wolschke-Bulmahn in this volume and Gröning and Wolschke-Bulmahn, *Drang*, 196–97. Seifert claimed that Himmler had promised a redesigning of the entire East according to his ideas "after the war," but handed down the task to his colleague Guido Erxleben. Seifert to Erxleben, 16 May 1940, ASP, 126. In his most outspoken display of (more than merely tactical) racism, Seifert competed with Wiepking over who would be the more ardent Antisemite: Thomas Zeller, "'Ich habe die Juden möglichst gemieden': Ein aufschlußreicher Briefwechsel zwischen Heinrich Wiepking und Alwin Seifert," *Garten+Landschaft: Zeitschrift für Landschaftsarchitektur*, no. 8 (August 1995): 4–5.

65. Seifert claimed he was too busy working on roads to work on camouflage projects. Todt to Hirsch, 23 September 1940, BAK, NS 26/1188; Seifert to Hirsch, 14 January 1940, ASP, 131; "Erfahrungen bei großen landschaftlichen Tarnungsaufgaben," Circular, 12 August 1940, 3–5, ASP, 117.

66. Himmler invited Seifert to inspect the experiments after he had received some of Seifert's publications. Reichsführer SS to Seifert, 12 August 1942 (copy), AGM Reichsführer SS Himmler.

67. Martin Broszat, ed., *Rudolf Höß: Kommandant in Auschwitz*, 13th ed. (Munich: Deutscher Taschenbuch Verlag, 1992), 178; Sybille Steinbacher, *"Musterstadt" Auschwitz: Germanisierungspolitik und Judenmord in Oberschlesien* (Munich: Saur, 2000), 246–47.

68. Anna Zieba, "Das Nebenlager Rajsko," *Hefte von Auschwitz* 9 (1966): 75–108; Military Government, Dr. Reuter, to the prosecuting attorney, Spruchkammer VII München, 21 August 1947, 3, AGM Akten der Spruchkammer München VII.

69. Gertrud Raila to Hauptspruchkammer München, 14 March 1949, AGM Akten der Spruchkammer München VII. For the herb garden, see Werner, *Anthroposophen,* 330–34; and Robert Sigel, "Heilkräuterkulturen im KZ: Die Plantage in Dachau," *Dachauer Hefte: Studien und Dokumente zur Geschichte der nationalsozialistischen Konzentrationslager* 4, no. 4 (1988): 164–73. While Werner seems to be convinced of the relatively benign treatment of the 800 to 1,200 prisoners there, Sigel speaks of "brutal" working conditions.

70. Werner, *Anthroposophen,* 334; Seifert to Pohl, 27 September 1944, AGM Reichsführer SS Himmler. Pohl was head of the "SS-Wirtschafts- und Verwaltungshauptamt," which oversaw the Dachau herb gardens, among many other enterprises.

71. "Eignungsbericht," 18 March 1943, Berlin Document Center, Research Alwin Seifert, 6.

72. "Aktenvermerk," Dr. Fuchs, Generalinspektor für das deutsche Straßenwesen, 15 January 1942 (copy), Bayerisches Hauptstaatsarchiv Munich, MK 58957.

73. Roderich Fick, Reichsbaurat Linz, to Streck, Dekan der Fakultät für Bauwesen, 4 May 1942, Bayerisches Hauptstaatsarchiv Munich, MK 58957.

74. Vormerkung, 8 March 1943; Vormerkung, 24 July 1943; Bormann to Fick, 27 June 1944 (copy); all Bayerisches Hauptstaatsarchiv Munich, MK 58957.

75. Seifert to the chair, Spruchkammer VII München, 8 April 1947, 20, AGM, VII 3702, Prof. Alwin Seifert. He called himself *getreuer Eckhart,* which alludes to the sage figure in the Tannhäuser myth who warned erring humans not to enter the tempting Mountain of Venus. Evidently, Seifert deemed himself to be the guardian of the German landscape, warning humans not to fall for the trappings of modernization—a position as lofty as his former role in Nazi Germany.

76. Seifert to the chair, 21, AGM, VII 3702.

77. In 1947, Seifert contacted the United States Soil Conservation Service and offered his services. Apparently, one of the Soil Conservation Service officers had visited him in 1939. Eight years later, Seifert presented himself as an apolitical conservationist with appropriate expertise. Seifert to Soil Conservation Service, 19 November 1947, ASP, 490.

78. Alwin Seifert, *Gärtnern, Ackern—ohne Gift* (Munich: Beck, 1991).

CHAPTER 7

Martin Heidegger, National Socialism, and Environmentalism

Thomas Rohkrämer

Over the last decade, researchers have discovered an increasing amount of evidence for the important role that academic professions played in the Third Reich. Many experts did not wait to be approached by the Nazis, but saw the new regime as an opportunity to realize their own goals. A large majority were attracted to Nazism or viewed it from a pragmatic career perspective. They approached the new power-holders to push competitors to the side, to gain access to more financial support, and to use a ruthless regime to overcome any hindrance to their own professional goals.

Association with National Socialism was also widespread among philosophers. While twenty philosophy professors were forced out of their positions, about thirty joined the Nazi Party in 1933 and almost half became party members by 1940. Moreover, it was not only, as many have assumed, "life philosophers" or radical Nietzscheans who supported the Nazis; the rival schools of neo-Kantians or "value philosophers" also had adherents who made the same political decision for very different reasons. Hans Sluga rightly draws our attention to the fact that "Heidegger's action was not unique. . . . We discover that other philosophers were involved for a longer time; that others were involved more deeply; that, unlike Heidegger, others had worked on philosophical ideas during the

Weimar period that clearly foreshadowed the new political ideology; and that others, unlike Heidegger, were willing after 1933 to adjust their philosophical thinking to political exigencies." The variety of often incompatible reasons, Sluga argues, "undermines the idea that there was a specific link between Heidegger's particular philosophy and National Socialism."[1]

While the political mistakes of others do not alter Heidegger's responsibility for his Nazism, they raise the question whether so many publications should focus on it. Even if Heidegger's detractors might have been frequently motivated, as he himself claimed, by the attempt to place a taboo on his uncompromising critique of modernity, the topic of Heidegger's Nazism surely deserves the attention it has received: while other Nazi philosophers have largely been forgotten, Heidegger has continued to exert a tremendous influence inside and outside his profession. Most relevant to us is that environmental thought increasingly draws on his work. Is a legacy of National Socialism thus unwittingly carried into the environmental movement? Or is Heidegger's environmental thought untainted by his involvement in the Third Reich? To answer this, I will discuss (1) Heidegger's reasons for becoming a Nazi and for his growing disillusionment, and (2) the reasons for his growing concern with questions connected with environmentalism. While there are obvious continuities in his work, I shall argue that his later writings, the part of his work most deeply connected with environmentalism, draw decisive lessons from his failed attempt at changing the course of history at the beginning of the Third Reich.

Heidegger and National Socialism

"Martin Heidegger? A Nazi, of course a Nazi!" On a purely factual level, this exclamation by Jürgen Habermas is fully correct.[2] Contrary to what Heidegger and Heideggerians have long maintained, historical research has demonstrated beyond doubt Heidegger's early enthusiasm for National Socialism.[3] Heidegger sympathized with the Nazis before 1933, he actively maneuvered to become rector, he publicly joined the Nazi Party on May Day, and the ceremony around his Rectoral Address included Nazi flags and the singing of the "Horst Wessel Song." While Jews and political opponents were removed from the university (like his teacher Edmund Husserl) or even forced to flee the country (like his intimate friend Hannah Arendt), Heidegger showed his enthusiastic support for the destruction of the Weimar Republic and for the new regime. He praised the

Führer principle for the university sector, while striving to attain such a position for himself. In speeches and newspaper articles he identified himself with Hitler's rule, going so far as to state in autumn 1933 that "the Führer himself and alone is and will be Germany's only reality and its law."[4] He not only approved in principle of the Nazi cleansing, but also tried to use the new regime to destroy the academic careers of colleagues, for example by initiating a Gestapo investigation.

Heidegger's initial enthusiasm soon waned. He decided to end his rectorship in spring 1934 and withdrew from all political involvement. Already in the lecture "An Introduction to Metaphysics," delivered in the summer term 1935, he voiced his critique of the bureaucratic management of the race of a *Volk,* and in his Nietzsche lectures (1936–40) he became increasingly critical of a modern will to power that, he believed, was behind the actions of all leading nations including Germany. Despite this, Heidegger's claim that he had opposed the regime since 1934 is not correct. He never left the Nazi Party, and his lectures were always accompanied by a Nazi salute. When he met his former student Karl Löwith, who (as a Jew) had fled Germany in 1936, he wore his party badge, reaffirmed his conviction that "National Socialism was the proper course for Germany," and agreed with Löwith's suggestion that his political conviction was based on his philosophy.[5] Passages from his war lectures show that, while seeing the whole war as a tragedy, he still sided with Germany.[6] While it is true that party spies listened in on his lectures and that attempts were made to stop the publication of one of his articles, this does not mean that the regime regarded him as an opponent. Rather, the Nazi movement was characterized by endless infighting: the philosophers Ernst Krieck (Heidegger's former ally in university politics) and Arthur Rosenberg tried to gather material to weaken the influence of a philosopher who was still regarded as a major player.[7]

Heidegger was an enthusiastic Nazi, at first. While his version of Nazism was not the ideology that won out in the Third Reich, the regime was well served by the initial support of a leading philosopher. From 1934 on, however, Heidegger's distance from the regime began to grow. It is difficult to put dates to this gradual process,[8] but Löwith's report strongly suggests that he still saw himself as a Nazi in 1936, despite disagreements on fundamental policy issues. By the time he delivered the Nietzsche lectures, the distance had grown to the extent that Heidegger should no longer be regarded as a Nazi, although to the end of his life he continued to hold two opinions which suggest that he never quite realized the unique dimension of the Nazi atrocities: he always failed to differentiate between Nazism and other forms of modern society in his sharp critique of the modern world; and he never questioned his chauvinistic belief that Germany was the most metaphysical nation, from which a positive historical turn was most likely to emerge. Lastly, Heidegger was typical of the widespread German reluctance to acknowledge personal responsibility for Nazism: in his statement immediately after the Third Reich about his rectorship, he still maintained that it had been better to try to exert a positive influence on National Socialism rather than stand aside.[9] He continued to play down the historical significance of his actions, and he tried to excuse his political error by pointing at the misjudgments of others.

What motivated Heidegger's political error?[10] Most fundamentally, Heidegger diagnosed an existential crisis of modernity and believed that the Nazi "awakening" offered the best chance for overcoming it. Heidegger shared Nietzsche's opinion that we live in an age of nihilism. For him, God was dead in the sense that there was no communal religion powerful enough to shape history. The horrors of the First World War, where all belligerent powers used God to legitimate their actions, showed that Christianity had lost its force to shape history; no metaphysical beliefs were left to guide humans in their communal existence. Humanity was largely lost in inauthentic everyday norms and attitudes instead of committing itself to a meaningful destiny, society was drifting apart because it lacked a sense of community based on shared beliefs, and academia had lost a common purpose in an age of specialization and vocational training.

Being and Time, Heidegger's main work of the Weimar period, outlined ways toward an authentic existence for the individual self, although it also touched on the concepts of heritage, historicity, and collective destiny. It called for the "cool conduct"[11] of resoluteness in honestly facing the realities of human existence: that we are thrown into a world; that choices we make are of essential importance because our life is limited in time (if we waste time on trivialities we can never regain it); and that we should aim for a life in accordance with our own destiny instead of living in accordance with *das Man,* that is, "the one," or "general opinion." The act of reflecting on the essence of human existence and on the relevance of our communal heritage was put forward as the way to question the platitudes of everyday life and to lead a more authentic existence.

This call for a conscious acceptance of the human condition in order to achieve an authentic individual existence continued throughout Heidegger's work. In the Weimar period, however, and especially in the crisis of the early 1930s, Heidegger was also increasingly influenced by the radical right.[12] He shared their contempt for constitutionalism, human rights, and democracy, favoring instead an emphasis on the well-being of the national community, rule by an elite, and the need for a Führer—which goes a long way toward explaining his agreement with the Nazi policy of brutal coordination.[13] He diagnosed a disintegration of society and feared a Marxist revolution, thinking that only the Nazis offered a viable alternative. He believed in their will to resolve class conflict by creating a true community of the people, he shared their commitment to overcoming the Versailles Treaty, and he hoped that they could give Germans a common destiny.[14] More generally, the many problems at the end of the Weimar Republic, combined with his general sense of an existential crisis of modernity on the one hand, and the belief in the chance for a national awakening through Nazism on the other, explain his belief that Germans faced a stark alternative: either be part of the general collapse of an allegedly nihilistic Western "moribund pseudocivilization" into "confusion" and suffocating "madness," or find a peculiarly German historic mission in which "we [Germans] as a historical-spiritual Volk will ourselves, still and again."[15]

After the Nazis gained power, Heidegger shared in the widespread sense of "the glory and greatness of this new beginning."[16] Associating contemporary events with the alleged enthusiasm of August 1914,[17] Heidegger felt that Germans were at last pulling together again under a communal will. While previously an "authentic existence" had mainly meant for him that *individuals* should work toward a resolute commitment to consciously accepted convictions, the term was now used as a call for supporting the new regime. "Authentic existence" came to mean a complete identification with the destiny of the German people as expressed by Hitler. This is why Heidegger could claim that the Führer was, as quoted above, "Germany's only reality and its law."[18]

Heidegger's political affinities with the radical right meant that he sympathized with many of the initial Nazi policies. He accepted the alleged need to destroy communism and weaken the Jewish influence.[19] He favored moves toward more social justice like the new labor service.[20] All service to the nation should be honored, Germany should find unity and greatness as a people in labor.[21] At the same time, Heidegger also shared the Nazi belief that social justice and respect for manual work should go hand in hand with a clear hierarchy according to "worth and achievement": "Only loyal obedience (*Gefolgschaft*) creates community."[22]

In unison with the extreme right and the Nazis, Heidegger celebrated the fallen soldiers of the First World War, calling for a commitment to the cause for which they had given their lives. He seems to have believed the propaganda line used to justify the rearmament program: we wish to live in peace with other nations, but demand full equality (that is, an end to the restrictions imposed by the Treaty of Versailles), and we aim for the integration of all ethnic Germans into the Reich. Rejecting "rootless and powerless thought," he praised "the struggle as the great test of all being, in which it is decided whether, in our own eyes, we are slaves or masters."[23]

In this period, Heidegger's texts are loaded with martial terminology. He called the students' life in the Third Reich a bloodless Langemarck,[24] because they would serve the nation in work service and the *Sturmabteilung* (SA).[25] He described the striving for an authentic existence as a dangerous battle, and he even perceived the human need to make sense of the world (for example by naming objects) as an act of risk and danger, violence and aggression. While one has to be cautious about reading a literally aggressive intent into the words (after all, it was a favorite pastime of Heidegger's to infuse new meanings into everyday words), the texts certainly show that Heidegger wanted to link the philosopher's work to that of the glorified soldier. Furthermore, he explicitly identified a struggle for survival in his lectures in summer 1935, in which Germans were called upon to decide the fate of the whole Occident by fighting Marxism and Americanism. "This Europe, in its ruinous blindness forever on the point of cutting its own throat, lies today in a great pincers squeezed between Russia on one side and America on the other. From a metaphysical point of view America and Russia are the same; the same dreary technological frenzy, the same unrestricted organization of the average man." Germany, as the nation in the center, allegedly suffered most under this pressure, but as "the most metaphysical of nations," "new spiritual energies" were also most likely to emerge from there.[26] Heidegger not only shared the long-standing determination of cultural criticism to fight "Americanism" in German culture, but even believed that only German thought could save the world. His utopian dream was thus equated with a global supremacy of German culture.

The critique of a "dreary technological frenzy" in the previous quotation leads to a question central to our topic: was Heidegger antimodern, and, if so, did his antimodernism attract him to National Socialism? Julian Young, for one, is highly critical on this point. While he, unlike some historians, rightly accepts that some versions of antimodernism are peaceful and harmless,[27] he claims that Heidegger intended "the 'Pol Pot' solution to the problem of modernism," that is, expansion into the East and displacement of the native population to create space for German settlement. In trying to realize his antimodern ideals, Heidegger allegedly advocated a criminal policy to break up cities and establish a traditional rural community for the German Volk.[28]

There can be no doubt that Heidegger had many romantic notions. Cultivating his rural artisan background, he idealized traditional peasant and artisan culture. In rejecting a professorship at Friedrich Wilhelm University in Berlin, he stressed that he had to stay in the province, as his thinking was deeply connected with the Black Forest.[29] He liked to retreat to his remote mountain hut for periods of study. His dress and style were inspired by the rather romantic youth movement, and he even organized a summer camp for students and colleagues in autumn 1933. Whenever he used positive examples of work or architecture, they were drawn from a traditional background. He was clearly in line with the German association Bund Heimatschutz, which tried to preserve the character of the traditional landscape, regional architecture, and old customs. Like many other German writers, he tended to judge cities negatively and glorify agriculture.[30]

The case, however, for regarding Heidegger as an *aggressive* antimodernist rests on a passage in a speech given in 1934 to men in the labor service, in which Heidegger listed a number of points allegedly essential for every German to know. Two of them were "to know to what point urbanization has brought the German people [and] how it should be brought back to soil and country through resettlement," and "[t]o know what is entailed by the fact that eighteen million Germans belong to the Volk but, because they are living outside the borders of the Reich, all the same do not belong to the Reich."[31] Julian Young reads the critique of urbanization as the authoritarian will to settle all Germans as farmers in rural areas and the second sentence as the will to violent expansion in order to create space for this resettlement program.

This interpretation goes too far and ignores the historical context. While the pan-German wish for all Germans to be part of the Reich was undoubtedly dangerously revisionist (although Heidegger did not say how such a greater German Reich could be achieved), it should not be confused with the quest for living space in the East: Heidegger did not call for the occupation and ethnic cleansing of space for the settlement of Germans, but shared the widespread belief that all ethnic Germans should be part of the Third Reich. His speeches on the German decision to leave the League of Nations further confirm that he wanted a strong Germany, whose allegedly legitimate claims had been satisfied, to live in harmony with its neighbors.[32] Also, the idea of a certain decentralization within Germany through rural settlements was not an idea peculiar to the Nazis; it was shared, for example, by the Brüning government, by the German engineers' association, and by members of the conservative resistance to Hitler. It did not necessarily imply the will to retreat into a rural past, but was usually aimed at finding a "better" balance between agriculture and industry and improving the living quality of workers. At the time, different groups and experts still believed that the land for this could be gained within Germany, through breaking up big estates in the eastern provinces and through cultivating wasteland.[33]

Also, an idealization of the past does not necessarily imply an intention to turn back the clock. Contrary to the claims of many historians, most voices seriously engaged in a critique of modernity in Germany since the 1880s were not those of Luddites. Many were nostalgic or tried to save aspects of the past, but their concepts for the future aimed at an alternative modernity as they tried to integrate positive features of the past into the framework of an industrially and technically advanced society.[34] Likewise, in a later publication, Heidegger explicitly stated that the use of a farmhouse as an exemplary building does not imply that all houses should be built that way, but should show how another time had a superior sense of dwelling and architecture.[35] His later work explicitly faced the difficult (and, I believe, necessary) balancing act between criticizing technology and realizing that there is no escape from it. In the early years of the Third Reich, however, he had not thought deeply about these questions; as a consequence, he probably adopted an ideal of the time without thinking through all its implications. A rather conventional romanticism, combined with his skepticism of modern society, probably made the "blood and soil" propaganda attractive to him, though he never made this a central point. Like the early environmental movement and related life-reform movements at the turn of the century, he favored a more natural lifestyle in harmony with the regional landscape for all Germans, supported at one point the ideal of a "German technology" in harmony with nature, and hinted that technology should not be a goal in itself, but incorporated within the vision of a destiny of the German Volk.[36] But all this remained peripheral and superficial in the early 1930s.

As we shall see later, it was only as a consequence of his disappointment with Nazism that the question of technology and environmentalism became central to Heidegger's thinking. In 1933, the green element in Nazi ideology was only one among many points that attracted Heidegger to National Socialism. What fascinated him most was not any particular ideological component (though, as described, he sympathized with many of them), but the feeling of a national awakening. Heidegger came from a strongly Catholic background and first studied theology in anticipation of becoming a priest. He later came to criticize Catholicism, because dogmatism seemed to have replaced personally felt convictions and an unreserved inquiry into the truth of Being. His disillusionment with Catholicism, however, did not mean that he lost a religious attitude. On the contrary: like many people of his time,[37] he remained, to put it in a nutshell, a religious man in search of a religion, and even in search of a religious age. Instead of powerless beliefs, dogmatism, or mere personal conviction, he desired strong collective religious feeling with the power to shape history. For a while, he believed that the Third Reich fulfilled this vision. Again and again he thus stressed that it was not the changed material reality that was decisive, but the commitment to a common German destiny embodied in Hitler. All Germans, he believed, should commit to this destiny and thus find an "authentic existence" collectively. He likened the Third Reich with his idealized vision of early Greece, where the perceptions of the whole community had allegedly been determined by their true poets, thinkers, and statesmen.[38]

From the beginning, Heidegger recognized negative aspects of the Third Reich, but, as he claimed in a letter of 4 May 1933, he was convinced that one should ignore "the lower and unpleasant things" and judge the movement instead "by its Führer and his great goals."[39] The belief that National Socialism could overcome the relativizing plurality of world views by forging the population into a coherent whole was so important to him that he never stopped to ask whether such a brutal authoritarian forging was legitimate and would not produce, in many cases, outward loyalty rather than true conviction. His utopia was the unanimous belief in *one* German destiny, or, in other words, a "*völkisch* totalitarianism."[40] If the Nazi world view was not all to his liking, he could live with this for a while, because he believed that Plato's vision of the philosopher as policy-making adviser to the ruler would now become reality. In a combination of naivety and delusion of grandeur, he was temporarily convinced that he himself would be *the* philosopher who would lead the Führer into realizing a Volk united in one belief. This conviction was supposed to draw on the purest Greek and German traditions and be religious in the best sense of the word. It would, he believed, overcome the deepest crisis of modernity, that is, nihilism.

Heidegger fell for the fatal attraction of National Socialism because he, like many other individuals and social groups with quite different orientations, believed that the Third Reich would offer an ideal chance to realize his own utopia of a people united in one völkisch belief. With such high hopes, Heidegger was in for a big disappointment. First he came to realize that he would not exercise significant influence over National Socialism as a whole or even within Freiburg University. As early as spring 1934, Heidegger resigned as rector, and within the year he had withdrawn from all political involvement. In a lecture at the end of 1934 he generalized his political failure by claiming that all true philosophy is "essentially untimely" and could "never find an immediate resonance in its own time."[41] In his university lectures in the summer of 1935, Heidegger also began to criticize aspects of National Socialism. His initial enthusiasm was replaced by his more customary sense of crisis and decline, and he criticized the use of intelligence as a mere tool. Instead of thinking in order to discover truth, he argued, such intelligence only tries to achieve material advantages. Not only the Marxist's alleged focus on production served as an example, but also "the organization and regulation of a nation's vital resources and race." Furthermore, he called it a sign of nihilism "when mass meetings attended by millions are looked on as triumph." He still expressed his belief in the "inner truth and greatness" of Nazism, but had become skeptical of a unity orchestrated by the state. He wanted a spiritual awakening, not a eugenic strategy to improve the race. Instead of a search for practical solutions, he stressed the need for philosophical reflection.[42]

The last point marked a line of conflict that became increasingly obvious. While the Nazis called for a politicized science serving the goals of the Third Reich, Heidegger postulated a much more ambitious role for the university and art. Poets and thinkers were supposed to identify and express the destiny of the people, not serve a destiny laid down by politicians. Philosophy was supposed to reflect on existence, not define convenient norms. Thus, by the summer of 1935, Heidegger attacked other Nazi philosophers, and with time he became increasingly outspoken against an attitude that took thinking to be just another weapon in worldly struggles.[43]

Heidegger's most comprehensive criticism, however, expressed most sharply in the Nietzsche lectures from 1936 to 1940, was his analysis of the will to power. Especially in the later lectures, Nietzsche was presented as *the* Nazi philosopher and the will to power as *the* core of the Third Reich. For Heidegger, the will to shape the world according to the human will gradually became the most dangerous aberration: it was hubris to believe that humans could perfect the world, and this hubris led to a belief that regarded everything as a resource for the will. Humans became blind to the intrinsic value of things because they could only see them as means to an end. The world, including fellow human beings and even one's own self, became nothing but raw material for the endless ambition of a nihilistic will.[44]

While Nietzsche saw the will to power as the most fundamental human drive, Heidegger set out to historicize it in "The Age of the World Picture" (1938). The will to power and domination became the central feature of the modern age. This claim, however, fits better with Heidegger's "environmentalism," which will be discussed in the next section. At this point it suffices to note that the critique of the will to power and the modern delusion of grandeur was also implicit self-criticism. After all, Heidegger himself had exhibited Promethean ambitions in 1933–34, with his belief that he, as a Platonian philosopher to the statesman Hitler, could bring about the end of nihilism; after this had failed, it was necessary to draw philosophical lessons. As a Nazi official, he had been able to draw on activist concepts like "resoluteness" from *Being and Time,* but this work, together with the shorter *Essence of Truth* (1930), also offered ideas Heidegger could use for a reorientation. Elements of *Being and Time* made humans appear to be free agents (these were later stressed in French Existentialism), but it also contained concepts like "thrownness" (into a historical heritage) which suggested that humans do not chose their own destiny. After some wavering, these latter concepts became decisive for Heidegger from 1936 onwards.

Heidegger was no hero: to the end, he remained a member of the Nazi Party and outwardly loyal. In his thought, however, he broke with the Third Reich. Nazism is highly amorphous, but a voluntaristic "cult of the will" is clearly a necessary part of its ideology. Nazism was committed to the belief that will and force could achieve a national awakening, a renaissance of German strength, and a victory in the eternal Social Darwinist struggle for more land and a Nordic superrace. When Heidegger broke with the activist notion that humans could overcome the crisis of modernity by their own strength, at least his thinking ceased to be fascist.

Heidegger remained an undemocratic elitist to the end of his life. He believed that only exceptional personalities like himself could impart the necessary impulse for understanding the human condition and the historical destiny of a community. His political ideas thus remained suspect, and he continued to have little sympathy for a pluralist society. At least, however, he broke with the Platonic belief that a philosopher had the right to enforce his vision on a nation. As he stated in 1966, "In the realm of thinking there are no authoritative statements."[45]

Heidegger and Environmentalism

Heidegger's Nazism temporarily interrupted his deep reflections on the nihilism of modernity because he believed there was a concrete solution at hand. His disillusionment with both the Third Reich and his own political engagement within it meant, however, that the old problem returned with redoubled force. Heidegger, who always used his own experiences as starting point for his philosophy, came to realize the naivety of hoping that one could simply break with existing conditions. Although he maintained his anti-Americanism and anticommunism, he no longer saw an easy escape from modernity through the political revival of a "German way." Only a tireless reflection on existing conditions, and a cautious preparing of the ground in which the "saving powers" were to grow, could, he argued in his later years, provide the chance for an individual and an historical "turn."

How did Heidegger see the relationship between humans and their environment? As pointed out earlier, in the Weimar Republic, Heidegger shared with many others a nostalgic vision of traditional crafts and agriculture, while ignoring the industrial world in his work.[46] He idealized the human connection with *Heimat* and expressed his support for moving Germans from the cities into the countryside. On the other hand, his phenomenological ideas of the 1920s did not allow for a contemplative or theoretical relationship with the world, but only for instrumental action. We gain awareness of nature, he argued, in our attempts to use and dominate it. Nature is, for us, what we have ready at hand for practical purposes: the forest is potential timber, "the mountain quarry, the river water-power, the 'wind in the sails.'"[47] In *Introduction to Metaphysics* (1935), the relationship between humans and nature was still described in terms of conflict: humans are thrown into an overpowering environment, and they have to act forcefully in their attempt to establish an intelligible world by naming objects and establishing symbolic relations. A clear sense of a more expansive, meditative, and respectful attitude toward nature seems to have emerged only in his writings of the 1930s on art.

His engagement with topics relevant to environmental thought started with a critique of what he regarded as problematic aspects of our contemporary world: the world-forming dynamics of modern science and technology. His general unease about the modern world became more specific and thoughtful through the study of Ernst Jünger's essay "Total Mobilization" (1930) and *The Worker: Mastery and Form* (1932) in the early thirties and during the winter of 1939–40. While we do not know exactly what Heidegger thought at the first encounter,[48] we have a quotation from 1939–40 in which he accepts the concept of "total mobilization" as a true analysis of the contemporary world. For him, Jünger described the essence of modern existence accurately as a Nietzschean will to power under the conditions of a technological world: modern humans use all technical means to achieve power and force their will upon the human and nonhuman world. But Heidegger also saw a fundamental disagreement. While the early Jünger celebrated total mobilization, this vision became a dystopia for Heidegger. In contrast to Jünger's opinion in the early 1930s, Heidegger criticized and deconstructed this mobilization as the act of a godless and nihilistic historical epoch.[49] He was not prepared to accept what he took as the workings of a will to will, with no ulterior motive or purpose, an emptiness which concealed itself through a meaningless hyperactivity of arbitrary willing. While Heidegger valued the early Ernst Jünger as an astute observer of his age, his later orientation, especially his rejection of the will to power, is closer to that of Ludwig Klages, the sharp critic of an unchecked human will and the destructiveness of modern technology.

Modern science became Heidegger's first target for a deconstruction through historicizing. In the lecture "The Age of the World Picture" (1938)[50] he offered a history of metaphysics that in important respects anticipated Thomas Kuhn's theory of paradigms. For Heidegger, "metaphysics" meant the paradigm or horizon of truth that structures an historical epoch's perception of reality. Every horizon of truth determines the basic structure for the recognition and interpretation of reality. It determines what can be perceived, what is regarded as truth, and how one should act. Since one cannot step out of one's own horizon of truth, there is no universal criterion to evaluate or rank different truth horizons. Since they determine what is regarded as truth, one cannot question the truth of one's own truth horizon.

The metaphysical essence of modernity, Heidegger argued, was scientific and mechanical thought. While art was sidelined into aesthetics, that is, to personal taste and pleasure, and religion to a private attitude without relevance to the public sphere, a new form of science and technology had come to determine the realm of the real. Modern man approaches reality with the assumption that it can be understood in mathematical and mechanical ways, with the corollary being that only those phenomena which can be explained mathematically and mechanically are accepted as real. The experiment determines reality, and a successful experiment is potentially a technical application.

Why did this modern world picture emerge? It is, Heidegger argued, motivated by the search for security. Reality is understood in a way that implies certainty. This was already the case with metaphysical or theological systems of thought, ranging from Plato's ideas to dogmatic Catholicism, which abandoned the being-exposed to the mystery of existence for the security of a firm belief. Modern science, however, is seen to go further. It puts humans at the center of the world; they now define what should be regarded as truth. Instead of realizing that science operates out of one of many possible truth-disclosing horizons, the modern age believes that science is the only producer of truth. With Heidegger's concept of truth horizons, this claim of science to universality is, however, undermined. While scientific discoveries are right as they grasp some aspects of truth, they cease to be true if they take their own partial truth as the whole truth. The inexhaustibly multifaceted nature of reality is marginalized, repressed, or ignored in order to gain a sense of security and control.

The way of thinking by which humans put themselves in the center, define reality according to their own standards, and reduce phenomena to their usefulness, Heidegger named "humanism" in 1947.[51] He came to regard this attitude as the key reason for the nihilistic crisis of modernity. Earlier perceptions of reality, he argued, accepted to a greater extent that we are thrown into a world view which is not of our own making: a historical tradition and a language which largely determine our perspective on the world. He also believed that earlier perceptions had a stronger sense that every horizon of truth makes clear some aspects of the world, but simultaneously conceals others, so that the world as a whole and everything within it must always remain, in large part, a mystery. The pre-Socratic philosophers came to embody his ideal, as they, in his judgment, were still openly facing and reflecting on the mysteries of Being. Since then humanism had gradually expanded its powers, until Descartes even came to see the human mind as the very center of all existence. Heidegger not only regarded the Cartesian idea of an autonomous subject as naive, because it ignored that subjects only emerge within a language community which largely shapes all its members (which made him a central initiator of the so-called linguistic turn), he even regarded this attitude as positively dangerous: if the world and everything within it are seen only in relationship to an autonomous subject, then these objects tend to be regarded mainly as a resource for the subject's will to power. In this way, Heidegger came to regard Nazism as an extreme form of humanism—but, equally so, all other modern societies. Heidegger regarded the political differences between democratic, socialist, and fascist states as surface phenomena; essentially they were the same, as they were all based on modern science and its powerful twin, modern technology.

This analysis of science was only an intermediate step toward the core of Heidegger's critique of modernity, namely his analysis of technology worked out in "The Question Concerning Technology" (hereafter QCT), from 1953.[52] Here he came to see Newtonian physics only as a "herald" (QCT, 303) of the essence of the modern age, that is, technology. In its concrete points the article largely repeated the themes which Ludwig Klages had voiced as early as 1913 in "Man and Earth," which remained influential throughout the 1920s and which were raised again from very different quarters after the Second World War.[53] In the postwar period, the writer Friedrich Georg Jünger published a book in which he denounced modern technology as dangerously destructive and inhumane, the sociologist Alfred Weber talked about a world in which humans would take on characteristics of robots, the philosopher Günther Anders claimed that humans could no longer really comprehend the effects of their technical actions, and the critical theorists Max Horkheimer and Theodor W. Adorno voiced their fear that domination over outer nature would also entail domination over our own human nature.[54] The process of modernization has triggered continuous reflection on the opportunities, challenges, and dangers of modern technology, and a period of rapid change gave these themes particular prominence. The memories of the Second World War, the unprecedented dangers of the nuclear age, but also a certain unease about the emerging consumer society with its alleged hedonism, produced a wave of meditations on the "technological age" (Hans Freyer) at the beginning of the Federal Republic of Germany's "economic miracle."

Heidegger's topic was, then, rather common, but the grounding within the framework of Heidegger's philosophy made it highly original. Whereas previous cultural critics saw technology either as a tool that humans have to learn to use properly for the right purposes or as a demonic force that threatens to enslave humankind, Heidegger broke with them over the idea of regarding either humans or technology as autonomous agents. Humans are not transcendent subjects who use technology freely as a tool, but have been born into and shaped by the technical world. On the other hand, technology cannot be an autonomous agent either: this view, a misplaced personification, ignores the fact that humans created the technical world, that they are part of it and have developed a "technological mentality" within the process of technological modernization.

If all this is the case, then we cannot study technology from the outside or step out of the technological world, because its logic is part of our fundamental thought structure. Heidegger thus maintained his argument from "The Age of the World Picture" that our whole horizon of truth is scientific and technological; consequently, we cannot "unchoose" technology, as this would involve stepping out of the life-world that is historically given to us. Our horizon of truth makes us think and act technologically; we may work on realizing the limitations of this perspective, which Heidegger came to regard as imposing a partial blindness,[55] and on altering this way of seeing the world, but we cannot simply step out of it.

In contrast to the bleak picture drawn by Ludwig Klages and Friedrich Georg Jünger, Heidegger argued against a demonization of technology. He stressed that all technology was essentially a justified way of understanding and relating to the world. Technology is not just an arbitrary human activity; it "is a mode of revealing." On the most fundamental level it belongs to the "realm where revealing and unconcealment take place, where . . . truth happens" (QCT, 295). This, however, does not mean that Heidegger saw no danger in modern technology. On the contrary, the truth which modern, scientifically based technology reveals is, he claims, largely determined by human demands: while traditional technology lets things be, "modern technology is a challenging" (*herausfordern*). While the work of the traditional peasant lets the soil reveal something about itself and bring forth its inherent qualities without interfering too much, the earth is now challenged to reveal "itself as a coal-mining district, the soil as a mineral deposit" (QCT, 296–97).

While this example is drawn from the tradition of agrarian romanticism, others reveal a connection, though never explicitly stated, to the environmental movement. One of the central concerns of the early environmentalists was hydroelectric plants, because they dramatically interfered with often very beautiful and remote parts of nature. Shortly after its foundation, for example, the Bund Heimatschutz, supported by famous academics like Werner Sombart, Ernst Troeltsch, and Max Weber, fought to preserve spectacular waterfalls at the top of the Rhine near Laufenburg, and many other conflicts followed about the use of rivers and lakes to produce electricity.[56] It thus seems no accident that Heidegger uses an old bridge and a hydroelectric plant on the Rhine, the river closest to his hometown and rich in romantic connotations, to offer a prime example of the changed character of modern technology. In a thoughtful yet passionate, even enraged, tone, he criticizes the modern way of gaining power:

> The hydroelectric plant is set into the current of the Rhine. It sets the Rhine to supplying its hydraulic pressure, which then sets the turbines turning. This turning sets those machines in motion whose thrust sets going the electric current for which the long-distance power station and its network of cables are set up to dispatch electricity. In the context of the interlocking processes pertaining to the orderly disposition of electric energy, even the Rhine itself appears to be something at our command. The hydroelectric plant is not built into the Rhine River as was the old wooden bridge that joined bank with bank for hundreds of years. Rather, the river is dammed up into the power plant. What the river is now, namely, a water-power supplier, derives from the essence of the power station. In order that we may even remotely consider the monstrousness that reigns here, let us ponder for a moment the contrast that is spoken by the two titles: "The Rhine," as dammed up into the *power* works, and "The Rhine," as uttered by the *art* work, in Hölderlin's hymn by that name.

The possible objection that the river can be both useful and perceived as beautiful is brushed aside with a brief remark: "Perhaps. But how? In no other way than as an object on call for inspection by a tour group ordered there by the vacation industry" (QCT, 297).

Most environmentalists and conservationists past and present would be primarily concerned about the ecological and aesthetic impact of the power station on the surrounding landscape, but for Heidegger the main problem was, as the comment on the tourist industry shows, the lack of respect and arrogance implicit in such a usage. Nature, he argues, is challenged to provide what humans demand, it is regarded as *Bestand,* that is, as a "standing-reserve" or "raw material." Whether nature is material for energy or aesthetic pleasure or any other usage is ultimately irrelevant for Heidegger, as the frame of mind is decisive.

As explained earlier, Heidegger rejected the idea that *homo faber* can be or should be in the driver's seat. Not only does he become degraded into being seen as just another standing reserve, or "human resource," he also does not choose his own technical attitude. "When man, investigating, observing, pursues nature as an area of his own conceiving, he has already been claimed by a way of revealing that challenges him to approach nature as an object of research, until even the object disappears into the objectlessness of standing-reserve" (QCT, 300). This whole constellation of scientific and technological perspectives of humans on their environment Heidegger named *Gestell,* which is usually translated as "enframing." The fact that in modernity humans reveal the world as standing reserve is not something chosen, but destined. Modern science and technology are expressions of this essential horizon of truth, a purely instrumental perspective on reality.

Why did Heidegger see "enframing" as the greatest danger? Heidegger's main concern was not environmental pollution or degradation, and he did not mention material limits of growth, although these worries were already being voiced throughout his lifetime. Instead, he was primarily concerned about the reductionist relationship between humans and their world. Within the constellation of "enframing," the world reveals itself to us as nothing but raw material. Consequently, humans lack appreciation and respect for the world, which in turn makes an unscrupulous use of the environment appear legitimate and appropriate. We see everything without respect, as "stuff," and thus treat it as such—to the point, even, that we kill humans who do not seem to fit into our design. However, the practical consequences are secondary for Heidegger: the real damage is already done, once humans are alienated from their world. It is all the worse, for Heidegger, if the technical world functions well, because then we do not even feel the degradation and fail to see the problem. "Everything is functioning. This is exactly what is so uncanny, that everything is functioning and that the functioning drives us more and more to even further functioning, and that technology tears men loose from the earth and uproots them. I do not know whether you were frightened, but I at any rate was frightened when I saw pictures coming from the moon to the earth. We don't need any atom bomb. The uprooting of man has already taken place. The only thing we have left is purely technological relationships. This is no longer the earth on which man lives."[57]

A perfectly organized technological system which utilizes the world to its limits while avoiding all environmental damage—something wholly compatible with the ideals of pragmatic environmentalism—would thus be diametrically opposed to Heidegger's ideals. For him, the main problem of "enframing" is not the actual damage it causes, but that it blinds humans: lost in the delusion of grandeur called humanism, humans have come to believe that they chose the technical attitude toward the world, when it is really given to them, a "destiny," or *Geschick*. This misapprehension means that humans no longer know the essence of their existence: being placed into a truth horizon. "Enframing" also imposes a very reductionist perspective, which tends to deny "the call for a more primal [and thus, for Heidegger, higher] truth" (QCT, 309). Lastly, the greatest danger, for Heidegger, is that humankind may never find an alternative to "enframing." Since "enframing" tends to block the realization that it is only one of many possible perspectives, that there are other ways of relating to the world, and that the world as a whole remains a mysterious and holy place (we will soon come to this in more detail), there is every possibility that this perception of the world will become permanent.

If the later Heidegger stated that "enframing" is sent to us by Being (as our Geschick, or destiny), was he, then, despairing, or at least fatalistic? Is there no escape route, if "enframing" blocks other perspectives on reality? Can we do something about the dangers of "enframing," or do we have to wait and see whether destiny will send us a different truth horizon? Referring to the title of the *Spiegel* interview, "Only a God Can Save Us" (1966), many have read Heidegger as saying that human action cannot make a real difference. A widely accepted argument has further explained this alleged fatalism as a philosophical excuse for Heidegger's political error in 1933: if the whole historical development is taken as fate, then history should be blamed for National Socialism, and not individual supporters like Heidegger.

It is certainly true that Heidegger emphasized the limits of human capabilities. This conviction might have been partly motivated by the wish to excuse himself, but, more importantly, it also followed from his philosophy. If humans are born into a symbolic universe, then they are not autonomous agents, but shaped by historical circumstances. If the problem is seen as arising not from technical "hardware," but from humanism itself (that is, the belief in the human will's ability to judge and shape the world by its own standards), then, clearly, the will to change things cannot be the solution. The idea that one can will to break with the will is plainly self-contradictory. Thus Heidegger rejected any attempt to solve the existing crisis by way of an action plan or a technical fix.

However, Heidegger's rejection of the idea that humans can change the course of history by themselves does not imply that humans can do nothing, as some critics who think in terms of polar oppositions have claimed. While Heidegger sharply criticized the belief in the will's ability to freely shape things, he did not preach fatalism or passivity. "Destining is never a fate that compels," he stated in 1953 (QCT, 306), and in the interview with *Der Spiegel* he emphasized: "I do not see the situation of man in the world of global technology as a fate which cannot be escaped or unravelled" (111).

The first positive thing to do is what Heidegger did: to question technology and discover its essence. On the one hand, Heidegger regarded "enframing" as the greatest danger, because it tends to block all other relationships of humans to their environment. But, on the other hand, it also offers the greatest chance to discover the nature of revealing, that is, truth. With "enframing" holding such powerful sway, it becomes all the more apparent that humans do not choose their truth horizon, but that it is given. If we realize and accept this, then we have already broken with the humanist illusion. We realize that we do not perceive and act autonomously, but are given a relationship to the world by the historical situation in which we exist.

Does this mean that Heidegger wanted us to accept the horizon of truth as destiny or fate? To some extent, yes: he believed that we should not only accept, but also learn to appreciate, that our perspective was destined or granted to us. In his later writings, Heidegger maintained that humans fulfill their true role only if they meditate upon the facts of existence. When man "becomes one who listens," however, he does not simply have to obey (QCT, 306). While humans should not have the illusion that they can alter things just by their own strength, they play an important part in making change possible. "How can this happen? Here and now and in little things, that we may foster the saving power in its increase"

(QCT, 315). Humans could be compared with gardeners: they cannot make things grow, but can provide conditions in which the right things have a chance to grow.

But what should grow? First, humans should develop *Gelassenheit*, or "releasement," in their attitude toward technology. Heidegger emphasized that "what is dangerous is not technology" as such (QCT, 309), but, as already hinted at in 1935, an empty technological frenzy. If we have a clear idea to what purpose we want to use technology, we can integrate an instrumental attitude into our lives without devoting our lives to technology or falling victim to the reductionist attitude that the world contains nothing but raw material. Once we have developed a broader sense of existence, "our relationship to the technical world becomes miraculously easy and calm. We let technical things enter our everyday world and keep them simultaneously outside, that is we let them be things which are nothing absolute, but reliant on something more important."[58]

Heidegger's "releasement" may sound a bit too easy, convenient, and passive, but it was not meant to cover up the new technological reality with a traditional surface. Rather, we should come to realize that our truth horizon is given to us. We should meditate on our existence and learn to value the world around us. We should work on expanding our truth horizon and thus learn to see things more fully, in their four relations to sky and earth, mortals and divinities. We should learn to realize that the world is not just raw material, but a mysterious and holy place. Instead of aiming for humanist utopias, we should realize that we inhabit a wonderful world, if only we develop the ability to notice it, respect it, and care for it. If we realize that we are not autonomous subjects (not, as Klaus Michael Meyer-Abich puts it, invaders from outer space), but earthlings, then there is a chance that we may learn to truly dwell within our world. This hope is perhaps captured best in a Hölderlin quotation Heidegger loved to use: "poetically dwells man upon this earth."

There is not enough space here to develop Heidegger's vision in any detail, and it is not necessary. In his later writings, Heidegger no longer tried to prove specific points, but thought about ways toward a fuller, more satisfying, better life, in which we would realize more fully our human potential in harmony with the world around us: fellow humans, nature, and Gods. His later texts are still carefully thought through, but should not be taken as attempts to give definite answers. Rather, they are marking a path of fruitful thoughts[59] which try to motivate us to see reality in a fuller way, and thus to change attitudes, behavior, and actions.

They are written, one might say, on a basis of religious respect and awe toward Being. Heidegger did not preach a dogmatic belief, but religious appreciation and respect for the mysteries of our existence as dwellers in this world. We should meditate on existence because "questioning is the piety of thought" (QCT, 317); we should "prepare a sort of readiness, through thinking and poeticizing, for the appearance of the god or for the absence of the God"[60] because we cannot make a new belief arrive, but can hope for it and meditate on its current absence. In contrast to many deep ecologists (while again similar, however, to Ludwig Klages), Heidegger did not see humans in negative, but in ambivalent, terms. While he regarded them as the greatest danger so long as they were caught up in "enframing," they also had the potential to fulfill a highly important and unique role. Humans are the only beings who can think and meditate; thus, humankind has the potential and duty to be the "shepherd of Being," of Being's self-disclosure as world.[61]

Heidegger did not believe in an ethics separate from our perception of the world. For him, ethical values were just human ideas, which we adopt when it suits us, but drop when the going gets tough. Only a different perception of the world, he argued, could be trusted to change our behavior. If we perceive the world as a holy place in which we dwell, then we will no longer treat it as raw material, but with respect and care. Whether one accepts Heidegger's rejection of a separate realm of ethics or not, it seems clear that he called for a change of our thinking *and* acting. Heidegger's philosophy might sound abstract, but the consequences of a turn away from "enframing" to reverence and care would be, as Young has illustrated in his book *Heidegger's Later Philosophy,* radical. While Heidegger was not primarily concerned about the material destruction of the environment, his late philosophy clearly included a green attitude. It still lacked a political analysis or strategy (indeed, Heidegger's vague ideas about politics remained suspect to the end), but it offered a clear vision of an alternative way of life.

Heidegger suggested, as quoted above, that individuals should try to do "little things" in the "here and now" to foster a positive development. He was not content, however, with personal changes or any notion of personal salvation. Instead, his hope was still directed toward a world-historical "turning." While individual changes could prepare the ground, the course of history could only change, he believed, with the spread of a new set of collective beliefs that would break with the hubris of modernity. This hoped-for event he called the arrival of a new God or Gods. Heidegger could maintain such a hope for a complete change because he did not accept the idea of unchangeable human traits. As human characteristics of humanity were brought forth by history, humanity had the potential to be destructive or constructive. For Heidegger, our perception and understanding of the world determine our actions, and a true understanding of the world and our existence within it could turn humanity into a wholly positive force. In his radical historicizing of existence there was no place for a universal conception of human nature, or for an evil that would set limits to his hope for change.

One might deny the possibility of the rise of a completely different— and better—epoch, and Heidegger himself was highly skeptical. However, it was only logical for Heidegger to think in this direction. If our truth horizon is not individually chosen, but historically given, the possibilities for an individual to think beyond the collective truth horizon must be limited. According to Heidegger, an epoch does not completely determine an individual's vision, and true poets as well as true thinkers can alter and expand a society's horizon. But a real change must be a collective one, especially if it is to have the power to shape historical development. Humans cannot *make* a God return (that is, in my reading, they cannot produce a collective belief in something divine), but in the absence of a God we cannot avoid *Untergang,* or extinction. Thus, humanity can only be saved through a historical turn toward an age of religiosity. If this turn does not happen, then the only thing we can achieve, Heidegger argued, is that we do not just "die a wretched death (*verrecken*)," caught up in illusions about our condition in a nihilistic age, but instead die with dignity, reflecting on the fact that the God is absent.[62]

These thoughts about a collective turning toward the arrival of new Gods do not sit easily with a Western world that praises individualism and pluralism. Heidegger accepted that different communities have different Gods, but the pluralism of modern Western societies he regarded as a form of nihilism. The thought (so central, for example, to single-issue campaigns) that very different motivations can lead toward agreement on environmentally friendly policies remained alien to him. For one thing, he strongly rejected the idea that the environment could be managed by humanity; for another, he remained committed to the ideal of tightly connected communities like the Greek polis or early Christian congregations. This was partly because, for Heidegger, attitudes and actions were intrinsically and closely linked, partly because his prime concern remained humanity. Caring for the world was important to him, but mainly as part of a fulfilled human life. This included the connection with nature and fellow humans, but also with collective divinities.

Heidegger was a Nazi *and* he was "green," if one does not have too narrow an understanding of this term. This should not to be taken, however, as an illustration of the greenness of the Nazis, because Heidegger's serious environmental thought was not positively connected with his political involvement in the Third Reich. It is true that Heidegger was attracted by, among other and more important things, the Nazi "blood and soil" propaganda, because he was a romantic about traditional peasant life. But his analysis of modern science and technology as well as his vision of a more religious-meditative attitude only emerged as a result of his disillusionment with National Socialism, as an attempt to find a philosophical explanation for the failure of his political hopes. As long as he believed in a straightforward political solution to the alleged nihilism of his time, there was no reason to engage seriously with the realities of modern society. But once he came to see the Third Reich as essentially just another modern society, he gradually developed his critique of science and technology, along with a possible alternative to the humanist belief that the world is just raw material for realizing our ideals.

This is not the place to discuss the validity of Heidegger's opinion; suffice it to say that he is by no means the only person who saw National Socialism as a modern movement.[63] The central point for our argument, however, is that Heidegger's involvement with Nazism and his thoughts on environmentalism belong to different phases of his work. Heidegger himself recognized a turn in his thinking in the 1930s, and a majority of the secondary literature accepts this self-interpretation. His critique of the will to power is, to me, the decisive turning point. In his political speeches in favor of Nazism, Heidegger tended to assign an active and forceful role to human beings as "makers" of the turn away from nihilism toward a new age of communal identity and beliefs. The critique of power marked a break with this opinion—and a distancing from Nazi ideology, since, by any definition, a cult of the will must be regarded as an integral part of the ideology of the Third Reich. His thoughts on science, technology, and a more meditative attitude toward the world emerged at the same time as the critique of the will; they were thus part of a reflection that helped him to define his philosophical distance from National Socialism.

A turn does not mean a complete break. In many ways, Heidegger continued to draw on his early work in defining his new position. The central philosophical concepts he continued to use were largely those that even a severe critic like Jürgen Habermas distinguishes from Heidegger's political thought of the early thirties. In some respects, however, there was a continued affinity with the ideas of Weimar's radical conservatives. For example, Heidegger continued to believe that any real change would most likely have to be apocalyptic. Following Friedrich Hölderlin's "But where danger is, grows / The saving power also," in his later years Heidegger argued that a change for the better was most likely to occur once the bottom had been reached. The same belief had encouraged reckless attitudes and policies toward the end of the Weimar Republic, because many assumed—wrongly—that things could not get worse.[64] However, since Heidegger did not promote a willful policy of destruction to speed up the allegedly necessary apocalyptic change, one can with good reason regard his position as delusive, but not dangerous.

In his fundamental critique, however, together with his lack of clear thought on politics, Heidegger did fall prey to a serious danger: he lost sight of important differences within modernity. His rejection of "enframing" was so sweeping that he saw the fundamental distinction between democratic and totalitarian systems as merely superficial, and his despair over the lack of human rootedness in the world led him to compare this alienation with a nuclear holocaust. These examples show that Heidegger could lose sight of differences in human suffering and of differences in the opportunities for change, because he saw the difference between today's (nihilistic) existence and his vision of an ideal existence too much as a polar opposition. As far as we can tell by his writings, he never developed an explicit appreciation of human rights or of a political division of power.[65] However, at least he no longer called for a desperate all-or-nothing policy, but instead promoted a policy of little steps. Thus, one can diagnose a serious blind spot, but not discern a promotion of dangerous policies.

There are many other points in Heidegger to which different readers have objected. One could, for example, ask whether his skepticism about democracy is really justified, when one thinks of the alternatives; whether his fear of the will and bold action might be overcautious in times that demand far-reaching measures; whether his history of metaphysics does not downplay differences within particular epochs; whether he is not too pessimistic about the world in the age of "enframing," and too optimistic about a world in which humans would accept that they have a limited truth horizon; whether humans are really able to lead such a meditative and disinterested existence, as "shepherds of Being," so as to overcome all evil.

Independent of all this, however, it seems to me that Heidegger's later philosophy, in particular his *environmental* ideas, do not fall within the realm of Nazi ideology. It is very understandable that phrases like "rootedness," "Heimat," "back to the land," and "German destiny" have become deeply suspect, because nationalism was used as justification for ignoring the most basic rights of others. German history served as a spurious justification for territorial claims and military expansion, and settlement programs were intrinsically linked with murderous racist policies in the occupied East. Furthermore, the term "nature" was given a Social Darwinist meaning to justify unleashing a war of extermination against nations, ideologies, "races," and "parasites." But the similarities of terms and phrases in the later Heidegger to those of blood-and-soil ideology should not obscure fundamental differences.[66] In Romanticism and early environmentalism, an idealized concept of nature played an important role, but in völkisch and Nazi thought, "soil" played at most a marginal, secondary role. One can, after all, idealize agrarianism for very different reasons. For the main proponents of rural ideals in Nazism, Richard Walther Darré and Heinrich Himmler, "blood" was always the primary concept, representing the attempt to breed a Nordic superrace of as high a quality and in as great a quantity as possible, and rural life was largely appreciated as making for an ideal breeding ground. As far as agriculture was actually promoted, it was done only for practical purposes: partly, at first, to fight the high unemployment of the early 1930s, but mainly to achieve self-sufficiency as a necessary prerequisite for going to war. When Darré claimed that, in contrast to allegedly nomadic races like the Jews, the Nordic race had a special relationship to agriculture, he saw agriculture not in green terms, but as the most important human attempt to step out of nature and "control the environment."[67] Leading Nazis could appreciate practical environmental measures to avoid damage like soil erosion or to create a healthy environment as a means to strengthen the race. They could promote aesthetic criteria in altering the landscape in order to strengthen the formation of a national identity, or consider organic agriculture if it seemed to promise higher production. However, all the leading Nazis' dealings with the environment served only practical purposes. The same holds true for their attitude toward the past. Historical research was promoted in order to make claims on land outside of Germany, to strengthen an alleged Nordic identity, or as an inspiration for finding useful methods for solving practical problems—but if traditional inheritance laws seemed to hinder agriculture, or traditional gender norms the breeding ideals, the lack of respect for tradition became blatantly obvious.

Heidegger always held on to a chauvinistic arrogance about German culture and, more quietly, to prejudices against what he viewed, very stereotypically, as Jewish cultural traits. It is surprising and shocking that he could maintain these beliefs even after the crimes Germany committed between 1933 and 1945, but as far as I can see they do not shape his ideas relevant to environmentalism. In contrast to Nazi ideology, Heidegger repeatedly stated his strong opposition to any biological understanding of human beings or to biological racism. He used history not to legitimize the present, but as a means to question, deconstruct, and change current beliefs. His call for a closer and richer connection with the place one lives was aimed at promoting a fulfilled human life, intrinsically linked with an attitude of disinterested care for the environment. These ideas are much closer to bioregionalism and contemporary philosophies of place[68] than to Nazi blood-and-soil ideology.

I hope to have shown that, despite Heidegger's active involvement with National Socialism, his thoughts on our relationship to the world are legitimate opinions worthy of serious discussion. In particular, he makes a strong case that environmentalism can be and should be much more than just a purely pragmatic management of the world around us. While sustainability is an important goal in itself, a respectful and caring relationship to our surroundings would also mean a fuller realization of our human potential and the world's potential, and thus a qualitatively better life. Heidegger's thought is radical, but he is not a deep ecologist: in contrast to belief in the possibility of a biocentric perspective, he reminds us "that it is always we, who understand, and that always our own consciousness is playing a part, also when we confront something incomprehensible, strange."[69] Nor does he share the ideal of wilderness, but envisions, like most environmentalists in Germany, a well-arranged landscape with suitable buildings (for Heidegger and the *Heimatschutz,* preferably in a regional style), where nature flourishes and humans truly feel at home. Finally, Heidegger's attempt to point out the uniqueness of human beings is in some respects problematic, as we share so many important features with other forms of life. However, against misanthropic tendencies he makes a valuable suggestion: that humans do not *only* have the ability to be singularly destructive, that they can also care for nature, like a gardener, and that they are singular in giving the world self-consciousness.[70]

Notes

1. Hans Sluga, *Heidegger's Crisis: Philosophy and Politics in Nazi Germany* (Cambridge: Harvard University Press, 1993), 8, 9.

2. Jürgen Habermas, "Ein Gespräch mit Jürgen Habermas: Martin Heidegger? Nazi, sicher ein Nazi!" interview by Mark Hunyadi, in Jürg Altwegg, *Die Heidegger Kontroverse* (Frankfurt: Athenäum, 1988), 172–75.

3. See primarily Hugo Ott, *Martin Heidegger: A Political Life* (London: Fontana, 1994). See also Victor Farias, *Heidegger and Nazism* (Philadelphia: Temple University Press, 1989).

4. Martin Heidegger, *Gesamtausgabe,* vol. 16, *Reden und andere Zeugnisse eines Lebensweges* (Frankfurt: Klostermann, 2000), 184 (hereafter *Reden*).

5. Karl Löwith, "My Last Meeting with Heidegger in Rome, 1936," in *The Heidegger Controversy: A Critical Reader,* ed. Richard Wolin (Cambridge: MIT Press, 1998), 140–43.

6. Domenico Losurdo, *Die Gemeinschaft, der Tod, das Abendland: Heidegger und die Kriegsideologie* (Stuttgart: Metzler, 1995). He also expressed his hope for a German victory in a private letter to Fabricius, 10 March 1940 (*Reden,* 357).

7. Ott, *Heidegger,* 255–60.

8. For the most useful discussions of this question, see Julian Young, *Heidegger, Philosophy, Nazism* (Cambridge: Cambridge University Press, 1997); Richard Wolin, *The Politics of Being: The Political Thought of Martin Heidegger* (New York: Columbia University Press, 1990); Otto Pöggeler, "Heidegger's Political Self-Understanding," in *Heidegger Controversy* (see note 5), 198–244; and Charles Bambach, *Heidegger's Roots: Nietzsche, National Socialism and the Greeks* (Ithaca: Cornell University Press, 2003).

9. Heidegger, "Das Rektorat 1933/34: Tatsachen und Gedanken" (1945), in *Reden,* 374, 376.

10. For my philosophical understanding of Heidegger, I am greatly indebted to Julian Young: to his books, to the many conversations we have had, and to his comments on this article.

11. Helmut Lethen, *Cool Conduct: The Culture of Distance in Weimar Germany* (Berkeley: University of California Press, 2002).

12. Habermas, "Work and Weltanschauung: The Heidegger Controversy from a German Perspective," in *Heidegger: A Critical Reader,* ed. Hubert L. Dreyfus and Harrison Hall (Oxford: Blackwell, 1992), 186–208; Michael E. Zimmerman, *Heidegger's Confrontation with Modernity: Technology, Politics, and Art* (Bloomington: Indiana University Press, 1990), division one.

13. Heidegger, *Introduction to Metaphysics* (New York: Doubleday, 1961), 39.

14. See, for example, Heidegger's explanation in "Brief an einen Studenten," in *Reden*, 568.

15. Heidegger, "The Self-Assertion of the German University," in *Heidegger Controversy* (see note 5), 38.

16. Ibid.

17. Sluga (see note 1), Losurdo (note 6), and Young (note 8) expand on the inspiration the "August-enthusiasm" offered for Heidegger. The very real effect of the "August myth" does not imply that a general enthusiasm really existed; see Jeffrey Verhey, *The Spirit of 1914: Militarism, Myth and Mobilisation* (Cambridge: Cambridge University Press, 2000).

18. Heidegger, "Aufruf zur Wahl" (10 November 1933), in *Reden*, 188. See also *Reden*, 190–93.

19. Heidegger continued to stress his anticommunism in his post-1945 justifications, while he rejected the accusation of anti-Semitism. Although his many contacts with Jews show that he held no prejudices against individual Jews, he believed that Jews had too much influence in Germany. This was even stated in a letter to his (Jewish) friend Hannah Arendt in the winter of 1932–33 (*Reden*, 68–69). Reiner Marten recalled that Heidegger counted off with a shake of his head the number of Jewish professors in Germany after 1945 (*Frankfurter Rundschau*, 27 September 1989).

20. See the Rectoral Address, "Die Selbstbehauptung der deutschen Universität" (27 May 1933), in *Reden*, 107–17, or "Arbeitsdienst und Universität" (14 June 1933), in *Reden*, 125–26.

21. Wolin, *Politics of Being*, 60.

22. Heidegger, "Rede zur Abiturfeier" (26 or 27 May 1934) in *Reden*, 282, 283. See also the Rectoral Address (note 20).

23. Heidegger, "Aufruf zur Reichstagswahl verbunden mit Austritt aus Völkerbund" (10 November 1933), in *Reden*, 192; Heidegger, "Rede zur Abiturfeier," in *Reden*, 192.

24. At the Battle of Langemarck in the First World War, many German students were supposed to have courageously sacrificed their lives.

25. Heidegger, "Rede bei der Immatrikulation" (25 November 1933), in *Reden*, 199.

26. Heidegger, *An Introduction to Metaphysics* (New Haven: Yale University Press), 37–38.

27. This argument is developed in my book *Die andere Moderne?: Zivilisationskritik, Natur und Technik in Deutschland, 1880–1933* (Paderborn: Schöningh, 1999).

28. Young, *Heidegger, Philosophy, Nazism,* 49.

29. Zimmerman, *Heidegger's Confrontation with Modernity,* 70–71.

30. Rohkrämer, *Eine andere Moderne,* 127–40 and passim (with further references); Klaus Bergmann, *Agrarromantik und Großstadtfeindschaft* (Meisenheim am Glan: Hain, 1970).

31. *Reden,* 232–37. Wolin, *Heidegger Controversy,* 59, translates the passage slightly differently.

32. See *Reden,* 188–93.

33. Rohkrämer, "Die Vision einer deutschen Technik: Ingenieure und das 'Dritte Reich,'" in *Utopie und politische Herrschaft im Europa der Zwischenkriegszeit,* ed. Wolfgang Hardtwig (Munich: Oldenbourg, 2003).

34. Rohkrämer, "Cultural Criticism in Germany 1880–1933, a Typology," in *History of European Ideas* 25 (1999): 321–39.

35. Heidegger, "Bauen Wohnen Denken," in *Vorträge und Aufsätze* (Pfullingen: Neske, 1990), 155. In looking at the body of work, Zimmerman concludes: "Heidegger usually conceded that Germany could not return to an earlier mode of production. Germany's task was to return to its primal origins in order to initiate an authentic future in which a more satisfactory relation could obtain between productive activity, on the one hand, and the German *Geist* on the other" (*Heidegger's Confrontation with Modernity,* 156–57).

36. Heidegger, "Immatrikulationsrede" (25 November 1933), in *Reden,* 198–208, especially 200–201. This also explains why he does not focus on technology as such, but on the "technological frenzy," in his critique of America and Russia. In Heidegger's later work the idea that technology must be incorporated into a wider vision of reality and existence is most clearly expressed in his concept of "releasement." The concept of a "German technology" was most clearly expressed by Alwin Seifert and in particular influenced the building of the motorways. These ideas, combined with the sense that National Socialism promised a wider vision of the world which technology would serve, could explain why Heidegger still maintained in 1966 that National Socialism at first "went in the direction" of a healthy attitude toward technology (*Reden,* 677)

37. From the growing literature about the contemporary widespread religiosity, the following are particularly useful: Klaus Vondung, "'Gläubigkeit' im Nationalsozialismus," in *Totalitarismus und Politische Religion: Konzepte des Diktaturvergleichs,* vol. 2, ed. Hans Maier and Michael Schäfer (Paderborn: Schöningh, 1997), 15–28; Wolfgang Hardtwig, "Political Religion in Modern Germany: Reflections on Nationalism, Socialism, and National Socialism," *Bulletin of the German Historical Institute* 28 (Spring 2001): 3–27.

38. This is most clearly expressed in Heidegger, *Introduction to Metaphysics*, and "The Origin of the Work of Art," in *Poetry, Language, Thought* (New York: Harper and Row, 1971).

39. *Reden*, 93.

40. Young, *Heidegger, Philosophy, Nazism*, 48. For Heidegger's belief that he could lead the Führer, expressed in a conversation with Karl Jaspers, see ibid., 20, and Sluga, *Heidegger's Crisis*, 172–78.

41. Heidegger, "Die gegenwärtige Lage und die künftige Aufgabe der deutschen Philsophie," in *Reden*, 318.

42. Heidegger, *Introduction to Metaphysics*, 47, 38, and 199.

43. Silvio Vietta, *Heideggers Kritik am Nationalsozialismus und an der Technik* (Tübingen: Niemeyer, 1989), 10.

44. Heidegger, *Nietzsche*, 4 vols. (San Francisco: Harper and Row, 1977).

45. Heidegger, "'Only a God Can Save Us': Der Spiegel's Interview with Martin Heidegger (1966)," in *Heidegger Controversy* (see note 5), 114. See also Sluga, *Heidegger's Crisis*, 236.

46. See Celia Applegate, *A Nation of Provincials: The German Idea of Heimat* (Berkeley: University of California Press, 1990); and Michael Neumeyer, *Heimat: Zu Geschichte und Begriff eines Phänomens* (Kiel: Kieler Geographische Schriften, 1992).

47. Heidegger, *Sein und Zeit*, 70. See also Michael Großheim, *Ökologie oder Technokratie?: Der Konservatismus in der Moderne* (Berlin: Duncker & Humblot, 1995), 72–91.

48. Heidegger stressed in his dispute with Ernst Cassirer that he conceived the present situation in terms of Jünger's work (Pöggeler, "Heidegger's Political Self-Understanding," 211), but not whether he shared Jünger's affirmative stand. Michael E. Zimmerman, *Heidegger's Confrontation with Modernity*, has shown Heidegger's relation to Jünger in most detail, though he overstates the case.

49. Heidegger, *Zur Seinsfrage* (Frankfurt: Klostermann, 1956).

50. Heidegger, "Die Zeit des Weltbildes," in *Holzwege* (Frankfurt: Vittorio Klostermann, 1950); and Heidegger, "The Age of the World Picture," in *Off the Beaten Track*, ed. and trans. Julian Young and Kenneth Haynes (Cambridge: Cambridge University Press, 2002), 57–85.

51. Heidegger, "Letter on 'Humanism,'" in *Martin Heidegger: Basic Writings*, ed. David F. Krell (London: Routledge, 1978), 189–242.

52. In Krell, ed., *Martin Heidegger: Basic Writings*, 283–318.

53. Ludwig Klages, "Mensch und Erde," in *Sämtliche Werke*, vol. 3 (Bonn: Bouvier, 1974), 614–36.

54. Friedrich Georg Jünger, *Die Perfektion der Technik* (Frankfurt: Klostermann, 1953); Alfred Weber, *Der dritte oder der vierte Mensch: vom Sinn des geschichtlichen Daseins* (Munich: Piper, 1953); Günther Anders, *Die Antiquiertheit des Menschen: Über die Seele im Zeitalter der zweiten industriellen Revolution* (Munich: Beck, 1956); Max Horkheimer and Theodor W. Adorno, *Dialectic of Enlightenment* (1947; New York: Seabury Press, 1972). A book like Huxley's "Brave New World" shows that these fears were not restricted to Germany.

55. While Heidegger regarded the technical attitude toward the world as "right," because it reveals part of the truth, it turned into an illusion or an "enchantment" if this perspective was accepted as the whole truth. He thus turns around Max Weber's influential concept of disenchantment, which also plays a central role in Horkheimer and Adorno's *Dialectic of Enlightenment*, by calling it an illusion.

56. See the contributions of Reinhard Falter and Ulrich Linse in *Von der Bittschrift zur Platzbesetzung: Konflikte um technische Großprojekte*, ed. Ulrich Linse et al. (Berlin: Dietz, 1988). More generally, see Mark Cioc, *The Rhine: An Eco-Biography, 1815–2000* (Seattle: University of Washington Press, 2002).

57. Heidegger, "Only a God Can Save Us," 105–6.

58. Heidegger, *Gelassenheit* (Stuttgart: Neske, 1999).

59. Otto Pöggeler, *Der Denkweg Martin Heideggers* (Stuttgart: Neske, 1994).

60. Heidegger, "Only a God Can Save Us," 107.

61. Heidegger, "Letter on Humanism," 210.

62. Heidegger, "Only a God Can Save Us." This is my translation from the original (*Reden*, 671), because the translation in Wolin misses this aspect of the meaning.

63. For a recent overview, see Riccardo Bavaj, *Die Ambivalenz der Moderne im Nationalsozialismus: Eine Bilanz der Forschung* (Munich: Oldenbourg, 2003).

64. Klaus Vondung, *Die Apokalypse in Deutschland* (Munich: Deutscher Taschenbuch Verlag, 1988).

65. In hindsight, Heidegger excused his involvement with Nazism by drawing attention to his lack of political experience. But, as Pöggeler has rightly asked, "is it a privilege of German professors to take on tasks without being qualified for them?" (*Denkweg*, 324).

66. For the following, see in particular Mathias Eidenbenz, *"Blut und Boden": Zu Funktion und Genese der Metaphern des Agrarismus und Biologismus in der nationalsozialistischen Bauernpropaganda R. W. Darrés* (Bern:

Lang, 1992), 34 and passim; Josef Ackermann, *Heinrich Himmler als Ideologe* (Göttingen: Musterschmidt, 1970); Gustavo Corni, *Hitler and the Peasants: Agrarian Policy of the Third Reich, 1930–1939* (New York: Berg, 1990); and Frank-Lothar Kroll, *Utopie als Ideologie: Geschichtsdenken und politisches Handeln im Dritten Reich* (Paderborn: Schöningh, 1998).

67. Darré, *Das Bauerntum als Lebensquell der Nordischen Rasse* (Munich: Lehmanns Verlag, 1933), 39. In contrast, the negatively viewed nomad supposedly adapts to the environment.

68. See, for example, Jeff Malpas, *Place and Experience: A Philosophical Topography* (Cambridge: Cambridge University Press, 1999).

69. Quoted in Pöggeler, *Denkweg*, 258.

70. This view was previously advanced by Johann Gottfried Herder and Ludwig Klages.

CHAPTER 8

Blood or Soil?

The Völkisch Movement, the Nazis, and the Legacy of Geopolitik

Mark Bassin

> Es ist eines, den geographischen Raum als statisches oder dynamisches
> Gebilde und als Objekt politischen Handelns zum Primärfaktor der Politik
> schlechthin zu erklären; ein anderes, in den Rassen das Movens der
> Geschichte zu sehen und daraus den Anspruch der eigenen, biologisch
> ausgezeichneten Rassen auf die Weltherrschaft abzuleiten.
>
> *Karl-Georg Faber*

DOWN TO THE PRESENT, scholarly interest in the phenomenon of Geopolitik in interwar Germany has been driven almost exclusively by the question of collusion. Did the geopoliticians influence National Socialist ideology and policy formulation, and if so, to what extent and toward what ends? Questions like these were being asked about Geopolitik already during the war, at which time a Svengali-like influence was attributed to its chief proponent, Karl Haushofer. Reputed to operate out of a vast and mysterious Institute for Geopolitics in Munich, Haushofer was described in sensational terms as an "important ideological tool for the Führer," the "man who gave Hitler his ideas," and the "master magician of the Nazi party."[1] This view is still with us, although it has been largely displaced by an alternative perspective that began to emerge in the 1970s and 1980s. Despite significant resonances between Geopolitik and National Socialism, it now seems quite clear that the former was never able to play anything approaching the influential political-advisory role for the Nazis that has been attributed to it. The reasons for this are complex. In the case of Haushofer, they involve a cluster of factors that were at once personal (his half-Jewish wife), political (his tireless advocacy of a Soviet-German alliance), and ideological (his failure fully to embrace the "racial science" that was so important to the Nazis). While it was obviously appealing to explain the delusion of Lebensraum (living space) and its expansionist implications as the product of an intoxicating geopolitical elixir brewed by the wily Bavarian Merlin, this perspective is no longer sustainable.[2]

But if the problem of collusion now stands clarified, other issues have emerged to claim our attention. Perhaps the most significant of these relates to a new interest in how ecological ideas in Germany crossed lines with social theory and, more specifically, how they may have influenced or been used by political ideologies.[3] Strictly speaking, such an interest is not new at all, for the study of conservative-nationalist sentiments in Germany in the nineteenth and twentieth centuries and their evolution into National Socialism has always highlighted their naturalistic and crypto-ecological underpinnings.[4] What is new is how the subject is approached. Earlier research generally considered these underpinnings themselves to be part of the larger aberration of the German experience. The very appeal to the authority of organicist-ecological principles for guidance in interpreting society and political organization, in other words, was seen as a fundamental aspect of what fascism was all about. We are now beginning to take a rather different view of this problem, largely because our own growing engagement with ecological issues and ideas in the contemporary world allows us to cast a more sensitized and nuanced eye back on the German experience. While in no way readjusting our fundamental judgments about fascism, we increasingly appreciate that the confluence of ecological and political thinking was complex and multi-faceted, and—importantly—that fascism per se was only one of its possible results. Thus, while an earlier literature was content simply to note the general presence and effect of an organicist-ecological perspective, we now are inclined to press rather further, to critically investigate its specific assumptions and implications and try to flesh out its inner ambivalences and tensions.

This chapter takes up the latter point through a study of geopolitics, the ideology of *Blut und Boden* ("blood and soil"), and National Socialism. Both the "political geography" of the Wilhelmine period and its Weimar reincarnation Geopolitik based their theories of political organization and evolution on ecological-naturalist principles. To this extent, they were in principle fully at one with the *völkisch* and "blood and soil" movements, and indeed this particular association was an important one at the time. An examination of the doctrinal and ideological underpinnings, however, reveals subtle clefts in the ways in which organicism and naturalism were interpreted and deployed in social theory. In the final analysis, these divergences proved to be of immense significance, and powerfully influenced the fate of Geopolitik in Nazi Germany. More generally, they provide fundamental insights into the sort of contending dynamics and potentialities that inhere in the political appropriation of ecological principles.

The Dilemma of *Naturbedingtheit*

As a set ideological formula, the expression Blut und Boden was coined in the mid-1920s. Its sources, however, derive from völkisch-nationalist beliefs and attitudes that had been crystallizing in Germany since the middle of the nineteenth century. At the center of these preoccupations was a naturalistic vision of the national community as a cohesive organic entity, effectively a sort of Volk-organism.[5] In its genuine state, the Volk was seen as an integral part of the ecology of the natural world, providing the conditions for the latter's existence while being dependent upon it in turn. This existential integration into and dependency upon the natural world was referred to as the Volk's *Naturbedingtheit*, or "natural determination." Like all natural organisms, the Volk derived its most vital impulses and sustaining energies from these ecological interconnections, and it was only by maintaining them in a healthy state that the health of the nation could be insured. The organicism of the völkisch perspective was markedly influenced by the antirationalist Romanticism of the early nineteenth century, but at the same time—and paradoxically—it drew equal inspiration from the hyperpositivist cult of natural science that spread across Europe in the wake of the Darwinian revolution. In this latter regard, it is highly indicative that the scientific concept of ecology itself was coined by Ernst Haeckel, an early and important representative of the völkisch movement.[6]

The inherent need for an enduring "inner correspondence" and "intrinsic unity" between Volk and the natural universe was expressed through the image of the *Bodenständigkeit*—roughly, the "organic territoriality"—of the Volk-organism and its "rootedness" (*Verwurzelung*) in the natural environment.[7] On the one hand, rootedness was used metaphorically in the sense of a deep spiritual-psychological communion, but at the same time it was understood in a literal and material sense as well. Thus, a Volk could be genuinely integrated into the matrix of the natural world only to the extent that it was literally anchored in the earth or soil and attuned to their natural rhythms. In this way, the geographical entities of *Heimat* (homeland), *Landschaft* (landscape), and *Kulturlandschaft* (cultural landscape) acquired a transcendent significance for the völkisch movement, for they represented the most palpable demonstration of a healthy "organic symbiosis" between Volk and the natural world.[8] It was the apprehension that these connections were being progressively ruptured by the chaotic forces of modernization in Germany—above all the growth of industry and shiftless, rootless urban populations—that provided the movement's general political impetus and direction.

But what was it, precisely, that made the Volk natural? What specifically did natural determination mean? The term suggested dependency upon organic forces and elements, but which of these were ultimately the most effective and influential? We may note at once that although rootedness may have been an essential condition of the Volk's existence, völkisch writers would not for the most part have identified terrestrial phenomena such as soil or landscape per se as *determining* sources of the Volk's natural essence. The agent that made the Volk organic and natural was understood very differently, and was identified, rather, in the fact that the individual members of the Volk were fused together by ties of blood into what was effectively a biological and racial community. The fundamental natural qualities and characteristics of the Volk were thus racial qualities and characteristics. These had been determined in some primordial process of ethnogenesis and were fixed forever in an *Erbmasse* (or "genetic plasma") which was passed on from generation to generation and which set the absolute parameters for the Volk for all time. The genetic character of any given Volk-race was both absolutely unique and absolutely immutable. Alteration could only mean degradation, and could happen only through the infusion of racially foreign elements. Within the framework of this racialism, "natural determination" necessarily meant internal or genetic determination, and by the late nineteenth century this perspective had become nearly universal for the völkisch movement. It was both supported and stimulated by the emergence across Europe of so-called racial science, expounded in the writings of Arthur de Gobineau, H. S. Chamberlain, and many others.[9]

The belief in a fundamental racial identity was not, however, the only way that a völkisch natural essence could be conceived of or natural determination understood. In effect, an alternative was available which, in logical terms, at least, was no less suitable for establishing the natural-organic character of the Volk community. Instead of a preestablished and timeless genetic configuration that controlled the nature and evolutionary trajectory of the organism from within, the locus of connection with the natural world and the source of determining natural influences could be identified externally, in the material conditions of that natural-geographical environment in which the life history of the Volk had unfolded. The conditions in question encompassed a wide variety of specific factors, including climate, topography, soil type, vegetation cover, natural resources, proximity to the oceans, location respective to other groups, and so on. We will call this alternative perspective "environmentalism" or environmental (geographical) determinism. It relied on a distinction that was at once highly subtle and enormously important, namely that the organic territoriality which was the marker of human communities qua natural entities was a matter not merely of "connection with the earth" (*Erdgebundenheit*) but of "determination by earthly forces and conditions" (*Erdbedingtheit*). Environmental determinism was well supported by the natural science of the day, and the work of notables such as the Comte de Buffon, Jean Baptiste Lamarck, and indeed Charles Darwin himself provided a highly sophisticated framework for the analysis of human societies as organic elements of the natural world, subject like all other natural elements to the determining influences of the external environment. Beyond the realm of natural science, moreover, there was a well-established and respected intellectual tradition of explaining human affairs in terms of their determination by the external conditions of the natural world.[10]

The position of environmentalism within the wider matrix of völkisch preoccupations and priorities was inherently unstable. On the one hand, in principle it could serve no less effectively than racialism as the foundation for a naturalist and organic vision of the Volk community. The heavy völkisch stress on rootedness, moreover, suggested that environmentalism was perhaps even more amenable to and readily assimilable with völkisch perspectives. Soil and landscape were obviously geographical phenomena, after all, and it seemed a small and logical step to bridge the distinction just noted and move from a sense of organic interconnection between nature and Volk to the assumption of a causal environmentalist relationship. In the event, however, such a transition proved to be remarkably problematic, for the assumptions and implications associated with racialism and geographical determinism could spin—at least potentially—in entirely different directions. The suggestion that the geographical environment exercised a deciding role in the constitution of the Volk, for example, meant that capabilities of the latter were in a fundamental sense limited, and such a position was difficult to bring into line with the insistence on the indomitable omnipotence of the Germanic Volk-race articulated by ideologues already in the nineteenth century. It was, moreover, impossible to reconcile fully a rigorous environmentalist perspective, which looked at how an external milieu shaped a national community, with the critical völkisch concept of the cultural landscape (Kulturlandschaft), which stressed influences in precisely the opposite direction. Finally, for the more subtle völkisch critics, environmentalism was fatally flawed by its perceived ideological association with the humanist universalism of the Enlightenment and with contemporary forces of reformist liberalism. While such an association was in fact by no means clear-cut or unambiguous, it was true that geographical determinism assumed as its point of departure both the essential plasticity and the essential uniformity of the human species. Racialism, by contrast, was premised on the countervailing assumption of the absolute immutability and unbridgeable inequality of peoples and races, and it was the latter perspective that better corresponded to völkisch inclinations.

It is important to note that these sorts of ideological dissonances were not widely recognized in the Wilhelmine period, and geographical determinism did figure significantly in völkisch perspectives. Environmentalist principles were logically implicit, for example, in the virulent antiurbanism that was a hallmark of the movement. They were deployed more explicitly as well, albeit in a carefully qualified manner. Most commonly, this took the form of backdating environmental influences to a remote period of prehistory, when geographical conditions were broadly acknowledged to have played a formative role in the process of racial genesis. Thus, it was popularly believed that the geographical provenance of the Jews in a desert environment had been critically important in determining their particular racial characteristics. Once these characteristics had become fixed in their genetic plasma, however, they were no longer subject to environmental influences. Even such a qualified accommodation of geographical determinism, however, would ultimately prove to be unstable.

Anthropogeographie and the Völkisch Movement

A clear indication of the ideological stakes involved in race-space juxtaposition, and of the disruptive potential of geographical determinism for the völkisch *Weltanschauung*, can be seen in the work of the geographer

Friedrich Ratzel. Ratzel was a leading academic mandarin in Wilhelmine Germany, and was also an influential conservative-nationalist spokesman on public affairs. In both capacities, he was closely identified with the völkisch movement.[11] He was a passionate and effective proponent of German colonial expansion, and was heavily involved in colonial advocacy groups in the 1870s and early 1880s. Later, he figured among the founding members of the Pan-German League (Alldeutscher Verein).[12] More important than this organizational work, however, was his ideological contribution to the expansionist cause. Most notably, the concept of Lebensraum that he authored became a basic keyword in völkisch and, later, "blood and soil" discourses.[13] Ratzel's major scientific achievement was the founding of a new academic discipline, anthropogeography, or human geography, devoted to the study of human society in terms of the principles and laws of Darwinian natural science. He identified the fundamental challenge of this perspective in völkisch terms, as the investigation of the significance of rootedness for social and political life. Ratzel published widely in the völkisch press, and several of his students, notably Paul Langhans and Peter Johannes Thiel, went on to become prominent activists in the völkisch movement.

Through to his doctorate, Ratzel's training had been as a zoologist, and subsequently he always argued that organic territoriality was a universal natural law, extending beyond human society to include all organic life. "As different from each other as plants, animals, and human beings may be, they all stand and move on the same soil. They came to life on the same soil. . . . Life is always bound to the earth . . . and cannot, partially or as a whole, be separated from the earth and its soil."[14] The preoccupation of his human geography, however, was specifically with the consequences of this natural law for human social and political organization. His most innovative insights in this regard came with regard to what he called "political geography": an elaborate and highly original perspective on human political organization that identified the political state as a natural organism and studied its emergence and behavior in terms of its organic territoriality. In addition to political geography, Ratzel studied the evolution of a distinctively German national landscape through centuries of interaction and interconnection between a distinctive natural environment and the German Volk. All of Ratzel's work carried enormous scientific authority in his day, and it was of particular significance for the elaboration of völkisch perspectives. The value of his geographical perspective to the popular "organismic state" theories of the late nineteenth century was widely acknowledged,[15] and his significance for the development of the study of cultural landscape has been compared to that of Wilhelm Heinrich Riehl.[16]

Ratzel's ultimate objective, however, was not limited to merely indicating the ecological-organic quality of the Volk's connections with the rest of the natural world. Beyond this, he sought to specify and explain the dynamics of this interrelationship, and in this regard his thinking was rather less typical for the völkisch movement. Ratzel argued that the ecological relationship between society and the natural world was a causal relationship, and that the line of causation ran directly from the latter to the former. The natural milieu therefore exercised an important, indeed decisive influence on the existence of all organic life and on the direction of its evolutionary development. In elaborating this environmentalist perspective, Ratzel's inspiration came less from the cultural studies of Riehl than from the Darwinian biology and natural science he learned from his mentors Moritz Wagner and Haeckel himself, and also from the teleological geo-determinism of his immediate predecessor in the field of geography, Carl Ritter.[17] In his first magnum opus, *Anthropogeographie* (1882–91), Ratzel elaborated his own geo-determinist position in a universal, world-historical framework, and in his second, *Politische Geographie* (1897), he applied geographical determinism more specifically to the study of the political state as a natural organism.[18] As noted, the organic nature of the state was manifested most importantly in its Bodenständigkeit, and Ratzel was clear that for him this involved the "dependency" (*Abhängigkeit*) of the state-organism on the natural-geographical conditions of the region in which it had developed.[19]

Within the corpus of Ratzel's work as a whole, his principled geographical determinism gave rise to a number of significant dissonances with more mainstream völkisch views. Perhaps the most fundamental example was the critical notion of *Raum* (space) that was at the center of his thinking. His prioritization of the external milieu led him to an abstract and essentially generic notion of geographical space as the terrestrial space of the globe. This space differed in terms of local natural conditions, of course, but at the same time he stressed its universality and commonality. The specific implication was that Lebensraum itself similarly had a universal generic quality. Effectively, it referred to global space, and this meant that Germany's political quest to secure the vital Lebensraum it needed for future prosperity could be, indeed had to be, an intercontinental or global project. Such a perspective obviously corresponded to the global nature of imperialism in his day, and well suited his argument that Germany must take an active part in the global competition for territorial acquisition and advantage. In one of his more memorable exhortations he insisted that even such apparently worthless spaces as the sandy deserts of Africa offered a real value as future German Lebensraum and were thus worth competing for. Within the völkisch movement, by contrast, the emphasis on the Volk led to an essentially more limited sense of Lebensraum as Germany's "lived space" or *Heimatboden*, that is to say the specific historical-cultural space of the nation. Ratzel's geodeterminist perspective, moreover, heavily colored his treatment of the cultural landscape. The emphasis on the autonomous agency of the Volk as a molder and transformer of the natural world was obviously at odds with his own prioritization of environmental influences, and thus the cultural landscape as such in fact fit very awkwardly into his system as a whole. His popular association with the term and the tradition of Riehl is not without paradox, for the cultural landscape did not figure in his most important analyses and indeed he used the term extremely rarely, pointedly preferring the designation "historical landscape" (*historische Landschaft*).[20] At those moments when he did discuss the German cultural landscape, he tended to emphasize the importance of primordial "natural regions" (*Naturräume*) and "natural landscapes" (*Naturlandschaften*), and treated the emergence of cultural landscapes in these zones largely as a process of accommodation to preexisting natural conditions.[21]

Environmentalism further influenced Ratzel's understanding of the nature of the Volk itself. An extended sojourn in the United States during his early career as a journalist suggested to him that the open empty spaces of the North American continent had a decisive impact on shaping the character of an emergent American nationality; subsequently he generalized these conclusions into a universal principle of environmental influences.[22] "One sees the insular inclinations in the British character, and among the Norwegians and the Spanish the effects of their [geographically] isolated position. Is it possible to doubt that its habitat (*Wohnsitz*) influences the Volk's spirit and the body?"[23] Ratzel understood very well that his choice of external environmental influences as the formative factor in determining the nature of the Volk came at the cost of discounting internal factors of "relationship based on blood" (*Blutverwandschaft*), and ultimately of race itself. The claim that the populations of modern states such as Germany still retained the qualities of primordial racial purity and homogeneity was a bald fiction, he argued, for the historical growth of nations always involved the assimilation of new populations, and in every instance this meant racial mixture (*Blutmischung*). "All races are mixtures [of other races]," he wrote in one of his earliest essays, and he stood by this judgment to the end of his life.[24] Germany was no exception, and he coolly pointed out that his compatriots had Celtic, Roman, and even Slavic blood "flowing in their veins."

This mixing of races, moreover, was not only historically inevitable but desirable as well, for racial heterogeneity offered distinct cultural and civilizational advantages. "The belief that the more [racially] uniform a Volk is, the stronger it is in all respects, is completely erroneous."[25] Ratzel did not deny the existence of racial divisions, nor did he maintain that these divisions were without significance. He did, however, reject the racialist notion that different racial groups were located at different points on the evolutionary scale, and that on this basis they could be ranked as relatively "advanced" or "backward." Faithful to the environmentalist spirit extending back to Herder and Montesquieu, he repeatedly stressed the basic unity of all humankind. He took an uncompromising stand against contemporary prophets of "racial science" (*Rassenkunde*) such as Chamberlain and Gobineau, whom he dismissed simply as "race fanatics" (*Rassenfanatiker*). His identification of their basic errors was telling: they erred on the one hand in their unfounded belief in the absolute immutability of races, and on the other in their neglect of the all-important "influence of geographical conditions."[26] Ultimately Ratzel tended toward what was essentially a statist perspective on the nature of the Volk, which defined the latter in terms of its identification with the political organism that subsumed it. His position on this point remained ambivalent, to be sure, and he never entirely rejected the significance of ethnographic-racial factors, but it is highly indicative that he almost always identified the political state itself, and not the Volk, as the natural-organismic subject.[27]

Ratzel expanded upon this distinctly un-völkisch diminution of the significance of racial-ethnographic factors by arguing that modern states must not define their ultimate raison d'être in terms of them. The quest for political consolidation and self-determination on the part of ethnically or racially homogeneous populations, in other words, cannot by itself serve as a rationale for state formation. With this, Ratzel was challenging the basic principle of the modern nation-state, represented in the formula *ein Land, ein Volk*—"one country, one people." This had of course provided the inspiration and rationale for German unification in the mid-nineteenth century, and it continued powerfully to motivate the völkisch movement in his own day. The problem, in his view, was that such an imperative was essentially detached from those natural-geographical conditions which ought to have precedence. "A pure *Nationalpolitik*," he insisted, "is characterized by the attempt to detach itself from the geographical conditions of the earth." In the end, however, "it will always be conquered by the latter and will adapt itself to it."[28] Ratzel pointed to the example of Switzerland, where geographical conditions provided the basis for enduring political cohesion among no less than four different nationalities. As a principle for establishing political states and political boundaries, he concluded, *Nationalitätenpolitik* represented an unacceptable "regression into the un-territorial."[29] Ratzel's preferred alternative was what he called a "geographical politics" which recognized that the material conditions of life rooted in the natural endowments and configuration of geographical regions were more important for political and state cohesion than ethnic or Volk affinities. Ratzel did not hesitate, moreover, to press the direct implications of this perspective for a cause at the very center of völkisch concerns of his day, namely the issue of the German irridenta. He was expressly untroubled by the fact that "parts" of the German Volk—in Switzerland, Austria, or Russia—had been left outside the political boundaries of the unified German state created in 1871, and he was plainly skeptical as to whether their reincorporation would bring either them or the German Reich itself any real benefit.[30]

What was really at stake in the juxtaposition of *geographische Politik* and *Nationalpolitik*, it should be noted, was the imperative of state expansion. It was Ratzel's abiding belief that states in the modern world were existentially constrained to expand territorially or perish, and his entire theory of Lebensraum was founded on this principle. However, the principle of ethnic-national consolidation—and the corresponding alternative sense of Lebensraum as the "soil of the homeland" (*Heimatboden*)—worked, in his view, directly against this. While the formation of a state which incorporated the entirety of a Volk-organism such as Germany might well involve political-territorial expansion, this expansionist impetus would expire as soon as such a state entity was created, and territorial growth would necessarily come to an end.[31] Ratzel's more generic vision of Lebensraum, by contrast, and the more general series of biological "laws for the spatial growth of states" that he elaborated, were geographically open-ended, with geopolitical implications that were radically global.[32]

Geopolitics in the Weimar Republic

The reactionary ruralism and antimodernism of the völkisch movement carried over powerfully into the postwar period, and by the mid-1920s had been reconfigured under the novel rubric "blood and soil."[33] "Blood and soil" continued to reinforce a sort of naturalistic view of the national community as a biological organism, fused into a cohesive whole by ties of blood and racial affinity.[34] The pointed juxtaposition of blood and soil, moreover, indicated a persisting preoccupation with the organic territoriality of the Volk-organism, and the conviction that its future welfare could be insured only by strengthening the roots that fixed it in and bonded it to the soil of its native homeland. The deterioration of Germany's position after World War I—including foreign occupation and the loss of substantial portions of its national territory—and the establishment of a regime dedicated to the "individualistic" principles of liberal democracy served to insure that the völkisch apprehensions of the prewar period would become ever more intense.

Most importantly for our purposes, the ideological juxtaposition of blood and soil involved the same dual options for defining völkisch natural determination that we have identified in the Wilhelmine period. Once again, precedence was largely accorded to the identity of the Volk as a racial entity, conditioned by the immutable qualities of its genetic constitution. This privileging of race over the conditions and forces of the external milieu was endorsed in the 1930s by the very highest authority, that is to say Adolf Hitler himself. The limited natural endowments of a particular geographical region, Hitler observed, "may stimulate one race to the highest achievements, but for another [the same space] may be the source of the bitterest poverty and inadequate nutrition, with all of consequences that this brings. It is the inner predisposition of a Volk that determines the way in which external conditions influence it."[35] This perspective was elaborated in the writings of an array of "blood and soil" theorists, perhaps most notably by the agronomist Richard Walther Darré. Darré, who served as minister of agriculture in the Third Reich, was one of the original proponents of "blood and soil" doctrine, and his particular ideological formulations of it were of special significance in that they provided the version eventually embraced by Nazis.[36] Darré described how Volk and land interacted organically, "growing into each other" to produce a single entity that was at once natural and national. In this process, the soul of the Volk-race becomes rooted in its "native landscape" (*Heimatlandschaft*) and, "in the proper sense, always grows out of it." His careful reference to "proper sense" here was intended precisely to specify that "growing into each other" did not mean that the Volk was subject to causal determination by its natural milieu. Darré repeated the völkisch concession to environmentalism by allowing that geographical conditions had exerted a formative influence in the primeval process of racial formation, but, once formed, races ceased to be subject to them. The suggestion that the environment might actually "shape a race or a Volk" in the present day he rejected "as emphatically as possible."[37]

Although Darré spoke of the "dependency" of the German or Nordic race on the soil, he viewed the latter exclusively as a passive external condition of völkisch existence, not as an active agent in its own right.[38] Very much to the contrary, the existentially active agent was the Volk, and as such it was the "Volk itself [that] configures its relationship to the soil."[39] For Darré, and for "blood and soil" doctrine more broadly, soil was not so much a counterpole to blood as a dependent category, an externalized arena for racial activity, and a "medium," as Mathias Eidenbenz put it, for the race's development of its interior qualities.[40] "Labor on the land of one's forebears, the struggle with the forces of nature, the cultivation of plants and the tending of animals through the various seasons"—all of this called forth a "spiritual force" (*Seelenkraft*) and "inner sense" in the Volk, out of which emanated creative powers that were "determined by race" alone. Ultimately, it was by exercising these innate capacities for organization and rational husbandry that the Germanic "farmer race" (*Bauernrasse*) could develop its racial potential, and progress thereby from the mastery of its native agricultural landscape to become "master" (*Beherrscher*) of the world.[41] This emphasis on the anthropogenic domination of the natural world was an essential part of the activist ethos of National Socialism, and became ever more pronounced throughout the 1930s.[42]

At the same time, however, the environmentalist legacy of Ratzelian human geography also carried over after 1918, and continued to provide geo-determinist impulses within the corpus of "blood and soil" doctrine. In the early years of the twentieth century, the scattered principles of Ratzel's political geography were reorganized by the Swedish political scientist Rudolf Kjellén into a systematic view of the state as an animate and geographically dynamic organism. Kjellén christened this perspective "Geopolitik," and his writings—translated and broadly disseminated in Germany during the First World War—struck an immediate chord.[43] This resonance intensified after the war, for Germany's territorial losses substantially accelerated the fateful perception of a national "need for space" (*Raumbedürfnis*) that had motivated Ratzel's theories of territorial expansion in the first place. As a self-proclaimed spatial science (*Raumwissenschaft*) which promised to offer the necessary scientific bases for future boundary rearrangements and the reacquisition of vital German Lebensraum, Geopolitik was enthusiastically embraced in the Weimar Republic.[44] Its appeal, indeed, extended across the political spectrum,[45] but was greatest among those radical-conservative forces who rejected both the Weimar Republic in toto and the rearrangement of European political space promulgated at Versailles. The principal architect of Geopolitik was Karl Haushofer, whose indefatigable academic and organizational efforts brought this new "science" to prominence across Germany and with whose name it consequently became widely associated. Like Ratzel with his political geography, Haushofer's highest ambition was that Geopolitik would play the role of an applied political science, which, through an analysis of the natural laws determining the spatial behavior and needs of the political state-organism, could indicate the sorts of practical policies that had to be pursued.

The ideological interplay between these different tendencies in the interwar period, however, was much more intricate than what we have observed in the case of Ratzel. The simple reason for this was that the resonances between Haushofer's Geopolitik and the doctrines of "blood and soil" were at once more genuine and more intimate than those linking Ratzel to the völkisch movement. Most importantly, Haushofer's understanding of the Volk as a "living organism" (*Lebewesen*) corresponded in important ways to the mainstream "blood and soil" position. Thus, he consistently acknowledged the salience of race as a factor, and specifically emphasized the relevance of racial theories as developed by important racial biologists such as Wilhelm Schallmeyer for his own larger conception of Geopolitik.[46] His own treatment of race was not unproblematic, as we shall see, but he effectively promoted racial science by featuring it from the outset as an important topic in his influential *Zeitschrift für Geopolitik*.[47] Beyond this, Haushofer embraced a genuinely völkisch position by accepting the principle of ethnic-racial homogeneity as the proper basis for the consolidation of modern states. A cohesive Volk-organism in its entirety, in other words, became not merely a proper but indeed the necessary subject of political-territorial sovereignty. In the interwar period, German nationalists borrowed the novel notion of "national self-determination" from the contemporaneous anticolonial movement to express this position, and Geopolitik took a lead in demanding that Germany be accorded this natural and inalienable "right" through the repatriation of alienated national territories and populations.[48]

That the proponents of Geopolitik might have taken any other position in this period was unthinkable, to be sure, but this fact should not obscure its significance as a departure from the Ratzelian legacy. Inevitably, and again in full resonance with the spirit of "blood and soil," Haushofer's Geopolitik moved the notion of Lebensraum away from Ratzel's more generic conception of absolute global space to refer specifically to German Heimatboden, that is to say the circumscribed historical space of the German nation.[49] This did not of course mean that Lebensraum ceased to be an expansionist project for Haushofer. Very much to the contrary, his conception of it mandated territorial expansion, in order first to repatriate those parts of the old Reich lost at Versailles, and then further to achieve the original pan-German vision of the genuine consolidation of all Germans and German territories into a single political-national entity. In this spirit, Haushofer developed a theory of "organic" or moveable political boundaries, and his Geopolitik broadly endorsed and disseminated novel geographical concepts such as *Kulturboden* (regions of historical German habitation) and *Volksboden* (regions where Germans were still living), which were used to determine "objectively" and "scientifically" the full geographical extent of German Heimatboden.[50] Haushofer brought all of these strands together in his essay *The National-Socialist Idea in the World*, written as the Nazis assumed power in 1933. This work represented a public declaration of fidelity on the part of Geopolitik to the now-official dogmas of "blood and soil." In this spirit, he described the ultimate goal as the reconstitution of Germany "on soil which has been [historically] preserved as a sacred object, in a space congenial to blood and race."[51]

The fact that such an essay was written at all stands as testament to a final dimension of Haushofer's conformity to "blood and soil," namely his ambitions of having his new science adopted as a sort of official state science—the "geographical conscience of the state," as he evocatively put it—providing a "necessary bridge" over which "political knowledge" would cross into "political action."[52] Haushofer's ambitions were well-founded, for he enjoyed a close personal proximity to the leadership of the Nazi Party. He was a friend and intimate of Rudolf Hess, who had fought under his command during the war and later studied with him at the university in Munich, and through Hess he came into contact with Adolf Hitler himself. Haushofer strongly sympathized with the antimodern, antiurban, and antidemocratic ethos of this radical-conservative milieu. His early commitment to the cause was demonstrated by his frequent visits to Hitler and Hess during their internment in Landsberg Prison in 1924, when Hitler was busy dictating *Mein Kampf* to Hess. Haushofer later boasted how he left behind him in the prison cell a "well-read" copy of Ratzel's *Politische Geographie,* implying that in this way the precepts of Geopolitik had made their way into the very "foundations" of National Socialist thought.[53] Haushofer's völkisch credentials were robust enough for him to be appointed in the mid-1930s to the influential office of president of the Deutsche Akademie, an association of German academics devoted to promoting ties with ethnic German communities across eastern Europe.[54]

The obvious sincerity of Haushofer's ideological allegiance to the spirit of Germany's new order was, however, undermined by the fact that significant elements of Geopolitik did not sit easily with the precepts of "blood and soil." Into the early 1930s, for example, Geopolitik presented itself as a traditional positivist science that analyzed objective and incontrovertible natural laws; indeed, its emphatic claims to scholarly authority were founded precisely on this. Haushofer repeatedly stressed the point that Geopolitik, as an objective science, operated entirely above the realm of political persuasion and prejudice. "Geopolitical knowledge that is genuine and scientific must of necessity remain outside the considerations of party politics, and must be true in equal measure for the extreme left as for the extreme right."[55] Haushofer left no doubt, moreover, about his genuine commitment to this principle. In his *Zeitschrift für Geopolitik* he published not only the work of moderate liberals such as the Jewish scholar Hans Kohn but also the highly polemical geopolitical deliberations of the young Karl Wittfogel, at the time one of the leading intellectual forces of the German Communist Party.[56] No less striking was Haushofer's outspoken enthusiasm for the "pivot of history" and "heartland" theories of the British geographer and diplomat Sir Halford Mackinder. Despite the fact that Mackinder spoke for the interests of the British Empire—which Haushofer considered to be Germany's greatest single enemy—he accepted Mackinder's geopolitical arguments and conclusions essentially without reservation. All he did was rearrange Mackinder's political prescriptions, and in an inverted form use them as the basis for his own vision of a "continental bloc" based on a German-Soviet alliance—the most important (and ultimately fateful) policy position of his career.[57]

Together with the positivistic claim to scientific objectivity, the continuing fidelity of Weimar Geopolitik to the Ratzelian legacy can be seen in its geographical determinism. In the final analysis, Haushofer argued, geopolitical analysis demonstrated "the dependence of all political events on the enduring conditions of the physical environment," such that political life in general followed a "path determined by Nature." He conceded that subjective forces, such as the intervention of strong leaders, could affect the course of history—by arousing the passions of the masses they could lift them momentarily "above the conditions of the natural world" and lead them away from the "path determined by Nature"[58]—but in the end this influence remains ephemeral. The environment will always reassert its precedence, and society will eventually settle back into the proper course of historical development dictated by it. "At this point," he explained to a radio audience in 1931, "geopolitics takes the place of political passion, and development determined by natural law reshapes the work of the arbitrary transgression of human will. The natural world, beaten back in vain with sword or pitchfork, reasserts itself with justice on the earth's mantle and in its face. This is geopolitics!"[59] The utter incompatibility of this environmentally derived circumscription of the subjective power of strong leadership with the *Führerkult* then being actively fostered by the Nazis need hardly be emphasized.

Geographical determinism was not merely a characteristic feature of Weimar Geopolitik. More than this, it effectively represented Geopolitik's defining element. It was the one aspect that offered a common appeal across the political spectrum, for all parties wanted to share in the cachet of objectivity and scientific veracity that it promised to provide.[60] Favorite concepts of the period such as "spatial destiny" (*Raumschicksal*) or "locational destiny" (*Lageschicksal*) are comprehensible only in terms of it. One geopolitical study, for example, connected the dynamics of Germany's "locational destiny" to the factors of geographical space and landscape in the following manner:

> Those forces that have an effect across history originate out of the womb of the landscape, out of space. It is incorrect to equate these forces with those human individuals through whom they work. The force and power of Völker grow out of the soil of the landscape. . . . Landscape is the static aspect of history, and space is the dynamic pole. The dy-

namic forces that develop out of both are the driving forces of world history.[61]

Although the language of this passage is suffused with a völkisch inspiration, the prioritization of the factor of space is evident. Haushofer's colleague and friend, the political geographer Richard Hennig, presented what proved to be a particularly significant formulation of the environmentalist underpinnings of Geopolitik. In his study *Geopolitik: Die Lehre vom Staat als Lebensform,* Hennig spoke of a "parallelogram" of geopolitical (i.e., natural-geographical) forces which determine the development and operations of all states, irrespective of subjective factors of human intentionality. Because these geopolitical forces remained constant throughout history, or at least changed extremely slowly, the political personality and imperatives of any given state remained largely constant as well. Thus he argued that the foreign policies of England under Oliver Cromwell were not substantially different from those of the Elizabethan period, and he illustrated the principle in the contemporary world by suggesting that the policies of Tsarist Russia were (indeed could not but be) virtually identical to those of the Soviets. The political unification of Germany itself, he insisted, had been the result of objective geopolitical imperatives, and not the subjective designs or inclinations of its leaders. He did not deny Bismarck's political and diplomatic genius, but ultimately judged that—like Martin Luther and Christopher Columbus before him—he had acted "merely" as a "consummator of natural laws."[62]

Inevitably, this vigorous environmentalism affected Geopolitik's treatment of the factor of race. Haushofer acknowledged the general salience of race, as we have indicated, but his understanding of it diverged markedly from that of other "blood and soil" enthusiasts. As had been the case for Ratzel, race for him did not represent a fixed quality but rather was malleable and plastic, and as such was specifically subject to what he called the "racially formative" (*rassenbildende*) influence of Lebensraum and geographical space. In an early study on the geopolitics of Southeast Asia, he identified ongoing processes of "racial blending" (*Rassenverschmelzung*) in the region, which were producing the sorts of hybrid "mixed races" (*Mischrassen*) that Ratzel as well had identified. All of this racial recombination was driven by the conditions of the geographical environment.[63] Hennig went yet further and effectively dismissed race as largely irrelevant for geopolitical analysis. The character of the Volk was formed not by a preconfigured genetic Erbmasse but rather by the conditions of the physical environment, and he located himself in the tradition of Herder and others who sought to link this character to geographical factors such as climate.[64] Indeed, not only national character but a people's historical destiny itself was shaped by possibilities and restrictions that were inherent in the physical milieu. In an example that was subsequently to cause him no little difficulty, Hennig explained the emergence of northern Germany as the dominant power in the Baltic region, and the associated ascendance of the Hansa, not in terms of a primordial *Volkscharakter* but rather out of an economic imperative to conquer and control the richest fishing regions and the most lucrative markets. Hennig further argued that it had been the exigencies of Germany's economic life—specifically, the need to create a single market—that lay behind its eventual unification.[65]

Blood vs. Soil

The increasingly stringent ideological vigilance that came in the wake of the Nazi ascendance to power finally brought the tensions between the two contrasting options for Naturbedingtheit into the open as a major ideological issue. The position of Haushofer's Geopolitik in the early years of the Nazi regime was ambiguous. His prodigious efforts to present his perspective as harmonious with and indeed essential for National Socialism had paid off, initially at least, and the Nazis clearly wanted to make what use of him they could. They were impressed that the "science" of Geopolitik offered valuable intellectual cachet and scientific legitimacy for their perspectives on the rootedness of all political life in the soil and on the state as a biological organism.[66] This related most importantly to the question of territorial expansion, which figured of course among the most fundamental principles of the Nazi regime. With concepts such as Lebensraum, Raumbedürfnis, and Volks- und Kulturboden, Geopolitik possessed a convincing scholarly-analytical lexicon which seemed to provide scientific legitimation for a proactive program of territorial aggrandizement.[67] Finally, there were a number of very practical reasons for the Nazis to take Haushofer seriously. His *Zeitschrift für Geopolitik* was an influential journal which was broadly disseminated in Germany and abroad and which maintained an extensive network of foreign contacts and correspondents.[68] They were, moreover, impressed with its relative sophistication in dealing with issues of foreign policy and world politics, areas where their own provincialism was particularly apparent.[69] More than anything, however, it was Geopolitik's broad popularity that made it appealing to the Nazis. Haushofer himself was something of a media personality, well known through frequent newspaper commentaries and regular radio addresses on geopolitical themes, and Hess was not alone in his estimation that Geopolitik offered great value as a medium for propaganda and a "tool for political education."[70] A Nazi publication confirmed this in 1934: "Geopolitical training for all parts of the party is extremely valuable for political training, as is the dissemination of geopolitical thought overall."[71] Geopolitik quickly proliferated in public education, and by mid-decade it was estimated that every schoolchild had some exposure to geopolitical concepts.[72]

At the same time, however, the ideological arbiters of "blood and soil" were never really convinced by the self-professed conformity of the geopoliticians to the principles of the new order, and their skepticism found expression at the highest levels. Even before 1933, the principal Nazi formulator of "blood and soil" ideology, Darré, had had a strong interest in Geopolitik, which eagerly spoke his language and—with its emphasis on Bodenständigkeit—appeared to share his perspective. There was, additionally, a personal link through Haushofer's son Heinz, who like Darré was an agronomist by training. The younger Haushofer published articles in the latter's journal *Odal*, and the minister of agriculture apparently thought quite highly of him.[73] In 1932, Darré instructed his Agrarian-Political Department to organize a "Working Group for Geopolitics" (Arbeitsgemeinschaft für Geopolitik). The intention was that it would work in cooperation with Haushofer in order to develop the theory and teaching of geopolitics, bring it more fully into the Nazi Party, and facilitate connections between geopoliticians and political activists.[74] On the one hand, the formation of such a group was a clear indication of the importance the Nazis were according Geopolitik. At the same time, however, it was also intended to provide some sort of mechanism for the political supervision of the geopoliticians and their journal. From the outset, the Arbeitsgemeinschaft für Geopolitik retained for itself "the right to make suggestions, and to carry them out."[75]

The need for supervisory intervention was quickly felt, and indeed in regard to fundamental issues of ideological orientation. Darré's early reservations about geo-determinism have already been noted, and after 1933 his frustration with this particular aspect of geopolitical discourse grew ever more pronounced. He finally brought the point to public attention in 1935, in an address to the Academy of German Law. Darré began by lauding Geopolitik, which had focused scientific attention on "the connection of a state to a geographical region," and he observed that its study of "the influence of space on historical processes" had uncovered "numerous valuable interconnections" that should become a part of the "intellectual arsenal" of a statesman. However, he proceeded immediately to critique the specific manner in which Geopolitik represented the vital connection between Volk and Boden. "The connection of the Volk to the soil on which it lives," he maintained, "is not limited to the natural influence exerted by the characteristics, productivity, and resources of the latter on the economy and the material conditions of the cultural life of the former." It was necessary "to go beyond the general effect that the soil exerts on the conditions of existence for a particular race and for the life of a particular Volk" and focus instead on "the special way in which a Volk itself shapes its relationship to the soil, and in what form it owns and manages this native soil." Ultimately, Boden "is subordinated to the laws of the life forces of the Volk."[76] This point framed the remainder of his lecture, which was devoted to legal systems of land ownership. Darré was concerned enough about the issue to call a special meeting in the same year between Haushofer and the Arbeitsgemeinschaft für Geopolitik. Although the tone of the meeting was conciliatory, Haushofer was confronted with the demand that Geopolitik must accord a "racial orientation" (*Rassedenken*) the same importance as a "spatial orientation" (*Raumdenken*).[77]

Criticism of Geopolitik also appeared in the pages of scholarly and popular-political publications, and here the tone was far less conciliatory. Functionaries of the Arbeitsgemeinschaft für Geopolitik aggressively baited environmental determinism and accused it of association with the sort of rationalist "geographical materialism" that had been characteristic of the liberalism of the Weimar period and was embraced even by Marxists such as Wittfogel. More fundamentally problematic, however, was the issue identified by Darré. Geopolitik's emphasis on geographical causation, together with its inclination to identify the Volk as a racial community determined by space (*raumbedingte Rassegemeinschaft*) rather than blood, suggested that it viewed "qualities of race" as no more than incidental, a perspective which led inevitably to a "neglect of those vital forces that reside in Volk and race."[78] Although Haushofer was implicated in this critique, the brunt of it was directed against his colleague Hennig, who in the early 1930s had gained further visibility as the coauthor of a highly popular introductory text to Geopolitik.[79] This work was denounced for its putative "liberal foundations," a transgression aggravated variously by its "indulgence" in a theory of environmental determinism, its confusion of the proper völkisch principle of Raumgebundenheit with the errant geo-fantasy of Raumbedingtheit, and—once again—the consequent failure to acknowledge the quintessential importance of race. Hennig neither drew the necessary fundamental distinctions between races, nor did he appreciate the cultural hierarchy into which all such groups had to fit.[80]

One commentator, writing in the journal of the National Socialist teachers' organization, pointed out indignantly that in Hennig's work the ancient Germanic tribes (*Stämme*) were "equated, without any trace of racial thinking, with Apaches, Mohicans, and the wild peoples of Africa who have yet to come under the domination and educational influence of the white man."[81] The basic independence of racial qualities from environmental influences was repeatedly affirmed: "the [same] geographical environment is not [necessarily] able to produce the same races."[82] Hennig's environmentalist explanation of the medieval rise of German power on the North Sea and the Baltic was inevitably taken as a major slight of Germanic racial virtue, and brought the full wrath of his critics down upon him. This geopolitician, they mocked, wanted them to believe that the Hansa was built not on the "daring spirit" of traders from Saxony but rather on the abundance of the local herring catch.[83] In exaggerating the formative power of Raum, Hennig simply could not understand that

> people do not become seafarers because the natural environment is conducive to it. Rather, people who sense strength and energy in themselves go to sea. It is not because the inhabitants of the Alps and the Himalayas, the Caucasus and the Hindu Kush must conduct a constant struggle with the natural environment that they are characteristically defiant and daring. Rather, they climbed into the mountains [in the first place] because they sensed in themselves the strength to defy the natural elements. It is above all inner qualities, that is to say the quality of genetic inheritance [Bluterbe], that allows some people to become seafarers and others mountaineers. Crudely put, a high-quality Volk will make the best of even a difficult spatial destiny, while a Volk with a limited Bluterbe will be unable to create a paradise out of even the best regions. . . . *The environment influences the form in which the life-energies are expressed, but it does not create them. These energies are rather innate values, and come from racial inheritance.*[84]

Hennig responded to these attacks with a vigorous reaffirmation of geopolitics as he had portrayed it in 1929. To the charge of "geographical materialism" he offered the defense that one of the tasks of geopolitics was indeed to demonstrate how "in very numerous cases material factors such as soil qualities and mineral, botanical, and animal resources have all influenced the policies of state, have driven their development and even brought on wars."[85] Regarding the more fundamental question of race, he repeated his conviction that racial characteristics were first and foremost a "product of cultivation and development by the environment." Genetic constitutions were subject to ongoing transformation as a result of environmental influence, and one of the primary tasks of geopolitics was precisely to study this process.[86] On its own, however, racial science simply had no place in geopolitical analysis, and in a letter to Haushofer he insisted that "a boundary between geopolitics and a science of race now has to be very clearly drawn"[87] Resurrecting a term first used by Ratzel, he denigrated his detractors in the Working Group by characterizing them as *Rassenprediger* ("race preachers"), and he ridiculed their sermonizing in mordant terms. "Truly heroic people never think about money or merchandise when they go to war. Rather, they seek out the battle for the sake of the battle, in order to win fame and because [their] blood and race drive them to do it."[88] One may well wonder how Hennig could possibly have failed to realize that with his sarcasm he was mocking the holiest of völkisch values.

Mindful of the political costs that this ideological contretemps was exacting, Haushofer sought to keep a low profile. He continued to maintain good relations with the Arbeitsgemeinschaft für Geopolitik, some of whose attacks on Hennig had drawn favorable comparisons with his own work, and indeed he even colluded by providing space for them in his journal.[89] The master did not, however, emerge entirely unscathed. A 1936 article in the popular Nazi publication *Das Volk* purported to explain to readers the "mistaken ways of Geopolitik as a world view."[90] Although Haushofer was not implicated by name, the fact that he was indeed the intended subject of the broadside was apparent from the cartoon caricatures illustrating the article, and from its content as well. The denunciation of environmentalism as "geographical materialism" was repeated, as was the castigation of Haushofer for his failure to appreciate the primacy of factors of race. Significantly, the fact that Geopolitik supported such a flawed perspective as geographical determinism now called into question the sincerity of its proclaimed fidelity to völkisch principles, and ulterior motives were alluded to. "It's known on every street corner how Geopolitik made elaborate efforts to do business with the new state as soon as it came to power," noted the essay, pointing out how Geopolitik presented itself as the official theory of the National Socialist state. The opportunism of this attempt "to maneuver its way" into a position of authority was transparent, for the geopoliticians' "fantasies about communities based on space" were in fact utterly irreconcilable with racial theory. All of their pious proclamations of faith to "blood and soil," therefore, were simply meaningless. "Blood-and-soil thinking is focused [exclusively] on the connection of a German peasant with his native soil," while the "geopolitical space" of Geopolitik "includes everyone who lives in it, regardless of whether or not they have a profession or whether they are German or Jewish."[91] Such a critique was all the more biting in that it was accurate, for neither Haushofer's nor Hennig's Geopolitik had any analytical basis for acknowledging the significance of these latter factors.

It was not in the pages of a national journal that Haushofer received the most telling critique of his environmentalism, however, but rather in private correspondence within the circle of his closest allies. The publisher of the *Zeitschrift für Geopolitik* and of many of Haushofer's books, Kurt Vowinckel, was also involved in defining the ideological framework of Geopolitik. As an early member of the Nazi Party, Vowinckel stood organizationally closer to the new order than Haushofer himself, and he was a formal member of the Arbeitsgemeinschaft für Geopolitik.[92] Haushofer and Vowinckel shared the same general perspective, as their close and fruitful collaboration for over two decades testifies, but the latter was nonetheless genuinely torn by the race-space juxtaposition. In a letter to Haushofer written soon after the German invasion of the USSR—a move which marked the ignominious collapse of a policy which Geopolitik had urged for over a decade—he finally gave vent to his frustrations. "So I ask you," he demanded in desperate exasperation, "what, after all, is Geopolitik?"

> It is always the case that the forces of the earth (*Kräfte der Erde*) are able to exert their influence on politics only through the medium of human agency. For this reason, simply to point to these earthly forces [in isolation] is utterly meaningless for the policy makers, whom we both agree it is our goal to serve. The results of our research will become useful for policy makers only when full consideration is given to the influence of

the forces of the earth on humankind [i.e., on human agency as a mediating force], and the rootedness between man and space.

"Thus," he concluded, "Geopolitik is precisely the theory of how political events are connected to nature and destiny" (die Lehre von der Natur- bzw. Schicksalsgebundenheit der politischen Vorgängen).[93] The significance of Vowinckel's observation is in his choice of words, for his reference was to the more general Naturgebundenheit, and he pointedly avoided specifying the latter in terms of a "connection to space and the land" (Raum- und Erdgebundenheit). Struggling with the two options for Naturbedingtheit, völkisch principle finally won out, and even this most committed supporter of Haushofer and his Geopolitik was unable to follow him in prioritizing the factor of geography.

As vociferous as this barrage of negative critique may have been, however, it did not at any point call for a principled rejection of Geopolitik. Very much to the contrary, Geopolitik continued to be seen as a valuable element in the propaganda arsenal of the new state. At the same time that the Arbeitsgemeinschaft für Geopolitik was delivering its criticisms of Hennig and Haushofer, it was urging the expansion of Geopolitik as a subject in schools and universities.[94] All that was needed was to bring it into genuine ideological alignment with the principles of Volkstümlichkeit and National Socialism. The geopoliticians must stop treating their subject as scientific analysis, much less as an independent academic discipline, and assimilate instead the perspective of the Arbeitsgemeinschaft. Thus, Geopolitik was not so much a "science" as a sort of "inner mood" or "spiritual attitude," which offered an essentially metaphysical perspective on a völkisch "spatial destiny" (Raumschicksal) formed by the timeless organic forces of "blood and soil."[95] And, of course, Geopolitik needed above all to discard the flawed precepts of environmental determinism and accept instead the truly völkisch priority of race.

The issue of race had specific implications for how a genuinely völkisch Geopolitik should treat the matter of Landschaft. Rather than follow Ratzel in emphasizing how the physical-geographical qualities of a natural or primeval landscape (Urlandschaft) had influenced the course of history and shaped national characteristics, Geopolitik should focus exclusively on the cultural landscape. Indeed, the rejection of the earlier perspective was important enough for the claim now to be made that there was no such thing as a German natural landscape at all.[96] The point was to invert the causal relationship and investigate how an active and self-conscious Volk had across centuries of habitation imprinted its own characteristics and its *Weltbild* on the natural environment. Race was the formative factor in this process, and the cultural landscape acquired significance as a sort of materialization and visual embodiment of an encoded racial essence. "Just like the pages of an open book, the basic features of a [cultural] landscape tell us about the race which shaped it." These features of a "racial geography" would remain constant, even if the natural conditions were to change, a point immediately apparent in the fact that German emigrant communities always reproduced their native agricultural and settlement patterns in the very different environmental conditions of the Americas or Africa. The local indigenous population, by contrast, was, despite all efforts, prevented from emulating these European patterns by its "different racial constitution."[97]

This particular sense of cultural landscape was closely aligned with the conception noted above of Lebensraum as Heimatboden, in other words, those native regions in which a given Volk has become spiritually rooted over the course of its historical existence.[98] The Arbeitsgemeinschaft für Geopolitik considered Geopolitik to be "suitable for developing völkisch convictions" because, working with concepts such as Volks- and Kulturboden, it was devoted to determining the boundaries of the legitimate Lebensraum of the German peoples, and this was an important means for developing the "national-political will."[99] The insistence on the Volk as the active agent shaping an inert and subject landscape, moreover, related not merely to the historical process of Kulturlandschaft formation. Beyond this, it also embodied Darré's characterization of the Volk as the master (Beherrscher) and transformer of the natural environment. The Volk, that is to say, continued in the present day to exercise its formative agency, by altering and shaping the natural world in its own image and for its own purposes. Thus, Gehl pointed out that a genuinely völkisch Geopolitik would move from a perspective focusing on the "spatial determination" (*Raumbedingtheit*) of a Volk to a looser sense of "spatial connection" (*Raumgebundenheit*), and beyond this to a positive vision of the Volk's eventual mastery and "overcoming of space and its influences" (*Raumüberwindung*).[100]

We may note in conclusion that a völkisch Geopolitik conceived in this spirit had indeed begun to take shape and in a sense to displace the more hybrid version on offer by Haushofer, Hennig, and others. The political geographer Otto Maull was a close associate of Haushofer from the beginning, and collaborated with him in the late 1920s on an influential collection of geopolitical essays.[101] He shared Haushofer's environmentalism, but was always careful in his analyses to balance geographical influences against the subjective autonomy of the Volk. Thus, while he postulated a "law of the causal dependency" of humans on the geographical environment, he immediately qualified it with a countervailing "law of the variability of the relations between man and nature," noting that similar geographical conditions will not necessarily elicit the same responses from different groups.[102] His *Das Wesen der Geopolitik,* first published in the mid-1930s with a laudatory preface from Haushofer, indicated a subtle but significant evolution in his thinking. He now argued that a triad of factors influenced the course of political events: the earth "in the broadest sense of the term," the cultural-geographical shaping of the natural landscape, and finally the "racial and völkisch character" of human groups themselves.[103] These elements were not, however, significant in the same way. Maull now categorically rejected geographical determinism as "materialist," insisting instead that true Geopolitik was "idealist" in its inspiration and that it identified the rooted völkisch "spirit" itself as "the cause of all political developments." Primary attention was now focused precisely on the subjective category of personality that Haushofer and Hennig had dismissed, and Maull invoked the authority of Kant in pronouncing its essential "freedom and independence from the mechanisms of the natural world." The Volk itself now became the "quintessential agent of activity and determination" to which the natural-geographical milieu was correspondingly subordinated and by which it was instrumentalized as nothing more than "a task, a goal, and a purpose." Far from being constrained by the natural conditions in which it exists, a Volk demonstrates its worthiness through its success in an endless struggle to overcome and, eventually, to conquer them.[104]

The troubled cohabitation of the racially founded doctrines of "blood and soil" and the environmentalism of Geopolitik points to underappreciated complexities in the way political ideologies incorporate and deploy natural-scientific theory. The scope of the problem can be readily illustrated by considering the logical limitations that inhere in the concept of Social Darwinism. As a very loose designation for the attempt to formulate a theory of society on the basis of laws governing the operation of the natural world, the term has a certain meaning. This immediately begins to fracture, however, in the face of the fact that the "Darwinism" in question—to say nothing of natural science in general—refers to a varied and jumbled assemblage of theories that in the final analysis diverge wildly in their assumptions, conclusions, and implications. For this reason, a political Weltanschauung that is self-avowedly "biological" or "ecological" or "Darwinian" always remains ideological in the sense that it always has to make essential decisions about which aspects of biological or ecological or Darwinian theory to emphasize, how these should be interpreted, and what sorts of social and political consequences should be attached to them. Indeed, it is ultimately these latter decisions, and not the original natural or ecological science per se, that are important, a point that I would suggest we can see clearly in the remarkable sensitivities that ultimately transformed Geopolitik into such a political problem. Bringing these considerations back into the context of the present study, it is clear that simple references to völkisch sentiment or "blood and soil" doctrines as founded in ecological or bio-organic principles are insufficient. Beyond this, it is important to recognize that this naturalism had different options available to it, and that these different options were open to contending ideological significations.

Notes

The epigraph to this chapter is taken from Karl-Georg Faber's "Zur Vorgeschichte der Geopolitik: Staat, Nation, und Lebensraum im Denken deutscher Geographen vor 1914":

> It is one thing to understand geographical space—as a static or dynamic entity and as an object of political activity—as the primary factor of politics; it is something very different to see race as the moving force of history and to derive from this fact the claim of one's own biologically distinguished race to world domination.

In Heinz Dollinger, Horst Gründer, and Alwin Hanschmidt, eds., *Weltpolitik, Europagedanke, Regionalismus: Festschrift für Heinz Gollwitzer zum 65. Geburtstag* (Münster: Aschendorff, 1982), 389.

1. Edmund A. Walsh, "The Mystery of Haushofer," *Life*, 16 September 1946, 106–20; Walsh, *Wahre anstatt falsche Geopolitik für Deutschland* (Frankfurt: G. Schulte-Bulmke, 1946), 5; G. Etzel Pearcy and Russell H. Fifield, *World Political Geography* (New York: Thomas Y. Crowell, 1948), 23–33; Trevor Ravenscroft, *The Spear of Destiny: The Occult Power behind the Spear Which Pierced the Side of Christ* (London: Neville Spearman, 1972), 223; Louis

Pauwels and Jacques Bergier, *The Dawn of Magic,* trans. Rollo Myers (London: Anthony Gibbs & Phillips, 1963), 195–96; Hans-Adolf Jacobsen, ed., *Karl Haushofer: Leben und Werk,* 2 vols. (Boppard am Rhein: H. Boldt, 1979), 1:451–52. The characterization of Haushofer as a magician refers to his well-documented interest in the occult and allegedly comes from Hess himself. Haushofer shared this fascination with the Nazis, of course, and it provides the basis for some of the most wildly exaggerated claims for his influence over them. For useful correctives, see Nicholas Goodrick-Clarke, *The Occult Roots of Nazism: Secret Aryan Cults and Their Influence on Nazi Ideology* (New York: New York University Press, 1992), 219–21; Helmut Zander, "Sozialdarwinistische Rassentheorien aus dem okkulten Untergrund des Kaiserreichs," in *Handbuch zur "Völkischen Bewegung," 1871–1918,* ed. U. Puschner, W. Schmitz, and J. H. Ulbricht (Munich: Saur, 1996), 233n; David T. Murphy, *The Heroic Earth: Geopolitical Thought in Weimar Germany, 1918–1933* (Kent, OH: Kent State University Press, 1997), 54–55, 108; and Dan Diner, "Knowledge of Expansion: On the Geopolitics of Karl Haushofer," in *Beyond the Conceivable: Studies on Germany, Nazism, and the Holocaust,* ed. Dan Diner (Berkeley: University of California Press, 2001), 41.

2. Jacobsen, *Karl Haushofer;* Mark Bassin, "Race *Contra* Space: The Conflict between German *Geopolitik* and National Socialism," *Political Geography Quarterly* 6, no. 2 (1987): 115–34; Dan Diner, "'Grundbuch des Planeten': Zur Geopolitik Karl Haushofers," *Vierteljahresheft für Zeitgeschichte* 32, no. 1 (1984): 1–28; Diner, "Knowledge of Expansion"; G. Bakker, *Duitse Geopolitiek, 1919–1945: Een Imperialistische Ideologie* (Assen: Van Gorcum, 1967); R. Mattern, "Karl Haushofer und seine Geopolitik in den Jahren des Weimarer Republik und des Dritten Reiches" (PhD diss., Universität Karlsruhe, 1978). The 1990s saw a resurgence of interest in Haushofer, as part of a more general renaissance of Geopolitik in Germany after unification. The old view of the geopolitician as Hitler's mentor and the ideological source of National Socialism was resurrected, and indeed in its most comprehensive presentation to date: Bruno Hipler, *Hitlers Lehrmeister: Karl Haushofer als Vater der N-S Ideologien* (St. Ottilien: EOS Verlag, 1996). The opposite position was argued in Ebeling's dense monograph on Haushofer, albeit with the novel intention of disassociating Haushofer from the Nazis in order to rehabilitate his geopolitical theories. Frank Ebeling, *Karl Haushofer und seine Raumwissenschaft, 1919–1945* (Berlin: Akademie, 1994). On contemporary views of Haushofer, see Mark Bassin, "Between Realism and the 'New Right': Geopolitics in Germany in the 1990s," *Transactions of the Institute of British Geographers* 28, no. 3 (2003): 350–66.

3. Anna Bramwell, *Ecology in the 20th Century: A History* (New Haven: Yale University Press, 1989).

4. George Mosse's classic study is the best example of this. George Mosse, *The Crisis of German Ideology: Intellectual Origins of the Third Reich* (New York: Universal Library, 1964).

5. On the völkisch movement, see Jost Hermand, *Old Dreams of a New Reich: Völkisch Utopias and National Socialism* (Bloomington: Indiana University Press, 1992); Mosse, *Crisis;* Uwe Puschner, *Die völkische Bewegung in wilhelmischen Kaiserreich: Sprache, Rasse, Religion* (Darmstadt: Wissenschaftliche Buchgesellschaft, 2001); Puschner, "'One People, One Reich, One God': The *Völkische Weltanschauung* and Movement," *Bulletin of the German Historical Institute London* 24, no. 1 (May 2002): 5–28; Klaus von See, *Die Ideen von 1789 und die Ideen von 1914* (Frankfurt: Athenaion, 1975); von See, *Freiheit und Gemeinschaft: Völkisch-nationales Denken in Deutschland zwischen Franzöischer Revolution und Erstem Weltkrieg* (Heidelberg: C. Winter, 2001); Rolf Peter Sieferle, *Fortschrittsfeinde? Opposition gegen Technik und Industrie von der Romantik bis zur Gegenwart* (Munich: Beck, 1984).

6. Daniel Gasman, *The Scientific Origins of National Socialism: Social Darwinism in Ernst Haeckel and the German Monist League* (London: Macdonald, 1971).

7. Mosse, *Crisis,* 15–19.

8. Sieferle, *Fortschrittsfeinde,* 187.

9. George Mosse, *Toward the Final Solution: A History of European Racism* (Madison: University of Wisconsin Press, 1985), esp. 77–94.

10. The classic study of environmentalism is Clarence J. Glacken, *Traces on the Rhodian Shore: Nature and Culture in Western Thought from Ancient Times to the End of the Eighteenth Century* (Berkeley: University of California Press, 1967), which, however, stops around 1800. For other general works, see Armin Hajman Koller, *The Theory of the Environment: An Outline of the History of the Idea of Milieu, and Its Present Status* (Menasha, WI: G. Banta, 1918); and Franklin Thomas, *The Environmental Basis of Society: A Study in the History of Sociological Thought* (New York: Century, 1925).

11. Puschner, *Die völkische Bewegung,* 93, 101, 107, 153, 352n; Kay Dohnke, "Völkische Literatur und Heimatliteratur," in *Handbuch der "Völkischen Bewegung," 1871–1918,* ed. U. Puschner, W. Schmitz, and J. H. Ulbricht (Munich: Saur, 1996), 666n. For a warm, völkisch appreciation, see the obituary by Gustav Antze, "Dem Andenken Friedrich Ratzel," *Politisch-Anthropologische Revue* 3 (1904): 517–19.

12. Woodruff D. Smith, *The Ideological Origins of Nazi Imperialism* (New York: Oxford University Press, 1986), 147–48; Michael Peters, "Der 'Alldeutsche Verband,'" in *Handbuch der "Völkischen Bewegung," 1871–1918,* ed. U. Puschner, W. Schmitz, and J. H. Ulbricht (Munich: Saur, 1996), 303.

13. Friedrich Ratzel, "Über den Lebensraum," *Die Umschau* 1, no. 21 (1897): 363–67; Ratzel, *Der Lebensraum: Eine biogeographische Studie* (Tübingen: Laupp'sche Buchhandlung, 1901); Woodruff D. Smith, "Friedrich Ratzel and the origin of *Lebensraum*," *German Studies Review* 3, no. 1 (1980): 51–68; Mark Bassin, "Imperialism and the Nation-State in Friedrich Ratzel's Political Geography," *Progress in Human Geography* 11 (1987): 479–84.

14. Friedrich Ratzel, *Die Erde und das Leben: Eine vergleichende Erdkunde,* 2 vols. (Leipzig: Bibliographisches Institut, 1901–2), 2:554 (quote); Ratzel, *Anthropogeographie,* 2nd ed., 2 vols. (Stuttgart: J. Engelhorn, 1899–1912), 1:63, 67, 2:xxiv.

15. See, for example, the evaluation by the Austrian political scientist Ludwig Gumplowicz. *Geschichte der Staatstheorien* (Innsbruck: Verlag der Wagner'schen Buchhandlung, 1905), 530–31, 537.

16. Friedrich Ratzel, "Die deutsche Landschaft," in *Kleine Schriften* (Munich: Oldenbourg, 1906 [1896]), 1:127–50; Ratzel, "Die deutsche Kulturlandschaft," in *Deutschland: Einführung in die Heimatkunde* (Leipzig: Fr. Wilh. Grunow, 1898), 255–72; Ratzel, "Die deutsche historische Landschaft," *Die Grenzboten* 57, no. 44 (1898): 251–59. Mosse in particular highlights Ratzel's influence on the völkisch movement, although he is apparently unaware of the latter's status as a prominent scholar and describes him merely as a "romantic writer" (*Crisis,* 18, 220). On Ratzel and Riehl, see Johannes Steinmetzler, *Die Anthropogeographie Friedrich Ratzels und ihre ideengeschichtlichen Wurzeln,* Bonner Geographische Abhandlungen 19 (Bonn: Selbstverlag des Geographischen Instituts der Universität Bonn, 1956), 133–37; Willi Oberkrome, *Volksgeschichte: Methodische Innovation und völkische Ideologisierung in der deutschen Geschichtswissenschaft, 1918–1945* (Göttingen: Vandenhoeck & Ruprecht, 1993), 41, 44–45; H. Overbeck, "Ritter—Riehl—Ratzel: Die grossen Anreger zu einer historischen Landschafts- und Länderkunde Deutschlands im 19. Jahrhundert," in *Kulturlandschaftsforschung und Landeskunde: Ausgewählte, überwiegend methodische Arbeiten,* Heidelberger Geographische Arbeiten 14 (Heidelberg: Selbstverlag des Geographischen Instituts der Universität Heidelberg, 1965), 88–103; F. Metz, "Wilhelm Friedrich Riehl und die deutsche Landeskunde," *Berichte zur deutschen Landeskunde* 8 (1950): 286–95.

17. Steinmetzler, *Die Anthropogeographie Friedrich Ratzels,* 86–99, 109–14.

18. Ratzel, *Anthropogeographie,* 1:48. On the "organismic state" theory more generally, see Francis W. Coker, *Organismic Theories of the State: Nineteenth-Century Interpretations of the State as an Organism or a Person* (New York: AMS Press, 1967 [1910]).

19. Friedrich Ratzel, *Politische Geographie, oder die Geographie der Staaten, des Verkehrs, und des Krieges,* 3rd ed. (Munich: Oldenbourg, 1923 [1897]), 129; Ratzel, "Politisch-geographische Rückblicke," *Geographische Zeitschrift* 4 (1898): 268. On determinism in Ratzel, see Steinmetzler, *Die Anthropogeographie Friedrich Ratzels,* 59–69; and Mark Bassin, "Friedrich Ratzel," *Geographers: Bio-Bibliographical Studies* 11 (1987): 125–28.

20. Overbeck, who argues strongly for the Ratzel-Riehl connection, draws attention to fact that Ratzel devoted "very little attention" to the problem of *Kulturlandschaft.* Overbeck, "Ritter—Riehl—Ratzel," 99.

21. See, for example, Ratzel, "Die deutsche Kulturlandschaft."

22. Friedrich Ratzel, *Kulturgeographie der Vereinigten Staaten von Nordamerika . . .* (Munich: Oldenbourg, 1880); Ratzel, *Anthropogeographie,* 1:47, 250; Mark Bassin, "Friedrich Ratzel's Travels in the United States: A Study in the Genesis of his Anthropogeography," *History of Geography Newsletter* 4 (1984): 11–22.

23. Friedrich Ratzel, "Nationalitäten und Rassen," in *Kleine Schriften* (Munich: Oldenbourg, 1906 [1903]), 2:487.

24. Friedrich Ratzel, "Die Beurteilung der Völker," *Nord und Süd: Eine deutsche Monatsschrift* 6 (1878): 193.

25. Ratzel, "Nationalitäten und Rassen," 472 (quote), 465–74; Ratzel, "Die Beurteilung der Völker," 192–93.

26. Ratzel, "Nationalitäten und Rassen," 487 (quote), 482–87; Mathias Eidenbenz, *"Blut und Boden": Zu Funktion und Genese der Metaphern des Agrarismus und Biologismus in der nationalsozialistischen Bauerenpropaganda R. W. Darrés* (Bern: Peter Lang, 1993), 131; Heinz Gollwitzer, *Geschichte des weltpolitischen Denkens,* 2 vols. (Göttingen: Vandenhoeck & Ruprecht, 1972–82), 2:56–60.

27. As Gumplowicz emphasizes, the Volk for Ratzel was not a *Naturganzes,* or natural-organic entity. Gumplowicz, *Geschichte der Staatstheorien,* 537. Also see Oberkrome, *Volksgeschichte,* 45; Faber, "Zur Vorgeschichte der Geopolitik," 392, 398.

28. Ratzel, *Politische Geographie,* 163.

29. Ratzel, "Die Beurteilung der Völker," 190; Ratzel, *Anthropogeographie,* 1:242; Ratzel, *Politische Geographie,* 141, 25; Faber, "Zur Vorgeschichte der Geopolitik," 395.

30. Ratzel, "Die Beurteilung der Völker," 198; Ratzel, "Nationalitäten und Rassen," 477–78.

31. Ratzel, *Politische Geographie,* 162–63.

32. See, for example, Friedrich Ratzel, "Die Gesetze des räumlichen Wachstums der Staaten," *Petermanns Mittheilungen* 42 (1896), 97–107.

33. The term was apparently coined by the renegade Social Democrat August Winnig. Anna Bramwell, *Blood and Soil: Richard Walther Darré and Hitler's Green Party* (Bourne End, Buckinghamshire, UK: Kensal, 1985), 55; Heinz Haushofer, *Ideengeschichte der Agrarwirtschaft und Agrarpolitik im deutschen Sprachgebiet*, 2 vols. (Munich: Bayerischer Landwirtschaftsverlag, 1958), 2:167. On the *Blut und Boden* movement, also see Eidenbenz, "*Blut und Boden*"; Gustavo Corni and Horst Gies, "*Blut und Boden*": *Rassenideologie und Agrarpolitik im Staat Hitlers* (Idstein: Schultz-Kirchner Verlag, 1994); Bramwell, *Blood and Soil*; Klaus Bergmann, *Agrarromantik und Grossstadtfeindschaft*, Marburger Abhandlungen zur Politischen Wissenschaft 20 (Meisenheim am Glan: Anton Hain, 1970).

34. Heinz Haushofer, *Ideengeschichte der Agrarwirtschaft*, 2:167–69, 172–73; Bergmann, *Agrarromantik und Grossstadtfeindschaft*, 219–29.

35. Hitler's words were quoted by the geographer Hans Schrepfer, "Landschaft und Mensch im deutschen Lebensraum," *Zeitschrift für Erdkunde* 4 (1936): 174, and cited in Hans-Dietrich Schultz, *Die deutschsprachige Geographie von 1800 bis 1970* (Berlin: Selbstverlag des Geographischen Instituts der FU Berlin, 1980), 209.

36. Bergmann, *Agrarromantik und Grossstadtfeindschaft*, 311–12.

37. Cited in Schultz, *Die deutschsprachige Geographie*, 347.

38. R. Walther Darré, "Blut und Boden als Lebensgrundlagen der nordischer Rasse" [1930], in *Um Blut und Boden* (Munich: Zentralverlag der NSDAP, 1940), 20–21; Bergmann, *Agrarromantik und Grossstadtfeindschaft*, 302.

39. R. Walther Darré, "Blut und Boden: ein Grundgedanke des nationalsozialistischen Rechts" [1935], in *Um Blut und Boden*, 297.

40. Eidenbenz, "*Blut und Boden*," 45, 49, 53, 56, 64.

41. R. Walther Darré, *Neuadel aus Blut und Boden* (Munich: Lehmann, 1930), 90; Heinz Haushofer, *Ideengeschichte der Agrarwirtschaft*, 2:172.

42. See Schultz, *Die deutschsprachige Geographie*, 203–4, 346.

43. Rudolf Kjellén, *Die Ideen von 1914: Eine weltgeschichtliche Perspektive*, trans. Carl Koch (Leipzig: S. Hirzel, 1915); Rudolf Kjellén, *Der Staat als Lebensform*, 5th ed., trans. J. Sandmeier (Berlin: Kurt Vowinckel, 1924).

44. For general treatments of Geopolitik, see Murphy, *Heroic Earth*; Klaus Kost, *Die Einflüsse der Geopolitik auf Forschung und Theorie der politischen Geographie von ihren Anfängen bis 1945*, Bonner Geographische Abhandlungen 76 (Bonn: Ferd. Dümmlers Verlag, 1988); Rainer Sprengel, *Kritik der Geopolitik: Ein deutscher Diskurs, 1914–1944* (Berlin: Akademie, 1996); Michel Korinman, *Quand l'Allemagne pensait le monde: Grandeur et décadence d'une géopolitique* (Paris: Fayard, 1990).

45. Adolf Grabowsky, "Das Problem der Geopolitik," *Zeitschrift für Politik* 22 (1933): 765. The appeal of Geopolitik in interwar Germany extended to the Social Democrats and even to the Communists. Murphy, *Heroic Earth,* 44, 57–58, 68–69, and passim; Mark Bassin, "Nature, Geopolitics, and Marxism: Ecological Contestations in Weimar Germany," *Transactions of the Institute of British Geographers,* n.s., 21, no. 2 (1996): 315–41.

46. Karl Haushofer, "Politische Erdkunde und Geopolitik" [1925], in Jacobsen, *Karl Haushofer,* 1:513, 514, 522; Haushofer, "Geopolitische Grundlagen" [1934], ibid., 1:559–60; Haushofer, *Der Nationalsozialistische Gedanke in der Welt* (Munich: G. W. Callway, 1933).

47. Thus, in the journal's earliest issues, from 1924, conservative notables such as Oswald Spengler were reprimanded for neglect and imprecision in their treatment of racial categories, and within a decade the journal was freely discussing issues of racial hygiene and the creation of administrative departments for racial matters (*Rasseämter*) across Germany. Hans Harmsen, "Ziele und Möglichkeiten deutscher Bevölkerungspolitik," *Zeitschrift für Geopolitik* 10 (1933): 212; Murphy, *Heroic Earth,* 243, 266n.

48. It is something of a tribute to Haushofer's consistency that he treated national self-determination as a universal right and spoke repeatedly in support of anticolonial movements in Asia and Africa. Haushofer, *Nationalsozialistische Gedanke,* 29–30. The main object, of course, was not the benefit of independence for the indigenous nations so much as the weakening of rival European powers.

49. Hugo Hassinger, "Geographie und Deutschlandskunde," *Nation und Staat* 7, no. 1 (1933): 285; Joachim Petzold, *Konservative Theoretiker des deutschen Faschismus: Jungkonservative Ideologen in der Weimar Republik als geistige Wegbereiter der faschistischen Diktatur* (Berlin: Deutscher Verlag der Wissenschaft, 1982), 82; Murphy, *Heroic Earth,* 61. On Haushofer's use of Lebensraum, see Jacobsen, *Karl Haushofer,* 1:249, 463, 643; Diner, "Knowledge of Expansion," 41–43.

50. Michael Fahlbusch, "*Wo der Deutsche . . . ist, ist Deutschland!" Die Stiftung für deutsche Volks- und Kulturbodenforschung in Leipzig, 1920–1933* (Bochum: Brockmeyer, 1994); Oberkrome, *Volksgeschichte.*

51. Haushofer, *Nationalsozialistische Gedanke,* 13 (quote), 4; Haushofer, "Geopolitische Grundlagen," 558ff. In the middle of the war, Haushofer reconfirmed his spiritual commitment to Blood and Soil in his poem, "The Meaning of Geopolitik":

> *Wenn Blut- und Boden-Kräfte sich durchdringen,*
> *Bis sich ein Völkerschicksal d'raus gestaltet,*

> *Das über wachsenden Geschlechtern waltet,*
> *Bis ihnen ihre Sendung will gelingen,*
> *Dann Kraft um Kraft in's Gleichgewicht zu schalten,*
> *Das muss die Geopolitik erringen,—*
> *Die Widerstande geistig zu bezwingen,*
> *Dem Erdkreis Schwung und Stete zu erhalten.*

(Jacobsen, *Karl Haushofer,* 1:[1])

52. Karl Haushofer, "Zur Geopolitik" [1931], in Jacobsen, *Karl Haushofer,* 1:545 (quote), 547.

53. Karl Haushofer, "Friedrich Ratzel als raum- und volkspolitischer Gestalter," in *Erdenmacht und Völkerschicksal: Eine Auswahl aus seinen Werken,* by Friedrich Ratzel (Stuttgart: Kröner, 1940), xxvi. On Hitler's use of geopolitical concepts, in particular the term "Lebensraum," see Karl Lange, "Der Terminus 'Lebensraum' in Hitlers *Mein Kampf,*" *Vierteljahresheft für Zeitgeschichte* 13, no. 4 (1965): 426–37; Smith, *Ideological Origins,* 231–58.

54. Murphy, *Heroic Earth,* 244.

55. Haushofer, "Zur Geopolitik," 545 (quotes), 511, 514.

56. Hans Kohn, "Übersicht über den Vorderen Orient," *Zeitschrift für Geopolitik* 7 (1930): 791–94. Haushofer's relationship with Kohn was close enough for the latter to request a letter of reference from the geopolitician in support of his application for a teaching position at Hebrew University in Jerusalem. Jacobsen, *Karl Haushofer,* 1:458n; Diner, "Knowledge of Expansion," 33. Haushofer's interest in Wittfogel, with whom he shared a strong interest in the Far East, was yet more striking. In a series of reviews, he rated the latter's work as the "very best" research available on its subject, notwithstanding the "ultra Marxism" of the exposition. Karl Haushofer, review of *Das erwachende China,* by Karl Wittfogel, *Zeitschrift für Geopolitik* 4 (1927): 187–90; Haushofer, review of *Wirtschaft und Gesellschaft Chinas,* by Karl Wittfogel, *Zeitschrift für Geopolitik* 8 (1931): 170; Haushofer, review of *Aufzeichnungen eines chinesischen Revolutionärs,* by Sun Yat-sen, ed. and intro. Karl Wittfogel, *Zeitschrift für Geopolitik* 5 (1928): 608–9. Most remarkable of all, however, was Haushofer's decision in 1932 to publish excerpts of an extended essay by Wittfogel on geopolitics that had appeared some years earlier in the scholarly organs of the German and Soviet Communist parties. Although Wittfogel conceived his essay as a critique of Geopolitik, and indeed of Haushofer himself, the geopolitician correctly perceived that Wittfogel was, actually, merely rearranging certain basic concepts, and he affirmed

that the communist's perspective was not without "scientific value." Karl August Wittfogel, "Geopolitik, geographischer Materialismus, und Marxismus," *Zeitschrift für Geopolitik* 9 (1932): 581–91. For the original, see Karl August Wittfogel, "Geopolitik, geographischer Materialismus, und Marxismus," *Unter dem Banner des Marxismus* 3 (1929): 17–51; 5 (1929): 485–522; 7 (1929): 698–735; K. Vitfogel, "Geopolitika, geograficheskii materializm, i Marksizm," *Pod Znamenem Marksizma* 2 (1929): 16–43; 6 (1929): 1–29; 7/8 (1929): 1–28. There was a telling coda to the Haushofer-Wittfogel association. Wittfogel was arrested the following year in the initial Nazi crackdown on political opponents, and his wife—aware of Haushofer's influential connections with the Nazi leadership—appealed to him to intervene on her husband's behalf. Haushofer did indeed speak with Hess about Wittfogel, but Hess was unmoved by Haushofer's appeal on behalf of the author of "the best German book on Chinese economics." G. L. Ulmen, *The Science of Society: Toward an Understanding of the Life and Work of Karl August Wittfogel* (The Hague: Mouton, 1978), 162.

57. Karl Haushofer, *Der Kontinentalblock: Mitteleuropa—Eurasien—Japan* (Munich: Zentralverlag der NSDAP, 1941). On Haushofer and Mackinder, see Haushofer, "Politische Erdkunde und Geopolitik," 513, 519; Haushofer, *Geopolitik der Pan-Ideen* (Berlin: Zentral-Verlag, 1931), 17; Diner, "Knowledge of Expansion," 31, 36.

58. Haushofer, "Politische Erdkunde und Geopolitik," 512, 511.

59. Haushofer, "Zur Geopolitik," 547.

60. Thus, Haushofer's Geopolitik was carefully criticized by political opponents such as Grabowsky and Wittfogel not for its geographical determinism per se but for the incorrect or excessive manner in which he used it. Grabowsky, "Das Problem der Geopolitik," esp. 783–84; Otto Maull, *Politische Geographie* (Berlin: Gebrüder Borntraeger, 1925), 45. Wittfogel's extensive argument is particularly interesting, for it raises the important problem of environmentalism and the interpretation of nature in the Marxist tradition. Mark Bassin, "Nature, Geopolitics, and Marxism," 328–332; Bassin, "Geographical Determinism in *Fin-de-Siècle* Marxism: Georgii Plekhanov and the Environmental Basis of Russian History," *Annals of the Association of American Geographers* 82, no. 1 (1992): 3–22.

61. Hermann Overbeck, *Raum und Politik in der deutschen Geschichte: Geopolitische Betrachtungen zum deutschen Lageschicksal* (Gotha: 1929), 13, cited in Schultz, *Die deutschsprachige Geographie*, 387.

62. Richard Hennig, *Geopolitik: Die Lehre vom Staat als Lebensform* (Leipzig: B. G. Teubner, 1928), 7.

63. Haushofer, "Politische Erdkunde und Geopolitik," 518; Karl Haushofer, *Zur Geopolitik der Selbstbestimmung: Südostasiens Wiederaufsteig zur Selbstbestimmung* (Munich: Rösl, 1923), 92–93, 119.

64. Hennig, *Geopolitik*, 2, 62.

65. Ibid., 53, 6.

66. Smith, *Ideological Origins*, 218; also see Joachim C. Fest, *The Face of the Third Reich: Potraits of the Nazi Leadership*, trans. Michael Bullock (New York: Pantheon, 1970), 250–57.

67. R. Walther Darré, "Stellung und Aufgaben des Landstandes in einem nach Lebensgesetzlichen Gesichtspunkten aufgebauten deutschen Staate" [1930], in *Um Blut und Boden* (Munich: Zentralverlag der NSDAP, 1940), 213; Eidenbenz, "*Blut und Boden*," 57–59; Corni and Gies, "*Blut und Boden*," 22; Bergmann, *Agrarromantik und Grossstadtfeindschaft*, 307–10.

68. Kurt Vowinckel, *Kurt Vowinckel Verlag, 1923–1973* (n.p., 1973), 6.

69. Richard Wagner, "Ziele der Arbeitsgemeinschaft für Geopolitik," in Jacobsen, *Karl Haushofer*, 2:153.

70. R. Hess to Richard Wagner (6 March 1934), in Jacobsen, *Karl Haushofer*, 2:1

71. *Verordnungsblatt der Reichsleitung der NSDAP*, Folge 65 (15 January 1934), cited in Hans F. Zeck, "Was ist Geopolitik?" *Zeitschrift für Erdkunde* 4 (1936): 975.

72. Ravenscroft, *Spear of Destiny*, 227; Murphy, *Heroic Earth*, 106–7, 242–43. Ravenscroft reckons this a propaganda feat "that even Goebbels was never able to match!"

73. Heinz Konrad Haushofer, "Die Auswirkungen der Marktordnung auf den Hof," *Odal: Monatsschrift für Blut und Boden* 4, no. 4 (1935): 317–25; Jacobsen, *Karl Haushofer*, 1:383. Heinz Haushofer's enduring commitment to these principles was apparent in his useful but subtly apologetic history of ruralist ideology in Germany, published in the late 1950s. Heinz Haushofer, *Ideengeschichte der Agrarwirtschaft*.

74. P. Gemeinder to K. Haushofer (23 February 1932), in Jacobsen, *Karl Haushofer*, 2:123.

75. Wagner, "Ziele der Arbeitsgemeinschaft für Geopolitik," 153–54; "Denkschrift: Geopolitik als nationale Staatswissenschaft," *Zeitschrift für Geopolitik* 10, no. 5 (1933): 301–5.

76. Darré, "Blut und Boden: Ein Grundgedanke des nationalsozialistischen Rechts," 296–97.

77. "Aussprache über Geopolitik in Bad Saarow," *Geographische Wochenschrift* 3 (1935): 715.

78. W. Seddin, "Der Irrweg einer 'Geopolitik' als Weltanschauung," *Das Volk: Kampfblatt für völkische Kultur und Politik,* May 1936, 60 (quote), 62. "Seddin" was apparently a pseudonym for W. Staudinger, an official in Darré's ministry. Hans Schrepfer, "Geopolitik und Erdkunde," *Zetischrift für Erdkunde* 4 (1936): 966.

79. Richard Hennig and Leo Korholz, *Einführung in die Geopolitik* (Leipzig: Teubner, 1933). By 1938 the book had gone through eight editions.

80. Walther Gehl, review of *Einführung in die Geopolitik,* by Richard Hennig and Leo Körholz, *Deutsche Höhere Schule* 2, no. 16 (1934–35): 589–90; Schrepfer, "Geopolitik und Erdkunde," 966.

81. Gehl, review of *Einführung in die Geopolitik,* 589.

82. Konrad Bahr, "Die Rassenfrage im Erdkundeunterricht," *Deutsche Höhere Schule* 2, no. 4 (1934–35): 110.

83. Gehl, review of *Einführung in die Geopolitik,* 590.

84. Zeck, "Was ist Geopolitik?" 976 (emphasis added).

85. Richard Hennig, "Geographischer Materialismus?" *Zeitschrift für Erdkunde* 4 (1936): 970.

86. Ibid., 972, 974. Also see R. Hennig to K. Haushofer (18 July 1936), in Jacobsen, *Karl Haushofer,* 2:254–55.

87. R. Hennig to K. Haushofer (18 June 1936), in Jacobsen, *Karl Haushofer,* 2:254.

88. Hennig, "Geographischer Materialismus?" 970.

89. "Geopolitik und Kochkunst," *Zeitschrift für Geopolitik* 12, no. 10 (1936): 651; "Protokoll über die Sitzung des Beirats der Arbeitsgemeinschaft für Geopolitik" (10 December 1936), in Jacobsen, *Karl Haushofer,* 1:300–305. For positive comparisons of Haushofer, see Zeck, "Was ist Geopolitik?" 975; Gehl, review of *Einführung,* by Hennig and Körholz, 590. However, Haushofer's correspondence with Hennig indicates how disturbed he was by this onslaught against his Geopolitik. See, for example, K. Haushofer to R. Hennig (19 July 1936), in Jacobsen, *Karl Haushofer,* 2:255–56.

90. Seddin, "Irrweg einer 'Geopolitik,'" 59–64. Jacobsen, *Karl Haushofer,* 2:354n.

91. Seddin, "Irrweg einer 'Geopolitik,'" 60–62, 63.

92. Indeed, Vowinckel later claimed that the original idea of forming the Arbeitsgemeinschaft was his. Most of his brief memoir is devoted to his long collaboration with Haushofer. Vowinckel, *Kurt Vowinckel Verlag, 1923–1973.*

93. K. Vowinckel to K. Haushofer (26 August 1941), in Jacobsen, *Karl Haushofer,* 521–22.

94. "Aussprache über Geopolitik," 718.

95. Ibid., 716–17; Zeck, "Was ist Geopolitik?" 975; Schrepfer, "Geopolitik und Erdkunde," 924; Murphy, *Heroic Earth*, 302n.

96. "Eine deutsche Naturlandschaft gibt es nicht, wohl aber eine deutsche Kulturlandschaft." Robert Gradmann, "Die Wissenschaft im Dienste der deutschen Volkstumspolitik: Rede zur Reichgrundungsfeier," *Erlanger Universitäts-Reden* 12:9, cited in Schultz, *Die deutschsprachige Geographie*, 389.

97. Oskar Sauer, "Rasse, Volk, und Lebensraum," *Deutsche Höhere Schule* 2, no. 16 (1934–35): 581; Bahr, "Die Rassenfrage im Erdkundeunterricht," 111.

98. Rudolf Völkel, "Die Erdkunde im Umbruch," *Deutsche Höhere Schule* 2, no. 19 (1934–35): 692–93.

99. "Aussprache über Geopolitik," 715.

100. Gehl, review of *Einführung*, by Hennig and Körholz, 590.

101. Karl Haushofer et al., eds., *Bausteine zur Geopolitik* (Berlin: Kurt Vowinckel, 1928).

102. Maull, *Politische Geographie*, 44–46.

103. Otto Maull, *Das Wesen der Geopolitik*, 3rd ed. (Leipzig: B. G. Teubner, 1941), 20.

104. Ibid., 60–62.

CHAPTER 9

Violence as the Basis of National Socialist Landscape Planning in the "Annexed Eastern Areas"

Joachim Wolschke-Bulmahn

LANDSCAPE ARCHITECTS AND urban planners enjoyed an unusually high status within the political and social structure of Nazi Germany, and nowhere was their influence more apparent than in the so-called Annexed Eastern Areas of the former Republic of Poland. After defeating Poland in September 1939, Nazi leaders set out to "Germanize" their annexed territories through murder, expulsion, expropriation, and other forms of ethnic cleansing. Nazi-era architects and planners, for their part, welcomed the opportunity to re-sculpt Poland's rural and urban landscape as they saw fit. Ultimately, Nazi exterminationists created an "empty space" that landscape and urban planners "filled" in accordance with the conceptual ideals (*Idealvorstellungen*) they had developed inside Germany.[1]

Although "landscape cleansing" reached its apex under National Socialism, the Nazis were by no means the first to redesign spatial environments in an authoritarian and violent manner. Time and again, feudal rulers expropriated land and expelled peasants in order to create parks and hunting preserves designed for their exclusive pleasures. The parks of Chatsworth in England and Pavlovsk in Russia are but two examples where whole villages were relocated in order to create an Arcadian environment for the ruling classes. The same can be said of the parks and wilderness areas of the modern era: Native Americans were forcefully re-moved to create Yellowstone National Park in Wyoming, just as native blacks were displaced to establish Serengeti National Park in Tanzania.

Conceptions of an "ideal" environment are connected not only to the spatial environment itself—that is, to the natural and built landscape—but also to specific notions of what constitutes an "ideal" human being and an "ideal" human society. During World War I, for instance, the Sec-ond Reich made plans to colonize the conquered portions of Polish-speaking Europe with German settlers.[2] In what can be viewed as a dress rehearsal for a later era, many urban planners and landscape architects in Germany planned for the permanent occupation of conquered terri-tories without feeling any need to take existing social and spatial struc-tures into consideration.

No doubt these architects and planners had mixed and overlapping motives. Many probably just wanted to enhance their status as civilian "soldiers" of the Second Reich. Others were probably just frustrated by the way in which existing social structures and property relations thwarted their ability to redesign their home cities and regions to the de-gree that they would have liked. A few, however, were already beginning to take this logic to its ultimate extreme and embrace the notion that an "empty" landscape offered unique opportunities. Thus, at the outset of World War I, the eminent landscape architect Hermann Koenig candidly expressed his vision for eastern Europe's future: "Instead of clay huts and thatched and tiled roofs, there could soon be charming pictures of vil-lages and little towns along the lines envisaged by the Settlement Com-mission (Ansiedlungskommission) in Poznan, all the more so if the garden-city idea receives a fair hearing. By partially reconstructing the larger places and towns, it should easily be possible to eliminate the urban-development sins of past decades. The dictatorial power of the victor will offer our generation the rare chance to operate artistically on totally new ground. . . . Our experiences so far entitle us to demand that, by the reorganization of so many things, the proper influence will be secured also for the field of garden art."[3]

Koenig's remarks clearly indicate a propensity among some German planners toward an authoritarian perspective long before the Nazi take-over. Under National Socialism, however, "the dictatorial power of the victor" took on new dimensions and opened up new vistas for landscape architects and urban planners. By 1939, they were no longer thinking sim-ply in terms of designing individual projects such as gardens and parks but in terms of redesigning entire regions. And whereas the authoritarian ideal had resonated earlier with only a handful of planners, now almost the whole profession was keen on participating in these endeavors.

Policy Making in the Annexed Eastern Areas

Dictatorial planning had fatal consequences for millions of human beings in the Annexed Eastern Areas. The German army occupied the western regions of Poland in 1939 in accordance with the terms of the Nazi-Soviet Pact, and soon thereafter landscape cleansing began. For administrative purposes, the Nazi government divided the territory into four districts (Wartheland, Danzig-Westpreussen, Ciechanów, and Katowice) and then incorporated them directly into the Reich. (A separate General Government was also established in Cracow to oversee the administration of an occupied rump Poland). German planners immediately began to prepare blueprints that foresaw the demolishing of towns, villages, and rural landscapes, and their reconstruction along Nazi ideals. As Alwin Seifert, the Reich landscape advocate and a fanatic anti-Semite, stated in 1941: "If the East is to become home for Germans from all over Germany, and if it is to flourish and become as beautiful as the rest of the Reich, then it is not enough just to cleanse the towns of past Polish mismanagement and construct clean and pleasant villages. The entire landscape must be Germanized."[4] The participation of numerous planners in this "Germanization" project demonstrates a support for, and legitimizing of, Nazi rulership and its policy of conquest. Many of the planners were apparently thrilled by the opportunity to re-sculpt the eastern territories in their totality, even if it meant the suppression, exploitation, and extermination of the people who lived there. By obliterating the visual structures of Polish culture, they participated in their own unique way in the implementation of the "final solution."[5]

Heinrich Himmler was of particular importance for Nazi landscape and city planning activities in occupied Poland, for it was under his supervision that a special planning team was established to Germanize the annexed territories.[6] Nazi ideologues saw this project in Social Darwinist terms: Germany needed "living space" (Lebensraum) to guarantee its long-term survival. They also saw it as a necessary buffer zone against the "danger from the East," that is, the Soviet Union. The German farmers who were to be settled there, so went the argument, needed to feel at home in a Germanized landscape so that they would be motivated to defend this new frontier. From the outset, German landscape planning was inextricably linked to annexation, colonization, and border defense.

Nothing demonstrates this commonality of interests better than Hitler's secret decree of 7 October 1939, which elevated Himmler to the position of Reich commissioner for the strengthening of Germandom (Reichskommissar für die Festigung deutschen Volkstums). The decree entrusted Himmler with the task of achieving the following goals: (1) the repatriation of German citizens and ethnic Germans currently living outside the Reich; (2) the "elimination of the harmful influence of such alien portions of the population as constitute a danger to the Reich and the German community"; and (3) the establishment of new German territories for the purpose of fostering resettlement, especially for those Germans returning from foreign communities.[7]

Of these three tasks, Himmler was mostly interested in the third: the formation of new territories for German settlements. He also quickly came to realize that the existing boards and agencies that dealt with city and regional planning—most notably Hanns Kerrl's Reich Office for Spatial Order (Reichsstelle für Raumordnung)—were not designed to take on a task of this "universal and historically unique character."[8] He therefore decided to create his own planning board under the supervision of Konrad Meyer, a member of the Nazi Party and the SS. Meyer, who had been serving as head of the Institute for Agriculture and Land Politics at the University of Berlin since 1934, was well known for his totalitarian approach to landscape planning. "For us National Socialists," he wrote in 1941, "planning results in responsibility to people and state. More than the complete planning of space and economy, it aspires to the creation of a healthy social structure and a permanent configuration of our living space as befits Teutonic German men."[9]

Another leading member of this planning board was Heinrich Friedrich Wiepking-Jürgensmann. He touted the idea that Germans had a close relationship to their home landscapes, and argued that it was necessary to replicate these homelands in the conquered territories. Much like Meyer, Wiepking had been named chair of the Institute for Landscape Design at the University of Berlin in 1934 and was later appointed by Himmler to become a special representative for questions concerning landscape formation. Wiepking was even more effusive than Meyer about his new assignment. In late 1939, shortly after the invasion of Poland, he published an article in the journal *Die Gartenkunst*, entitled "The German East: A Priority Task for our Students," which predicted "a golden age for the German landscape and garden designer that will surpass everything that even the most enthusiastic among us had previously dreamed."[10]

The "elimination of the harmful influence of such alien portions of the population as constitute a danger to the Reich and the German community" (Hitler); the "permanent shape of our living space as befits Teutonic German men" (Meyer); the "golden age for the German landscape and garden designer" (Wiepking)—these effusive proclamations were all predicated on the use of violence. They were, in fact, nothing less than euphemisms thinly veiling the expropriation, expulsion, and extermination of Poles, especially Jewish Poles.[11]

Meyer even defined this "planning freedom" in terms that left no doubt as to its exterminationist implications: "It is essential to a real planning freedom that, firstly, one's own *Volk* are available in sufficient numbers and are of appropriate ability to claim new space and, secondly, that property which is not owned by members of one's own Volk is available in a sufficient amount."[12] For him, "planning freedom" in the Annexed Eastern Areas was not being carried far enough. He wanted more territory brought into the eastern realm, as foreseen in such army planning documents as "General Plan East":

> All in all, the "Annexed Eastern Areas" that once belonged to the Polish state, namely the district of Danzig–Western Prussia and parts of Eastern Prussia and Upper Silesia, as well as the space won in the west in Lower Styria and South Carinthia, have alleviated our land shortage to some degree. Since the property of Poles, Jews, and other alien and state-adversarial individuals was confiscated for the Reich, additional space has been won. However, this newly acquired property is by no means sufficient in terms of size and condition to satisfy all of the demand which has arisen in the Reich. Furthermore, because of the transfer of more than 550,000 ethnic Germans [*Volksdeutscher*] from abroad, a significant additional demand for agricultural land for settlement has arisen. Only the abolishing of Soviet rule and the incorporation of additional eastern spaces into our European living space will return full planning freedom to the Reich and enable us to open up new settlement areas. This shows the fundamental difference between planning in the old Reich before 1939 and planning after the conquest of the new territories: while the former Reich was constrained by the affliction of too little space, the new one has the opportunity for creative design.[13]

Meyer's colleagues in the planning section of the Reich Commission also saw the aggressive policies of the Nazis as a legitimate way to create what they considered the prerequisites for planning. In 1942, for instance, Erhard Mäding published *Landespflege: Die Gestaltung der Landschaft als Hoheitsrecht und Hoheitspflicht*. In it, he offered a particularly aggressive definition of "living space," in which conquering other countries and exploiting their populations was an integral part of landscape care.[14]

Landscaping as a Tool of Ethnic Cleansing

Those involved with the Reich Commission plainly knew that terror and force lay at the foundation of all planning in the Annexed Eastern Areas; the commission controlled the fate of the local inhabitants just as it controlled the use of the land and soil. One can see this policy of expulsion and elimination in one of the Reich Commission's own documents, "Basics of Planning for the Building-up of the Eastern Areas." Its bland title notwithstanding, it stated in part: "In the following material, it is taken for granted that the entire Jewish population of this area, roughly 560,000 people, has already been evacuated or will leave the area in the course of this winter. Therefore it is practical to count on a population of nine million people."[15] In order to augment the German population in the Annexed Eastern Areas to at least 50 percent (the percentage of Germans that allegedly lived there before the outbreak of World War I), "the number of Germans now living in this area [1.1 million] should be increased by 3.4 million so that it reaches 4.5 million. At the same time, 3.4 million Poles should be deported, little by little."[16] Meyer announced these "planning basics" at a conference in Poznań on 24 January 1940, only four weeks after the conquest of Poland. In the audience were the landscape and regional planners responsible for the Annexed Eastern Areas as well as local representatives of the Reich Commission for the Strengthening of Germandom.

From the outset, the Reich Commission's plan was to create a new home for ethnic Germans by rendering millions of people who lived in the Annexed Eastern Areas homeless. Many were summarily expelled from their houses on such short notice that they had no time to take their possessions with them. (At first, the German occupiers seemed to have no idea what to do with the expellees; they were simply transported elsewhere in boxcars and then "unloaded.") There are no reliable statistics to evaluate the total number of Poles who were ultimately expelled from their homes. Nor are there any reliable data to determine the number of Polish children who were taken from their parents and forcibly "Germanized."[17]

The link between evacuation and landscape planning can be seen clearly in the blueprints of Himmler's Reich Commission. One of the first things that the planners undertook was a climatic-geographical survey of each of the Annexed Eastern Areas (Wartheland, Danzig-Westpreussen, Ciechanów, and Katowice districts) to determine what was "typical" of each landscape. They then tried to match the landscapes to the expectations of potential colonists, on the premise that Germans would only feel "rooted" in regions that were similar to what they knew back home. As Herbert Frank stated in 1942, they "put into practice the principles of planning that had until now been considered theoretically by the various agencies."[18] For instance, the Saybusch (Żywiec) region of the Katowice district was judged to be a mountainous landscape best suited for those Germans accustomed to a higher and colder climate. Small farms predominated, too small, in the opinion of the Nazi administrators, for a German family to live comfortably. Therefore, between September and December 1940, in the so-called Saybusch Action, the Nazis forcibly deported 17,413 Poles and created farms of around 15 hectares (approximately 37 acres) in size, on average displacing nine Polish families just to settle one German family. This was the incarnation of the "planning freedom" that Meyer and others demanded.

It can be proven that the planners knew about these matters. For instance, the expulsion of Poles from the Annexed Eastern Areas to those regions of Poland under the control of the General Government was not concealed; it was graphically detailed in a public exhibition called "Planning and Building in the East," sponsored by the Reich commissioner for the strengthening of Germandom. One of the panels presumably produced for this exhibit was even entitled "The Transfer of Population." The pattern of discrimination against the Polish populace was also codified in the "General Guidelines" issued by Himmler regarding the design of villages, towns, and landscapes. For instance, General Guideline 7/II, entitled "Basics and Guidelines for Rural Build-up in the New Eastern Territories," stipulated the segregation of cheap foreign labor: "Insofar as it is necessary to utilize Polish rural workers, their housing must be located apart from German settlements."[19]

Administrators discussed the planned evacuations at a number of meetings. A memorandum to the planning staff of the Reich commissioner included a discussion among the officers of the Reich Office for Spatial

Order concerning questions of planning in the Eastern territories: "In particular, there have been complaints about insufficient cooperation in implementing the evacuations, which are often taking place without any prior contact with the General Government. The evacuated persons should not be put to work. They should be taken directly from the transport trains, divided into small groups, spread as evenly as possible across the country, and then left to fend for themselves. One can thereby avoid a massing together of troublesome elements, in view of possible turbulence throughout the country."[20] Similarly, when the spatial planner Gerhard Isenberg wrote in 1941 about the "carrying capacity of the German East regarding agricultural and commercial populations," and about the fact that the Reich would be putting displaced Poles in the General Government "for the time being," he was clearly signaling that the planners were well aware of these forced measures.[21]

The existence of extermination camps was also known to the planners. This can be documented, for instance, by examining an agreement between the Reichsführer SS and the Reich Office for Spatial Order, according to which the Reichsführer SS announced all planning intentions to the Reich Office and other planning agencies, including those plans that dealt with concentration camps and satellite work camps.[22] There is other documentation as well. The landscape architect Werner Bauch, for instance, worked at the Auschwitz concentration camp.[23] And Reich Landscape Advocate Alwin Seifert would occasionally allude indirectly to concentration camps by using the term "Jews," a colloquial term among construction workers to describe faulty masonry.[24]

One of the most active professionals in propagating Nazi planning ideology was Wiepking-Jürgensmann, Himmler's special appointee for landscape design. He emphasized that an absolute freedom over property was the defining characteristic of conditions in the Annexed Eastern Areas. As a professor in Berlin, he also saw this as offering a special opportunity for his students. In 1943, for instance, he told one of his graduate students to write a master's thesis on the topic of planning for the new city of Auschwitz. In explaining his choice of topic, he wrote: "The narrow limitation of city planning on (mostly insufficient) city-owned land has to be contrasted with the possibility of viewing city planning and rural planning as a unity, and of designing, in all its details, where property ownership plays no special role."[25]

There is, however, more to the story than simply the fact that planners had foreknowledge of the use of force and terror. Many planners enthusiastically embraced the Nazi ideology of the master race in their scholarly publications. They thereby contributed to the image of Poles and Russians as "subhumans" (*Untermenschen*), which in turn helped legitimize (because they spoke as "experts") the policies of expulsion and annihilation. Among landscape designers, Wiepking-Jürgensmann's writings were particularly egregious. He vilified eastern Europeans as incapable of designing landscapes or properly maintaining their natural resources. In publication after publication, he depicted Poles and Russians as alien figures who had to be removed in order to save the landscape. For instance, in his book *Landschaftsfibel* (The Landscape Primer, 1942), he stated:

> The landscape is always a form, an expression, and a characteristic of the people [*Volk*] living within it. It can be the gentle countenance of its spirit and soul, just as it can be the grimace of its soullessness [*Ungeist*] and of human and spiritual depravity. In any case, it is the infallible, distinctive mark of what a people feels, thinks, creates, and does. It shows, with inexorable severity, whether a Volk is constructive and a part of the divine creative power, or part of a destructive force. The German landscape—like the German people—differs in every way from those of the Poles and the Russians. The murders and atrocities of the Eastern peoples are engraved, in a razor-sharp manner, in the grimaces of their native landscapes.[26]

Through the selective use of photographs and commentary, Wiepking-Jürgensmann tried to "prove" the inadequacies of the Poles. Hence a photo of a Polish farmhouse was accompanied by the caption, "Suggestion: Removal of the 'Farmers' and Afforestation."[27] A similarly racist vision of landscape design comes through in two articles ("The Landscape of the Germans" and "Against the Steppe Spirit") that appeared under his name in the main journal of the SS, *Das Schwarze Korps,* in 1942. The same can be said of a paper ("The Tasks and Goals of German Landscape Policy") that Wiepking-Jürgensmann wrote in 1940 for *Die Gartenkunst:*

> Whoever believes in the equality of Eastern populations, should not be allowed to be there. There were and are no commonalities between Germans and what are collectively known as "Poles," unless we are willing to give up our notions of *völkisch* and racial science! A German farmer is more fit for life, in the sense of having a higher calling, than a Polish baron, and every German worker possesses more creativity than the

Polish intellectual elite. Four millennia of Germanic evolution point to an irrevocable chain of evidence.[28]

Finally, a booklet entitled *Der Untermensch* (The Subhuman) also appeared in 1942. It was published by the Reichsführer SS without attribution, and it too contrasts the harmonious German landscape to the supposed devastated landscape of eastern Europe in an attempt to demonstrate the shortcomings of the eastern peoples:

> It is only man who can leave an imprint on a landscape. Therefore, we find orderly fertility, planned harmony of fields, and well-thought-out villages on the one side of Germany; beyond we see zones of impenetrable thicket, steppe, and endless primeval forests, through which silted-up rivers are grinding their way. This badly used yet fertile lap of black soil could be a paradise, a California of Europe, but in reality it is run down, coarsely untended, imprinted with the seal of a cultural disgrace without precedent, an eternal accusation against the subhuman being and his rule.[29]

Articles and pamphlets such as these clearly formed the intellectual backdrop for plans to destroy Polish villages and towns. Many architects and urban planners argued for the complete destruction of Polish towns and cities in order to create a tabula rasa for future planning. "One has to question whether it is worth trying to save parts of the Polish legacy," Ewald Liedecke wrote in 1940, in reference to Polish towns such as Ciechanów (Zichenau). "It makes more sense to build the German administrative and commercial centers from the ground up and to abolish the old towns one by one, as all-too-haunting reminders of the Polish way."[30] In a similar fashion, the architect Walter Wickop (who worked in the Wartheland district) welcomed the opportunity for planning in a "total" way that did not have to take existing property structures into consideration: "In the east of the Warthegau, in former 'Russian territory,' there are wide areas where there is hardly anything worth preserving, except for some through roads. . . . Where one does not have to take anything into consideration except for existing political boundaries, traffic roads, and the naked earth itself (its soils and contours), one is confronted with the necessity of deciding what one most wants to create."[31]

"Where one does not have to take anything into consideration"—this phrase of Wickop's accurately depicts the freedom of action given to the planners in the Annexed Eastern Areas who worked for the Reich commissioner for the strengthening of Germandom, for Himmler, and for other Nazi institutions. Urban architecture and landscape design were inextricably linked to the terror regime of the Nazis. Planning professionals for the most part enthusiastically welcomed these new realities and legitimized them. Their ideal conceptions for designing villages, towns, and landscapes were based on disenfranchising, dispossessing, and exterminating human beings.

Moreover, though these racist landscape planners really came into their own during the Nazi years, they did not suddenly disappear with the death of Hitler in 1945. Wiepking-Jürgensmann, Meyer, Wickop, and many others continued their careers as professors and consultants. A genuine "denazification of landscape architecture" never really took place in the Federal Republic, any more than it did in the former East Germany. Whether and how this has influenced the development of the discipline after the liberation from National Socialism needs to be examined further.[32]

Notes

1. For a more detailed discussion of this aspect of German landscape architecture history, see Gert Gröning and Joachim Wolschke-Bulmahn, *Der Drang nach Osten: Zur Entwicklung der Landespflege im Nationalsozialismus und während des Zweiten Weltkriegs in den "eingegliederten Ostgebieten,"* Arbeiten zur sozialwissenschaftlich orientierten Freiraumplanung 9 (Munich: Minerva Publikation, 1987). This essay is a revised version of "Gewalt als Grundlage nationalsozialistischer Stadt- und Landschaftsplanung in den 'eingegliederten Ostgebieten,'" in *Der "Generalplan Ost": Hauptlinien der nationalsozialistischen Planungs- und Vernichtungspolitik,* ed. Mechtild Rössler and Sabine Schleiermacher, in collaboration with Cordula Tollmien (Berlin: Akademie Verlag, 1993), 328–38. I am grateful to Mark Cioc and Thomas Zeller for their assistance in translating portions of this article from German to English.

2. See for more detail Robert Lewis Koehl, *RKFDV: German Resettlement and Population Policy, 1939–1945; A History of the Reich Commission for the Strengthening of Germandom* (Cambridge: Harvard University Press, 1957).

3. Hermann Koenig, "Zur Frage des Wiederaufbaus zerstörter Ortschaften im Osten und Westen," *Die Gartenkunst* 27 (1914), 295–96.

4. Alwin Seifert, "Die Zukunft der ostdeutschen Landschaft," *Flüssiges Obst* 12, no. 1/2 (1941): 108–10. Seifert is handled in greater detail in chapter 6

of this anthology. See also Joachim Wolschke-Bulmahn, "Political Landscapes and Technology: Nazi Germany and the Landscape Design of the *Reichsautobahnen* (Reich Motor Highways)," in *Nature & Technology,* ed. Gina Crandell, Selected CELA Annual Conference Papers 8 (Washington, DC, 1996), 157–70.

5. Nevertheless, it should be pointed out that during the war one possible motivation for participating in these planning activities was exemption from military service. For instance, this argument was made by city planner Josef Umlauf (see Gröning and Wolschke-Bulmahn, *Der Drang nach Osten,* 215–16).

6. The following passages are taken from Joachim Wolschke-Bulmahn and Gert Gröning, "The National Socialist Garden and Landscape Ideal: *Bodenständigkeit* (Rootedness in the Soil)," in *Art, Culture, and Media under the Third Reich,* ed. Richard A. Etlin (Chicago: University of Chicago Press, 2002), 80–83.

7. Adolf Hitler, decree of 7 October 1939, Bundesarchiv Berlin (hereafter BAB), R 49/20.

8. Konrad Meyer, "Der Osten als Aufgabe und Verpflichtung des Germanentums," *Neues Bauerntum* 34 (1941): 205–8.

9. Konrad Meyer, "Planung und Ostaufbau," *Raumforschung und Raumordnung* 5 (1941): 392–96.

10. Heinrich Friedrich Wiepking-Jürgensmann, "Der deutsche Osten: Eine vordringliche Aufgabe für unsere Studierenden," *Die Gartenkunst* 52 (1939): 193.

11. See Czeslaw Madajczyk, *Die Okkupationspolitik Nazideutschlands in Polen, 1939–1945* (Cologne: Pahl-Rugenstein, 1988).

12. Konrad Meyer, *Reichsplanung und Raumordnung im Lichte der volkspolitischen Aufgabe des Ostaufbaus* (n.p.: [1942?]), 12.

13. Ibid., 13.

14. Mäding defined "Lebensraum" in this way:

> The Lebensraum of a Volk is not defined by national borders. It includes at the very least the Volksboden (that is, the space entirely or predominantly settled by one's own ethnicity), especially those regions where settlements are thickest and property rights well established. Lebensraum is a larger concept than Volksboden: it includes the space that is needed to satisfy the necessities of life (including fishing and hunting grounds and areas with resources), even if it is inhabited by an alien population which has not developed an adequate Volk personality. Apart from these immediately controlled areas (the more strictly

defined Lebensraum, for which an effective exercise of state power and an ability to provide the population with essential goods can be assumed), a Volk can reach out and incorporate wider areas, the Lebensraum of other populations, indirectly into its own Lebensraum more widely defined—through leadership exercised politically, organizationally, culturally, or economically, and whether circumstance has it that for biogeographical reasons these areas form a unity with the Volk's own Lebensraum, or they complement one another—in the form of a comprehensive area of autarky, an immense space.

Erhard Mäding, *Landespflege: Die Gestaltung der Landschaft als Hoheitsrecht und Hoheitspflicht* (Berlin: Deutsche Landesbuchandlung, 1942), 141.

15. "Planungsgrundlagen für den Aufbau der Ostgebiete," BAB, R 113/10.

16. Ibid.

17. Czeslaw Luczak, "The Deportation of Polish Population by the Occupation Nazi Authorities in the Years 1939–1945," *Studia Historiae Oeconomicae* 3 (1968): 243–54.

18. Herbert Frank, "Das Dorf im Osten und sein Lebensraum," *Der Landbaumeister* 6 (1942): 1–2.

19. "Allgemeine Anordnung Nr. 7/II des Reichsführers SS, Reichskommissars für die Festigung deutschen Volkstums vom 26. November 1940, Betr.: Grundsätze und Richtlinien für den ländlichen Aufbau in den neuen Ostgebieten," cited in *Neues Bauerntum* 33 (1941): 1, 36–37.

20. BAB, R 49/895.

21. Gerhard Isenberg, *Die Tragfähigkeit des deutschen Ostens an landwirtschaftlicher und gewerblicher Bevölkerung, Gemeinschaftswerk im Auftrage der Reichsarbeitsgemeinschaft für Raumforschung* (1941), part 5.

22. BAB, R 113/1713.

23. Westmeyer to Seifert, 6 January 1943, Alwin Seifert Papers (ASP). See also chapter 6 of this volume.

24. Alwin Seifert, "Die Wiedergeburt landschaftsgebundenen Bauens," *Die Straße* 8, no. 1/2 (1941): 286–89. As noted in chapter 6, Seifert's team of landscape architects was mainly displaced in the East in favor of Wiepking-Jürgensmann's group.

25. Heinrich Friedrich Wiepking-Jürgensmann, "Diplom-Hausaufgabe für den Kandidaten der Landschafts- und Gartengestaltung Max Fischer," typewritten manuscript, 1943.

26. Heinrich Friedrich Wiepking-Jürgensmann, *Die Landschaftsfibel* (Berlin: Deutsche Landbuchandlung, 1942), 13.

27. Heinrich Friedrich Wiepking-Jürgensmann, "Aufgaben und Ziele deutscher Landschaftspolitik," *Die Gartenkunst* 53 (1940): 89.

28. Ibid., 6, 113.

29. Reichsführer SS, ed., *Der Untermensch* (Berlin: n.p., 1942), 2.

30. Ewald Liedecke, "Der neue deutsche Osten als Planungsraum," *Neues Bauerntum* 32, no. 4/5 (1940): 135–37. With the last words of this quote, Liedecke refers to "polnische Wirtschaft," a familiar pre-1945 derogatory locution regarding Poles.

31. Walter Wickop, "Grundsätze und Wege der Dorfplanung," *Der Landbaumeister* 6 (1942): 2–8.

32. Currently, Peter Fibich is working with the author on this question in relation to East Germany.

Glossary

Akademie für Deutsches Recht: Munich-based Academy for German Law

Anthropogeographie: Human geography

Arbeitsgemeinschaft für Geopolitik: Working Group for Geopolitics

Autobahn: Superhighway or interstate highway

Blut: Blood

Bluterbe: Genetic inheritance

Blut und Boden: Blood and soil

Boden: Soil

Bodenhaftigkeit: Attachment to the soil

Bodenständigkeit: Rootedness in the soil

Dauerwald: Perpetual forest, or eternal forest

Erbhof (pl. Erbhöfe): Inheritance estate(s)

Erbhofbauer: The peasant male heir and chief beneficiary of the Erbhof Law

Erbhof Law: Law of Hereditary Entailment

Erbmasse: Genetic material

Erdbedingtheit: Determination by earthly forces and conditions

Erde: Earth

Erdgebundenheit: Connection with the earth

Führerkult: Leadership cult, Hitler idolatry

Führerstaat: A dictatorship, or rule based on the Führer

Geographische Politik: Geography-based policy

Geopolitik: Geopolitics

Gestell: Enframing

Gleichschaltung: Synchronization, coordination of all political forces to move in one direction

Heimatbewegung: Homeland protection movement

Heimatboden: The specific historical-cultural space of a nation

Heimatschutz: Homeland protection

Historische Landschaft: Historical landscape

Kulturboden: Cultural earth, i.e., the soil-based essence of culture

Kulturlandschaft: Cultural landscape

Land (pl. Länder): Federal state(s)

Landschaftspflege: The care of the landscape, landscape preservation

Lebensraum: Living space

Nachhaltigkeit: Sustained yield

Nationalpolitik (pl. Nationalitätenpolitik): Nation-based policy, nationalistic policy

Naturbedingtheit: Determination by nature, nature as destiny

Naturdenkmal (pl. Naturdenkmäler): Natural monument(s)

Naturlandschaft: Natural landscape

Naturraum (pl. Naturräume): Natural space(s)

Naturschutz: Nature conservation

Naturschutzgebiet (pl. Naturschutzgebiete): Nature conservation area(s)

Normalwald: Normal forest

Politische Geographie: Political geography

Rassenkunde: Race-based science, ethnology

Raum: Space

Raumbedürfnis: The need for space

Raumordnung: Spatial planning

Reichsarbeitsdienst: Reich Labor Service

Reichsforstamt: Reich Forest Office

Reichsforstmeister: Reich master of forestry

Reichsinnenministerium: Reich Ministry of the Interior

Reichskommissar für die Festigung des deutschen Volkstums: Reich commissioner for the strengthening of Germandom

Reichsminister für Bewaffnung und Munition: Reich minister for armament and ammunition

Reichsnährstand: Reich Food Estate

Reichstelle für Naturschutz: Reich Nature Protection Office

Reichstelle für Raumordnung: Reich Office for Spatial Planning

Reichswirtschaftsministerium: Reich Ministry of Trade and Commerce

Verwurzelung: Rootedness

Volk: The nation, the people, or the "common ethnic German"

völkisch: Adhering to the values of the Volk

Volksboden: The Volk's essential substrate

Volksgemeinschaft: National community or people's community

Volkstum: Folklore, the culture of the Volk

Volkstümlichkeit: Popular celebration of Volkstum

Selected Bibliography

Adolf, Heinrich. "Technikdiskurs und Technikideologie im Nationalsozialismus." *Geschichte in Wissenschaft und Unterricht* 48 (1997): 429–44.

Anderson, Dennis LeRoy. *The Academy for German Law, 1933–1944.* New York: Garland, 1987.

Applegate, Celia. *A Nation of Provincials: The German Idea of Heimat.* Berkeley: University of California Press, 1990.

Bassin, Mark. "Imperialism and the Nation-State in Friedrich Ratzel's Political Geography." *Progress in Human Geography* 11 (1987): 473–95.

———. "Nature, Geopolitics, and Marxism: Ecological Contestations in Weimar Germany." *Transactions of the Institute of British Geographers,* n.s., 21, no. 2 (1996): 315–41.

———. "Race *Contra* Space: The Conflict between German *Geopolitik* and National Socialism." *Political Geography Quarterly* 6, no. 2 (1987): 115–34.

Bergmann, Klaus. *Agrarromantik und Großstadtfeindschaft.* Meisenheim am Glan: Hain, 1970.

Biehl, Janet, and Peter Staudenmaier. *Ecofascism: Lessons from the German Experience.* Edinburgh: AK Press, 1995.

Bode, Wilhelm, and Elisabeth Emmert. *Jagdwende: Vom Edelhobby zum ökologischen Handwerk.* 3rd ed. Munich: Beck, 2000.

Bode, Wilhelm, and Martin von Hohnhorst. *Waldwende: Vom Försterwald zum Naturwald.* 4th ed. Munich: Beck, 2000.

Borrmann, Norbert. *Paul Schultze-Naumburg, 1869–1949: Maler—Publizist—Architekt.* Essen: Bacht, 1989.

Bramwell, Anna. *Blood and Soil: Richard Walther Darré and Hitler's Green Party.* Bourne End, Buckinghamshire, UK: Kensal Press, 1985.

———. *Ecology in the 20th Century: A History.* New Haven: Yale University Press, 1989.

Brose, Eric Dorn. "Generic Fascism Revisited: Attitudes toward Technology in Germany and Italy, 1919–1945." *German Studies Review* 10 (1987): 273–97.

Brüggemeier, Franz-Josef. *Tschernobyl, 26. April 1986: Die ökologische Herausforderung.* Munich: Deutscher Taschenbuch Verlag, 1998.

———. *Das unendliche Meer der Lüfte: Luftverschmutzung, Industrialisierung und Risikodebatten im 19. Jahrhundert.* Essen: Klartext, 1996.

Brüggemeier, Franz-Josef, and Thomas Rommelspacher, eds. *Besiegte Natur: Geschichte der Umwelt im 19. und 20. Jahrhundert.* 2nd ed. Munich: Beck, 1989.

———, eds. *Blauer Himmel über der Ruhr: Geschichte der Umwelt im Ruhrgebiet, 1840–1990.* Essen: Klartext, 1992.

Cioc, Mark. *The Rhine: An Eco-Biography, 1815–2000.* Seattle: University of Washington Press, 2002.

Confino, Alon. *The Nation as a Local Metaphor: Württemberg, Imperial Germany, and National Memory, 1871–1918.* Chapel Hill: University of North Carolina Press, 1997.

Corni, Gustavo. *Hitler and the Peasants: Agrarian Policy of the Third Reich, 1930–1939.* New York: Berg, 1990.

Corni, Gustavo, and Horst Gies. *"Blut und Boden": Rassenideologie und Agrarpolitik im Staat Hitlers.* Idstein: Schultz-Kirchner Verlag, 1994.

———. *Brot, Butter, Kanonen: Die Ernährungswirtschaft in Deutschland unter der Diktatur Hitlers.* Berlin: Akademie, 1997.

Deichmann, Ute. *Biologists under Hitler.* Cambridge: Harvard University Press, 1996.

Diner, Dan. "Knowledge of Expansion: On the Geopolitics of Karl Haushofer." In *Beyond the Conceivable: Studies on Germany, Nazism, and the Holocaust,* ed. Dan Diner, 26–48. Berkeley: University of California Press, 2001.

Ditt, Karl. "Nature Conservation in England and Germany, 1900–1970: Forerunners of Environmental Protection?" *Contemporary European History* 5, no. 1 (1996): 1–28.

———. "The Perception and Conservation of Nature in the Third Reich." *Planning Perspectives* 15 (2000): 161–87.

———. *Raum und Volkstum: Die Kulturpolitik des Provinzialverbandes Westfalen, 1923–1945.* Münster: Aschendorff, 1988.

Dominick, Raymond. *The Environmental Movement in Germany: Prophets and Pioneers, 1871–1971.* Bloomington: Indiana University Press, 1992.

Eidenbenz, Mathias. *"Blut und Boden": Zu Funktion und Genese der Metaphern des Agrarismus und Biologismus in der nationalsozialistischen Bauernpropaganda R. W. Darrés.* Bern: Peter Lang, 1993.

Eisel, Ulrich, and Stefanie Schultz, eds. *Geschichte und Struktur der Landschaftsplanung.* Berlin: Technical University, 1991.

Emmerich, Wolfgang, and Carl Wege, eds. *Der Technikdiskurs in der Hitler-Stalin-Ära.* Stuttgart: Metzler, 1995.

Falk, Susanne. "'Eine Notwendigkeit, uns innerlich umzustellen, liege nicht vor': Kontinuität und Diskontinuität in der Auseinandersetzung des Sauerländischen Gebirgsvereins mit Heimat und Moderne, 1918–1960." In *Politische Zäsuren und gesellschaftlicher Wandel im 20. Jahrhundert: Regionale und vergleichende Perspektiven,* ed. Matthias Frese and Michael Prinz, 401–17. Paderborn: Schöningh, 1996.

———. *Der Sauerländische Gebirgsverein: "Vielleicht sind wir die Modernen von übermorgen."* Bonn: Bouvier, 1990.

Farias, Victor. *Heidegger and Nazism.* Philadelphia: Temple University Press, 1989.

Farquharson, John E. *The Plough and the Swastika: The NSDAP and Agriculture in Germany, 1928–1945.* London: Sage, 1976.

Fehn, Klaus. "Rückblick auf die 'nationalsozialistische Kulturlandschaft' unter besonderer Berücksichtigung des völkisch-rassistischen Mißbrauchs von Kulturlandschaftspflege." *Informationen zur Raumentwicklung,* no. 5/6 (1999): 279–90.

Frei, Norbert. *National Socialist Rule in Germany: The Führer State, 1933–1945.* Oxford: Blackwell, 1993.

Gerhard, Gesine. "Das Ende der deutschen Bauernfrage: Ländliche Gesellschaft im Umbruch." In *Der lange Abschied vom Agrarland: Agrarpolitik, Landwirtschaft und ländliche Gesellschaft zwischen Weimar und Bonn,* ed. Daniela Münkel, 124–42. Göttingen: Wallstein, 2000.

———. "Politische Bauernbewegungen zwischen Systemkonformität und Opposition: Der Deutsche Bauernverband (DBV) und die politische Eingliederung der Bauern in die Bundesrepublik Deutschland." *Österreichische Zeitschrift für Geschichtswissenschaft* 13, no. 2 (2002): 129–38.

Gerlach, Christian. *Krieg, Ernährung, Völkermord: Deutsche Vernichtungspolitik im Zweiten Weltkrieg.* 2nd ed. Zürich: Pendo Verlag, 2001.

Gispen, Kees. "National Socialism and the Technological Culture of the Weimar Republic." *Central European History* 25 (1992): 387–406.

Gröning, Gert, and Ulfert Herlyn, eds. *Landschaftswahrnehmung und Landschaftserfahrung: Texte zur Konstitution und Rezeption von Natur als Landschaft.* Munich: Minerva, 1990.

Gröning, Gert, and Joachim Wolschke-Bulmahn. *Grüne Biographien: Biographisches Handbuch zur Landschaftsarchitektur des 20. Jahrhunderts in Deutschland.* Berlin: Patzer, 1997.

————. *Die Liebe zur Landschaft.* Part 1, *Natur in Bewegung: Zur Bedeutung natur- und freiraumorientierter Bewegungen der ersten Hälfte des 20. Jahrhunderts für die Entwicklung der Freiraumplanung.* Munich: Minerva, 1986.

————. *Die Liebe zur Landschaft.* Part 3, *Der Drang nach Osten: Zur Entwicklung der Landespflege im Nationalsozialismus und während des Zweiten Weltkriegs in den "eingegliederten Ostgebieten."* Munich: Minerva, 1987.

————. "Some Notes on the Mania for Native Plants in Germany." *Landscape Journal* 11 (1992): 116–26.

Grossheim, Michael. *Ökologie oder Technokratie? Der Konservatismus in der Moderne.* Berlin: Duncker & Humblot, 1995.

Grundmann, Friedrich. *Agrarpolitik im "Dritten Reich": Anspruch und Wirklichkeit des Reichserbhofgesetzes.* Hamburg: Hoffmann und Campe, 1979.

Gugerli, David, ed. *Vermessene Landschaften: Kulturgeschichte und technische Praxis im 19. und 20. Jahrhundert.* Zurich: Chronos, 1999.

Harrington, Anne. *Reenchanted Science: Holism in German Culture from Wilhelm II to Hitler.* Princeton: Princeton University Press, 1996.

Haushofer, Heinz. *Ideengeschichte der Agrarwirtschaft und Agrarpolitik im deutschen Sprachgebiet.* 2 vols. Munich: Bayerischer Landwirtschaftsverlag, 1958.

Heidegger, Martin. *Gesamtausgabe.* Vol. 16, *Reden und andere Zeugnisse eines Lebensweges.* Frankfurt: Klostermann, 2000.

————. "The Question Concerning Technology." In *Martin Heidegger: Basic Writings*, ed. David F. Krell, 283–318. London: Routledge, 1978.

————. *Vorträge und Aufsätze.* 6th ed. Pfullingen: Neske, 1990.

Heim, Susanne. *Kalorien, Kautschuk, Karrieren: Pflanzenzüchtung und landwirtschaftliche Forschung in Kaiser-Wilhelm-Insituten 1933–1945.* Göttingen: Wallstein, 2003.

Heinemann, Isabel. *"Rasse, Siedlung, deutsches Blut": Das Rasse- und Siedlungshauptamt der SS und die rassenpolitische Neuordnung Europas.* Göttingen: Wallstein, 2003.

Herf, Jeffrey. *Reactionary Modernism: Technology, Culture and Politics in Weimar and the Third Reich.* Cambridge: Cambridge University Press, 1984.

Hermand, Jost. *Grüne Utopien in Deutschland: Zur Geschichte des ökologischen Bewußtseins.* Frankfurt: Fischer, 1991.

Heske, Franz. *German Forestry.* New Haven: Yale University Press, 1938.

Heuser, Marie-Luise. "Was grün begann endete blutigrot: Von der Naturromantik zu den Reagrarisierungs- und Entvölkerungsplänen der SA und SS." In *Industrialismus und Ökoromantik: Geschichte und Perspektiven der*

Ökologisierung, ed. Dieter Hassenpflug, 43–64. Wiesbaden: Deutscher Universitäts-Verlag, 1991.

Hoebink, Heinrich. *Mehr Raum—Mehr Macht: Preussische Kommunalpolitik im rheinisch-westfälischen Industriegebiet*. Essen: Klartext, 1990.

Huchting, Friedrich. "Abfallwirtschaft im Dritten Reich." *Technikgeschichte* 48 (1981): 252–73.

Jacobsen, Hans-Adolf, ed. *Karl Haushofer: Leben und Werk*. 2 vols. Boppard am Rhein: H. Boldt, 1979.

Jarausch, Konrad H. *The Unfree Professions: German Lawyers, Teachers and Engineers, 1900–1950*. New York: Oxford University Press, 1990.

Josephson, Paul, and Thomas Zeller. "The Transformation of Nature under Hitler and Stalin." In *Science and Ideology: A Comparative History*, ed. Mark Walker, 124–55. London: Routledge, 2003.

Kerbs, Diethart, ed. *Handbuch der deutschen Reformbewegungen, 1880–1933*. Wuppertal: Peter Hammer, 1998.

Klenke, Dietmar. "Autobahnbau und Naturschutz in Deutschland: Eine Liaison von Nationalpolitik, Landschaftspflege und Motorisierungsvision bis zur ökologischen Wende der siebziger Jahre." In *Politische Zäsuren und gesellschaftlicher Wandel im 20. Jahrhundert: Regionale und vergleichende Perspektiven*, ed. Matthias Frese and Michael Prinz, 465–98. Paderborn: Schöningh, 1996.

Kloepfer, Michael. *Zur Geschichte des deutschen Umweltrechts*. Berlin: Duncker & Humblot, 1994.

Klose, Hans. *Fünfzig Jahre staatlicher Naturschutz: Ein Rückblick auf den Weg der deutschen Naturschutzbewegung*. Giessen: Brühlscher Verlag, 1957.

Klueting, Edeltraud, ed. *Antimodernismus und Reform: Beiträge zur Geschichte der deutschen Heimatbewegung*. Darmstadt: Wissenschaftliche Buchgesellschaft, 1991.

Koehl, Robert Lewis. *RKFDV: German Resettlement and Population Policy, 1939–1945; A History of the Reich Commission for the Strengthening of Germandom*. Cambridge: Harvard University Press, 1957.

Korinman, Michel. *Quand l'Allemagne pensait le monde: Grandeur et décadence d'une géopolitique*. Paris: Fayard, 1990.

Körner, Stefan. *Der Aufbruch der modernen Umweltplanung in der nationalsozialistischen Landespflege*. Berlin: Technical University, 1995.

Koshar, Rudy. *German Travel Cultures*. Oxford: Berg, 2000.

———. *Germany's Transient Pasts: Preservation and National Memory in the Twentieth Century*. Chapel Hill: University of North Carolina Press, 1998.

Küppers, Günter, Peter Lundgreen, and Peter Weingart. *Umweltforschung—die gesteuerte Wissenschaft? Eine empirische Studie zum Verhältnis von Wissenschaftsentwicklung und Wissenschaftspolitik.* Frankfurt: Suhrkamp, 1978.

Küster, Hansjörg. *Geschichte der Landschaft in Mitteleuropa: Von der Eiszeit bis zur Gegenwart.* Munich: Beck, 1995.

———. *Geschichte des Waldes: Von der Urzeit bis zur Gegenwart.* Munich: Beck, 1998.

Lange, Karl. "Der Terminus 'Lebensraum' in Hitlers *Mein Kampf*." *Vierteljahresheft für Zeitgeschichte* 13, no. 4 (1965): 426–37.

Lehmann, Joachim. "Herbert Backe—Technokrat und Agrarideologe." In *Die Braune Elite II: 21 weitere biographische Skizzen*, ed. Ronald Smelzer, Enrico Syring, and Rainer Zitelmann, 1–12. Darmstadt: Wissenschaftliche Buchgesellschaft, 1993.

Lekan, Thomas. *Imagining the Nation in Nature: Landscape Preservation and German Identity, 1885–1945.* Cambridge: Harvard University Press, 2004.

———. "Regionalism and the Politics of Landscape Preservation in the Third Reich." *Environmental History* 4 (1999): 384–404.

Lekan, Thomas, and Thomas Zeller, eds. *Germany's Nature: Cultural Landscapes and Environmental History.* New Brunswick, NJ: Rutgers University Press, 2005.

Lenz, Gerhard. *Verlusterfahrung Landschaft: Über die Herstellung von Raum und Umwelt im mitteldeutschen Industriegebiet seit der Mitte des neunzehnten Jahrhunderts.* Frankfurt: Campus, 1999.

Linse, Ulrich. *Ökopax und Anarchie: Eine Geschichte der ökologischen Bewegungen in Deutschland.* Munich: Deutscher Taschenbuch Verlag, 1986).

Luczak, Czeslaw. "The Deportation of Polish Population by the Occupation Nazi Authorities in the Years 1939–1945." *Studia Historiae Oeconomicae* 3 (1968): 243–54.

Ludwig, Karl-Heinz. "Politische Lösungen für technische Innovationen, 1933–1945: Eine antitechnische Mobilisierung, Ausformung und Instrumentalisierung der Technik." *Technikgeschichte* 62 (1995): 333–44.

———. *Technik und Ingenieure im Dritten Reich.* Düsseldorf: Droste, 1974.

Maasen, Sabine, Everett Mendelsohn, and Peter Weingart, eds. *Biology as Society, Society as Biology: Metaphors.* Dordrecht: Kluwer, 1995.

Madajczyk, Czeslaw. *Die Okkupationspolitik Nazideutschlands in Polen, 1939–1945.* Cologne: Pahl-Rugenstein, 1988.

Maier, Helmut. "Kippenlandschaft, 'Wasserkrafttaumel' und Kahlschlag: Anspruch und Wirklichkeit nationalsozialistischer Naturschutz- und Energiepolitik." In *Umweltgeschichte: Methoden, Themen, Potentiale. Tagung des Hamburger Arbeitskreises für Umweltgeschichte,* ed. Günter Bayerl, Norman Fuchsloch, and Torsten Meyer, 247–66. Münster: Waxmann, 1996.

———. "Nationalsozialistische Technikideologie und die Politisierung des 'Technikerstandes': Fritz Todt und die Zeitschrift 'Deutsche Technik.'" In *Technische Intelligenz und "Kulturfaktor Technik": Kulturvorstellungen von Technikern und Ingenieuren zwischen Kaiserreich und früher Bundesrepublik Deutschland,* ed. Burkhard Dietz, Michael Fessner, and Helmut Maier, 253–68. Münster: Waxmann, 1996.

———. "'Unter Wasser und unter die Erde': Die süddeutschen und alpinen Wasserkraftprojekte des Rheinisch-Westfälischen Elektrizitätswerks (RWE) und der Natur- und Landschaftsschutz während des 'Dritten Reiches.'" In *Die Veränderung der Kulturlandschaft: Nutzungen—Sichtweisen—Planungen,* ed. Günter Bayerl and Torsten Meyer, 139–75. Münster: Waxmann, 2003.

———. "'Weiße Kohle' versus Schwarze Kohle: Naturschutz und Ressourcenschonung als Deckmantel nationalsozialistischer Energiepolitik." *WerkstattGeschichte,* no. 3 (1992): 33–38.

Martin, Bernd, and Alan S. Milward, eds. *Agriculture and Food Supply in the Second World War.* Ostfildern: Scripta Mercaturae Verlag, 1985.

Mehrtens, Herbert. "Kollaborationsverhältnisse: Natur- und Technikwissenschaften im NS-Staat und ihre Historie." *Medizin, Naturwissenschaft, Technik und Nationalsozialismus: Kontinuitäten und Diskontinuitäten,* ed. Christoph Meinel and Peter Voswinckel, 13–32. Stuttgart: GNT, 1994.

Mosse, George. *The Crisis of German Ideology: Intellectual Origins of the Third Reich.* New York: Universal Library, 1964.

Mrass, Walter. *Die Organisation des staatlichen Naturschutzes und der Landschaftspflege im Deutschen Reich und in der Bundesrepublik Deutschland seit 1935, gemessen an den Aufgabenstellungen einer modernen Industriegesellschaft.* Stuttgart: Ulmer, 1970.

Murphy, David T. *The Heroic Earth: Geopolitical Thought in Weimar Germany, 1918–1933.* Kent, OH: Kent State University Press, 1997.

Oberkrome, Willi. *Volksgeschichte: Methodische Innovation und völkische Ideologisierung in der deutschen Geschichtswissenschaft, 1918–1945.* Göttingen: Vandenhoeck & Ruprecht, 1993.

Olsen, Jonathan. *Nature and Nationalism: Right-Wing Ecology and the Politics of Identity in Contemporary Germany.* New York: St. Martin's Press, 1999.

Osterhammel, Jürgen. "Die Wiederkehr des Raumes: Geopolitik, Geohistoire und historische Geographie." *Neue Politische Literatur* 43 (1998): 374–97.

Ott, Hugo. *Martin Heidegger: A Political Life*. London: Fontana, 1994.

Patel, Kiran Klaus. "Neuerfindung des Westens—Aufbruch nach Osten: Naturschutz und Landschaftsgestaltung in den Vereinigten Staaten von Amerika und in Deutschland." *Archiv für Sozialgeschichte* 43 (2003): 191–223.

————. *"Soldaten der Arbeit": Arbeitsdienste in Deutschland und den USA, 1933–1945*. Göttingen: Vandenhoeck & Ruprecht, 2003.

Petzold, Joachim. *Konservative Theoretiker des deutschen Faschismus: Jungkonservative Ideologen in der Weimar Republik als geistige Wegbereiter der faschistischen Diktatur*. Berlin: Deutscher Verlag der Wissenschaften, 1982.

Pfister, Christian. "Landschaftsveränderung und Identitätsverlust: Akzentverschiebungen in der Modernisierungskritik von der Jahrhundertwende bis um 1970." *Traverse* 4, no. 2 (1997): 49–68.

Potthast, Thomas. *Die Evolution und der Naturschutz: Zum Verhältnis von Evolutionsbiologie, Ökologie und Naturethik*. Frankfurt: Campus, 1999.

Proctor, Robert N. *The Nazi War on Cancer*. Princeton: Princeton University Press, 1999.

Puschner, Uwe. *Die völkische Bewegung im wilhelminischen Kaiserreich: Sprache, Rasse, Religion*. Darmstadt: Wissenschaftliche Buchgesellschaft, 2001.

Radkau, Joachim. *Natur und Macht: Eine Weltgeschichte der Umwelt*. 2nd ed. Munich: Beck, 2002.

Radkau, Joachim, and Frank Uekötter, eds. *Naturschutz und Nationalsozialismus*. Frankfurt: Campus, 2003.

Riechers, Burkhardt. "Nature Protection during National Socialism." *Historical Social Research* 21, no. 3 (1996): 34–56.

Riordan, Colin, ed. *Green Thought in German Culture: Historical and Contemporary Perspectives*. Cardiff: University of Wales Press, 1997.

Rohkrämer, Thomas. "Antimodernism, Reactionary Modernism and National Socialism: Technocratic Tendencies in Germany, 1890–1945." *Contemporary European History* 8, no. 1 (1999): 29–50.

————. "Contemporary Environmentalism and its Link with the German Past." In *The Culture of German Environmentalism: Anxieties, Visions, Realities*, ed. Axel Goodbody, 47–62. New York: Berghahn Books, 2002.

————. *Eine andere Moderne? Zivilisationskritik, Natur und Technik in Deutschland, 1880–1933*. Paderborn: Schöningh, 1999.

Rollins, William. *A Greener Vision of Home: Cultural Politics and Environmental Reform in the German Heimatschutz Movement*. Ann Arbor: University of Michigan Press, 1997.

————. "Whose Landscape? Technology, Fascism, and Environmentalism on the National Socialist *Autobahn*." *Annals of the Association of American Geographers* 85 (1995): 494–504.

Rössler, Mechtild. "'Area Research' and 'Spatial Planning' from the Weimar Republic to the German Federal Republic: Creating a Society with a Spatial Order under National Socialism." In *Science, Technology, and National Socialism*, ed. Monika Renneberg and Mark Walker, 126–38. Cambridge: Cambridge University Press, 1994.

Rössler, Mechtild, and Sabine Schleiermacher, in collaboration with Cordula Tollmien, eds. *Der "Generalplan Ost": Hauptlinien der nationalsozialistischen Planungs- und Vernichtungspolitik.* Berlin: Akademie, 1993.

Rozsnyay, Zoltán, and Uta Schulte. *Der Reichsforstgesetzentwurf von 1942 und seine Auswirkungen auf die neuere Forstgesetzgebung.* Frankfurt: Sauerländer, 1978.

Rubner, Heinrich. *Deutsche Forstgeschichte 1933–1945: Forstwirtschaft, Jagd und Umwelt im NS-Staat.* 2nd ed. St. Katharinen: Scripta Mercaturae Verlag, 1997.

———. *Forstgeschichte im Zeitalter der Industriellen Revolution.* Berlin: Duncker & Humblot, 1967.

Schama, Simon. *Landscape and Memory.* New York: Alfred A. Knopf, 1995.

Schütz, Erhard, and Eckhard Gruber. *Mythos Reichsautobahn: Bau und Inszenierung der "Straßen des Führers," 1933–1941.* Berlin: Links, 1996.

See, Klaus von. *Freiheit und Gemeinschaft: Völkisch-nationales Denken in Deutschland zwischen Französischer Revolution und Erstem Weltkrieg.* Heidelberg: C. Winter, 2001.

Sieferle, Rolf Peter. *Fortschrittsfeinde? Opposition gegen Technik und Industrie von der Romantik bis zur Gegenwart.* Munich: Beck, 1984.

———. *Rückblick auf die Natur: Eine Geschichte des Menschen und seiner Umwelt.* Munich: Luchterhand, 1997.

Sluga, Hans. *Heidegger's Crisis: Philosophy and Politics in Nazi Germany.* Cambridge: Harvard University Press, 1993.

Smith, Woodruff D. "Friedrich Ratzel and the Origin of *Lebensraum.*" *German Studies Review* 3, no. 1 (1980): 51–68.

Speitkamp, Winfried. "Denkmalpflege und Heimatschutz in Deutschland zwischen Kulturkritik und Nationalsozialismus." *Archiv für Kulturgeschichte* 70 (1988): 149–93.

Sprengel, Rainer. *Kritik der Geopolitik: Ein deutscher Diskurs, 1914–1944.* Berlin: Akademie, 1996.

Steinbacher, Sybille. *"Musterstadt" Auschwitz: Germanisierungspolitik und Judenmord in Oberschlesien.* Munich: Saur, 2000.

Steinmetzler, Johannes. *Die Anthropogeographie Friedrich Ratzels und ihre ideengeschichtlichen Wurzeln.* Bonn: Selbstverlag des Geographischen Instituts der Universität Bonn, 1956.

Steinsiek, Peter-Michael, and Zoltán Rozsnyay. "Grundzüge der deutschen Forstgeschichte 1933–1950 unter besonderer Berücksichtigung Niedersachsens." Special issue, *Aus dem Walde (Mitteilungen aus der Niedersächsischen Landesforstverwaltung)*, no. 46 (1994).

Stephens, Piers H. G. "Blood, not Soil: Anna Bramwell and the Myth of 'Hitler's Green Party.'" *Organization & Environment* 14 (2001): 173–87.

Trepl, Ludwig. *Geschichte der Ökologie: Vom 17. Jahrhundert bis zur Gegenwart*. Frankfurt: Athenäum, 1987.

Troitzsch, Ulrich. "Die technikgeschichtliche Entwicklung der Verkehrsmittel und ihr Einfluß auf die Gestaltung der Kulturlandschaft." *Siedlungsforschung: Archäologie—Geschichte—Geographie* 4 (1986): 127–43.

Uekötter, Frank. *Naturschutz und Nationalsozialismus: Erblast für den Naturschutz im demokratischen Rechsstaat?* Bielefeld: Archiv Forum Museum, 2002.

Uekötter, Frank. *Von der Rauchplage zur ökologischen Revolution: Eine Geschichte der Luftverschmutzung in Deutschland und den USA, 1880–1970*. Essen: Klartext, 2003.

Vietta, Silvio. *Heideggers Kritik am Nationalsozialismus und an der Technik*. Tübingen: Niemeyer, 1989.

Vogt, Gunter. *Entstehung und Entwicklung des ökologischen Landbaus im deutschsprachigen Raum*. Bad Dürkheim: Stiftung Ökologie und Landbau, 2000.

Voigt, Wolfgang. "The Garden City as Eugenic Utopia." *Planning Perspectives* 4, no. 3 (1989): 295–312.

Vondung, Klaus. *Die Apokalypse in Deutschland*. Munich: Deutscher Taschenbuch Verlag, 1988.

Weiner, Douglas. "Demythologizing Environmentalism." *Journal of the History of Biology* 25 (1992): 385–411.

Werner, Uwe. *Anthroposophen in der Zeit des Nationalsozialismus (1933–1945)*. Munich: Oldenbourg, 1999.

Wettengel, Michael. "Staat und Naturschutz: Zur Geschichte der Staatlichen Stelle für Naturdenkmalpflege in Preußen und der Reichsstelle für Naturschutz." *Historische Zeitschrift* 257, no. 2 (October 1993): 355–99.

Wey, Klaus-Georg. *Umweltpolitik in Deutschland: Kurze Geschichte des Umweltschutzes in Deutschland seit 1900*. Opladen: Westdeutscher Verlag, 1982.

Williams, John. "'The Chords of the German Soul are Tuned to Nature': The Movement to Preserve the Natural *Heimat* from the Kaiserreich to the Third Reich." *Central European History* 29, no. 3 (1996): 339–84.

Wolin, Richard, ed. *The Heidegger Controversy: A Critical Reader.* 3rd ed. Cambridge: MIT Press, 1998.

———. *The Politics of Being: The Political Thought of Martin Heidegger.* New York: Columbia University Press, 1990.

Wolschke-Bulmahn, Joachim. "Political Landscapes and Technology: Nazi Germany and the Landscape Design of the *Reichsautobahnen* (Reich Motor Highways)." In *Nature & Technology*, ed. Gina Crandell (Selected CELA Annual Conference Papers 8), 157–170. Washington, DC, 1996.

Wolschke-Bulmahn, Joachim, and Gert Gröning. "The National Socialist Garden and Landscape Ideal: *Bodenständigkeit* (Rootedness in the Soil)." In *Art, Culture, and Media under the Third Reich*, ed. Richard A. Etlin, 80–83. Chicago: University of Chicago Press, 2002.

Young, Julian. *Heidegger, Philosophy, Nazism.* Cambridge: Cambridge University Press, 1997.

Zebhauser, Helmuth. *Alpinismus im Hitlerstaat: Gedanken, Erinnerungen, Dokumente.* Munich: Bergverlag Rother, 1998.

Zeller, Thomas. "'Ich habe die Juden möglichst gemieden': Ein aufschlußreicher Briefwechsel zwischen Heinrich Wiepking und Alwin Seifert." *Garten+Landschaft: Zeitschrift für Landschaftsarchitektur*, no. 8 (1995): 4–5.

———. "'The Landscape's Crown': Landscape, Perceptions, and Modernizing Effects of the German *Autobahn* System, 1934–1941." In *Technologies of Landscape: Reaping to Recycling*, ed. David Nye, 218–38. Amherst: University of Massachusetts Press, 1999.

———. "Landschaft als Gefühl und Autobahn als Formel: Der Autobahnbau in der frühen Bundesrepublik als Abgrenzungsversuch gegen die 'Straßen Adolf Hitlers.'" *WerkstattGeschichte* 7, no. 21 (1998): 29–41.

———. *Straße, Bahn, Panorama: Verkehrswege und Landschaftsveränderung in Deutschland 1930 bis 1990.* Frankfurt: Campus, 2002.

Zimmerman, Michael E. *Heidegger's Confrontation with Modernity: Technology, Politics, and Art.* Bloomington: Indiana University Press, 1990.

Zundel, Rolf, and Ekkehard Schwartz. *50 Jahre Forstpolitik in Deutschland.* Münster-Hiltrup: Landwirtschaftsverlag, 1996.

Contributors

Mark Bassin is reader in the Department of Geography, University College, London. As a cultural geographer, his research interests include the intersection of territory, politics, and ideologies of national identity. His book *Imperial Visions: Nationalist Imagination and Geographical Expansion in the Russian Far East, 1840–1865* was published in 1999.

Franz-Joseph Brüggemeier is professor of economic and social history in the History Department, University of Freiburg, Germany. His publications include *Das unendliche Meer der Lüfte: Luftverschmutzung, Industrialisierung und Risikodebatten im 19. Jahrhundert* (1996) and *Tschernobyl, 26. April 1986: Die ökologische Herausfordernung* (1998).

Mark Cioc is professor of history at the University of California, Santa Cruz, and editor of the journal *Environmental History*. His book *The Rhine: An Eco-Biography, 1815–2000* was published in 2002. He is currently working on a book entitled *The Game of Conservation: International Treaties to Protect the World's Migratory Animals, 1900–1948*.

Charles Closmann is assistant professor of history at the University of North Florida in Jacksonville. He received his PhD from the University of Houston in 2002 and has worked as a research fellow in environmental history at the German Historical Institute, Washington, DC.

Gesine Gerhard is assistant professor in the Department of History at the University of the Pacific in Stockton, California. She received her PhD in modern German history from the University of Iowa in 2000. Her dissertation was entitled "Peasants into Farmers: Agriculture and Democracy in Modern Germany."

Michael Imort is assistant professor in the Department of Geography and Environmental Studies at Wilfrid Laurier University in Waterloo, Ontario, Canada. He has also taught at the International Study Centre at Herstmonceux Castle in East Sussex, United Kingdom. His work focuses on the political representations of the German forest landscape.

Thomas Lekan is associate professor in the Department of History at the University of South Carolina. His book *Imagining the Nation in Nature: Landscape Preservation and German Identity, 1885–1945* was published in 2004. He received his PhD in 1999 from the University of Wisconsin at Madison.

Thomas Rohkrämer teaches modern Germany in the Department of History at Lancaster University, United Kingdom. In 1999, he published *Eine andere Moderne? Zivilisationskritik, Natur und Technik in Deutschland, 1880–1933*.

Frank Uekötter has published monographs on the history of air pollution in Germany and the United States (*Von der Rauchplage zur ökologischen Revolution*, 2003) and the history of conservation in postwar North Rhine-Westphalia (*Naturschutz im Aufbruch*, 2004). He is currently a research assistant in the Department of History, University of Bielefeld, with a project on the history of agricultural knowledge.

Joachim Wolschke-Bulmahn is professor in the history of open-space planning and landscape architecture in the Department of Landscape Architecture, University of Hanover, Germany, and has worked at the Dumbarton Oaks Research Institute in Washington, DC. His publications include *Die Liebe zur Landschaft*, parts I and III (with Gert Gröning).

Thomas Zeller is assistant professor in the Department of History at the University of Maryland, College Park, and a visiting research fellow at the German Historical Institute in Washington, DC. His book *Straße, Bahn, Panorama: Verkehrswege und Landschaftsveränderung in Deutschland, 1930 bis 1990* was published in 2002; a revised version is forthcoming in English. He is currently working on a book entitled *Consuming Landscapes*.

Index

Academy for German Law, 10–11
    air pollution, 102, 103, 105, 115–16,
      126n76
    Committee on Land Law, 106–8
    Nation's Code, 105
Adorno, Theodor W., 185
Africa, 212, 225, 229, 244
agricultural interest organizations, 133,
    142n22
air pollution
    Academy for German Law and, 102,
      103, 105, 115–16, 126n76
    Civil Code (BGB) and, 103
    Federal Republic, 119–20
    Hitler and, 102
    law of 13 December 1933, 104
    law of 18 October 1935, 104
    Reich Food Estate and, 102
    Third Reich, 114–16
    Weimar Republic, 113–16
    World War I, impact of, 111
    World War II, impact of, 116–18
Alpers, Friedrich, 58
Alps, 157, 161, 225
American Society for Environmental
    History, 14
Ammon, Otto, 24
Anders, Günther, 185
Anderson, Dennis LeRoy, 103
Annexed Eastern Areas, 158, 243, 245
    anti-Semitism, 34, 247–48
    exterminationist planning for, 247
    landscape planning and evacuation,
      34, 249
    "Planning and Building in the East"
      exhibition, 249

anthropogeography, 210–11
Anthroposophical Society, 138–39,
    145n53, 157
anti-Americanism, 176, 182
anticommunism, 175, 182
antimodernism, 81, 89, 214
    Heidegger and, 176–78
    Rudorff and, 24
anti-Semitism, 2, 5, 6, 12, 14, 130, 245
    Annexed Eastern Areas, 158, 243, 245
    blood and soil doctrine, 131, 209
    Darré and, 140, 142n21
    Heidegger and, 173, 175, 196–97, 199n19
    Hitler and, 133
    Nazi policies concerning, 132, 172
    Schwenkel and, 32
    in Warthegau, 34, 247–48
antiurbanism, 209
Arendt, Hannah, 101, 172
Arndt, Ernst Moritz, 131
Artamanen, 132
Association of German Engineers
    (Verein Deutscher Ingenieure,
    VDI), 120
Auschwitz, 118–19, 250
    Himmler and, 158–59
    Seifert and, 158–59
autobahn project, 87
    Seifert and, 11–12, 148–49, 151–53, 161
    See also road building

Backe, Herbert, 130, 135, 137
Battle for Production, 76, 81, 92, 136. *See
    also* Four Year Plan
Bauch, Werner, 250
Bauhaus, 150

Bavaria, 23, 31, 64, 150, 151, 205
environmental protection legislation, 28
Ministry of War, 112
Beautification Society for the Siebengebirge, 75
"Beautiful City" exhibition, 88–89
Bialowieża Forest, 34
Bielefeld, 114, 116–17
billboards, 25, 27, 80, 88
biodynamic farming, 138–39, 157. *See also* organic farming
Birkenau, 119
Bismarck, Otto von, 221
Black Forest, 177
Blätter für Naturschutz, 32
blood and soil (Blut und Boden), 12, 19, 26, 73, 90, 93. *See also* völkisch ideology
eastern Europe, conquest and settlement of, 129
ecological ideas and, 205–6
euthanasia program and, 129
geopolitics and, 230–31
Heidegger and, 194
impacts, 130
racism and, 215–16
Seifert and, 162
sources, 206–7
Volksgemeinschaft and, 30
Bodenständigkeit. See indigenous (bodenständig) species
Borchardt, Rudolf, 149–50
Bormann, Martin, 130, 137
Bramwell, Anna, 2, 19, 141n5, 142n21
Blood and Soil, 18, 130
Darré and, 137–39
Nazi racial extermination policies, 142n21
Brüning, Heinrich, 178
Buffon, Comte de, 208
Bund Heimatschutz, 177, 187
Bund Naturschutz, 151

capitalism, alienation and, 24
Catholicism, Heidegger and, 179, 184
centralism and centralization, 6, 10, 19, 74, 76, 82–83, 161, 178
Reich Forest Bill and, 57, 63–64, 65–66
See also polycentrism and polycracy; regionalism; synchronization (Gleichschaltung)

Chamberlain, H. S., 207, 213
civilization (Zivilisation), 82, 175
Cologne, 77, 86, 87, 92
communism, 175, 182, 219
Conwentz, Hugo, 23–24, 29, 75, 78
cultural landscape (Kulturlandschaft), 149, 150, 207
Czechoslovakia, 66

Dachau, 159
dams, hydroelectricity, and hydroengineering, 13, 81, 85, 92, 155, 157, 161, 187–88
Danube, 157
Darré, Richard Walther, 11, 12, 19, 26, 62, 65, 77
air pollution, 108–11
Backe and, 130, 135, 137
Bauerntum als Lebensquell der nordischen Rasse, 132
blood and soil, 131–32, 215–16
Bramwell and, 137–39
geopolitics, 223
as head of SS Race and Settlement Office, 133–34
Himmler and, 137–38
Hitler and, 132–33
as Minister of Agriculture, 133–36
Neuadel aus Blut und Boden, 132
Reich Food Estate and, 137
as Reich Peasant Leader, 129
Seifert and, 155–56
SS Race and Settlement Office, 141n2
Volk, concept of, 229
Wilhelmstrasse proceedings, 136–38
Working Group for Geopolitics (Agrarian-Political Department), 223–24, 226, 227, 228
Darwin, Charles, 208
Dauerwald doctrine, 9, 43–45, 66–68
"close-to-nature commercial forest" concept, 58–59
decrees, 59
economic context, 50–52
federalism, 49
Göring and, 48–49, 51–52, 54
Nazi propaganda and, 52–57
property rights, 50–51
racism, 53
tenets of, 47–48
Volksgemeinschaft and, 52–53, 55–56, 69n13

DBH. *See* Homeland Protection Association of Germany (DBH)
denazification, 119, 136–37, 159–60, 161, 253
desertification (Versteppung), 154–55, 160–61
Deutsche Technic, 154
Ditt, Karl, 19, 21
Dominick, Raymond, 19, 37n16
Düsseldorf, 77, 86, 89
Dust Bowl (U.S.), 155

eastern Europe, conquest and settlement of, 158. *See also* Annexed Eastern Areas
Eidenbenz, Mathias, 216
Eiser, Ernst, 103, 110–11
Enlightenment, 3, 209
environmentalism, 2, 182–92, 194
Erbhof law (1933), 109–10, 134–36, 139
ethnic cleansing, 243
eugenics, 82, 99n70, 136, 180
euthanasia, 56, 129
Existentialism, 181

Faber, Karl-Georg, 231
Feder, Gottfried, 85
federalism, 20, 28, 31, 64–65
Federal Nature Conservancy Law (1976), 62
Federal Republic of Germany, 3, 61
  air pollution, 119–20
  forestry laws, 65
  Ministry of Defense, 119
  road building, 161
Fighting League for German Culture, 83
Finland, 66
forestry, 9, 21–22, 31
  national afforestation program, 59–60
  Third Reich, 60–68
  Weimar Republic, 61
  See also Dauerwald doctrine; Reich Forest Bill
Forestry and Hunting Affairs, Law Concerning the Transfer to the Reich, 50
Four Year Plan, 57, 76, 81, 109–10, 112, 136. *See also* Battle for Production
France, 22, 66, 116
Frank, Herbert, 249
Frankfurt am Main, 108

Freyer, Hans, 186
Frick, Wilhelm, 31

Garden Cities, 85, 94, 244
Gartenkunst, Die, 246–47, 251
Gayer, Karl, 46
Gehl, Walther, 229
General Government (Cracow), 245, 250
General Plan East, 13–14, 247
geographical (environmental) determinism, 208–11, 220–21, 223–26, 228, 230
geopolitics (Geopolitik), 204–5
  blood and soil, 230–31
  Darré and, 223
  Third Reich, 222–30
  Weimar Republic, 215–22
"Germanization," 248–49
German Labor Front (Deutsche Arbeitsfront, DAF), 83, 90, 134
"German landscape" (Landschaft), 5, 207
  care of (Landschaftspflege), 21, 74, 76, 79–81, 90, 93
  historical, 212, 228
Gestapo
  Darré and, 138
  Heidegger and, 173
Gewerkschaft Zinnwalder Bergbau, 108
Gleichschaltung. *See* synchronization (Gleichschaltung)
Gobineau, Arthur de, 207, 213
Göring, Hermann, 9, 20, 30–31, 43, 83, 92
  blood and soil concept and, 130
  Dauerwald doctrine and, 48–49, 54
  as head of Four Year Plan, 92, 136–37
  as head of Reich Forest Office, 20, 57–58, 62
  as Prussian prime minister, 48–49
  as Reich master of forestry, 49–51, 57–59
Great Britain, 24, 26, 116, 157, 159, 243
Great Depression, 51
Green Party, Greens, 1, 2, 11, 14n1, 18, 43, 130, 136, 138–39
Guenther, Konrad, 55
Guha, Ramachandra, 2

Haake, Heinrich, 76, 83–85, 88–89
  Volksgemeinschaft and, 84
Haardt Forest, 92

Habermas, Jürgen, 172, 195
Haeckel, Ernst, 206, 211
Hamburg, 93
Hard, Gerhard, 149
Haushofer, Heinz, 223
Haushofer, Karl, 204–5, 217–24, 231n1,
    232n2, 237n48, 238–39n56
    Hess and, 218–19
    National-Socialist Idea in the World,
        The, 218
    Nazi military strategy and, 12–13
    racism and, 226–30
Haverbeck, Werner, 83
Heidegger, Martin, 12
    "Age of the World Picture, The," 181,
        183–84, 186
    antimodernism, 176–78
    anti-Semitism, 173, 175, 196–97,
        199n19
    Being and Time, 174–75, 181
    blood and soil, 194
    Catholicism and, 179
    "enframing," 188–92
    environmentalism, 182–92, 194
    Essence of Truth, 181
    Introduction to Metaphysics, 173,
        182–83
    Lebensraum, 17
    National Socialism and, 172–82
    Nietzsche and, 173, 174, 181
    "Question Concerning Technology,
        The," 185, 186–88, 190–92
    racism, 197
    radical right, 174–76
    "releasement," 191, 199–200
    ruralism, 182–83
    technology, 185–87, 200n36
    völkisch ideology, 175, 179–80, 197
    "völkisch totalitarianism," 179–80
    Weimar Republic and, 172–73
Heimatschutz movement, 6, 73–75,
    81–82, 84, 90, 207
    Bund Heimatschutz, 177, 187
    Homeland Protection Association of
        Germany (DBH), 5, 6, 7, 10, 25, 79
    leadership, 83–84
    Nazi agrarian ideology and, 131
    Reich Nature Protection Law (RNG)
        and, 21, 79–80
    residential planning, 88
Hennig, Richard, 221–22, 225–26
Herder, Johann Gottfried von, 213, 222

Hess, Rudolf, 138, 160, 162, 223
    Haushofer and, 218–19, 231–32n1,
        238–39n56
    Seifert and, 156, 157–58
Hesse, Hermann, 23
hiking, 80, 152
Himmler, Heinrich, 13, 130, 136
    Annexed Eastern Areas, 13, 245
    Auschwitz, 158–59
    Darré and, 137–38
    "General Guidelines," 249
    ideology, 196
    as Reich commissioner for the
        strengthening of Germandom,
        138, 245–46, 249
    as SS commander, 137
Hitler, Adolf, 2, 4, 11, 29, 66
    Mein Kampf, 12, 219
    policymaking, 102
Hoemann, Reinhold, 87
Hoffmann, Rudolf, 92
Hölderlin, Friedrich, 195
Holocaust, 2, 3
Homeland Protection Association of
    Germany (DBH), 5, 7, 10, 79
    racism and, 6
Horkheimer, Max, 185
Hueck, Kurt, 34
Husserl, Edmund, 172
hydroengineering. *See* dams, hydroelec-
    tricity, and hydroengineering

indigenous (bodenständig) species, 88,
    90, 223
    autobahn and, 151, 153–54
    Dauerwald and, 47, 52–53, 56
    Volk and, 206–9, 211
Isenberg, Gerhard, 250
Iven, Herbert, 87

Jews, 6, 12, 14, 209, 248
    blood and soil and, 131, 209
    Darré and, 140, 142n21
    Heidegger and, 73, 75, 196–97,
        199n19
    Hitler and, 133
    Nazi policies concerning, 132, 172
    in Warthegau, 34, 247–48
Joachim, Joseph, 6, 13
Jünger, Ernst, 183
    "Total Mobilization," 183
    Worker, The, 183

Jünger, Friedrich Georg, 185, 186
Juristische Wochenschrift, 104

Karpa, Oskar, 83, 87
Kerrl, Hanns, 246
Keudell, Walter von, 31, 48–49, 57, 59,
     77
Kjellén, Rudolf, 216–17
Klages, Ludwig, 183, 185–86, 192
Klausing, Friedrich, 105, 110
Klose, Hans, 31–32, 34, 35, 76–77, 87,
     158
Klueting, Edeltraud, 19
Koenig, Hermann, 244
Kohn, Hans, 219
König, Gottlob, 46
Kornfeld, Hans, 78, 81, 86
Krieck, Ernst, 173
Kuhn, Thomas, 183
Kulturlandschaft. *See* cultural landscape
     (Kulturlandschaft)
Kupferwerk Ilsenburg, 108

Lamarck, Jean Baptiste, 208
Land Requirements for the Public Ser-
     vice, Law Concerning the Regula-
     tion of, 79
landscape architecture, 150–51, 253
"landscape cleansing," 243–44
Landschaft. *See* "German landscape"
     (Landschaft)
Landschaftspflege. *See under* "German
     landscape"
Lane, Barbara Miller, 33
Langhans, Paul, 210
Law Concerning the Protection of the
     Racial Purity of Forest Plants
     (1934), 61–62
Law Concerning the Regulation of Land
     Requirements for the Public Ser-
     vice, 79
Law Concerning the Transfer of
     Forestry and Hunting Affairs to
     the Reich, 50
Law for the Reduction of Unemploy-
     ment, 59–60
League of Nations, 178
Lebensraum, 12, 73, 130, 210, 254–55n14
     architecture and, 89
     Eastern Europe, 130, 245
     environment and, 93
     Heidegger and, 17

racism, 76
     Ratzel and, 211–12, 214
     spatial planning, 79
Lehmann, Julius Friedrich, 132
Leipzig, 114, 116
Leopold, Aldo, 47–48, 161
Ley, Robert, 91–92, 134, 137
liberalism, 32, 73, 77, 80, 82, 85–87, 93,
     103–4, 209, 215, 220
Liedecke, Ewald, 252
Lienenkämper, Wilhelm, 90–91
Lindner, Werner, 80, 82, 88–89
Löns, Hermann, 7, 26
Löwith, Karl, 173–74
Lunebürger Heath, 93

Mackinder, Halford, 219
Mäding, Erhard, 248
Marxism, 175, 176, 188
Maull, Otto, 229–30
Mein Kampf (Hitler), 12, 219
Meyer, Konrad, 246, 247, 253
Meyer-Abich, Klaus Michael, 191
Middle Rhine Gorge Plan, 87–88, 94
military planning and Naturschutz
     movement, 92–93
modernity, 24, 77–78, 81, 85, 150, 162
     Heidegger and, 172–75, 178–85, 188,
     192–95
Möller, Alfred, 46–47, 68n5
Montesquieu, Charles-Louis de Secon-
     dat, Baron, 213
Muir, John, 26
Munich, 10, 11, 81, 102
     Seifert and, 147, 149, 150, 151, 152, 159,
     160
Münker, Wilhelm, 92

National Afforestation Program, 59–60
national parks (Germany), 22, 34, 62, 93
National Parks (U.S.), 26, 244
National Socialism, 1, 3–4, 8. *See also*
     völkisch ideology
     academic professions and, 170–72
     agrarian ideology, 13–14, 129–35,
     137–38, 187, 196 (*see also* Darré,
     Richard Walther)
     air pollution, 103–8
     District Leader Training School, 54–55
     geopolitics and, 222–28
     government, 19–20, 76–78, 83, 101–2,
     120–22

National Socialism (*cont.*)
  Heidegger and, 172–82
  ideology, 2, 18–19, 27–28, 32–35, 101–2
  "modernity" of, 3
  *National Socialist Handbook for Law
    and Legislation,* 104
  regionalism and, 83–84
  Volksgemeinschaft and, 76, 77, 107
National Socialist Cultural Community,
  83
*National Socialist Handbook for Law
  and Legislation,* 104
Nation's Code
  Academy for German Law, 105
native species. *See* indigenous (boden-
  ständig) species
nature protection areas (Naturschutzge-
  biete), 20–24, 29, 30, 62, 79
Naturschutz movement, 5–6, 18, 73–76,
  77–81, 90
  acceptance of, 25
  Bund Naturschutz, 151
  environmental imperialism and, 34–35
  funding, 84
  leadership, 82–83
  military planning and, 92–93
  Prussia, 84
  Reich Nature Protection Law (RNG)
    and, 18–20, 23, 26–30, 32, 90–94
  Rhineland, 86
Natur und Heimat, 32
Nazis. *See* National Socialism
Nazi-Soviet Pact, 245
Netherlands, nature protection laws in,
  22
Neumann, Franz, 101
Nietzsche, Friedrich, 171, 183
  Heidegger's lectures on, 173–74, 181
Nordau, Max, 24
"Nordic race," 130
"normal forest," 45–46
Norway, 66
Nuremberg trials, 140

Oberkirch, Karl, 92
organic farming, 11, 19, 130, 138–39,
  151–52, 160–61
organicism, 154–55, 160

Pan-German League (Alldeutscher
  Verein), 210
parkways, 151–53

phytosociology, 153, 154
"Planning and Building in the East" exhibition, 249
Pohl, Oswald, 159
Poland, 13–14, 23, 51, 66, 140, 243–50. *See
  also* Annexed Eastern Areas
  Nazi planning in, 34
polycentrism and polycracy, 30, 35, 44,
  65, 76, 101–2, 120–22. *See also* centralism and centralization; regionalism; synchronization (Gleich-
  schaltung)
private property rights, concepts of,
  28–30, 250–51
"Productive People" exhibition, 89
propaganda, 4, 19, 32–33, 129, 133
  autobahn and, 152–53
  blood and soil as, 129, 178, 194
  Dauerwald as, 9, 48, 52–57, 67–68
  Geopolitik as, 223, 228
Provincial Museum for Natural History
  (Westphalia), 75
Prussia, 31
  environmental protection legislation,
    20, 28
  Field and Forest Police Law, 25
  Göring and, 48–49
  Institute for Water, Soil, and Air Hy-
    giene, 114–15, 117–18
  Law Against the Disfigurement of
    Exceptionally Scenic Areas, 25, 78
  Ministry of Public Welfare, 113–14
  Ministry of War, 111–12
  Naturschutz movement, 84
  Office for the Care of Natural Monu-
    ments, 20, 23, 27, 30, 75, 91
  private property rights, 28–30
  Silviculture Decree of 30 May 1934,
    59
  State Forest Office, 49–50
  Trading Regulations, 111
  Weimar Republic, 40n57

Racial Purity of Forest Plants, Law Concerning the Protection of, 61–62
"racial science," 205, 207, 213, 217, 226,
  251
racism, 2, 5
  agrarian ideology and, 130
  conservation and, 8, 20, 90
  Haushofer and, 226–30
  Heidegger and, 197

Homeland Protection Association of
Germany (DBH) and, 6
landscape design and, 251
Ratzel, Friedrich, 12, 210–14, 216–21, 226,
228
Anthropogeographie, 211
Lebensraum, 211–12, 214
Politische Geographie, 211, 219
Raumordnung. *See* spatial planning
regionalism, 10, 25, 28, 30, 33–34
as anticentralism, 6
National Socialism and, 83–84
Rhenish Regional Planning Society, 90
synchronization (Gleichschaltung)
and, 74–76, 78, 82–84
Volksgemeinschaft and, 77
See also centralism and centraliza-
tion; polycentrism and polycracy;
synchronization (Gleichschaltung)
Reich Commission for the Strengthen-
ing of Germandom, 245, 248, 253
Reich Food Estate (RNS), 11, 62, 115, 121,
134
air pollution and, 102, 108–11
Reich Forest Bill
failure of, 65–66
federalism and, 64–65
goals, 64
Göring and, 65–66
lumber industry and, 66
Reich Forest Office, 49
legislative goals, 57
nature conservancy branch, 62
Reich Hunting Law, 31
Reich Labor Service (RAD), 91–92, 156
Reich League for Volkstum and Heimat
(RVH), 83
Reich Ministry of the Interior, 104, 117, 118
Reich Ministry of Trade and Commerce, 109, 111, 112, 117, 118
Reich Nature Protection Book, 79, 80, 86
Reich Nature Protection Law (RNG),
8–10, 18–26, 62–63, 74, 93–94
blood and soil and, 78
bureaucratic power and, 30
drafting of, 29–30
federalism and, 20, 27, 31
Göring and, 8–10
Heimatschutz movement and, 21,
79–80
ideological and environmental limits,
90–94

landscape protection, 79–80
land-use planning, 21
Nazi ideology and, 26–35
open-space provisions, 20–21
and private property rights, 29
and regional synchronization, 74–76,
78, 82–84
Reich Forest Office, 20
Reich Nature Protection Areas, 21
Reich Nature Protection Office, 20,
34, 83
Rhine Valley and, 87
spatial planning, 81
Volksgemeinschaft and, 32, 93
Reich Nature Protection Office, 20, 34,
79, 83
Reich Office for Spatial Planning, 79,
246, 250
Reich peasant leader, 108–11
Reichsführer SS, 250, 252
Reichskommissar für die Festigung
deutschen Volkstums. *See* Reich
Commission for the Strengthen-
ing of Germandom
Reichsnährstand. *See* Reich Food Estate
(RNS)
Reichsnaturschutzgesetz. *See* Reich Na-
ture Protection Law (RNG)
Reichsstelle für Raumordnung. *See*
Reich Office for Spatial Planning
Rein, Robert, 77–78
Research Institute for Air Pollution
Damage, 109
residential planning, 88–89
Rhineland, 10
Homestead Association, 90
land-use planning, 74–75
Provincial Association, 76
Regional Planning Society, 90
Reich Nature Protection Law (RNG)
and, 78
Society for Monument Preservation
and Homeland Protection
(RVDH), 75
Society for Spatial Planning, 85
Rhine Province, 85
Rhine River, 86, 187
Rhine Valley, 75, 86–88, 91, 92
Riehl, Wilhelm Heinrich, 81–82, 131, 211
Ritter, Carl, 211
RNG. *See* Reich Nature Protection Law
(RNG)

RNS. *See* Reich Food Estate (RNS)
road building, 77, 152–54, 157–58
  and RNG, 25
  Rhine Valley, 84, 85, 87, 91
  See also autobahn
Rodderberg, 85
Romania, 66
Romanticism, 8, 9, 23–24, 25, 29, 74, 79,
  89, 151
  blood and soil, 131–32, 136, 139
  Heidegger and, 177–78, 187, 196
  Naturbedingtheit and, 206
Rosenberg, Alfred, 26, 83
Rosenberg, Arthur, 173
Roßmäßler, Adolf, 46
Rudorff, Ernst, 6, 23–25, 27, 81–82
Ruhr area (Ruhrgebiet), 75–77, 78–79, 92
Ruhr Settlement Association, 75–76, 92
Russia, 22, 46, 176, 214, 221, 243. *See also*
  Soviet Union
Rust, Bernhard, 29, 31

Saxony, 28, 54–55, 108, 225
Saybusch Action, 249
Schacht, Hjalmar, 136
Schallmeyer, Wilhelm, 217
Schama, Simon, 19
Schiffer, Heinz, 103, 105–6
Schoenichen, Walther, 32–34, 35, 42n87,
  87–88
  commercialism, 28
  Kulturlosigkeit, 27
  Nazi ideology, 94
  parliamentarism, 28
  Volksgemeinschaft, 32
Schultze-Naumburg, Paul, 6, 8, 79,
  81–83, 90
  "Creation of the Landscape," 81–82
  Fighting League for German Culture,
  83
  Nazi ideology and, 94
Schürmann, Wilhelm, 85–87
Schwenkel, Hans, 28, 32–33, 79, 79–80,
  82
scientific forestry, 43, 45–57
Sears, Paul, 155
Seifert, Alwin, 11–12, 81, 90, 138, 245,
  250
  Auschwitz, 158–59
  autobahn landscaping, 11–12, 148–49,
  151–53, 161
  blood and soil, 162

Dachau, 159
Danube hydroelectric plant in Ybbs-
  Persenbeug, 157
Darré and, 155–56
denazification proceedings and,
  159–60, 161
desertification of Germany, 154–55
education, 150
Hess and, 157–58
organic farming, 151
as Reich landscape architect, 148
Todt and, 151–54, 156–60, 162
völkisch ideology, 155–56
Settlement Commission, 244
shelterbelts, 155
Siebengebirge, 85
Silviculture Decree of 30 May 1934, 59
Sluga, Hans, 171–72
social Darwinism, 12, 56, 230, 245
Soil Conservation Service (U.S.), 155
Sombart, Werner, 187
Soviet Union, 51, 118, 245
  alliance with, 12, 205, 219–20, 245
  nature protection laws, 22
  See also Russia
spatial planning (Raumordnung), 79,
  81–85, 214, 217, 246, 250
Speer, Alfred, 117
Spiegel, 189
SS Race and Settlement Office, 129, 132,
  137–38
Stahlhelm, 132
Stalinism, 22
Steiner, Rudolf, 138–39, 151, 156, 156–57,
  160
Sturmabteilung (SA), 176
Sudetenland, 66
sustainability, 44, 45, 60–61, 64, 73, 197
Sweden, 66
Switzerland, 214
synchronization (Gleichschaltung), 49,
  74–76, 82–88, 90, 93–94, 133. *See*
  also centralism and centralization;
  polycentrism and polycracy; regionalism

Technische Anleitung, 118
Thiel, Peter Johannes, 210
Third Reich, 4, 19–20, 76–78, 83, 101–2,
  120–22
  Civil Code (BGB), 103–4
  environmental legislation, 19–20

Forestry and Hunting Affairs, Law Concerning the Transfer of to the Reich, 50
ideological confusion, 34
Interior Ministry, 65–66
Land Requirements for the Public Service, Law Concerning the Regulation of, 79
Ministry of the Interior, 104
Ministry of Trade and Commerce, 109, 111, 112, 117
Office for Spatial Order, 246, 250
polycentrism, 101–2, 120–22
Racial Purity of Forest Plants, Law Concerning the Protection of, 61–62
Unemployment, Law for the Reduction of, 59–60
Todt, Fritz, 77, 138, 151–54, 156–60, 162
"Total Mobilization" (Jünger), 183
town planning, 81
Trading Regulations, 109, 119
    Paragraph 22a, 111–12, 115, 119, 120
travel and tourism, 27, 76, 86–87, 188
Troeltsch, Ernst, 187

Ukraine, 136
Unemployment, Law for the Reduction of, 59–60
United Kingdom, 26
    nature protection laws, 21–22
United States, 26, 212
Urfelder Heath, 85
Urlandschaft, 228

Vereinigte Deutsche Metallwerke, 108
Versailles, Treaty of, 175, 176
Versteppung. *See* desertification (Versteppung)
Volk, Das, 226
völkisch ideology, 5–7, 27, 56, 81, 139, 178
    air pollution and, 107
    cultural landscapes and, 207, 209, 229
    environmentalism and, 208–9, 216, 221, 226–27, 230
    Heidegger and, 175, 179–80, 197
    national character and, 212–13
    "natural determination" and, 206–9
    organicism of, 206–8, 210–11, 215, 218, 228, 231
    race and, 228–29, 230–31
    totalitarianism and, 179–80

Volksgemeinschaft, 28
    blood and soil and, 30
    Dauerwald doctrine and, 52–53, 55–56, 69n13
    Haake and, 84
    National Socialism and, 76, 77, 104, 107
    regionalism and, 77
    Reich Nature Protection Law (RNG) and, 32, 93
Volksgesetzbuch. See Nation's Code
Voluntary Labor Service, 60
Vowinckel, Kurt, 227–28

Wagner, Moritz, 211
Wahner Heath, 85, 92
Warthegau, 34, 252
Weber, Alfred, 185
Weber, Max, 187
Weimar Republic, 4, 7, 28
    air pollution regulation, 113–16
    environmentalism and, 77
    land-use planning in, 73
    philosophers, 171–72
Westphalia, 92, 117
    land-use planning in, 74–75, 76, 77
    Reich Nature Protection Law (RNG) in, 78
Westphalian Homeland Association, 75
Wickop, Walter, 252–53
Wiepking-Jürgensmann, Heinrich Friedrich, 158, 246, 250–53
Wilhelmstrasse proceedings, 136–40
Wirtschaftsgruppe Chemische Industrie, 109
Wirtschaftsgruppe Metallindustrie, 108
Witthaus, Wernher, 73
Wittfogel, Karl, 219, 224, 238n56
Working Group for Geopolitics (Agrarian-Political Department), 223–24, 226, 227, 228, 229
World War I, 5, 6–7, 111, 174, 244
World War II, 116–18
Württemberg, 79, 112

Yellowstone National Park, 26, 244

Zeitschrift für Geopolitik, 217, 219, 222, 227
Zivilisation. *See* civilization (Zivilisation)